Historical and Philosophical Foundations of Education

Selected Readings

Gerald L. Gutek

Loyola University Chicago

Merrill
Prentice Hall

Upper Saddle River, New Jersey
Columbus, Ohio

Library of Congress Cataloging-in-Publication Data

Gutek, Gerald Lee.

Historical and philosophical foundations of education: selected readings / Gerald L. Gutek.
   p.cm

Includes bibliographical references and index.

ISBN 0-13-012233-5

   1. Education—History—Sources. 2. Education—Philosophy. 3. Educators—Biography. I. Title.

LA11 .G79 2001

370—dc21   00-062417

Vice President and Publisher: Jeffery W. Johnston
Editor: Debra A. Stollenwerk
Editorial Assistant: Penny S. Burleson
Production Editor: Mary Harlan
Design Coordinator: Diane C. Lorenzo
Cover Design: Linda Fares
Cover Art: SuperStock
Text Design: Carlisle Publishers Services
Production Coordination: Larry Goldberg, Carlisle Publishers Services
Production Manager: Pamela D. Bennett
Director of Marketing: Kevin Flanagan
Marketing Manager: Amy June
Marketing Services Manager: Krista Groshong

This book was set in Life Roman by Carlisle Communications, Ltd. It was printed and bound by R.R. Donnelley & Sons Company. The cover was printed by The Lehigh Press, Inc.

Photo Credits: *pp. 2, 34, 59, 68, 126, 161, 169:* Reproduced from the Collections of the Library of Congress. *p. 10:* Reproduction from Charles F. Horne, ed., *Great Men and Famous Women.* New York: Selmar Hess. Publisher, 1894, p. 54. *p. 42:* Reproduction from *The New England Primer Improved.* Pittsburgh: United Presbyterian Board of Publications, n.d. *p. 125:* Reproduced from *The Standard Reference Work for the Home, School, and Library,* vol. 1. Chicago: The Interstate Publishing Company, 1912. *pp. 162, 212:* From the National Archives. *p. 179:* Barbara Schwartz/Merrill.

10 9 8 7 6 5 4

ISBN: 0-13-012233-5

*To my wife, Patricia,
my daughters, Jennifer and Laura,
and my granddaughter, Claire*

Preface

Historical and Philosophical Foundations of Education: Selected Readings developed from my more than three decades of teaching the history and philosophy of education at Loyola University Chicago and as a visiting professor at Northern Michigan University, the University of Glasgow in Scotland, and Otterbein College. It can be used as a companion volume with *Historical and Philosophical Foundations of Education: A Biographical Introduction,* or it can be used as a separate text. The overriding goal in the book is to provide teachers, prospective teachers, and educational administrators and personnel with an understanding of their profession by exploring its historical and philosophical roots through the writings of the world's great educational thinkers.

ORGANIZATION AND COVERAGE

The book provides primary source readings from the works of the world's leading thinkers on education. It is organized around three broad themes: major educational movements in world history, the biographies of leading educators, and the philosophies and ideologies that emanated from their ideas.

The identification of educational thinkers and the selected primary sources in the book reflect the major movements in world history: Plato, Aristotle, and Quintilian represent the Greek and Roman classical period; Thomas Aquinas, the Middle Ages; Erasmus, the Renaissance; John Calvin and Johann Amos Comenius, the Protestant Reformation; Jean-Jacques Rousseau and Johann Heinrich Pestalozzi, the Enlightenment and post-Enlightenment periods; Thomas Jefferson and Mary Wollstonecraft, the age of revolution; Horace Mann, the foundations of the American republic; Robert Owen, John Stuart Mill, and Herbert Spencer, the industrial revolution and the rise of ideologies; Friedrich Froebel and Maria Montessori, the development of new insights on early childhood education; Jane Addams and John Dewey, the progressive movement; Mohandas Gandhi, the end of imperialism in the postcolonial world; Mao Tze-tung, revolutionary Marxism; W. E. B. Du Bois, the rise of African American consciousness.

Each primary source is preceded by a biographical sketch and discussion of the thinker's principal ideas on education. These brief biographies and discussions are designed to give the great movements of educational history a human face and perspective. The selection is introduced by focusing questions, which guide the student in reading the selection. The reading is followed by suggestions for further reading.

The selections, which are situated in their historical contexts, were chosen because of their relevance to philosophical and ideological questions in education.

What did the educational thinker have to say about the nature of truth and value, the meaning of education, and the role of schooling? How did the thinker conceive of teaching and learning? For example, an examination of Plato's ideas leads to a consideration of philosophical Idealism; Aristotle's ideas, to Realism; Thomas Aquinas, to Thomism; Erasmus, to Humanism; Comenius, to Pansophism; Rousseau, to Naturalism; and Dewey, to Pragmatism.

The choice of selections is also designed to provide students with an understanding of ideology and how it influences educational policy. Here, Robert Owen provides insights into utopianism, Mary Wollstonecraft into feminism, John Stuart Mill into liberalism, Herbert Spencer into social Darwinism, Jane Addams into progressivism, Mao Tze-tung into Marxism, and W. E. B. Du Bois into Pan Africanism.

FORMAT

The book is divided into 22 chapters, each of which examines the life, ideas, and a primary source selection of one of the world's great educational thinkers. It builds, in chronological fashion, from the ancient classical Greek and Roman period to the modern thinkers of the twentieth century. Each chapter is organized into the following sections:

- A *Biographical Sketch* examines the key events in the educational thinker's life and work.
- An *Overview of Ideas on Education* creates a historical and philosophical framework for analyzing the selected primary source reading.
- *Focusing Questions* introduce the primary source selection and suggest ways of getting to its historical and philosophical relevance for educators.
- *The Primary Source* brings students directly to the thinker's own statement of educational philosophy and ideology.
- *Suggestions for Further Reading* include books both by and about the particular educational thinker.

FEATURES

Historical and Philosophical Foundations of Education: Selected Readings offers the following special features:

- It provides a knowledge base in the historical, philosophical, and ideological foundations of education that is based on primary sources.
- It encourages students to discover, in a guided and structured way, the foundational roots of education.
- It considers history, philosophy, and ideology of education in a single book.

ACKNOWLEDGMENTS

I appreciate the advice, support, and patience of Debbie Stollenwerk, my editor at Prentice Hall, who encouraged me to write and edit this book.

I want to thank my wife, Patricia, and my daughters, Jennifer and Laura, for their continuing love and interest in my work as a teacher and writer.

Gerald L. Gutek

Contents

Chapter 1   **Plato: Idealist Philosopher and
Educator for the Perfect Society**   1

From *The Republic of Plato*   5

Chapter 2   **Aristotle: Founder of Realism**   9

From *The Nicomachean Ethics of Aristotle*   12

Chapter 3   **Quintilian: Rhetorical Educator in Service of the Emperor**   19

From *Quintilian's Institutes of Oratory*   21

Chapter 4   **Thomas Aquinas: Scholastic Theologian and the
Creator of the Medieval Christian Synthesis**   24

From Berardus Bonjoannes' *Compendium of the Summa
Theologica of St. Thomas Aquinas*   28

Chapter 5   **Desiderius Erasmus: Renaissance Humanist and
Cosmopolitan Educator**   33

From *The Colloquies of Erasmus*   37

From Desiderius Erasmus' *The Praise of Folly*   39

Chapter 6   **John Calvin: Theologian and Educator of the Protestant
Reformation**   41

From John Calvin's *Tracts and Treatises on the Doctrine and
Worship of the Church*   46

Chapter 7   **Johann Amos Comenius: Pansophist Educator and
Proponent of International Education**   50

From *The Great Didactic of John Amos Comenius*   53

Chapter 8 **Jean-Jacques Rousseau: Prophet of Naturalism** **58**

From *Rousseau's Emile or Treatise on Education* 63

Chapter 9 **Johann Heinrich Pestalozzi: Proponent of Educating the Heart and Senses** **67**

From Pestalozzi's *Leonard and Gertrude* 75

From Johann H. Pestalozzi's *How Gertrude Teaches Her Children* 77

Chapter 10 **Thomas Jefferson: Advocate of Republican Education** **81**

From *The Papers of Thomas Jefferson* 87

Chapter 11 **Mary Wollstonecraft: Proponent of Women's Rights and Education** **91**

From Mary Wollstonecraft's *Thoughts on the Education of Daughters: With Reflections on Female Conduct, in the More Important Duties of Life* 97

From Mary Wollstonecraft's *Original Stories* 98

From Mary Wollstonecraft's *A Vindication of the Rights of Woman* 99

Chapter 12 **Horace Mann: Leader of the Common School Movement** **103**

From Horace Mann's "Twelfth Annual Report on Education (1848)," in *The Life and Works of Horace Mann* 109

Chapter 13 **Robert Owen: Utopian Socialist and Communitarian Educator** **114**

From *A Supplementary Appendix to the First Volume of The Life of Robert Owen* 118

From *The Life of Robert Owen* 120

Chapter 14 **Friedrich Froebel: Founder of the Kindergarten** **124**

From *Autobiography of Friedrich Froebel* 132

From Friedrich Froebel's *The Education of Man* 134

From Friedrich Froebel's *Mother-Play and Nursery Songs* 137

Chapter 15   **John Stuart Mill: Proponent of Liberalism**   **140**

From John Stuart Mill's *Autobiography*   144

From John Stuart Mill's "Inaugural Address,
University of Saint Andrews, February 1, 1867"   149

Chapter 16   **Herbert Spencer: Advocate of Individualism, Science,
and Social Darwinism**   **152**

From Herbert Spencer's *Education: Intellectual,
Moral, and Physical*   156

Chapter 17   **Jane Addams: Advocate of Socialized Education**   **160**

From Jane Addams' *Democracy and Social Ethics*   164

From Jane Addams' *The Spirit of Youth and the City Streets* 166

Chapter 18   **John Dewey: Pragmatist Philosopher and
Progressive Educator**   **168**

From John Dewey's *Democracy and Education:
An Introduction to the Philosophy of Education*   173

Chapter 19   **Maria Montessori: Proponent of Early Childhood Education**

From Maria Montessori's *The Montessori Method*   183

Chapter 20   **Mohandas Gandhi: Father of Indian Independence**   **188**

From *The Moral and Political Writings of Mahatma
Gandhi*   193

Chapter 21   **W. E. B. Du Bois: Scholar and Activist for African
American Rights**   **198**

From W. E. B. Du Bois' *The Souls of Black Folk:
Essays and Sketches*   204

Chapter 22   **Mao Tse-tung: The Revolutionary Educator**   **211**

From *Chairman Mao Talks to the People:
Talks and Letters: 1956–1971*   218

Index   **223**

1

PLATO: IDEALIST PHILOSOPHER AND EDUCATOR FOR THE PERFECT SOCIETY

BIOGRAPHICAL SKETCH

Plato (427–347 B.C.) was among the leading contributors to philosophy in the Western world. He was a founding figure in creating the intellectual foundations of Western civilization, and his ideas remain the point of departure for analyzing many educational issues that face us today.

Plato lived in Athens, a polis renowned as the cradle of Western democracy, though he resisted many of democracy's egalitarian tendencies. His resistance may have been influenced by his aristocratic family origins, or it may have come from his antagonism to the cultural and ethical relativism that he saw as a consequence of popular democracy.

Born into an established aristocratic Athenian family, Plato's father, Ariston, claimed to be descended from Codrus, Athens' last king before it became a democracy. Perictione, his mother, was descended from Solon, ancient Athens' famous lawmaker. Plato was the youngest of four children. He mentioned his brothers Glaucon and Adeimantus in *The Republic*. His sister Potone was the mother of Speusippus, who succeeded him at the Academy, the school of philosophy Plato established in Athens.[1]

During Plato's life, Athens experienced change caused by military defeat and economic development. After Sparta defeated Athens, a politically conservative pro-Spartan regime was installed. Critias, a relative of Plato, was among the Athenians who collaborated with the Spartans. When Athens' democratic faction regained power, the conservative officials were deposed and their families and friends were purged from state positions. Plato, who resented his family's fall from political power, resisted the social change taking place in Athens. Abandoning any interest in a political career, Plato turned increasingly to philosophical inquiries.

Plato received a conventional Athenian education. In primary school, he learned to read, write, and compute. He went to the palaestra, the special school for gymnastics and physical education. At the school of the citharist—another separate institution for the study of music, dancing, and singing—Plato learned the oral tradition, the stories of Greek heroes, that had been recounted since the age of Homer. At age 18, he served in the cavalry, fulfilling the year of military service required of Athenian young men.

1

Plato, Athenian philosopher, author of *The Republic*.

Plato's real education began, however, when as a young man of 22, he encountered the famous teacher Socrates (470–399 B.C.), who would become his mentor. Socrates and his students were pursuing the essential philosophical questions about truth, goodness, and beauty. Socrates asserted that leading a good life meant that the person was using reason to discover the truth and had determined to live according to it. For Socrates, the word "discover" was highly important in that he believed that each person possessed the ideas of truth but needed to bring them to consciousness. The teacher, according to the Socratic method, was to ask stimulating and challenging questions that motivate students to think critically and reflectively. In particular, Socrates challenged the Sophists, who claimed they could teach students to present a positive public image and manipulate public opinion by the clever combination of fact, myth, crowd psychology, and speech technique.[2]

As a consequence of his questioning of the prevailing authority and opinion, Socrates, accused of impiety to the gods and corrupting the youth of Athens, was tried, convicted, and sentenced to death by the Athenian court. He was sentenced to take his own life by drinking hemlock, a poison. Socrates' ordeal had a profound impact on Plato, who later wrote about it in his dialogue Crito.[3] Socrates' students begged him to save his life by fleeing from Athens or recanting his beliefs. Resisting their entreaties, Socrates accepted death saying he must be true to his ideas. To do otherwise would be denying the right to seek and to follow the truth. Socrates' trial was one of the earliest and most famous of a long line of cases involving academic freedom—the right of a teacher to teach and of a learner to learn without interference from arbitrary political authorities or a countervailing public opinion.

After Socrates' death, Plato departed Athens, journeying to the cultural centers of the Aegean and Mediterranean worlds. At Megara, he studied with Euclid, the famous scholar of geometry. In Egypt, he studied with the Pythagoreans, a circle of mathematicians. His travels took him to Sicily, an important outpost of Greek culture, ruled by Dionysius I. For political and personal reasons, he incurred the wrath of Dionysius I, who arrested and sold Plato into slavery. Fortunately, Plato's friend Anniceris purchased his freedom. Plato then returned to Athens.[4]

In 387 B.C., Plato founded the Academy, a school of higher education where his students followed a rigorous curriculum of arithmetic, geometry, astronomy, and harmonics, which were designed to prepare them for the study of philosophy.[5] In their work in philosophy, Plato's students examined questions dealing with metaphysics, the study of ultimate reality; epistemology, the study of knowledge; and axiology, the examination of ethical and aesthetic values. While directing the Academy, Plato wrote his leading philosophical works: *The Republic, The Apology,* and *Phaedo.* He remained at the Academy, lecturing, working with students, and writing until his death in 347 B.C.

OVERVIEW OF IDEAS ON EDUCATION

Plato's ideas on education were counterarguments to the Sophists, who claimed that what we call truths were merely temporary statements or opinions that depended on changing times and circumstances. The Sophists claimed that they gave their students a pleasing public persona, proper social bearing, correct style of speech, and effective political skills. For Plato, the Sophists' educational claims distorted and cheapened the true meaning of education. The Sophists were creating public images rather than searching for truth as Socrates had done.

Plato's educational goal was to penetrate through images and appearances to find reality's true underlying meaning. His search led him to develop philosophical idealism, which asserts that reality consists of eternally stable and universal unchanging ideas, or pure concepts. All ideas are derived from a superior, higher, and all-encompassing universal idea, the form of the good.[6] The objects that we see, touch, smell, and hear are imperfect representations of the perfect ideas of these objects in the form of the good. To know means to penetrate through the sensory image to reach the perfect world of ideas. The clearer our knowledge of these general concepts, the closer we are intellectually to the form of the good and the more accurate our knowledge of reality.

Rejecting the Sophists' ethical relativism, Plato argued that ethical and aesthetic values are universal regardless of place, time, and circumstances. What is good, right, and beautiful has been so throughout history and will be so in the future.

Plato explained how we search for truth through his famous "Allegory of the Cave" in which objects that appear to our senses are mere reflections of the idea of the perfect object. The aim of a true education is to discover the knowledge of ultimate and perfect ideas, the form of the good from which all ideas derive.

For Plato, we know truth by a process called "reminiscence," bringing to consciousness ideas we knew before our soul was encased in a physical body. Before birth, the soul, residing in a world of pure forms, knew these universal and perfect concepts. While we retain our knowledge of these ideas at birth, the shock of being born into the material world pushes them into our subconsciousness. Now, in the material world, we are overwhelmed by fleeting sensations, appetites, and false opinions. To really know, we need to penetrate through these sensations and opinions and rediscover the truth within us.[7]

Plato, like many other ancient Greek philosophers, grappled with the question, What kind of society would enable human beings to best realize their human potential and live according to justice? Plato tried to answer this question in *The Republic,* his major work on politics and education.[8] For Plato, living in justice meant that every citizen would do what was appropriate to his or her abilities.

Plato conceived his perfect society, the Republic, as a social organism, in which the societal, economic, political, and educational institutions serve the common good. Plato identified three classes—the philosopher-kings, the military, and the workers—that, functioning as interrelated and necessary parts of the body politic, performed the essential functions of the political organism or body. Membership in these three classes was determined by the person's capacity to perform the role appropriate to the particular class.

The philosopher-kings, who had the greatest intellectual capacity, enjoyed the highest status as the Republic's governors. Next came the military, the armed forces, who with the greatest capacity for physical courage and bravery were to defend the Republic from its enemies. At the bottom of the hierarchy were the workers, those with the greatest capacity to produce the goods and services needed to sustain the Republic's economic life.

Plato believed that basing occupational assignments on a person's aptitude would lead to the harmonious relationships of all classes in the Republic. The principle of justice was fulfilled by the harmonious relationship of all classes, which were organized according to their aptitude, with intellectuality given the highest ranking. Making a connection between the society and the individual, Plato reasoned that a person's mind, will, and body should be harmoniously organized in a way that was reflected in the larger society.

Plato's idealized society was hierarchical, with people ranked according to intellectual ability. The potential for abstract thinking, intellectual ability, was not inherited or ascribed on a socioeconomic class basis. For example, those born to lower ranked parents but who demonstrated intellectual ability would be assigned to a higher class.

In the Republic, Plato regarded early childhood as a highly important educational stage in a person's life. In the early years, the cultural, social, and intellectual predispositions of adult life were laid. Plato specified that young children, from birth to age 6, were to be reared in state-operated nurseries. There little children, free from corruptive vices, would develop the proper habits needed in an organic society. Also, teachers could begin to identify intellectually gifted children.

Children, from 6 to 18, attended schools where they learned music, literature, mathematics, and gymnastics.[9] Music was taught to develop the proper moral spirit, and literature, the study of the approved classics, was to help form character. Mathematics, Plato's favorite subject, was to develop abstract reasoning. Gymnastics was for physical development, skill, and strength.

When they reached their level of abstractive capacity, students left the school and took their place in the Republic. Those who showed a military disposition or who might become philosopher-kings continued in school for 2 more years, from ages 18 to 20. At 20, the military defenders assumed their roles. The future philosopher-kings continued their study for 10 more years. Pursuing mathematics and philosophy, they searched for the underlying principles of truth. When they were 30, there was still another selection. Those who reached their intellectual capacity were assigned to subordinate administrative and educational responsibilities. The brightest students, the future philosopher-kings, studied for 5 more years, concentrating on metaphysics by using the dialectical process of critical discussion. At 35, the philosopher-kings would assume the responsibility of governing the Republic. At age 50, the most able would become the policy makers of the Republic.

THE PRIMARY SOURCE

The primary source reading is from Book VII of Plato's *Republic,* in which the famous dialogue on the ascent from the cave appears. Here, Plato discusses how we come to know by using the analogy of prisoners in a dark cave. The prisoners are bound in such a way that they can see only the shadows, the distorted images, of objects that are passed in front of a fire that is behind them. When the prisoners are released from the cave and enter the world where the shining sun illuminates all that they see, they at first reject the clarity of illuminated vision. Plato is suggesting that human knowledge is similar. To know, the person needs to escape from the cave of sensation and opinion and seek the truth that is found in the contemplation of the Form of the Good.

FOCUSING QUESTIONS

As you read the selection, you might wish to consider the following questions:

1. Analyze the meaning of the shadows that the prisoners in the cave confuse with reality. Are there any similar shadows in contemporary society that confuses our vision of truth? How can teachers guide students in distinguishing between shadows and substance?
2. Consider the prisoners as students and analyze their confusion on leaving the cave. Why is it so difficult to "unlearn" an early childhood learning that is erroneous?
3. Plato is strongly suggesting that contemplation to try to understand the "Form of the Good" is the highest human intellectual activity. Do you agree or disagree with him? How would contemporary teachers and students react to such a goal for education?

FROM *THE REPUBLIC OF PLATO*

BOOK VII

Now then, I proceeded to say, go on to compare our natural condition, so far as education and ignorance are concerned, to a state of things like the following. Imagine a number of men living in an underground cavernous chamber, with an entrance open to the light, extending

From *The Republic of Plato,* translated by John L. Davies and David J. Vaughan. Cambridge, U.K.: Macmillan and Co., 1858, 264–270.

along the entire length of the cavern, in which they have been confined, from their childhood, with their legs and necks so shackled, that they are obliged to sit still and look straight forwards, because their chains render it impossible for them to turn their heads round: and imagine a bright fire burning some way off, above and behind them, and an elevated roadway passing between the fire and the prisoners, with a low wall built along it, like the screens which conjurors put up in front of their audience, and above which they exhibit their wonders.

I have it, he replied.

Also figure to yourself a number of persons walking behind this wall, and carrying with them statues of men, and images of other animals, wrought in wood and stone and all kinds of materials, together with various other articles, which overtop the wall; and, as you might expect, let some of the passers-by be talking, and others silent.

You are describing a strange scene, and strange prisoners.

They resemble us, I replied. For let me ask you, in the first place, whether persons so confined could have seen anything of themselves or of each other, beyond the shadows thrown by the fire upon the part of the cavern facing them?

Certainly not, if you suppose them to have been compelled all their lifetime to keep their heads unmoved.

And is not their knowledge of the things carried past them equally limited?

Unquestionably it is.

And if they were able to converse with one another, do you not think that they would be in the habit of giving names to the objects which they saw before them?

Doubtless they would.

Again: if their prison-house returned an echo from the part facing them, whenever one of the passers-by opened his lips, to what, let me ask you, could they refer the voice, if not to the shadow which was passing?

Unquestionably they would refer it to that.

Then surely such persons would hold the shadows of those manufactured articles to be the only realities.

Without a doubt they would.

Now consider what would happen if the course of nature brought them a release from their fetters, and a remedy for their foolishness, in the following manner. Let us suppose that one of them has been released, and compelled suddenly to stand up, and turn his neck round and walk with open eyes towards the light; and let us suppose that he goes through all these actions with pain, and that the dazzling splendour renders him incapable of discerning those objects of which he used formerly to see the shadows. What answer should you expect him to make, if some one were to tell him that in those days he was watching foolish phantoms, but that now he is somewhat nearer to reality, and is turned towards things more real, and sees more correctly; above all, if he were to point out to him the several objects that are passing by, and question him, and compel him to answer what they are? Should you not expect him to be puzzled, and to regard his old visions as truer than the objects now forced upon his notice?

Yes, much truer.

And if he were further compelled to gaze at the light itself, would not his eyes, think you, be distressed, and would he not shrink and turn away to the things which he could see distinctly, and consider them to be really clearer than the things pointed out to him?

Just so.

And if some one were to drag him violently up the rough and steep ascent from the cavern, and refuse to let him go till he had drawn him out into the light of the sun, would he not, think you, be vexed and indignant at such treatment, and on reaching the light, would he not find his eyes so dazzled by the glare as to be incapable of making out so much as one of the objects that are now called true?

Yes, he would find it so at first.

Hence, I suppose, habit will be necessary to enable him to perceive objects in that upper world. At first he will be most successful in distinguishing shadows; then he will discern the reflections of men and other things in water, and afterwards the realities; and after this he will raise his eyes to encounter the light of the moon and stars, finding it less difficult to study the heavenly bodies and the heaven itself by night, than the sun and the sun's light by day.

Doubtless.

Last of all, I imagine, he will be able to observe and contemplate the nature of the sun, not as it *appears* in water or on alien ground, but as it *is* in itself in its own territory.

Of course.

His next step will be to draw the conclusion, that the sun is the author of the seasons and the years, and the guardian of all things in the visible world, and in a manner the cause of all those things which he and his companions used to see.

Obviously, this will be his next step.

What then? When he recalls to mind his first habitation, and the wisdom of the place, and his old fellow-prisoners, do you not think he will congratulate himself on the change, and pity them?

Assuredly he will.

And if it was their practice in those days to receive honour and commendations one from another, and to give prizes to him who had the keenest eye for a passing object, and who remembered best all that used to precede and follow and accompany it, and from these data divined most ably what was going to come next, do you fancy that he will covet these prizes, and envy those who receive honour and exercise authority among them? Do you not rather imagine that he will feel what Homer describes, and wish extremely

'To drudge on the lands of a master,
Under a portionless wight,'

and be ready to go through anything, rather than entertain those opinions, and live in that fashion?

For my own part, he replied, I am quite of that opinion. I believe he would consent to go through anything rather than live in that way.

And now consider what would happen if such a man were to descend again and seat himself on his old seat? Coming so suddenly out of the sun, would he not find his eyes blinded with the gloom of the place?

Certainly, he would.

And if he were forced to deliver his opinion again, touching the shadows aforesaid, and to enter the lists against those who had always been prisoners, while his sight continued dim, and his eyes unsteady,—and if this process of initiation lasted a considerable time,—would he not be made a laughingstock, and would it not be said of him, that he had gone up only to come back again with his eyesight destroyed, and that it was not worth while even to attempt the ascent? And if any one endeavoured to set them free and carry them to the light, would they not go so far as to put him to death, if they could only manage to get him into their power?

Yes, that they would.

Now this imaginary case, my dear Glaucon, you must apply in all its parts to our former statements, by comparing the region which the eye reveals, to the prison-house, and the light of the fire therein to the power of the sun: and if, by the upward ascent and the contemplation of the upper world, you understand the mounting of the soul into the intellectual region, you will hit the tendency of my own surmises, since you desire to be told what they are; though, indeed, God only knows whether they are correct. But, be that as it may, the view which I take of the subject is to the following effect. In the world of knowledge, the essential Form of Good is the limit of our inquiries, and can barely be perceived; but, when perceived, we cannot help concluding that it is in every case the source of all that is bright and beautiful,—in the visible world giving birth to light and its master, and in the intellectual world dispensing, immediately and with full authority, truth and reason;—and that whosoever would act wisely, either in private or in public, must set this Form of Good before his eyes.

To the best of my power, said he, I quite agree with you.

That being the case, I continued, pray agree with me on another point, and do not be surprised, that those who have climbed so high are unwilling to take a part in the affairs of men, because their souls are ever loath to desert that upper region. For how could it be otherwise, if the preceding simile is indeed a correct representation of their case?

True, it could scarcely be otherwise.

Well: do you think it a marvellous thing, that a person, who has just quitted the contemplation of divine objects for the study of human infirmities, should betray awkwardness, and appear very ridiculous, when with his sight still dazed, and before he has become sufficiently habituated to the darkness that reigns around, he finds himself compelled to contend in courts of law, or elsewhere, about the shadows of justice, or images which throw the shadows, and to enter the lists in questions involving the arbitrary suppositions entertained by those who have never yet had a glimpse of the essential features of justice?

No, it is anything but marvellous.

Right: for a sensible man will recollect that the eyes may be confused in two distinct ways and from two distinct causes,—that is to say, by sudden transitions either from light to darkness, or from darkness to light. And, believing the same idea to be applicable to the soul, whenever such a person sees a case in which the mind is perplexed and unable to distinguish objects, he will not laugh irrationally, but he will examine whether it has just quitted a brighter life, and has been blinded by the novelty of darkness, or whether it has come from the depths of ignorance into a more brilliant life, and has been dazzled by the unusual splendour; and not till then will he congratulate the one upon its life and condition, and compassionate the other; and if he chooses to laugh at it, such laughter will be less ridiculous than that which is raised at the expense of the soul that has descended from the light of a higher region.

You speak with great judgment.

Hence, if this be true, we cannot avoid adopting the belief, that the real nature of education is at variance with the account given of it by certain of its professors, who pretend, I believe to infuse into the mind a knowledge of which it was destitute, just as sight might be instilled into blinded eyes.

True; such are their pretensions.

Whereas, our present argument shows us that there is a faculty residing in the soul of each person, and an instrument enabling each of us to learn; and that, just as we might suppose it to be impossible to turn the eye round from darkness to light without turning the whole body, so must this faculty, or this instrument, be wheeled round, in company with the entire soul, from the perishing world, until it be enabled to endure the contemplation of the real world and the brightest part thereof, which according to us, is the Form of Good. Am I not right?

You are.

Hence, I continued, this very process of revolution must give rise to an art, teaching in what way the change will most easily and most effectually be brought about. Its object will not be to generate in the person the power of seeing. On the contrary, it assumes that he possesses it, though he is turned in a wrong direction, and does not look towards the right quarter; and its aim is to remedy this defect.

So it would appear.

Suggestions for Further Reading

Annas, Julia. *An Introduction to Plato's Republic.* Oxford: Oxford University Press, 1981.

Barrow, Robin. *Plato and Education.* London: Routledge and Kegan Paul, 1976.

Cross, R. C., and A. D. Woozley. *Plato's Republic: A Philosophical Commentary.* New York: St. Martin's Press, 1966.

Gulley, Norman. *Plato's Theory of Knowledge.* London: Methuen, 1962.

Guthrie, W. K C. *Socrates.* London, U.K.: Cambridge University Press, 1971.

Hare, R. M. *Plato.* Oxford: Oxford University Press, 1982.

Lodge, Rupert C. *Plato's Theory of Education.* New York: Russell and Russell, 1970.

Mall, Robert W. *Plato.* London: Allen and Unwin, 1981.

Nettleship, R. L. *The Theory of Education in Plato's Republic.* New York: Teachers College Press, Columbia University, 1968.

Plato. *The Republic.* Translated by Allan Bloom. New York: Basic Books, 1968.

Shorey, Paul. *What Plato Said.* Chicago: University of Chicago Press, 1968.

Taylor, Alfred E. *Plato: The Man and His Work.* London: Methuen, 1966.

Notes

1. For biographical and philosophical commentaries on Plato, see Alfred E. Taylor, *Plato: The Man and His Work* (London: Methuen, 1966); Robert W. Hall, *Plato* (London: Allen and Unwin, 1981); Paul Shorey, *What Plato Said* (Chicago: University of Chicago Press, 1968).

2. For Socrates, see W. K. C. Guthrie, *Socrates* (London, U.K.: Cambridge University Press, 1971); Robert S. Brumbaugh, *The Philosophers of Greece* (Albany, N.Y.: State University of New York Press, 1981).

3. Erich H. Warmington and Philip G. Rouse, eds., *Great Dialogues of Plato,* trans. W. H. D. Rouse (New York: New American Library, 1956), 447–459.

4. G. C. Field, *Plato and His Contemporaries* (London: Methuen, 1962), 16–17.

5. Edward J. Power, *Evolution of Educational Doctrines: Major Educational Theorists of the Western World* (New York: Appleton-Century-Crofts, 1969), 55–56.

6. W. D. Ross, *Plato's Theory of Ideas* (Oxford: Oxford University Press, 1951).

7. Plato, "Meno," in *The Dialogues of Plato,* trans. B. Jowett (Indianapolis: Liberal Arts Press, Bobbs-Merrill, 1949), 37–45.

8. For translations and editions of *The Republic,* see Plato, *The Republic,* trans. Allan Bloom (New York: Basic Books, 1968); *The Republic,* trans. G. M. A. Grube (Indianapolis: Hackett, 1974).

9. Robert S. Brumbaugh and Nathaniel M. Lawrence, *Philosophers on Education: Six Essays on the Foundations of Western Thought* (Boston: Houghton-Mifflin, 1963), 40–43.

ARISTOTLE: FOUNDER OF REALISM

BIOGRAPHICAL SKETCH

Aristotle (384–322 B.C.), an ancient Greek philosopher, is significant as a founding father of Western philosophy and education. His Realism influenced the course of later thought, especially the Theistic Realism of Thomas Aquinas.

Aristotle was born in 384 B.C. in Stagira, in Macedonia, where his father, Nichomachus, was court physician to King Amyntas II. Little is known about Phoestis, his mother. From his father, Aristotle developed a lifelong interest in science and medicine.[1] At 17, Aristotle went to Athens, the center of Greek intellectual life, where he studied with Plato, the famous philosopher. For the next 20 years, from 367 B.C. to 347 B.C., Aristotle was a student at Plato's Academy.

While Aristotle was Plato's intellectual heir, he did not become his philosophical disciple. Rather than accepting Plato's doctrine that reality was nonmaterial, Aristotle developed a dualistic position that saw reality composed of matter and form. While Plato sought to overcome what he regarded as the distortions of reality caused by the senses, Aristotle argued that human knowing begins with sensation.

In 347 B.C., Aristotle toured Asia Minor to study the land, climate, politics, plants, and animals of the lands to the east of Greece. For several years Aristotle lived in the kingdom of Assos where he was adviser to its King, Hermias. Aristotle, a member of the court, married Hermias' niece Phythias. The couple had a daughter, Phythias. In 343 B.C., Aristotle joined the court of Philip of Macedon, where he was the tutor of Philip's son Alexander, who would later conquer the known world and be called Alexander the Great.

Aristotle returned to Athens, where he started a school, the Lyceum. Reflecting their teacher's many interests, Aristotle's students studied the natural sciences, politics, metaphysics, and ethics. Aristotle was a demanding teacher, and his lectures were logically organized and forcefully presented.

Aristotle developed a theory of natural progression in which natural phenomenon was organized in a hierarchy. At the hierarchy's base were lifeless minerals and then at the next higher rung came plants, which, though alive, had limited potentiality. Higher were the animals. At the summit were human beings who possessed rationality. From 336 B.C. until 323 B.C., Aristotle taught and wrote and gained repute as a commanding philosophical presence in Athens.

Aristotle, Greek philosopher, and tutor of Alexander the Great.

Aristotle was a prodigious scholar and writer, and most of his treatises began as lectures to his students. Among his works were his *Metaphysics*, which deals with his theory of reality, *Nicomachean Ethics,* which examines virtue, and his *Politics,* on government. His lectures and writings examined logic, the arts and sciences, psychology, physiology, political science, mathematics, zoology, botany, biology, law, metaphysics, epistemology, and astronomy.

After Alexander's death in 323 B.C., the Athenians revolted against Macedonian rule and Aristotle, who had been Alexander's tutor, decided to leave Athens. He retired to Chalcis in Euboea, where he died in 321 B.C.

OVERVIEW OF IDEAS ON EDUCATION

Aristotle's philosophy of education emphasizes human reason as the power that gives purpose and meaning to life. In contrast to the view that sees human destiny determined by irrational forces, Aristotle emphasized the human being's choice based on reason. Aristotle's philosophy emphasized that human excellence in all things, especially the pursuit of reason, was the overriding human goal.

Aristotle believed that we live in a world of objects that are external to us but that we can know. Using our senses and our reason, we study these objects and develop generalizations about their structure and function. These generalizations, or theory grounded on observation, are the surest guide we have for our behavior.

Aristotle's metaphysics rests on his matter-form hypothesis. All the objects that we perceive through our senses are composed of matter. Matter, which objects must have to exist, is arranged according to different designs, which Aristotle called form. Throughout his philosophy, Aristotle asserts the principle of dualism, that all things are divided into two elements. All objects—minerals, plants, and animals—can be analyzed according to their matter and their form, or structure. Human beings, too, are made of matter in that they have a body, but they possess the form, the structure, of a human person. For Aristotle, the power or potentiality at the core of the person is rationality. The aim of education is to develop the human potential of rationality to its highest possible level.

Aristotle explained the process of change through his theory of the four causes: material, formal, efficient, and final. Every object has matter, a material cause, which is that from which it is made. Every object has a structure or design, which is the formal cause that defines it and puts it in a class or category with similar objects. The efficient cause is the agent that brought about the change from the material to the formal. The final cause is that purpose for which the action is done.

Aristotle believed that the world in which we live is purposeful in that what takes place in its patterns is meaningful and is tending to an end. Everything that exists has a place in the ecology or great chain of being. Human life is purposeful, and human beings, by using rationality, have the power to make choices. For Aristotle, the purpose of life is happiness, the realization of all human potentiality, especially that of reason.

Aristotle's epistemology, how we know, is dualistic as is his metaphysics. It involves two phases, sensation and abstraction. By our senses we acquire information about the object's matter. Through abstraction, our minds, like a computer, sort this information to build concepts based on the object's form or structure.

Aristotle, a founder of science, emphasized classification of objects. From the basic classes of animal, vegetable, and mineral, it is possible to create a highly specialized system of classification. For example, the animal category can be divided into an immense array of subcategories such as biology, zoology, anthropology, anatomy, physiology, and so on.

Aristotle's philosophy of education emphasized liberal education through the arts and sciences. It is this knowledge that helps to realize a person's potential for rationality by informing the way in which we make choices. To act rationally, the human being needs to have alternatives upon which to act. It is in the knowledge provided by the arts and sciences that we can frame our choices and act on them.

For Aristotle, the highest ethical good is happiness, the exercise of rationality, a life governed by reason. Aristotle divided virtue into two categories, moral and intellectual. Moral virtue is a habit by which the individual exercises a prudent choice, a decision a rational person would make. Moral virtues are those that tend toward moderation, lying between extreme excess and extreme inhibition. The intellectual virtues contribute to the perfection of the human power to reason. Through the search for first principles, the human being develops a theory that arises from observation of the world. This theory, our best guide to conduct, has an explanatory power that informs us about the structure of the world and how it functions.

Aristotle continues to inspire contemporary educators who see the cultivation of the intellect as the primary purpose of education. Educational proposals such as the "Great Books" curriculum and the "Paideia" proposal rest on Aristotelian principles. His argument that human beings should be liberally educated remains a sustaining rationale for a liberal arts and sciences education.

THE PRIMARY SOURCE

The primary source is an excerpt from Aristotle's *Nichomachean Ethics.* Here, Aristotle considers the relationships between knowledge and virtue, between our knowing and our doing. Some highly significant principles of Aristotle's Realism, especially as they apply to ethical decisions, are discussed. Among them are:

1. Since we live in a purposeful world, our goals, in life and education, can and should be purposeful.
2. A proper education can illuminate our goals and the choices we make.
3. Ethical education, the early forming of human character, depends, to a large extent, on having learned the predispositions, the habits, that lead to virtue.
4. Virtuous behavior or desirable human character is based on moderation, a means that avoids excesses.
5. As rational creatures, we can and should use our reason to make our decisions and determine our choices.

FOCUSING QUESTIONS

As you read the selection, you may wish to consider the following questions:

1. Aristotle believes that we live in a purposeful and meaningful world. What do you think? Consider what your answer means for you as you create your own philosophy of education.
2. Reflect on how family and other early childhood experiences form your beliefs, your habits about what is right and wrong. In your own life, examine the role that is played by such ethical predispositions. Consider contemporary American society and reflect on the ethical predispositions that children acquire before coming to school. How do these predispositions have an impact on your teaching and on your students' development of character?
3. Do you agree or disagree that desired ethical behavior follows a mean of moderation between excess and repression? Consider your answer in terms of the standards of behavior found in contemporary American society and education.

FROM *THE NICOMACHEAN ETHICS OF ARISTOTLE*

Every art and every kind of inquiry, and similarly every act and purpose, seems to aim at some good; and so it has been well said that the good is that at which everything aims. But a difference is observable among these aims or ends. What is aimed at is sometimes the exercise of a faculty, sometimes a certain result beyond that exercise. And where there is an end beyond the act, there the result is better than the exercise of the faculty. Now since there are many kinds of actions and many arts and sciences, it follows that there are many ends also; the end of medicine is health, of shipbuilding, ships, of war, victory, and of economy, wealth. But when several of these are subordinated to some one art or science—as bridle-making and other arts concerned with horsemanship, and this in turn, along with all else the soldier does, to the art of war, and so

From *The Nicomachean Ethics of Aristotle,* translated by
F. H. Peters. London: Printed in the United Kingdom, 1886,
1–5, 10–12, 34–52.

on—then the end of the master-art is always more desired than the ends of the subordinate arts, since these are pursued for its sake. And this is equally true whether the end in view be the mere exercise of a faculty or something beyond that, as in the case of the sciences just mentioned.

If then in what we do there be some end which we wish for on its own account, choosing all the other ends as means to this, but not every end without exception as a means to something else (for so we should go on indefinitely, and desire would be left void and without object) this evidently will be the good or the best of all goods. And surely from a practical point of view it concerns us much to know this good; for then, like archers shooting at a target, we shall be more likely to get what we want. If this be so, we must try to indicate roughly what it is, and first of all to which of the arts or sciences it belongs. It would seem to belong to the highest art or science, that one which most of all deserves the name of master-art or master-science. Politics seems to answer this description. For politics prescribes which of the sciences a state needs, and which each man shall study, and how much; and to politics we see subordinated even the highest arts, such as economy [the management of a household], rhetoric, and war. Since then politics makes use of the other practical sciences, and since further it ordains what men are to do and from what to refrain, its end must include the ends or objectives of the others, and this end is the good of man. For though this good is the same for the individual as well as the state, yet the good of the state seems a larger and more perfect thing both to attain and to secure; and glad as one would be to do this service for a single individual, to do it for a people and for a number of city-states is nobler and more divine. This then is the aim of the present inquiry, which is political science.

We must be content if we can attain to so much precision in our statement as the subject will permit, for the same degree of accuracy is no more to be expected in all kinds of reasoning than in all kinds of manufacture. Now what is noble and just (with which political science deals) is so various and uncertain, that some think that these are merely conventional, and not natural, distinctions. There is a similar uncertainty also about what is good, because good things often do people harm; men have before now been ruined by wealth or have lost their lives through courage. Our subject then and our data being of this nature, we must be content if we can indicate roughly and in outline the truth; and if, in dealing with matters not subject to immutable laws, and reasoning from premises that are but probable, we can arrive at probable conclusions. The reader, on his part, should take each of my statements in the same spirit; for it is the mark of an educated man to require, in each kind of study, just so much exactness as the subject permits; it is equally absurd to accept probable reasoning from a mathematician, and to demand scientific proof from an orator.

Now each man can form a judgment about what he knows, and is called a good judge of that—that is of any special matter in which he has received special training. And the man who has received an all-round education is a good judge in general. And hence a young man is not qualified to be a student of politics; for he lacks experience of the affairs of life which form the data and the subject matter of political science. Further, since he is apt to be swayed by his passions, he will derive no benefit from a study whose aim is practical and not speculative. And it makes no difference whether he is young in years or young in character, for the young man's disqualification is not a matter of time, but is due to the fact that feeling or passion rules his life and directs all his desires. Men of this character turn the knowledge they get to no practical account, as we see with those we call incontinent; but those who direct their desires and ambitions by reason will gain much profit from a knowledge of these matters. So much, then, by way of preface as to the student, and the spirit in which he must accept what we say, and the object which we propose to ourselves. . . .

Let us return once more to the question of what this good can be of which we are in search. It seems to be different in different kinds of action and in different arts; it is different in medicine, in war, and in the other arts. What then is the good in each of these? Surely that for the sake of which all else is done. And that in medicine is health, in war is victory, in building is a house—a different thing in each case, but always the end in whatever we do and in whatever we choose. For it is always for the sake of the end that all else is done. If then there be one end of all that man does, this end will be the good achievable in action, and if there be more than one, these will be the goods achievable by action. Our argument has thus come round by a different path to the same point; this we must try to explain more clearly. We see that there are many ends. But some of these are chosen only as means, as wealth, flutes, and the whole class of instruments. And so it is plain that not all ends are final. But the best of all things must be something final. If then there be only one final end, this will be what we are seeking; or if there be more than one, then the most final of them.

Now that which is pursued as an end in itself is more final than that which is pursued as a means to something else, and that which is never chosen as a means than that which is chosen both as an end in itself and as a means, and that is strictly final which is always chosen as an end in itself and never as a means. Happiness seems more than anything else to answer this description, for we always choose it for itself, and never for the sake of something else; while honor and pleasure and reason, and all virtue or excellence, we choose partly for themselves (for, apart from any result, we should choose each of them), but partly also for the sake of happiness, supposing that they will help to make us happy. But no one chooses happiness for the sake of those things, or as a means to anything else at all.

We seem to be led to the same conclusion when we start from the idea of self-sufficiency. The final good is thought to be self-sufficing or all-sufficing. In applying this term we do not regard a man as an individual leading a solitary life, but we take account also of parents, children, wife, and in short, friends and fellow-citizens generally, since man is naturally a social being. Some limit must indeed be set for this; for if you go on to parents and descendants and friends of friends, you will never come to a stop. But this we will consider further on; for the present we will take self-sufficing to mean what by itself makes life desirable and in want of nothing. And happiness answers this description. And further, happiness is believed to be the most desirable thing in the world, and that not merely as one among other good things. If it were merely one among other good things [so that other things could be added to it] it is plain that the addition of the least of other goods must make it more desirable; for the addition becomes a surplus of good, and of two goods the greater is always more desirable. Thus it seems that happiness is something final and self-sufficing, and is the end of all that man does.

But perhaps the reader thinks that though no one will dispute the statement that happiness is the best thing in the world, yet a still more precise definition of it is needed. This will best be gained by asking, What is the function of man? For as the goodness and the excellence of the flute-player or the sculptor, or the practitioner of any art, and generally of those who have any business to do, lies in the function, so man's good would seem to lie in his function, if he possesses one. But can we suppose that, while a carpenter or a shoemaker has a function and a business of his own, man has no business and no function assigned to him as man by nature? Nay, surely as his several members, eye, hand, and foot, plainly have each its own function, so we must suppose that man also has some function over and above all of these. What then is it? Life evidently he has in common even with the plants, but we want that which is peculiar to man. We must exclude, therefore, the life of mere nutrition and growth. Next to this comes the life of sense; but this too he plainly shares with horses and cattle and all kinds of animals. There remains then the life whereby he acts—the life of his rational nature with its two aspects or divisions, one rational as obeying reason, the other rational as having and exercising reason. But as this expression is ambiguous, we must be understood to mean thereby the life that consists in the exercise of the faculties; for this seems to be more properly entitled to the name. The function of man, then, is the exercise of his soul on one side in obedience to reason, and on the other side with reason. But what is called the function of a man of any profession and the function of a man who is good in that profession are generically the same, that is to say, of a harper and of a good harper; and this holds in all cases without exception, only that in the case of the latter his superior excellence at his work is added; for we say a harper's function is to play the harp, and a good harper's function is to play the harp well. Man's function then being, as we say, a kind of life—that is, the exercise of his faculties and action of various kinds with reason—the good man's function is to do this well and nobly. But the function of anything is done well when it is done in accordance with the proper excellence of that thing. Putting all this together, then, we find that the good of man is the exercise of his faculties in accordance with excellence or virtue, or, if there be more than one, in accordance with the best and most complete virtue. But there must be a full term of years for this exercise; for one swallow or one fine day does not make a spring, nor does one day or any small space of time make a happy or virtuous man.

This, then, may be taken as a rough outline of the good; for this, I think, is the proper method: first to sketch the outline, and then to fill in the details. But it would seem that, the outline once fairly drawn, any one can carry on the work and fit in the several items which time reveals to us or aids us to discover. And this, indeed, is the way in which the arts and sciences have developed, for it requires no unusual genius to fill in the gaps. We must bear in mind, however, what was said earlier, and not demand the same degree of accuracy in all branches of inquiry, but in each case as much as the subject permits and as is proper to that kind of study. The carpenter and the geometer both look for the right angle, but in different ways; the former only wants such an approximation of it as his work requires, but the latter wants to know what constitutes a right angle, or what is its special quality—his aim is to find the truth. And so in other cases we must follow the same course, lest we spend more time on what is immaterial to our purpose than on the real business at hand. Nor must we in all cases alike demand the reason why. Sometimes it is sufficient if the undemonstrated fact be fairly pointed out, as in the case of the first principles of a science. Undemonstrated facts always form the first step or beginning of a science; and these first principles are arrived at some in one way and some in another way, some by induction, others by perception, others by some kind of training. But in each case we must attempt to apprehend them in the proper way, and do our best to define them clearly, for they have great influence upon the subsequent course of an inquiry. A good start is more than half the race, and our starting-point, once found, clears up a number of difficulties. . . .

Excellence or virtue, then, being of two kinds, intellectual and moral, intellectual excellence owes its birth and growth mainly to teaching, and so requires time and experience, while moral excellence is the result of habit or custom (*ethike*), and has accordingly received in our language [Greek] a name formed by a slight change from the word *ethos* (habit). From this it is plain that none of the moral excellencies or virtues is implanted in us by nature; for that which is by nature implanted within us cannot be altered by training. For example, a stone naturally tends to fall downward, and you could not train it to rise upward, though you tried to do so by throwing it up ten thousand times, nor could you train fire to move downward, nor accustom anything which naturally behaves in one way to behave in any other way. The virtues, then, come neither by nature nor contrary to nature, but nature gives us the capacity for acquiring them, and this is developed by training.

Again, where we do things by nature we get the power first, and put this power forth in act afterwards (as we plainly see in the case of the senses); for it is not by constantly seeing and hearing that we acquire those faculties, but, on the contrary, we had the power first and then used it, instead of acquiring the power by use. But we acquire the virtues by doing the acts, as is the case with the arts. We learn an art by doing those things which we wish to do when we have learned the art; we become builders by building, and harpists by playing the harp. And so by doing just and virtuous acts we become just and virtuous, and by doing acts of temperance and courage we become temperate and courageous. This is confirmed by what happens in states; for the legislators make their citizens good by training, and this is the wish of all legislators. Those who do not succeed in this miss their aim, and it is this that distinguishes a good from a bad constitution.

Again, both virtues and vices result from and are formed by the same acts in which they manifest themselves, as is the case also with the arts. It is by playing the harp that good harpers and bad harpers alike are produced; and so it is with builders and the rest, by building well they will become good builders and bad builders by building badly. Indeed, if it if were not so, they would not need anybody to teach them, but would all be born either good or bad at their trades. And it is just the same with the virtues also. It is by our conduct in our dealings with other men that we become just or unjust, and by acting in circumstances of danger, and training ourselves to feel fear or confidence, that we become courageous or cowardly. So too with our animal appetites and the passion of anger; for by behaving in this way or in that on occasions with which these passions are concerned, some become temperate and gentle, others profligate and ill-tempered. In a word, the several habits or characters are formed by the same kind of acts as those which they produce. Hence we ought to make certain that our acts be of a particular kind; for the resulting character varies as the acts vary. Instead of making a very small difference whether a man be trained from his youth up in this way or that, it makes a very great difference; indeed, it makes all the difference.

But our present study has not, like the rest, merely a theoretical aim. We are not inquiring simply to learn what excellence or virtue is, but in order to become good; for otherwise our study would be useless. We must ask therefore about these acts, and see of what kind they are to be; for, as we said, it is the acts that determine our habits or character. First of all, then, that they must be in accordance with right reason is a common characteristic of them, which we shall take for granted here, reserving for future discussion the question what this right reason is, and how it is related to the other excellencies or virtues. But let it be understood before we go on, that all reasoning on matters of practice must be in outline merely, and not scientifically exact; for as we said at the beginning the kind of reasoning demanded varies with the subject in hand, and in practical matters and questions of expediency there are no invariable laws, any more than in questions of health. And if our general conclusions are thus inexact, still more inexact is all reasoning about particular cases; for these fall under no system of scientifically established rules or traditional maxims, but the agent must always consider for himself what the special occasion requires, just as in medicine or navigation. In spite of this, however, we must try to give what help we can.

First of all then, we must observe that, in matters of this sort, to fall short and to go beyond are both fatal. To illustrate what we cannot see by what we can see: This is plain in the case of strength and health. Too much and too little exercise alike destroy strength, and to take too much meat and drink, or to take too little, is equally ruinous to health; but the proper amount produces and increases strength and health. So it is with temperance also and courage and the other virtues. The man who shuns and fears everything and never makes a stand becomes a coward; while the man who fears nothing at all, but will face anything, becomes foolhardy. So, too, the man who takes his fill of any kind of pleasure and abstains from none, is self-indulgent; but the man who avoids all pleasures (like a boor) lacks sensibility. For temperance and courage are destroyed both by excess and defect, but are preserved by moderation.

But habits or types of character are not only produced and preserved and destroyed by the same occasions and the same means, but they will also manifest themselves in the same circumstances. This is the case with obvious things like strength. Strength is produced by taking plenty of nourishment and doing plenty of hard work, and the strong man, in turn, has the greatest capacity for these. And the case is the same with the virtues. By abstaining from pleasure we become temperate, and when we have become temperate we are best able to abstain. And so with courage. By habituating ourselves to despise danger, and to face it, we become courageous; and when we have become courageous, we are best able to face danger.

The pleasure or pain that accompanies the acts must be taken as a test of the formed habit or character. He who abstains from the pleasures of the body and rejoices in the abstinence is temperate, while he who is vexed at having to abstain is self-indulgent. And, again, he who faces danger with pleasure, or at any rate, without pain is courageous, but he to whom this is painful is a coward. For moral virtue or excellence is closely concerned with pleasure and pain. It is

pleasure that moves us to do what is base and pain that moves us to refrain from what is noble. And therefore, as Plato says, man needs to be so trained from his youth as to find pleasure and pain in the right objects. This is what sound education means. Another reason why virtue has to do with pleasure and pain is that it has to do with actions and passions or affections; but every affection and every act is accompanied by pleasure or pain. This is indicated also by the use of pleasure and pain in correction; they have a kind of curative property, and a cure is effected by administering the opposite of the disease.

Again, as we said before, every type of character or habit is essentially relative to, and concerned with, those things that form it for good or for ill; but it is through pleasure and pain that bad characters are formed—that is to say, through pursuing and avoiding them at the wrong time, or in the wrong manner, or in any other of the various ways of going wrong that may be distinguished. And hence some people go so far as to define the virtues as a kind of impassive or neutral state of mind. But they make a mistake in saying this absolutely, instead of qualifying it by the addition of the right and wrong manner, time, etc. We may lay down, therefore, that this kind of excellence [moral excellence or virtue] makes us do what is best in matters of pleasure and pain, while vice or badness has the contrary effect. The following considerations will throw additional light on the point. There are three kinds of things that move us to choose and three that move us to avoid them. On the one hand, the beautiful or noble, the advantageous, the pleasant. On the other hand, the ugly or base, the hurtful, the painful. Now the good man is apt to go right, and the bad man to go wrong about them all, but especially about pleasure; for pleasure is not only common to man and animals, but also accompanies all pursuit or objects of choice; for even the noble and advantageous appear pleasant.

Again, the feeling of pleasure has been fostered in us all from our infancy by our training, and has thus become so ingrained in our life that it can scarcely be washed out. And, indeed, we all more or less make pleasure our test in judging actions. For this reason too, then, our whole study must be concerned with these matters; since to be pleased and pained in the right or wrong way has great influence on our actions. And lastly, as Heraclitus says, it is harder to fight with pleasure than with wrath; and virtue, like art, is always more concerned with what is harder; for the harder the task, the better is success. For this reason also, then, both moral virtue or excellence and political science must always be concerned with pleasures and pains; for he that behaves rightly with regard to them will be good, and he that behaves badly will be bad. We will take it as established then, that moral virtue or excellence has to do with pleasures and pains; and that the acts which produce virtue develop it, and also, when done differently, destroy it; and that it manifests itself in the same acts which produced it. . . .

We have thus found the genus to which virtue belongs; but we want to know, not only that it is a trained faculty, but also what species of trained faculty it is. We may safely assert that the virtue or excellence of a thing causes that thing both to be itself in good condition and to perform its function well. The excellence of the eye, for example, makes both the eye and its work good; for it is by the excellence of the eye that we see well. Similarly the excellence of the horse makes a horse both good in itself and good at running and at carrying its rider and at awaiting the attack of the enemy. If this is true in every case, therefore, the virtue of man also will be the state of character which makes a man good and which makes him do his own work well.

Every art or science, then, perfects its work in this way, looking to the mean and bringing its work up to this standard; so that people are wont to say of a good work that nothing could be taken from it or added to it, implying that excellence is destroyed by excess or deficiency, but secured by observing the mean. And good artists do in fact keep their eyes fixed on this in all that they do. Virtue therefore, since like nature it is more exact and better than any art, must also aim at the mean—virtue of course meaning moral virtue or moral excellence; for it has to do with passions and actions, and it is these that admit of excess and deficiency and the mean. For example, it is possible to feel fear, confidence, desire, anger, pity, and generally to be affected pleasantly and painfully, either too much or too little, in either case wrongly; but to be thus affected at the right times, and on the right occasions, and toward the right persons, and with the right object, and in the right fashion, is the mean course and the best course, and these are characteristics of virtue. And in the same way our outward acts also admit of excess and deficiency, and the mean or intermediate. Virtue then is concerned with feelings or passions and with outward acts, in which excess is wrong and deficiency is also blamed, but the mean is praised and is right; and being praised and being successful are both characteristics of virtue. Virtue, therefore, is a kind of moderation or mean as it aims at the mean or moderate amount. . . .

Virtue, then, is a habit or trained faculty of choice, the characteristic of which lies in observing the mean relatively to the persons concerned, and which is guided by reason, that is, by the judgment of the prudent man. And it is a moderation, firstly, inasmuch as it comes in the middle or the mean between two vices, one on the side of excess, the other on the side of deficiency; and secondly, inasmuch as, while these vices fall short of or exceed the mean or intermediate measure in feeling and in action, it finds and chooses the mean, middling, or moderate amount. Regarded in essence, therefore, or according to the definition of its nature, virtue is a moderation or middle state, but viewed in its relation to what is best and right it is the extreme of perfection.

SUGGESTIONS FOR FURTHER READING

Ackrill, J. L. *Aristotle: The Philosopher.* New York: Oxford University Press, 1981.

Aristotle. *Nichomachean Ethics.* Translated by Terence Irwin. Indianapolis: Hackett Publishing Co., l985.

_____. *The Poetics.* Buffalo, N.Y.: Prometheus Books, 1992.

_____. *On Rhetoric: A Theory of Civic Discourse.* New York: Oxford University Press, 1991.

Broadie, Sarah. *Ethics with Aristotle.* New York: Oxford University Press, 1991.

Burnet, John. *Aristotle on Education.* Cambridge, Mass.: Harvard University Press, 1928.

Davidson, Thomas. *Aristotle and Ancient Educational Ideals.* New York: Burt Franklin, 1969.

Edel, Abraham. *Aristotle and His Philosophy.* Chapel Hill, N.C.: University of North Carolina Press, 1982.

Evans, John D. G. *Aristotle.* New York: St. Martin's Press, 1987.

Irwin, Terence. *Aristotle's First Principles.* Oxford: Clarendon Press, 1988.

Johnson, Curtis N. *Aristotle's Theory of the State.* New York: St. Martin's Press, 1990.

McKirahan, Richard D. *Principles and Proofs: Aristotle's Theory of Demonstrative Science.* Princeton, N.J.: Princeton University Press, 1992.

Rankin, Kenneth. *The Recovery of the Soul: An Aristotelian Essay on Self-Fulfillment.* Montreal: McGill-Queen's University Press, 1991.

Reeve, C. D. C. *Practices of Reason: Aristotle's Nicomachean Ethics.* New York: Oxford University Press, 1992.

Salkever, Stephen G. *Finding the Mean: Theory and Practice in Aristotelian Political Philosophy.* Princeton, N.J.: Princeton University Press, 1990.

Spangler, Mary Michael. *Aristotle on Teaching.* Lanham, Md.: University Press of America, 1998.

Swanson, Judith A. *The Public and the Private in Aristotle's Political Philosophy.* Ithaca, N.Y.: Cornell University Press, 1992.

Verbeke, Gerard. *Moral Education in Aristotle.* Washington, D.C.: Catholic University of America Press, 1990.

White, Stephen A. *Sovereign Virtue: Aristotle on the Relation between Happiness and Prosperity.* Stanford, Calif.: Stanford University Press, 1992.

NOTES

1. G. E. R. Lloyd, *Aristotle: The Growth and Structure of His Thought* (Cambridge, Mass.: Cambridge University Press, 1968), 3.

3

QUINTILIAN: RHETORICAL EDUCATOR IN SERVICE OF THE EMPEROR

BIOGRAPHICAL SKETCH

Marcus Fabius Quintilianus, or Quintilian (35–95 A.D.), is significant as a prominent Roman rhetorician whose theory incorporated the integrated Greek and Roman concepts about oratorical education that became part of the Western educational heritage. In classical Rome, oratory or rhetoric was esteemed as a means of influencing people and shaping the course of events. Earlier, the Greeks gave an emphasis to the power of oratory.

Quintilian was born in 35 A.D. in Callagurris, a Roman city located in modern-day Spain. He was taught rhetoric by his father, a noted rhetorician. The Roman study of rhetoric, particularly Quintilian's education, had been shaped by their cultural interchange with the Greeks, a people whom they had conquered. A particularly strong influence on Quintilian came from his reading of Isocrates (436–338 B.C.), an influential teacher of rhetoric in Athens. Isocrates had written that the orator should be both a rational and ethical person as well as an effective and persuasive public speaker. Further, Isocrates' emphasis on the orator as a policy and decision maker was eagerly accepted by the Romans.

Well grounded in the theory of rhetoric, Quintilian, at age 16, journeyed to Rome, the capital of the empire, to work as an assistant to Domitius Afer, a distinguished lawyer. Here, he learned to put theory into practice. After Domitius' death, Quintilian returned to Callagurris to practice law.

Quintilian later returned to Rome, where he established a rhetorical school. His outstanding ability as a teacher of rhetoric brought him to the notice of the emperor Vespasian, who ruled from 70 to 79 A.D. Vespasian appointed Quintilian to the imperially endowed Chair of Latin rhetoric, a position he held from 72 to 92 A.D.[1] After retiring from the Chair of Latin rhetoric, Quintilian spent the next 2 years writing his most important work on education, *Institutio Oratoria*.

OVERVIEW OF IDEAS ON EDUCATION

Quintilian's *Institutio Oratoria* states his educational philosophy. He announced at the beginning of the work that he intended to educate "a good man" as well as a "perfect orator." His book, an early treatise on educational psychology as well as rhetorical education, described human beings as having many sides to their nature—intellectual, volitional, and emotional. Though giving reason the highest priority, Quintilian advised educators to develop all aspects of human character.

Quintilian's learning theory identified stages of human development that were marked with a readiness for a particular kind of learning and instruction. He saw a child's earliest years as especially important to form the correct habits and predispositions for later learning. From birth to 7, he said, children are not yet reasonable but are ruled by their instincts and impulses. Concerned with the development of speech, he cautioned parents to make sure that children heard correct speech patterns.[2]

A theorist who integrated Greek and Latin cultural ideas on education, Quintilian gave importance to Greek language and literature in rhetorical education. His students were to be bilingual in Greek and Latin.

At 7, the future orator attends the Roman primary school, the *ludus,* to learn reading, writing, and calculating. Quintilian wanted boys to go to school rather than be tutored at home since schooling created opportunities for peer group interaction that would benefit the orator in the future. At age 13, the boy was to attend the school of the grammaticus. Roman boys attended two parallel grammar schools— one that emphasized Greek and the other, Latin grammar and literature.

After completing his primary and secondary studies, the young man, if he had the aptitude, was to proceed to the rhetorical school. Here, the liberal arts were studied, including literature, poetry, drama, history, law and jurisprudence, philosophy, and oratory. Rhetoric, debate, declamation, and elocution were stressed since they were indispensable to the successful orator, who sought to perfect the human power of speech into eloquence, its highest and noblest expression.

Quintilian's ideal orator was to be an ethical leader who exemplified the Roman values of honor, responsibility, and duty to the state.

After early childhood came the stage of growing to cognitive and physical maturity. For Quintilian, these years were a time of developing literary skills, of learning subjects, and of being socialized with the right kind of peers. In the last stage of formal education, in the school of rhetoric, Quintilian stood firmly in the tradition of the liberal arts, which he regarded as essential in forming the properly educated human being. Quintilian broadened the concept of the orator from a skilled and persuasive public speaker to a person who was liberally educated, ethical, and committed to public service.

THE PRIMARY SOURCE

In this selection from *Quintilian's Institutes of Oratory,* Quintilian discusses the desirable characteristics of teachers of rhetoric or oratory. Many of these characteristics apply to teachers in general.

FOCUSING QUESTIONS
As you read the selection, you may wish to consider the following questions:

1. Reflect on Quintilian's prescriptions regarding the character of teachers. Do you think that his prescriptions are applicable to contemporary American schools? Why, or why not?

2. Consider Quintilian's belief that a teacher's expertise in teaching requires both knowledge of a subject and skill in the methods of teaching. Do contemporary programs of teacher education meet Quintilian's requirement regarding knowledge and method?
3. What is Quintilian's advice to teachers regarding their pupils' individual differences? Is his advice sound? In your own teaching, consider the problems of recognizing and attending to pupils' individual differences while providing group instruction.
4. What is Quintilian's advice to teachers regarding the education of gifted students? In your own teaching, what do you consider to be appropriate instruction for gifted students?

FROM *QUINTILIAN'S INSTITUTES OF ORATORY*

As soon therefore as a boy shall have attained such proficiency in his studies, as to be able to comprehend what we have called the first precepts of the teachers of rhetoric, he must be put under the professors of that art.

Of these professors the morals must first be ascertained; a point of which I proceed to treat in this part of my work, not because I do not think that the same examination is to be made, and with the utmost care, in regard also to other teachers, (as indeed I have shown in the preceding book) but because the very age of the pupils makes attention to the matter still more necessary. For boys are consigned to these professors when almost grown up, and continue their studies under them even after they are become men; and greater care must in consequence be adopted with regard to them, in order that the purity of the master may secure their more tender years from corruption, and his authority deter their bolder age from licentiousness. Nor is it enough that he give, in himself, an example of the strictest morality, unless he regulate, them by severity of discipline, the conduct of those who come to receive his instructions.

Let him adopt, then, above all things, the feelings of a parent towards his pupils, and consider that he succeeds to the place of those by whom the children were entrusted to him. Let him neither have vices in himself, nor tolerate them in others. Let his austerity not be stern, nor his affability too easy, lest dislike arise

From *Quintilian's Institutes of Oratory*, I, translated by John Selby Watson. London: Henry G. Bohn, 1856, excerpts from 99–101, 103–104, 122–25.

from the one, or contempt from the other. Let him discourse frequently on what is honourable and good, for the oftener he admonishes, the more seldom will he have to chastise. Let him not be of an angry temper, and yet not a conniver at what ought to be corrected. Let him be plain in his mode of teaching, and patient of labour, but rather diligent in exacting tasks than fond of giving them of excessive length. Let him reply readily to those who put questions to him, and question of his own accord those who do not. In commending the exercises of his pupils, let him be neither niggardly nor lavish; for the one quality begets dislike of labour, and the other self-complacency. In amending what requires correction, let him not be harsh, and, least of all, not reproachful; for that very circumstance, that some tutors blame as if they hated, deters many young men from their proposed course of study. Let him every day say something, and even much, which, when the pupils hear, they may carry away with them, for though he may point out to them, in their course of reading, plenty of examples for their imitation, yet *the living voice*, as it is called, feeds the mind more nutritiously, and especially the voice of the teacher, whom his pupils, if they are but rightly instructed, both love and reverence. How much more readily we imitate those whom we like, can scarcely be expressed.

The liberty of standing up and showing exultation, in giving applause, as is done under most teachers, is by no means to be allowed to boys; for the approbation even of young men, when they listen to others, ought to be but temperate. Hence it will result that the pupil will depend on the judgment of the master, and will think that he has expressed properly whatever shall have been approved by him. But that most mischievous *po-liteness*, as it is now termed, which is shown by students in their praise of each other's compositions, whatever be their merits, is not only unbecoming and theatrical, and foreign to strictly regulated schools, but even a most destructive enemy to study, for care and toil may well appear superfluous, when praise is ready for whatever the pupils have produced. Those therefore who listen, as well as he who speaks, ought to watch the countenance of the master, for they will thus discern what is to be approved and what is to be condemned; and thus power will be gained from composition, and judgment from being heard. But now, eager and ready, they not only start up at every period, but dart forward, and cry out with indecorous transports. The compliment is repaid in kind, and upon such applause depends the fortune of a declamation; and hence result vanity and self-conceit, insomuch that, being elated with the tumultuous approbation of their class-fellows, they are inclined, if they receive but little praise from the master, to form an ill opinion of him. But let masters, also, desire to be heard themselves with attention and modesty; for the master ought not to speak to suit the taste of his pupils, but the pupils to suit that of the master. If possible, moreover, his attention should be directed to observe what each pupil commends in his speeches, and for what reason; and he may then rejoice that what he says will give pleasure, not more on his own account than on that of his pupils who judge with correctness. . . . For my part, I do not consider him, who is unwilling to teach little things, in the number of preceptors; but I argue that the ablest teachers can teach little things best, if they will; first, because it is likely that he who excels others in eloquence, has gained the most accurate knowledge of the means by which men attain eloquence; secondly, because method, which, with the best qualified instructors, is always plainest, is of great efficacy in teaching; and lastly, because no man rises to such a height in greater things that lesser fade entirely from his view.

Is there not then, it may be asked, a certain height of eloquence too elevated for the immaturity of boyhood to comprehend it? I readily confess that there is; but the eloquent professor must also be a man of sense, not ignorant of teaching, and lowering himself to the capacity of the learner; as any fast walker, if he should happen to walk with a child, would give him his hand, relax his pace, and not go on quicker than his companion could follow. What shall be said, too, if it generally happens that instructions given by the most learned are far more easy to be understood, and

more perspicuous than those of others? For perspicuity is the chief virtue of eloquence, and the less ability a man has, the more he tries to raise and swell himself out as those of short stature exalt themselves on tiptoe, and the weak use most threats. As to those whose style is inflated, displaying a vitiated taste, and who are fond of sounding words, or faulty from any other mode of vicious affectation, I am convinced that they labour under the fault, not of strength, but of weakness, as bodies are swollen, not with health, but with disease, and as men who have erred from the straight road generally make stoppages. Accordingly, the less able a teacher is, the more obscure will he be. . . .

It is generally, and not without reason, regarded as an excellent quality in a master to observe accurately the differences of ability in those whom he has undertaken to instruct, and to ascertain in what direction the nature of each particularly inclines him; for there is in talent an incredible variety; nor are the forms of the mind fewer than those of the body. This may be understood even from orators themselves, who differ so much from each other in their style of speaking, that no one is like another, though most of them have set themselves to imitate those whom they admired. It has also been thought advantageous by most teachers to instruct each pupil in such a manner as to cherish by learning the good qualities inherited from nature, so that the powers may be assisted in their progress towards the object to which they chiefly direct themselves. As a master of palaestric exercises, when he enters a gymnasium full of boys, is able, after trying their strength and comprehension in every possible way, to decide for what kind of exercise each ought to be trained; so a teacher of eloquence, they say, when he has clearly observed which boy's genius delights most in a concise and polished manner of speaking, and which in a spirited, or grave, or smooth, or rough, or brilliant, or elegant one, will so accommodate his instructions to each, that he will be advanced in that department in which he shows most ability; because nature attains far greater power when seconded by culture; and he that is led contrary to nature, cannot make due progress in the studies for which he is unfit, and makes those talents, for the exercise of which he seemed born, weaker by neglecting to cultivate them. . . .

We must so far accommodate ourselves, however, to feeble intellects, that they may be trained only to that to which nature invites them; for thus they will do with more success the only thing which they can do. But if richer material fall into our hands, from which we justly conceive hopes of a true orator, no rhetorical excellence must be left unstudied. For though such a genius be more inclined, as indeed it must be, to the exercise of certain powers, yet it will not be averse to that of others, and will render them, by study, equal to those in which it naturally excelled; just as the skilful trainer in bodily exercise, (that I may adhere to my former illustration,) will not, if he undertakes to form a pancratiast, teach him to strike with his fist or his heel only, or instruct him merely in wrestling, or only in certain artifices of wrestling, but will practise him in everything pertaining to the pancratiastic art.

There may perhaps be some pupil unequal to some of these exercises. He must then apply chiefly to that in which he can succeed.

For two things are especially to be avoided; one, to attempt what cannot be accomplished; and the other, to divert a pupil from what he does well to something else for which he is less qualified. . . .

Having spoken thus fully concerning the duties of teachers, I give pupils, for the present, only this one admonition, that they are to love their tutors not less than their studies, and to regard them as parents, not indeed of their bodies, but of their minds. Such affection contributes greatly to improvement, for pupils, under its influence, will not only listen with pleasure, but will believe what is taught them, and will desire to resemble their instructors. They will come together, in assembling for school, with pleasure and cheerfulness; they will not be angry when corrected, and will be delighted when praised; and they will strive, by their devotion to study, to become as dear as possible to the master. For as it is the duty of preceptors to teach, so it is that of pupils to show themselves teachable; neither of these duties, else, will be of avail without the other. And as the generation of man is effected by both parents, and as you will in vain scatter seed, unless the furrowed ground, previously softened, cherish it, so neither can eloquence come to its growth unless by mutual agreement between him who communicates and him who receives.

SUGGESTIONS FOR FURTHER READING

Bonner, Stanley F. *Education in Ancient Rome.* Berkeley: University of California Press, 1977.

Gwynn, Aubrey. *Roman Education from Cicero to Quintilian.* New York: Russell and Russell, 1964.

Kennedy, George. *The Art of Rhetoric in the Roman World: 300 B.C.–A.D. 300.* Princeton, N.J.: Princeton University Press, 1972.

_____. *Quintilian.* New York: Twayne Publishers, 1969.

Murphy, James J. *Quintilian on the Teaching of Speaking and Writing.* Carbondale, Ill.: Southern Illinois University Press, 1987.

Quintilian. *The Institutio Oratoria.* Translated by H. E. Butler. London: William Heinemann, 1921.

NOTES

1. George Kennedy, *The Arts of Rhetoric in the Roman World: 300 B.C.–A.D. 300* (Princeton, N.J.: Princeton University Press, 1972), 487–514; and Aubrey Gwynn, *Roman Education from Cicero to Quintilian* (New York: Russell and Russell, 1964), 180–241.

2. Edward J. Power, *Evolution of Educational Doctrine* (New York: Appleton-Century-Crofts, 1969), 87–92.

4

THOMAS AQUINAS: SCHOLASTIC THEOLOGIAN AND THE CREATOR OF THE MEDIEVAL CHRISTIAN SYNTHESIS

BIOGRAPHICAL SKETCH

Thomas Aquinas is significant in the history and philosophy of education for his formation of the medieval Christian synthesis that integrated Christian doctrines with Aristotelian philosophy. Aquinas (1225–1274), one of the medieval period's most prominent theologians and philosophers, was born at the castle of Roccasecca, the estate of a wealthy landowning feudal family in the Italian province of Caserta, near Naples. His father was Landulf and his mother was Theodora de Aquino.[1] At age 5, his father enrolled Thomas at the monastic school of the famous Benedictine abbey at Montecassino, founded by St. Benedict in 529, on a hill overlooking the town of Cassino. The abbey was renowned for its large library of books on theology and philosophy, especially the writings of the early church fathers. Thomas studied in the monastery school from 1231 to 1239.[2]

In 1239, the 14-year-old Aquinas enrolled at the University of Naples to begin his study of the liberal arts. Naples, in the south of Italy, was accessible to intellectual currents from both Greece and the Arab world. Here, Thomas studied such classical authors as Aristotle, Boethius, Priscian, Donatus, Cicero, Euclid, and Ptolemy. His introduction to Aristotle would serve him well when he later wrote a comprehensive book, or summa, that united Aristotelian philosophy with Christian doctrine.[3] He completed his liberal arts studies in 1243, at age 18.

At Naples, Aquinas had encountered the Dominican order, which included some of the most highly regarded scholars of the period. He announced, in 1244, his intention to become a Dominican. His family, especially his mother, strongly opposed his decision. While not objecting to his entry into religious life, she did not want him to become a Dominican. As a Dominican, he could not inherit the family's wealth. His brothers abducted Thomas from Naples and confined him for a year at the family castle at Roccasecca. Finally, the family relented and Thomas was permitted to return to the Dominicans in 1245.[4]

Recognizing that he was intellectually gifted, Aquinas' Dominican superiors sent him for further study to the monastery of the Holy Cross in Cologne, Germany. From

24

1246 to 1252, he continued his liberal studies and learned the regula established by St. Dominic. Here he entered the Dominican order, was ordained a priest, and published one of his early essays, *On Being and Essence.*

Aquinas, in 1252, began his graduate studies in theology and was appointed as a lecturer at the University of Paris. He lectured on dogmatic theology, using Peter Lombard's *Libri Quator Sentiarium,* or *Book of Sentences,* as his text. Lombard's *Sentences,* an important scholastic text, contained a compilation of the writings of the leading Church fathers. Aquinas, following the scholastic method of teaching, would lecture on the text, reviewing arguments for and against a proposition, providing explanations, and drawing conclusions. Aquinas published his interpretations on Lombard's work as the *Commentary on the Sentences.* In 1256, he was awarded the licentiate, which qualified him as a fully approved professor.

Aquinas then wrote *Summa Contra Gentiles,* the *Summa Against the Gentiles,* which defended Christian doctrines against opposing religious views and was used as a manual for teaching Christian doctrines.[5] In responding to Arabic scholars' interpretation of Aristotle's work, Aquinas began his major effort of reconciling Aristotle's philosophy with Christianity, which would appear in his greatest work, the *Summa Theologiae.*

From 1259 to 1269, Aquinas was away from Paris, pursuing special assignments at the request of the Dominicans. When not traveling to perform these duties, he was in Rome, where Pope Urban IV encouraged his scholarly research and writing of the *Summa Theologiae.* In 1269, he returned to the University of Paris, where he completed his major work and continued teaching and writing until his death in 1274.

OVERVIEW OF EDUCATIONAL IDEAS

Thomas Aquinas was one of those rare scholars who was able to effect a great reconciliation of ideas and create an all-embracing synthesis. In building his synthesis in the *Summa Theologiae,* Aquinas sought to integrate two important principles: divine revelation as the ultimate source of truth, and the validity and efficacy of human reason. Aquinas was determined to use Aristotle's philosophy of natural Realism in building his synthesis of faith and reason. He believed that Aristotle's natural sciences, ethics, and politics, which expressed a belief in an intelligible natural order, could be raised to a higher spiritual dimension by the Christian faith. Aristotle's natural virtues, when infused by grace, could become supernatural virtues.

Thomism, the philosophy of Aquinas, was a variety of religious or Theistic Realism. Like Aristotle, who saw reality divided into form and matter, Aquinas also conceived of reality existing in two dimensions, the supernatural and the natural orders. Aquinas reasoned that the human being, as "a spirit in the world," possessed a spirit, grounded in the soul, and a body.[6] True to the Christian conception of human nature, Aquinas held that the soul, living after the body's death, would bring the person to the vision of God in the afterlife in heaven.

Aquinas, like Aristotle, recognized that the body positioned human beings in the natural order on earth. Though they shared many characteristics with the lower order animals, human beings, because of soul and mind, were raised by God to a higher level of existence.

Like Aristotle, Aquinas argued that human ideas originated through the senses, which experienced an external world of objects. The mind, in turn, formed concepts as it extracted the form of the objects conveyed with sensory data. Added to this natural power of cognition or conceptualization was the truth revealed by God through the Scriptures, which completed the knowledge that humans developed through their reason.

Human beings were endowed by God with intellect and free will, which empowered them to choose between alternatives. This power to make choices, while a rational activity for Aristotle, was raised to a spiritual plane by Aquinas, who believed that human reason could be guided by the Scriptures and the doctrines of the Church.

Aquinas, again like Aristotle, believed that human beings possessed the power of rationality. For Aristotle, human beings' highest and defining power was reason and the greatest human pleasure was in cultivating rational excellence. Aquinas agreed with Aristotle that reason was a highly important distinguishing human power. Again he added the Christian belief that reason needed faith to accept God's revealed truth. Although Aquinas concurred with Aristotle on the importance of reason, he believed that the greatest pleasure human beings could experience came from the supernatural life of the soul in the vision of God after death.

While Aquinas emphasized the spiritual side of human nature, he did not neglect the physical dimension by which humans lived in society, evolved governments, and sustained themselves through economic activities. What emerged in Thomistic thought was a hierarchical arrangement of human activities with religious studies at the summit, moving gradually downward to those that cultivated rationality, and finally reaching those bounded by space and time that dealt with society, government, and the economy.

Thomas Aquinas was both a philosopher who examined theological issues as well as a theologian who philosophized. As a teacher, he also wrote on educational themes. In *de Magistro,* he developed a theory of education that complemented his broader philosophical and theological work. His philosophy of education emphasized that:

1. Education, like life, is purposeful; it is a means to an end. Human beings' ultimate destiny is the beatific vision of God, and education should contribute to the achievement of that goal.
2. Reality exhibits two dimensions: one spiritual and the other physical. Education relates to both dimensions—to both soul and body. It should prepare people to live fulfilling and productive lives on earth and also prepare them for their ultimate goal of being with God in heaven.
3. Society and institutions, like reality, are hierarchically structured. Education, especially the curriculum, should be structured hierarchically with the most important subjects, those of greatest generality, located higher and receiving priority.

As a true scholastic teacher, Aquinas developed some important definitions and distinctions about education, schooling, teaching, and learning. Education, broadly construed, contributed to human beings' total formation. As the process of total human formation, education, while including schooling, was more than formal instruction. Formal education, or schooling, Aquinas called *disciplina*. Here, a teacher deliberately taught a skill or a subject to a learner. A subject was *scientia*, an organized body of knowledge in which first principles were logically developed and illustrated by analogies, cases, and examples. The Thomistic principles, resting on definite theological and philosophical foundations, emphasized teaching and learning of subjects in a structured and disciplined way. The school climate would include the religious elements that reflected Christian faith and doctrine. Schooling would have a moral purpose in nurturing the habits, dispositions, and outlooks that inclined students to a purposeful life of faith and reason. In such an environment, teachers were to be models of virtue that could be imitated by students. In addition to education and schooling, Aquinas recognized the importance of *Inventio,* self-learning that came from intuition and discovery without the aid of a teacher.[7]

Aquinas elevated teaching to the level of a vocation in which a person was "called" to the life of teaching in a way similar to a priest's or nun's call to religious service. The teacher's service to humanity was an act of love. In addition, to be a teacher meant that the person possessed a body of knowledge and the instructional skills to transmit it to students. The life of a teacher was highly integrated in that it was characterized by service, study, and action.

THE PRIMARY SOURCE

Bonjoannes has prepared an edition of Thomas Aquinas' *Summa Theologica* that summarizes the medieval theologian's important theological principles. The selections treat Thomas' principles of sacred doctrine, reasoning to the existence of God, creation by God, the human intellectual faculty, free will, and the knowledge possessed by children.

FOCUSING QUESTIONS

1. According to Aquinas, what is sacred doctrine and how is it related to the other sciences?
2. How does Aquinas go about presenting a case that it is possible to reason to the existence of God?
3. How is the concept of hierarchy expressed in Aquinas' interpretation of God's act of creation? Can this concept of hierarchy be applied to educational institutions and the curriculum?
4. Describe and analyze Aquinas' principles of human intellect and free will.
5. Consider Aquinas' method of presenting an argument. Is his approach to making a case relevant to contemporary education?

CHAPTER I

OF SACRED DOCTRINE: ITS NATURE AND EXTENT

It is necessary for the salvation of man that, besides the natural sciences, there should exist some doctrine received by revelation; for many things are made known by revelation which transcend reason. Moreover, that which is discoverable about God by human reason could be known only to a few, and that after much time, and not without a large admixture of error. It was good, therefore, for man to be taught by means of a doctrine divinely revealed; for salvation, which is in God, depends upon a knowledge of the truth.

This doctrine is a science proceeding from principles made known by the light of a higher science, as music proceeds from principles explained by arithmetic. For Sacred Doctrine proceeds from principles made known by the light of a higher knowledge, namely, the Divine Knowledge, and in it certain particulars are treated of, both as an example of life and in order that we may know clearly by what instrumentality this revelation is made.

Sacred Doctrine takes account of all things only in so far as they belong to the formal order of Divine revelation. This science is one, neither wholly practical nor wholly speculative; but being of a higher order it includes both, yet remains one, as God knows both Himself and what He does with the same knowledge. It is, however, more speculative than practical, for it treats more of Divine things than of human actions, being concerned with the latter only in so far as they are intended to lead man to the perfect knowledge of God, in which eternal beatitude consists.

And this science is higher in dignity than other speculative sciences, for these derive their certainty from human reason, which may err, while Sacred Doctrine, owing to the light of Divine Knowledge, can never be deceived; moreover, they consider only things which are below reason, while she treats principally of such as transcend reason. Sacred Doctrine is also higher in dig-

nity than other practical sciences, for, among such, that science is accounted the more honourable which is not subordinated to a further end, as military science is to civil; but the end of this doctrine, in as far as it is practical, is eternal beatitude, to which all other ends of the practical sciences are subordinate. . . .

CHAPTER II

THE EXISTENCE OF GOD

That God exists is in itself a self-evident truth; but it is not so to us who do not see the Essence of God; and it requires to be proved by those things which are more known as regards ourselves and less known in their nature, that is, by effects. Although we know God in a general way, we do not therefore know Him absolutely. It is possible to demonstrate the Existence of God by effects, which are more known to us than their cause, for effects being granted, a pre-existing cause there must be; and we call this *demonstratio quia,* not *propter quid,* for not even by effects do we know the Essence of God.

The Existence of God may be shown by five proofs. The First is drawn from the principle of motion. It is evident to our senses that motion exists. Whatever is moved must be moved by some external agent. Nothing is moved unless it is in potentiality (*in potentia*) to its term of motion. Motion is made accordingly as things are changed from the potential to the actual, and this requires some actual agent to move them from the potential state. Since it cannot be that anything should be both potential and actual as regards the same order, it follows that the mover and the moved cannot be identical. Thus, not to go on indefinitely, we must come at last to a First Cause immovable of motion; and there we find God.

The Second Proof consists in the order of Efficient Causes in sensible objects. Nothing can be its own efficient cause, for then it would exist before itself. In every order of being the first is the cause of the intermediate, and this latter the cause of the ultimate; so that if the cause be removed the effect ceases to be, and if the first is gone there can be neither the intermediate nor the ultimate. Hence, not to proceed indefinitely, there must be a First Efficient Cause; and there too we find God.

From Berardus Bonjoannes' *Compendium of the Summa Theologica of St. Thomas Aquinas,* translated by Fr. Wilfrid Lescher. London: Thomas Baker, 1906, 1–2, 5–7, 163–64, 200–02, 209–10, 254.

The Third Proof is taken from possible and necessary things. Some things may be or not be; they are possible, as they are subject to generation and decomposition; but everything could not be always thus, for what is not necessary at some time is not. If, therefore, all things may possibly not be, at some time there must have been nothing; and if this be true even now, there would be nothing, for what is not can only exist by that which is. All things, therefore, are not mere possibilities in their origin; there must exist some necessary thing. But whatever is necessary, either has cause for its necessity or it has not; and, not to proceed indefinitely, as regards necessary things with a cause for their being necessary, we are obliged to postulate something necessary in itself with no cause for its necessity, but itself the cause to other things of their necessity; and this is God.

The Fourth Proof proceeds from our finding some things better than others. A thing is said to be more or less as it approaches to that which is called most. There exists, therefore, something which is best and truest, the source to things of all goodness and truth, and of all their other perfections; and this we call God.

The Fifth Proof is drawn from the idea of government. Some things are without understanding, yet they work for an end, because often or always they work in the same way to obtain the best end; hence it is evident that they attain the end not by chance, but by intention; and since they must act towards the end not by their own but by some one's knowledge, they reach the end because they are directed by an Intelligent Being. There must, therefore, be such an Intelligent Being Who directs all natural things to their end; and Him we call God.

CHAPTER LXV

THE CREATION OF CORPOREAL CREATURES

Every corporeal creature is from God. For wherever unity is found in diversity, it must be referred to a single cause, because variety does not, by itself, unite things in one order. Since Being, therefore, is common to all things, however diverse, there must of necessity be some Principle of Being by which all things exist, whatever they are and according to whatever mode; and this Principle is God.

Corporeal creatures are created by God to manifest His Goodness, not by way of punishment; for every nature is good. Neither is the disposition of the universe accidental, but creatures all form parts of a whole, in which the parts exist for the sake of their utility and are ordered to the whole. The less noble are for the nobler, matter for form, single creatures for the universe, and the universe for God;—since it forms a representation of the Divine Goodness, by means of which rational creatures may, in a special manner, find their end in the love and knowledge of God.

The higher any cause is, the more it extends to variety in causation; but that which underlies things is always found to be more general than that which informs and individualizes them. Thus, Being is more general than life, and life than intelligence; and the more general anything is found to be, the more directly it proceeds from the First Cause; for no second cause can produce anything unless something be presupposed to the thing produced, either created or uncreated.

It remains, therefore, as before said, that God alone can create, and that corporeal forms are not produced from ideas (as taught by Plato and Origen); or created by lower intelligences (as held by Avicenna)—but that in the first constitution of things they are directly from God. And since there can be no transmutation from the potential to the actual in simple creation, we must admit that, in respect of its proper cause, matter is subject at command to God only, and that the forms of bodies are from God.

CHAPTER LXXIX

THE INTELLECTUAL FACULTY

The intellect is not the essence of the soul, but a faculty; for in God only, Whose operation is His Being, can intellect be the same as essence. Therefore faculty stands to operation, as essence to being; and understanding, in creatures, is a faculty of the being who understands.

Our intellect, indeed, is a passive power in respect of intelligible things, and at the first like a clean slate. For the human intellect is lowest in order of intelligence and furthest removed from the Intellect of God, as appears from the fact that at first it is only *in potentia* and afterwards is made actually intelligent. . . .

We see, also, that there must be some *intellectus agens* in the soul, because, although it participates in a higher intellect by which it is assisted, yet, owing to its discursive mode of understanding, and gradual conversion from the potential to the actual, it neither understands all things, nor perfectly. There must, therefore, be some virtue received from the Superior Intellect, inherent in the soul itself, by which things are made actually intelligible; as is the case with other perfect things. For besides causes which act universally there are infused virtues, proper to things, which are derived from the Superior Intellect, whereby the intellect of man is enabled to elucidate phantasms, elicit universal conditions from particular ones, and make things actually intelligible. . . .

But every action belongs to things in virtue of some principle formally inherent in them; therefore the power which is the principle of such action is something in the soul itself. And since the active intellect is something in the soul itself, it follows that it must be multiplied according to the plurality of souls; for the same power cannot belong to several subjects. While, if it were something separate, the intellect of all men would be one; which has been disproved above.

Memory also belongs to the intellectual part, if it be understood as the power of preserving species. Understood as the power of recalling the past, it belongs rather to the sensitive part; for the sensitive soul apprehends particulars.

Nor can there be any difference of faculties in the intellect except that of possible and acting. For there is a difference between the active faculty, which renders an object actual; and the passive faculty, which is moved by an object already existing. Thus the active faculty, compared with its object, is as actual being to being *in potentia;* and the passive faculty *vice versa:* because the faculty which receives and retains is not distinct from the intellect itself.

Nor is reason a faculty distinct from the intellect. For to understand is simply to apprehend intelligible truth; and to reason is to proceed from one intellection to another in order to arrive at the knowledge of intelligible truth. Thus the angels, who possess such knowledge perfectly, do not require to go through the process of reasoning, since they have by simple intelligence what man acquires discursively. Reasoning, therefore, compared to understanding, is as movement to rest or acquiring to possessing; which processes are the work of the same faculty, and differ only as the imperfect differs from the perfect.

Neither are the superior and inferior reason different faculties; they are distinguished only by their operations and diversity of use; for the medium and the end both belong to the faculty of reason. The act of reasoning, indeed, somewhat resembles that kind of motion in which the moveable passing through the medium is the same as that which arrives at the end; and thus wisdom is attributed to the superior reason and knowledge to the inferior. . . .

CHAPTER LXXXIII

FREE WILL

Man has freedom of choice. For some things act without judgment, as a stone falls; others with judgment but without freedom, as the lower animals, which judge by instinct, not by collating; while man acts by judgment, with the power of choosing diversely by seeking out reasons. By this means, as regards contingent objects, the understanding finds a way to reach an opposite conclusion, and since particular works are contingent, man stands towards them free and undetermined.

This free will is a faculty, not a habit: for if it were a habit it would have to be a natural one, since man possesses free will by nature; the things to which we are inclined by nature, however, are not the objects of free will; hence it is contrary to reason to ascribe free will to a natural habit. Secondly, habits are the result of our passions, or of our good or bad acts; but free will stands indifferently to the choice of good or evil; hence it is not a habit; we conclude, therefore, that it is a faculty.

It is, moreover, an appetitive faculty, since election is its virtual act; for we can refuse one thing and choose the other, which is election, in which something is due to the understanding, *i.e.* counsel, while acceptance belongs to the concurrence of the will. But because things which conduce to the end are conceived as good in virtue of being useful, Aristotle inclines to the opinion that election belongs chiefly to the will.

And this freedom of choice is one faculty with the will, not another; for as intellect, which is simple intelligence, stands to reason which is discursive, so the will which is the end stands to that freedom of choice which is the way to the end. Thus they are diverse acts of the same faculty.

CHAPTER CI

OF THE STATE OF CHILDREN AS REGARDS KNOWLEDGE

Children, in a state of innocence, would not have been perfect in knowledge; since it is natural to man to acquire knowledge through the senses. Moreover, the body is united to the soul because it is necessary to its operation, and if the soul had knowledge from the beginning it would no longer require to make use of the sensitive faculties. Children, therefore, would have acquired knowledge gradually, though without difficulty, by means of instruction and investigation.

Nor could new-born infants have had the full use of reason; because reason depends upon the organs of the sensitive faculties, which are imperfect in infancy through excess of moisture; thus perfection would only have been reached with maturity; they would, however, have possessed a fuller use of reason than now, in regard of things suitable to their age.

SUGGESTIONS FOR FURTHER READING

Aquinas, Thomas. *Saint Thomas Aquinas: The Treatise on Law*. Notre Dame: University of Notre Dame Press, 1993.

———. *On the Truth of the Catholic Faith*. Translated by Anton C. Pegis. Garden City, N.Y.: Image Books, 1955.

Blanchette, Oliva. *The Perfection of the Universe According to Aquinas: Teleological Cosmology*. University Park, Pa.: Pennsylvania State University Press, 1992.

Davies, Brian. *The Thought of Thomas Aquinas*. New York: Oxford University Press, 1991.

Donohoe, John W., S. J. *St. Thomas Aquinas and Education*. New York: Random House, 1968.

Elder, Leo. *The Metaphysics of Being of St. Thomas Aquinas in a Historical Perspective*. Leiden and New York: E. J. Brill, 1992.

Fatula, Mary Ann. *Thomas Aquinas: Preacher and Friend*. Collegeville, Minn.: Liturgical Press, 1993.

Gilson, Etienne. *The Christian Philosophy of St. Thomas Aquinas*. Notre Dame, Ind.: University of Notre Dame Press, 1994.

Hall, Pamela M. *Narrative and the Natural Law: An Interpretation of Thomistic Ethics*. Notre Dame, Ind.: University of Notre Dame Press, 1994.

Kenny, Anthony. *Aquinas*. New York: Hill and Wang, 1980.

———. *Aquinas on Mind*. New York: Routledge, 1992.

Klauder, Francis J. *A Philosophy Rooted in Love: The Dominant Themes in the Perennial Philosophy of St. Thomas Aquinas*. Lanham, Md.: University Press of America, 1994.

McInerny, Ralph M. *Aquinas on Human Action: A Theory of Practice*. Washington, D.C.: Catholic University of America Press, 1992.

———. *A First Glance at St. Thomas Aquinas: A Handbook for Peeping Thomists*. Notre Dame, Ind.: University of Notre Dame Press, 1990.

Nelson, Daniel M. *The Priority of Prudence: Virtue and Natural Law in Thomas Aquinas and the Implications for Modern Ethics*. Washington Park, Pa.: Pennsylvania State University Press, 1992.

Selman, Francis J. *Saint Thomas Aquinas: Teacher of Truth*. Edinburgh: T&T Clark, 1994.

Weisheipl, James, O. P. *Friar Thomas d'Aquino: His Life, Thought, and Work*. New York: Doubleday, 1974.

Woznicki, Andrew N. *Being and Order: The Metaphysics of Thomas Aquinas in Historical Perspective*. New York: Peter Lang, 1990.

NOTES

1. James A. Weisheipl, O. P., *Friar Thomas d'Aquino: His Life, Thought, and Work* (New York: Doubleday, 1974), 3–9.

2. John W. Donohoe, S. J., *St. Thomas Aquinas and Education* (New York: Random House, 1968), 23–57.

3. Ibid., 26–31.

4. Ibid., 27–33.

5. Thomas Aquinas, *On the Truth of the Catholic Faith,* trans. Anton C. Pegis (Garden City, N.J.: Image Books, 1955), 17.

6. John W. Donohoe, S. J., *St. Thomas Aquinas and Education* (New York: Random House, 1968), 62–96.

7. Ibid., 58–96.

5

DESIDERIUS ERASMUS: RENAISSANCE HUMANIST AND COSMOPOLITAN EDUCATOR

Desiderius Erasmus (1466–1536) is significant in the history and philosophy of education as one of the leading classical humanist scholars and educators of the Renaissance. Known for the revival of humanism, artistic innovation, and exploration, the Renaissance spanned the late fourteenth through the early sixteenth centuries. The Renaissance was one of those periods of intellectual intensity that saw a number of significant contributions to arts, letters, and education. Niccolo Machiavelli wrote *The Prince,* a treatise on power politics, to guide his patron in gaining, using, and maintaining power. Baldesar Castiglione wrote about educating the courtier, an intellectually and politically capable gentleman equally effective in statecraft, diplomacy, or poetry, depending upon the situation.[1] Thomas Elyot, author of *The Boke Named the Governour,* translating Isocrates' works, prescribed the appropriate education for the statesman. Louis Vives, a student of Erasmus, wrote *de Institutione Feminae Christianae,* on educating noblewomen in classics. Roger Ascham, tutor of Queen Elizabeth I, in *The Scholemaster* stressed writing Latin according to Cicero's elegant style.

Erasmus, destined to be foremost among the humanists, was born on October 27, 1466, in Rotterdam, in the Netherlands. He is alleged to have been the illegitimate child of Roger Gerard, a priest, and Margaret Rogerius, a physician's daughter who was employed as Gerard's housekeeper. Sensitive about his illegitimate birth, Erasmus never revealed his father's last name. In 1497, he added the name Desiderius and later adopted the name of the city of his birth, Rotterdam.[2] He attempted to create an appearance of legitimacy by altering his birth date and claimed that his father had not been ordained until after his mother's death.[3]

When he was 6, Erasmus was enrolled in the Latin school of Saint Lebuin's Church at Deventer, conducted by the Brethren of the Common Life, a lay religious association, which he attended from 1478 to 1483. The Brethren, founded by the Dutch religious reformer Gerhard Groote (1340–1384), were not a conventional religious order but were an organization of individuals who performed charitable and educational works.[4] Under the Brethren's tutelage, Erasmus

An engraving of Erasmus,
by Albrecht Dürer.

studied the usual primary subjects of reading, writing, arithmetic, and religion. Additionally, the Brethren's schools, exemplifying morality and charity in the imitation of Christ, emphasized studying the Gospels, the writings of the church fathers, and the lives of the saints.

Erasmus, a gifted intellectual, showed an early tendency toward the criticism that he later perfected in his life. Criticizing his education with the Brethren, he contended they were preoccupied with performing empty rituals, exaggerating their own self-importance, and keeping strict discipline rather than with genuine learning. Though he found little to commend about his teachers, Erasmus would write that teaching was the "noblest of occupations" by which dedicated and skilled teachers had the opportunity of imbuing the young with "the best literature and the love of Christ."[5] The importance of good literature, which to him was the Greek and Latin classics, and true Christian morality were persistent themes in Erasmus' philosophy of education.

From 1486 to 1492, Erasmus studied with the Augustinians at St. Gregory's at Steyn. On April 25, 1492, Erasmus, at age 23, was ordained as a priest under the jurisdiction of the Augustinian religious order.[6] He was still associated with the Brethren of the Common Life, who were supervised by the Augustinians. St. Augustine, for whom the order was named, was an early father of the church who had defended Greek and Latin classics in the foundations of a Christian education. For the next 2 years, Erasmus was engaged in advanced study at the Augustinian monastery at Steyn, where he wrote a treatise, *On the Contempt of the World,* which defended monastic life.

Erasmus' superiors recognized his intellectual promise and sent him in 1494 to the renowned College de Montaigu at the University of Paris for advanced studies in languages and Scripture. While at the university, he was a tutor in Latin grammar and rhetoric, subjects that would engage him throughout his life. His work as a tutor stimulated his interest in teaching, which in turn inspired him to write his *Colloquies,* with the revealing subtitle *Formulas of Familiar Conversations by Erasmus of Rotterdam, Useful Not Only for Polishing a Boy's Speech but for Building His Character.*[7] The *Colloquies* featured dialogues in which participants, engaged in intellectual conversations, followed correct patterns of grammar and style and exemplified proper ethical values. The dialogues reflected Erasmus' conviction that good literature and morality were mutually reinforcing. Using conversation as a teaching method, the *Colloquies* demonstrated Erasmus' strong belief in the educational possibilities of the free interchange of ideas between persons of knowledge and cultivation.

Erasmus enjoyed travel as a means of education that enlarged a person's perspective. He made a journey to England in 1499 and located for a time at Oxford University. Here, he joined a circle of humanist scholars such as John Colette, dean of St. Paul's Cathedral and school, and Thomas More, the gifted jurist and diplomat. He returned to Paris in 1500.

In 1499, Erasmus published *Adages,* or *Familiar Quotations from the Classics,* a book that combined literary and moral instruction. Enjoying a distinguished scholarly reputation, Erasmus was appointed as professor of Divinity and Greek, in 1511, at Cambridge University in England. He continued his research and writing in classical languages and biblical scholarship. In 1512, he published *de Copia,* a compendium of words, phrases, and idioms designed for use in teaching Latin. In 1516, Erasmus completed his Greek version of the New Testament.

In *Encomium Moriae, The Praise of Folly,* the caustic Erasmus turned his critical pen against arrogant and pompous pseudo-intellectuals. He ridiculed those teachers who were obsessed with trivial points of grammar rather than genuine learning. Some supposedly erudite philosophers he found were building imaginary "castles in the air" rather than exploring important issues that would liberate people from ignorance and prejudice. Further, he found too many theologians were interested in provoking rather than resolving doctrinal divisions.[8]

In his great work on political philosophy and education, *The Education of the Christian Prince,* in 1516, Erasmus portrayed the ideal ruler as prudent, gentle, humane, and well-educated.[9] A student of history and geography, the Christian prince learns everything possible about his realm and its people, especially the location, economy, and demographics of its regions and localities. Educated in the humanities and in religious principles, the prince should have a classical education. The Christian prince should be a model for his subjects, the personification of ethical and moral behavior. Recognizing the importance of education to the long-term prosperity and order of his subjects, the prince should establish schools taught by well-educated and trustworthy teachers. Erasmus' *The Education of the Christian Prince* was also a treatise on peace and international education. Fearing religious strife and nationalist-inspired wars, he advised the prince to study peacekeeping. An early proponent of international arbitration, he urged conflict resolution by international tribunals.

During the Reformation, Erasmus engaged in a written debate against Luther. His *On the Freedom of the Will,* in 1524, was followed by *On Restoring the Harmony of the Church,* in 1533. Erasmus died on July 12, 1536, while in Basel, Switzerland, interpreting the Bible.

OVERVIEW OF EDUCATIONAL IDEAS

Erasmus' educational ideas need to be considered in the context of Renaissance classical humanism. He excelled in the qualities of scholarship and education that marked this era of Western history, which gave high priority to knowledge of the ancient texts of Greece and Rome. Eramus' scholarly research, criticism, and publication demonstrate his mastery of the classics. Like the other humanists of the time, he looked back to a "golden age" for the sources of knowledge. The sources of the classical past were in the languages of antiquity, Greek and Latin, which the humanist teacher needed to master if he was to join the educated elite.

Like most Renaissance humanists, Erasmus was an elitist who saw himself as an expert whose mission was to interpret the classical heritage. Expertise was not seen as an egalitarian possibility to be shared by all but rather was the hallmark of those initiated into scholarship. The humanist scholar was a critic, a commentator, and an interpreter who stood between the body of knowledge and the public. Classical humanist education was not intended to be a popular product diffused to the masses but rather carried with it marks of selectivity and elitism.

Erasmus and his humanist colleagues, like the earlier Plato and Aristotle, reasserted the conception of the educated person as a generalist, who was versatile, knowledgeable, and comfortable in a variety of situations. Though definitely not a specialist, the humanist did not believe that everyone could learn to practice educated versatility or be a critic of society, art, and literature. However, it was possible to have an elite of educated generalists, who could be the dispassionate, just, fair, and humane leaders of nations and guardians of the intellectual heritage.

A true classical humanist educator of the Renaissance, Erasmus placed intrinsic value in translating and interpreting the ancient Greek and Latin texts. In addition to their scholarly merit, the classical texts along with the Bible were, he believed, of great value in educating knowledgeable and ethical persons. Encompassing both the classics and Christianity, Erasmus' educational ideas were broadly conceived as the formation of the educated person according to the principles of a Christian *paideia.*

Like other humanist educators, Erasmus concentrated on the teaching of the ancient Greek and Latin languages and literature. Teachers of the classics, he advised, needed to be well-educated individuals who, possessing a thorough scholarly knowledge in their subjects, avoided pedantry. By reviewing the classical texts, humanist teachers would also be led to archaeology, astronomy, history, and mythology. Warning humanist teachers to avoid the empty formalism and memorization that masqueraded as erudition, Erasmus told them to emphasize the understanding of content and meaningful interpretation. He developed a teaching method by which the teacher was to:

1. Discuss the biography of the author of the text being studied.
2. Identify the type of work.
3. Discuss the theme or plot.

4. Comment on the author's writing style.
5. Comment on the work's moral implications.
6. Reflect on the work's location and implications in the larger areas of culture, art, politics, and philosophy.[10]

Erasmus did not intend for teachers to follow these steps in a rigid routine but rather saw them as a means of guiding instruction. Most important, he believed, was learning by sharing ideas through lively intellectual dialogues in which the teacher and students, through conversation, explored an author's ideas, style, and meaning.

THE PRIMARY SOURCES

In the selection from *The Colloquies,* Erasmus, taking the figure of Desiderius, presented a dialogue in which he discusses the progress of a student, Erasmius. The dialogue emphasized the value of the liberal arts and the expenditure of time and energy needed in their study.

In the selection from *The Praise of Folly,* Erasmus criticizes the pomposity and arrogance of members of certain professions, such as lawyers, theologians, and philosophers. He was a critic of his day, prone to deflate pseudo-intellectuals.

FOCUSING QUESTIONS
As you read the selections, you might wish to consider the following questions:

1. Consider the value of a dialogue such as that used here as an educational device. Can you identify any contemporary uses of such devices in education?
2. How does Erasmus advise his student to approach his studies?
3. Reflect on the educator as critic. What role would such a person perform in contemporary education?

FROM *THE COLLOQUIES OF ERASMUS*

Desiderius: How do your studies progress, Erasmius?

Erasmius: I'm not the Muses' darling, apparently. But studies would go better if I could get something from you.

Desid: Anything you ask, provided it be to your advantage. Just tell me what's the matter.

Eras: I'm sure none of the abstruse arts has escaped you.

From *The Colloquies of Erasmus,* edited by Craig R. Thompson. Chicago: University of Chicago Press, 1965, 459–461.

Desid: I wish you were right!

Eras: I hear there's a certain method that enables a fellow to learn all the liberal arts thoroughly with a minimum of trouble.

Desid: How's that? Have you seen the book?

Eras: I've seen it, but only seen it, because I didn't have the resources of a teacher.

Desid: What was in the book?

Eras: Various figures of animals—dragons, lions, leopards—and various circles with words written in them, partly Greek, partly Latin, partly Hebrew, and others in barbarous tongues.

Desid: The title promised a knowledge of the arts within how many days?

Eras: Fourteen.

Desid: A splendid promise, surely, but do you know anybody who emerged a learned man through this method of instruction?

Eras: No indeed.

Desid: Neither has anyone else ever seen one, or ever will, unless we first see someone made rich through alchemy.

Eras: Well, I wish there *were* a true method!

Desid: Perhaps because you're reluctant to buy learning at the cost of so much labor.

Eras: Of course.

Desid: But heaven has so decreed. Riches in the ordinary sense—gold, jewels, silver, palaces, a kingdom—it sometimes grants to the slothful and worthless; but it has ordained that what are true riches, and peculiarly our own, must be won by toil. The labor by which wealth so great is achieved should not seem grievous to us when we see many men struggle, through terrible dangers, through countless labors, for wealth that is both temporary and quite ignoble if compared with learning; they don't always get what they seek, either. And the drudgery of studies has a generous mixture of sweetness, too, if you advance a little in them. Now getting rid of a large part of the irksomeness depends on you.

Eras: How do I do it?

Desid: First, by persuading yourself to love studies. Secondly, by admiring them.

Eras: How shall this be done?

Desid: Observe how many men learning has enriched, how many it has brought to the highest honor and power. Reflect at the same time how much difference there is between man and beast.

Eras: Good advice.

Desid: Next you must discipline your character in order to win self-control and to find delight in things productive of utility rather than pleasure. For what are in themselves honorable, even if somewhat painful at first, prove agreeable by becoming habitual. So it will come about that you will tire the tutor less and understand more easily by yourself; according to the saying of Isocrates, which should be painted in golden letters on the title page of your book: "If you are a lover of learning, you will learn much."

Eras: I'm quick enough at learning, but what's learned soon slips away.

Desid: A jar with holes in it, you mean.

Eras: You're not far wrong. But what's the remedy?

Desid: The chink must be stopped up to prevent leaks.

Eras: Stopped up with what?

Desid: Not moss or plaster but industry. Whoever learns words without understanding the meaning soon forgets, for words, as Homer says, are "winged" and easily fly away unless held down by the weight of meaning. Make it your first task, therefore, to understand the matter thoroughly; next to review it and repeat it frequently to yourself; and in this respect your mind (as I remarked) must be disciplined so that whenever necessary it may be able to apply itself to thought. If one's mind is so wild that it can't be tamed in this way, it's unfit for learning.

Eras: How hard this is I understand only too well.

Desid: One who is so giddy-minded that he can't concentrate on an idea is incapable of paying attention for long when somebody is speaking, or of fixing in memory what he's learned. A thing can be stamped on lead to stay; on water or quicksilver nothing can be stamped, since they are always fluid. But if you can subdue your nature in this respect, then, through constant association with learned men, whose daily conversation affords so much that is worth knowing, you'll learn a great deal with a minimum of effort.

Eras: True enough.

Desid: For besides the table talk, besides the daily conversations, immediately after lunch you hear half a dozen witty sayings, selected from the best authors; and as many after dinner. Now just reckon how large a sum these amount to every month and year.

Eras: Splendid—if I could remember them!

Desid: In addition, since you hear nothing but good Latin spoken, what's to prevent you from learning Latin within a few months, when uneducated boys learn French or Spanish in a very short time?

Eras: I'll follow your advice and see whether this nature can be broken to the yoke of the Muses.

Desid: For my part, I know no other art of learning than hard work, devotion, and perseverance.

FROM DESIDERIUS ERASMUS' *THE PRAISE OF FOLLY*

Among the learned, the lawyers claim the highest rank, nor could anyone be more self-satisfied than they are as they endlessly roll the stone of Sisyphus, stringing together six hundred laws in one breath—no matter whether they are relevant—piling gloss on gloss <and opinion on opinion> to make their profession seem the most difficult of all. For they imagine that whatever is laborious is automatically also preeminent.

Let us join to them the dialecticians and disputants, a race of men more noisy than 'a steeple-full of brass bells,' any one of whom could be matched in a talking contest with twenty women specially chosen for the occasion. But they would be happier if they were only loudmouthed and not also quarrelsome, fighting to the bitter end over some hair-splitting quibble and, often enough, missing the truth entirely by fighting too much about it. But their self-love places them in such felicity that once they are equipped with two or three syllogisms, they are immediately bold enough to challenge anyone at all to a verbal duel on any subject whatever. But then their persistence renders them invincible, even if their opponent is downright Stentorean.

After them come the philosophers, venerable with their beards and robes, who assert that they alone are wise, all other mortals being mere fleeting shades by comparison. How delightfully they are deluded as they build up numberless worlds; as they measure the sun, the moon, the stars and their orbits as if they were using a ruler and plumb line; as they recite the causes of lightning, winds, eclipses, and other unfathomable phenomena, without the slightest hesitation, as if they were confidential secretaries to Na-

---

From Desiderius Erasmus' *The Praise of Folly*, translated by Clarence H. Miller. New Haven: Yale University Press, 1979, 85–87.

ture herself, the architect of all things, or as if they came to us straight from the council chamber of the gods. At the same time, Nature has a grand laugh at them and their conjectures. For that they have actually discovered nothing at all is clear enough from this fact alone: on every single point they disagree violently and irreconcilably among themselves. Though they know nothing at all, they profess to know everything; and though they do not know themselves, and sometimes can't see a ditch or a stone in their path (either because most of them are blear-eyed or because their minds are wool-gathering), nevertheless they claim that they can see ideas, universals, separate forms, prime matter, quiddities, ecceities—things so finespun that no one, however 'eagle-eyed,' would be able, I think, to perceive them. But their arrogant scorn of the unwashed multitude is most notable when they bewilder uneducated people with their triangles, tetragons, and circles, and such mathematical figures, superimposing one on another to produce what looks like a labyrinth, and then lining up series of letters as if in battle lines and repeating them first in one order and then in another. In this group there is also no lack of those who predict the future by consulting the stars and who promise to perform miracles beyond any magician, and they are even lucky enough to find people who believe them.

As for the theologians, perhaps it would be better to pass them over in silence, *'not stirring up the hornets' nest'* and 'not laying a finger on the stinkweed,' since this race of men is incredibly arrogant and touchy. For they might rise up en masse and march in ranks against me with six hundred conclusions and force me to recant. And if I should refuse, they would immediately shout "heretic." For this is the thunderbolt they always keep ready at a moment's notice to terrify anyone to whom they are not very favorably inclined.

SUGGESTIONS FOR FURTHER READING

Augustijn, C. *Erasmus: His Life, Works, and Influence.* Toronto: University of Toronto Press, 1991.

Bainton, Roland H. *Erasmus of Christendom.* New York: Charles Scribner's Sons, 1969.

Demolen, Richard, ed. *Erasmus of Rotterdam: A Quincentennial Symposium.* New York: Twayne Publishers, 1971.

Dorey, T. A., ed. Erasmus. London: Routledge and Kegan Paul, 1970.

Erasmus, *Desiderius: Adages.* Translated by Craig R. Thompson. Chicago: University of Chicago Press, 1962.

———. *Colloquies.* Translated by Craig R. Thompson. Chicago: University of Chicago Press, 1965.

———. *Controversies.* Toronto: University of Toronto Press, 1993.

———. *The Education of the Christian Prince.* Translated by Lester K. Born. New York: Columbia University Press, 1936.

———. *The Erasmus Reader.* Toronto: University of Toronto Press, 1990.

———. *The Praise of Folly.* Translated by Hoyt H. Hudson. Princeton, N.J.: Princeton University Press, 1941.

———. *Poems.* Toronto: University of Toronto Press, 1990.

Gordon, Walter E. *Humanist Play and Belief: The Seriocomic Art of Desiderius Erasmus.* Toronto: University of Toronto Press, 1990.

Halkin, Leon E. *Erasmus: A Critical Biography.* Oxford, U.K., and Cambridge, Mass.: Blackwell, 1993.

Hillerbrand, Hans J., ed. *Erasmus and His Age.* New York: Harper and Row, 1970.

Hyma, Albert. *The Youth of Erasmus.* New York: Russell and Russell, 1968.

Jardine, Lisa. *Erasmus, Man of Letters: The Construction of Charisma in Print.* Princeton, N.J.: Princeton University Press, 1993.

McConica, James. *Erasmus.* Oxford, U.K., and New York: Oxford University Press, 1991.

Schoeck, Richard J. *Erasmus of Europe: The Making of a Humanist, 1467–1500.* Savage, Md.: Barnes & Noble Books, 1990.

———. *Erasmus Grandescens: The Growth of a Humanist's Mind and Spirituality.* Nieuwkoop, Netherlands: De Graaf, 1988.

Notes

1. Baldesar Castiglione, *The Book of the Courtier,* trans. Charles S. Singleton (New York: Doubleday, 1959).

2. Albert Hyma, *The Youth of Erasmus* (New York: Russell and Russell, 1968), 51–53, 55–56, 59.

3. Christopher Hollis, *Erasmus* (New York: Bruce Publishing Co., 1933), 4–6.

4. Theodore P. Van Ziji, *Gerhard Groote, Ascetic and Reformer, 1340–1384* (Washington, D.C.: Catholic University of America Press, 1963), 31–39.

5. Hans J. Hillerbrand, ed., *Erasmus and His Age* (New York: Harper and Row, 1970), 92.

6. J. Huizinga, *Erasmus of Rotterdam* (London: Phaido Press, 1952), 9–16.

7. Erasmus, *Colloquies,* trans. Craig R. Thompson (Chicago: University of Chicago Press, 1965).

8. Frank E. Schacht, "The Classical Humanist: Erasmus," in Paul Nash, Andreas Kazamias, and Henry Perkinson, eds., *The Educated Man: Studies in the History of Educational Thought* (New York: John Wiley and Sons, 1965), 140–162.

9. Erasmus, *The Education of the Christian Prince,* trans. Lester K. Born (New York: Columbia University Press, 1936).

10. Gerald L. Gutek, *A History of the Western Educational Experience* (Prospect Heights, Ill.: Waveland Press, 1995), 123–124.

JOHN CALVIN: THEOLOGIAN AND EDUCATOR OF THE PROTESTANT REFORMATION

BIOGRAPHICAL SKETCH

John Calvin (1509–1564), a leading Protestant reformer, is significant for his theology of Evangelical Protestantism, which was an important force on social, economic, and educational thought as well as on religion. Calvin's religious doctrines, which sanctioned economic industriousness, provided a rationale for the rising professional and business middle classes. It encouraged the movement to universal education.

John Calvin, the second son of Gerard and Jeanne Lefranc Calvin, was born on July 10, 1509, in Noyon, France. Gerard, who was a clerk at Noyon's ecclesiastical court, was solidly positioned in the town's middle class.[1] John Calvin's orientation as an adult was shaped by his father's legal and administrative work as an official of the ecclesiastical court.

Young John Calvin benefited by being the recipient of several educational opportunities. His father's position also brought Calvin's family into contact with Charles de Hangest, Noyon's bishop. The bishop, recognizing John's intellectual talent, encouraged and supported his education at the College des Capettes. Here, young Calvin excelled as a student of religion and the humanities. When he was 12 another opportunity came John's way when he was invited to reside with the Montmors family, which enabled him to receive personal instruction from the family tutor, who introduced him to liberal arts.[2]

In 1521, John Calvin was attending the College de la Marche in Paris, where he enrolled in the grammar course, a preparatory step toward the arts degree. The grammar course in Latin was necessary since instruction in the liberal arts was given in that language. Again, John Calvin had an educational opportunity in that his teacher was Mathurin Cordier, one of France's preeminent Latin scholars.

At 14, John Calvin began the liberal arts course in the College de Montaigu, which was directed by Jean Standonck. The college was known for its orderliness, academic rigor, and strict discipline. Though he demonstrated ability in humanities and theology, Calvin left the institution. His father had advised him to transfer to the University of Orleans to study civil law, his father's profession. Throwing himself into his studies, Calvin displayed the order and discipline that characterized his later life

This page from *The New England Primer* illustrates the emphasis of religious themes in schooling.

as a religious reformer. Gaining academic distinction, he was asked to substitute for instructors when they were absent from their classes.

Although Calvin's education was moving along smoothly, events in Europe were to enter and affect his life. Europe was caught up in the ferment of the Protestant Reformation. Although France was Roman Catholic, the ideas emanating from the Reformation had entered its academic institutions. Martin Luther's challenge to the Pope's authority and to the Roman Catholic Church was shaking the foundations of Western Christianity. Calvin encountered Melchior Wolmar, a German student, who introduced him to Luther's religious ideas.[3]

Completing his legal studies, Calvin was awarded his licentiate degree. However, he was preoccupied with religion rather than law. He devoted time to studying the Bible and the writings of early church fathers. Trained in the law, he approached his scriptural study like a lawyer. He constructed a theological brief that found the Roman Catholic Church in conflict with his interpretation of the Bible. During his scriptural investigations, Calvin had an intense religious experience, a personal conversion, which, "like a flash of light," illuminated his quest for spiritual truth.[4]

Calvin then returned to Paris, where he met with those who supported Luther in his challenge to the Catholic Church. He appeared at meetings and began to speak on behalf of Protestantism. Addressing one of these meetings on November 1, 1533, Calvin, who proclaimed that faith alone was necessary for salvation, joined the Protestant cause. Comparing the Catholic Church to a decaying structure, Calvin asserted, "The building is too rotten to be patched up. It must be torn down and instead a new one must be built."[5]

Calvin's *Institutes of the Christian Religion* was published in 1536 and recognized as the definitive statement of Evangelical Protestant doctrines.[6] In this work, Calvin completely rejected the Roman Catholic hierarchical system of ecclesiastical governance and organization. He further rejected Catholicism's sacramental system and elaborate ceremonial rituals. He asserted that those who would be saved were predestined for salvation by God's grace, not through their own actions. Calvin proclaimed the Evangelical church as the true successor of the early Christian church.

Facing mounting persecution from the French monarchy, Calvin sought refuge in Geneva, Switzerland, a city already committed to Protestantism. The Protestant ministers and city officials of Geneva invited him to assist in creating a reformed church. Accepting their invitation, Calvin set to work to make Geneva into a citadel of Evangelical Protestantism.

Calvin prepared a "confession of faith" designed to guide the adherents of reformed Christianity.[7] The articles of faith emphasized the authority of the Bible, the importance of a personal experience of guilt for sin, and the need to be reconciled to God through the redemptive act of Jesus Christ. Calvin's proclamation of the Bible as the only infallible rule of faith contrasted with the Roman Catholic emphasis on the dual authority of the Scriptures and the tradition of the Church. The confession of faith was presented to and accepted by the Council of Two Hundred, Geneva's ruling legislative body. This document provided the theological basis for the Heidelberg Catechism, which was widely used in the reformed churches.

Turning to education, Calvin used the catechistic method to teach the correct version of Christianity to children. The doctrines in *Institutes* were simplified and condensed into a catechism, a book of questions and answers, that children could study and memorize in school.

Calvin's projected reformation of Geneva encountered opponents who resisted what they considered to be arbitrarily imposed social control. In 1538, Calvin's opponents, taking control of the city's government, exiled him.

From 1538 to 1541, the exiled Calvin found refuge in Strasbourg, where he served as pastor of a Protestant church established by Protestants who had fled France. Here, he met and wed Idelette de Buren. During the 9 years of their marriage, which ended with Idelette's death, the couple had three children, all of whom died shortly after their birth. The diligent Calvin, using exile in Strasbourg to refine his theological doctrines, expanded on the *Institutes* and wrote commentaries on the Last Supper and St. Paul's Epistle to the Romans.

In 1541, Calvin's supporters, regaining control of the city council, recalled him to Geneva. After a triumphal return, he resumed his efforts to make Geneva into a solidly Evangelical Protestant city. Here, he worked until his death 23 years later on May 27, 1564.

OVERVIEW OF IDEAS ON EDUCATION

Calvin's religious doctrines emphasized the Bible as the exclusive authority of the reformed faith. Calvin, Luther, and other Protestant reformers wanted the Bible to be translated in the various European languages so that it could be read by the people.

The Bible became more available because the invention of the printing press made inexpensive editions possible. Worship centered on the reading of the Bible and sermons to explain and illustrate its meaning and application. Like Luther, Calvin believed the laity needed to be literate so that they could read the Bible and participate in religious services. Further, Calvin associated the orderly, disciplined, and productive life with literacy and education.

Calvin and other Evangelical Protestant leaders were strongly committed to schools. Not content with merely providing schools, they enlisted civil authorities to make sure that children attended them. Calvin's emphasis on schools was based on his belief that a mutually supportive relationship existed between education, religious orthodoxy, civil order, and economic prosperity. Calvinism, in particular, emphasized creating and supporting primary schools to teach basic literacy, reading and writing, and religion to both boys and girls. As a result, a strong movement began for creating systems of primary schools in Calvinist areas in Europe and North America. By law, the children of Geneva and other Calvinist communities were to attend school, and parents were held accountable in making sure that their children were present for classes. Parents who failed to meet their responsibilities were subject to civil law and might be fined. Children from families too poor to pay tuition were educated at public expense.

Though committed to primary education in the vernacular language spoken by the people, Calvin, who had been educated as a classical humanist as well as a lawyer, believed that the leaders of church and state needed a classical education in the Greek and Latin languages and literatures. These languages, along with Hebrew, provided knowledge necessary for scriptural study. The classical humanist schools, like the Latin Grammar school in colonial New England, prepared the educated elite for higher university studies.

Calvinism had great appeal to the middle classes of Western Europe and North America. Situated between the aristocratic nobles and the agricultural peasants, the middle classes, the new economic class, consisted of merchants, industrialists, bankers, lawyers, and other professionals. In ideological terms, Calvinism provided a religious justification to the middle classes. According to Calvin's doctrine of predestination, the elect, those destined for salvation, were to live righteous, industrious, and productive lives. The wealth that the middle classes produced was not an impediment to their salvation but was a manifestation of God's pleasure in their work. Further, the middle classes, as stewards, were to use their wealth for constructive social and religious purposes. Where the middle class presence was strong, Calvinism attracted members. In Switzerland, the Calvinist Church was the Reformed Church; in the Netherlands, it was the Dutch Reformed Church; and in Scotland, the Presbyterian Church. In North America, the Calvinists were the Puritans who settled in Massachusetts.

The Puritans of Massachusetts enacted the earliest ordinances requiring education in North America. The laws of 1642 and 1647 required the towns to ensure that children learned to read, write, and know the principles of religion and laws of the commonwealth. The law of 1647 required larger towns to provide a Latin master to prepare promising young men in classical languages, the Greek and Latin needed for admission to Harvard College.

Calvinism's economic beliefs came to be known as the "Protestant ethic." The ethic of Evangelical Protestantism in the United States strongly encouraged establishing common or public schools to prepare a literate, law-abiding, Bible-reading, and economically productive citizenry. Skills and values conducive to economic productivity were taught along with reading, writing, and arithmetic. Values such as the importance of time and punctuality, diligence in work, the need to achieve, repression of immediate needs for long-term success, and orderly behavior moved from the Protestant ethic into the patterns of school routines.

THE PRIMARY SOURCE

The selection from Calvin's "Catechism of the Church of Geneva," in his *Tracts and Treatises on Doctrine and Worship of the Church,* illustrates the importance and use of the catechism and the catechetical method as a means of religious education. During the Reformation and post-Reformation periods, virtually each church, be it Protestant or Roman Catholic, viewed other churches as rival institutions based on erroneous doctrines. An important element in the education of the young was devoted to building religious commitment, particularly in conformity to the doctrines certified as correct by the parent church. Young members of the particular denomination also were prepared to defend their faith against rival antagonists. To this end, the catechism became a popular teaching device. Constructed as a series of questions and answers, the catechism's responses contained religious principles. Students were to memorize the catechism, thereby instilling in their minds correct religious positions.

The catechisms, used by many of the Christian churches, were organized in a question-answer format. In the catechism's text, the teacher, or master, would ask a question that raised an important doctrine of the church. This would be followed by the student's answer. An important requirement in this kind of instruction was that both the question and the answer be memorized. It was believed that the student, by using the catechetical method, would internalize the doctrines of the church and be prepared to defend the faith against those who challenged it. The catechetical method was so widespread that the approach was also used to teach other subjects such as arithmetic, history, and geography. The selection illustrates the doctrines of the purpose of human life and justification by faith.

FOCUSING QUESTIONS

As you read the selection, you might wish to consider the following questions:

1. During the Protestant Reformation, what was the purpose of the catechism? Why was it used so widely? Is the catechetical method relevant to contemporary education? Explain your answer.
2. Were the religious doctrines, beliefs, and values conveyed by the catechism directly made, or did they leave room for individual decision making? Compare and contrast the catechism's approach to character and values education with contemporary approaches.
3. How would a teacher using the catechism react to the problems of disorder and violence found in some American schools?
4. Consider Calvin's doctrine of "justification by faith." What are the educational implications of this doctrine?

FROM JOHN CALVIN'S *TRACTS AND TREATISES ON THE DOCTRINE AND WORSHIP OF THE CHURCH*

TO THE READER

It has ever been the practice of the Church, and one carefully attended to, to see that children should be duly instructed in the Christian religion. That this might be done more conveniently, not only were schools opened in old time, and individuals enjoined properly to teach their families, but it was a received public custom and practice, to question children in the churches on each of the heads, which should be common and well known to all Christians. To secure this being done in order, there was written out a formula, which was called a Catechism or Institute. Thereafter the devil miserably rending the Church of God, and bringing upon it fearful ruin, (of which the marks are still too visible in the greater part of the world,) overthrew this sacred policy, and left nothing behind but certain trifles, which only beget superstition, without any fruit of edification. Of this description is that confirmation, as they call it, full of gesticulations which, worse than ridiculous, are fitted only for apes, and have no foundation to rest upon. What we now bring forward, therefore, is nothing else than the use of things which from ancient times were observed by Christians, and the true worshippers of God, and which never were laid aside until the Church was wholly corrupted.

CATECHISM OF THE CHURCH OF GENEVA OF FAITH

Master: What is the chief end of human life?

Scholar: To know God by whom men were created.

M: What reason have you for saying so?

S: Because he created us and placed us in this world to be glorified in us. And it is indeed right that our life, of which himself is the beginning, should be devoted to his glory.

M: What is the highest good of man?

S: The very same thing.

M: Why do you hold that to be the highest good?

S: Because without it our condition is worse than that of the brutes.

M: Hence, then, we clearly see that nothing worse can happen to a man than not to live to God.

S: It is so.

M: What is the true and right knowledge of God?

S: When he is so known that due honour is paid to him.

M: What is the method of honouring him duly?

S: To place our whole confidence in him; to study to serve him during our whole life by obeying his will; to call upon him in all our necessities, seeking salvation and every good thing that can be desired in him; lastly, to acknowledge him both with heart and lips, as the sole Author of all blessings.

M: To consider these points in their order, and explain them more fully—What is the first head in this division of yours?

S: To place our whole confidence in God.

M: How shall we do so?

S: When we know him to be Almighty and perfectly good.

M: Is this enough?

S: Far from it.

M: Wherefore?

S: Because we are unworthy that he should exert his power in helping us, and show how good he is by saving us.

M: What more then is needful?

S: That each of us should set it down in his mind that God loves him, and is willing to be a Father, and the author of salvation to him.

M: But whence will this appear?

S: From his word, in which he explains his mercy to us in Christ, and testifies of his love towards us.

M: Then the foundation and beginning of confidence in God is to know him in Christ?

S: Entirely so. . . .

M: Do we conceive faith of ourselves, or do we receive it from God?

S: Scripture teaches that it is the special gift of God, and this experience confirms.

M: What experience do you mean?

S: Our mind is too rude to be able to comprehend the spiritual wisdom of God which is revealed to us by faith, and our hearts are too prone either to dif-

From John Calvin's, *Tracts and Treatises on the Doctrine and Worship of the Church.* II, translated by Henry Beveridge. Grand Rapids, Mich.: Wm. B. Eerdmans Publishing Co., 1958, 37–38, 53–56.

fidence or to a perverse confidence in ourselves or creatures, to rest in God of their own accord. But the Holy Spirit by his illumination makes us capable of understanding those things which would otherwise far exceed our capacity, and forms us to a firm persuasion, by sealing the promises of salvation on our hearts.

M. What good accrues to us from this faith, when we have once obtained it?

S: It justifies us before God, and this justification makes us the heirs of everlasting life.

M: What! are not men justified by good works when they study to approve themselves to God, by living innocently and holily?

S: Could any one be found so perfect, he might justly be deemed righteous, but as we are all sinners, guilty before God in many ways, we must seek elsewhere for a worthiness which may reconcile us to him.

M: But are all the works of men so vile and valueless that they cannot merit favour with God?

S: First, all the works which proceed from us, so as properly to be called our own, are vicious, and therefore they can do nothing but displease God, and be rejected by him.

M: You say then that before we are born again and formed anew by the Spirit of God, we can do nothing but sin, just as a bad tree can only produce bad fruit? (Matt. vii. 18.)

S: Altogether so. For whatever semblance works may have in the eyes of men, they are nevertheless evil, as long as the heart to which God chiefly looks is depraved.

M: Hence you conclude, that we cannot by any merits anticipate God or call forth his beneficence; or rather that all the works which we try or engage in, subject us to his anger and condemnation?

S: I understand so; and therefore mere mercy, without any respect to works, (Titus iii. 5,) embraces and accepts us freely in Christ, by attributing his righteousness to us as if it were our own, and not imputing our sins to us.

M: In what way, then, do you say that we are justified by faith?

S: Because, while we embrace the promises of the gospel with sure heartfelt confidence, we in a manner obtain possession of the righteousness of which I speak.

M: This then is your meaning—that as righteousness is offered to us by the gospel, so we receive it by faith?

S: It is so.

M: But after we have once been embraced by God, are not the works which we do under the direction of his Holy Spirit accepted by him?

S: They please him, not however in virtue of their own worthiness, but as he liberally honours them with his favour.

M: But seeing they proceed from the Holy Spirit, do they not merit favour?

S: They are always mixed up with some defilement from the weakness of the flesh, and thereby vitiated.

M: Whence then or how can it be that they please God?

S: It is faith alone which procures favour for them, as we rest with assured confidence on this— that God wills not to try them by his strict rule, but covering their defects and impurities as buried in the purity of Christ, he regards them in the same light as if they were absolutely perfect.

M: But can we infer from this that a Christian man is justified by works after he has been called by God, or that by the merit of works he makes himself loved by God, whose love is eternal life to us?

S: By no means. We rather hold what is written—that no man can be justified in his sight, and we therefore pray, "Enter not into judgment with us." (Ps. cxliii. 2.)

M: We are not therefore to think that the good works of believers are useless?

S: Certainly not. For not in vain does God promise them reward both in this life and in the future. But this reward springs from the free love of God as its source; for he first embraces us as sons, and then burying the remembrance of the vices which proceed from us, he visits us with his favour.

M: But can this righteousness be separated from good works, so that he who has it may be void of them?

S: That cannot be. For when by faith we receive Christ as he is offered to us, he not only promises us deliverance from death and reconciliation with God, but also the gift of the Holy Spirit, by which we are regenerated to newness of life; these things must necessarily be conjoined so as not to divide Christ from himself.

M: Hence it follows that faith is the root from which all good works spring, so far is it from taking us off from the study of them?

S: So indeed it is; and hence the whole doctrine of the gospel is comprehended under the two branches, faith and repentance.

M: What is repentance?

S: Dissatisfaction with and a hatred of sin and a love of righteousness, proceeding from the fear of God, which things lead to self-denial and mortification of the flesh, so that we give ourselves up to the guidance of the Spirit of God, and frame all the actions of our life to the obedience of the Divine will.

M: But this second branch was in the division which was set down at first when you showed the method of duly worshipping God.

S: True; and it was at the same time added, that the true and legitimate rule for worshipping God is to obey his will.

M: Why so?

S: Because the only worship which he approves is not that which it may please us to devise, but that which he hath of his own authority prescribed.

Suggestions for Further Reading

Bouwsma, William J. *John Calvin: A Sixteenth-Century Portrait.* New York: Oxford University Press, 1988.

Calvin, John. *Institutes of the Christian Religion.* Translated by Henry Beveridge. Grand Rapids, Mich.: Eerdmans Publishing Co., 1933.

———. *Calvin's Ecclesiastical Advice.* Louisville, Kentucky: Westminster/John Knox Press, 1991.

———. *Tracts and Treatise on the Doctrines and Worship of the Church.* Translated by Henry Beveridge. Grand Rapids, Mich.: Eerdmans Publishing Co., 1958.

Estep, William R. *Renaissance and Reformation.* Grand Rapids, Mich.: Eerdmans Publishing Co., 1986.

Gamble, Richard C., ed. *The Biography of Calvin.* New York: Garland, 1992.

Graham, W. Fred. *The Constructive Revolutionary: John Calvin and His Socioeconomic Impact.* Richmond: John Knox Press, 1971.

Luke, Carmen. *Pedagogy, Printing and Protestantism: The Discourse on Childhood.* Albany: State University of New York Press, 1989.

McGrath, Alister E. *A Life of John Calvin: A Study in the Shaping of Western Culture.* Oxford, U.K., and Cambridge, Mass.: Basil Blackwell, 1990.

Mullett, Michael. *Calvin.* London: Routledge, Chapman, and Hall, 1989.

Parker, Thomas H. *John Calvin: A Biography.* Philadelphia: Westminster Press, 1975.

Schreinter, Susan E. *The Theater of His Glory: Nature and the Natural Order in the Thought of John Calvin.* Durham, N.C.: Labyrinth Press, 1991.

Towns, Elmer L., ed. *A History of Religious Educators.* Grand Rapids, Mich.: Baker Book House, 1975.

Walker, Williston. *John Calvin: The Organizer of Reformed Protestantism.* New York: Schocken Books, 1969.

Warfield, Benjamin B. *Calvin and Calvinism.* New York: Oxford University Press, 1931.

Notes

1. Williston Walker, *John Calvin: The Organizer of Reformed Protestantism* (New York: Schocken Books, 1969), 23; also see Thomas H. Parker, *John Calvin: A Biography* (Philadelphia: Westminster Press, 1975).

2. Parker, 4.

3. Walker, 49.

4. Emanuel Stickelberger, *Calvin,* translated by David G. Gelzer (London: J. Clarke, 1959) 16.

5. Ibid., 23.

6. John Calvin, *Institutes of the Christian Religion,* translated by Henry Beveridge (Grand Rapids, Mich.: Eerdmans Publishing Co., 1933).

7. John Calvin, *Tracts and Treatises on the Doctrine and Worship of the Church.* II, translated by Henry Beveridge (Grand Rapids, Mich.: Eerdmans Publishing Co., 1958), 137–62.

JOHANN AMOS COMENIUS: PANSOPHIST EDUCATOR AND PROPONENT OF INTERNATIONAL EDUCATION

BIOGRAPHICAL SKETCH

Johann Amos Comenius (1592–1670) is significant in the history and philosophy of education as a pioneering figure who, at a time of intense religious intolerance and persecution, urged the development and diffusion of general enlightenment to create a more tolerant and humane world order. His life coincided with the period of intense religious and nationalistic conflict that swept Europe during the Thirty Years War.

Comenius was born on March 28, 1592, in Moravia, now part of the Czech Republic. The Komensky family ("Comenius" in Latin) lived in the town of Uhersky Brod, where Johann received his elementary education. The family were members of a small Protestant denomination, the "Unity of the Brethren." His parents died in 1604 when he was 12 years old. Despite the loss of his parents, he was able to attend the Universities of Herborn and Heidelberg. Upon completing his university studies, Comenius returned to Moravia and was ordained a minister in the Unity of the Brethren in 1616. He was appointed pastor to the congregation of Brethren at Fulnek in 1618, where he was also principal of the local school.[1]

The early seventeenth century, the post-Reformation period, was a time of intense religious and political conflicts. After the Protestant army was defeated in 1620 at the Battle of White Mountain, Comenius, his family, and his church suffered persecution. From 1620 to 1627, Comenius, his wife, and two small children took refuge in a number of hiding places to avoid arrest. His wife and children died, victims of the plague. On the basis of his experiences as a hunted victim of intolerance, Comenius wrote *The Labyrinth of the World,* which portrayed the trials of a pilgrim's unsatisfied search to find peace in the world. The pilgrimage was satisfied only by union with Christ.

In 1628, Comenius fled to Poland to begin 42 years as a refugee and exile from his native Moravia. He settled in Leszno, where he ministered to the Brethren, wrote, and taught. In 1632, now a bishop of the Brethren, he published *Janua Linguarum Reserata,* a book on teaching languages. Again, he was a victim of intolerance when an invading army burned his home and library of books and manuscripts.[2]

50

Because of his educational writings, Comenius had gained an international reputation. In 1641, he visited England at the invitation of the educational reformer Samuel Hartlib (1596–1662), an associate of Oliver Cromwell. He published *The Way of Light,* an early work on international education. Once again religious and political strife interfered with his educational work. Civil War between King James' followers and Cromwell's supporters forced him to leave England in 1642.

Comenius took up residence in Prussia. He tried to persuade the Swedish government, led by Chancellor Oxenstierna (1583–1654), to protect the Brethren and regain their right to return to Bohemia and Moravia. However, Comenius' attempts to gain Swedish support failed.

In 1656, Comenius moved to Amsterdam in the Netherlands, where he was financially supported by Ludovicus de Geer. Free from financial pressures, Comenius dedicated himself to writing. His major book on education, *Opera Didactica,* appeared in 1657, followed by *Orbis Pictus,* an illustrated textbook, in 1658. His *Via Lucis, The Way of Light,* a proposal for ecumenical understanding, was published in 1668. His great work on education, *Opera Didactica Omnia,* a comprehensive effort to encompass all the world's knowledge, was published in installments from 1657 to 1668.[3] At the time of his death in 1670, Comenius had won renown and respect for his work as an educator.

OVERVIEW OF IDEAS ON EDUCATION

Comenius' philosophy of education, Pansophism, an attempt to embrace all knowledge, was drawn from theology, philosophy, and science. Pansophism sought to provide human beings with universal knowledge, which, in turn, would lead to God, the source of all truth and goodness. Comenius based his theological principles on Pietism, a religious persuasion based on what was called the "religion of the heart," love of God and love of human beings. His theory of knowledge was based on sense Realism, the belief that people acquired knowledge about the objects in the world through sensation. He viewed science, knowledge about the natural world, as complementing the Bible, a higher source of truth.[4] While the Bible was the superior guide to human conduct, Comenius believed that scientific knowledge, which also came from God, gave people a complementary way of knowing God's creation.

A victim of religious and political intolerance, Comenius believed that war and conflict were caused by ignorance, which produced hatred, bigotry, discrimination, and prejudice. Complete knowledge, the way to conquer ignorance, he argued, would bring people closer to God and to each other. As an international or peace educator, Comenius wanted educational institutions to have a peacemaking function. It was important that schools become agencies that cultivated an ecumenical vision of a peaceable kingdom in which all could live in mutual respect.

Comenius developed insights into child psychology and development, which he applied to teaching and learning. He based many of his principles of education on his observations of nature. Among his guiding principles were:

1. Like nature, human beings have a time, a readiness, for growth and development.

2. Human education, like natural development, should be orderly and sequential in that each stage is related.
3. Teaching and learning, following nature, should proceed slowly and gradually and not be forced or rushed.[5]

Child development, according to Comenius, can be seen in terms of sequential stages, each of which has its own readiness and appropriate experiences. Teachers were to learn to recognize these stages of development and base their teaching on them. In his effort to teach universal knowledge, Comenius was concerned that instruction be done as efficiently but also as humanely and kindly as possible.

Comenius designed a complete sequence of schools. In what he called the School of Infancy, children, from birth until age 6, were to be educated by their parents, especially by their mother, the first and best teacher. Comenius advised parents to create a secure and emotionally healthy home environment. They were encouraged to play with their children and develop their readiness for later learning.

From ages 6 through 12, children attended primary school, where they learned reading, writing, religious education, mathematics, history, geography, music, art, and crafts. An early proponent of what is currently known as "effective schooling," Comenius advised teachers to group children so that they could pursue the same lesson simultaneously and interact collaboratively. He advised teachers to use objects and pictures to make instruction more meaningful to children. His book, *Orbis Pictus,* provided illustrations of the language lessons. Comenius strongly opposed using corporal punishment and psychological repression as a form of classroom management. Teachers were to be gentle, and discipline was to be fair and administered without anger.[6]

After primary school, students continue for another 6 years, from ages 12 to 18, in the Latin grammar school, a secondary institution. Here, the curriculum consisted of Greek, Latin, and Hebrew, languages then part of a conventional secondary education that prepared students for university admission. They also studied mathematics, geometry, physical and natural sciences, astronomy, history, ethics, rhetoric, music, and theology.[7]

At the summit of Comenius' projected system of educational institutions was the Pansophist university, where students would study the entire range of knowledge.

THE PRIMARY SOURCE

In the selection from his most important book, *The Great Didactic of John Amos Comenius,* Comenius sets forth his guiding principles of education. In the original text, Comenius first states the principle, provides an example from nature, indicates how the principle is imitated or applied in human culture, describes how teachers and schools deviate from the principle, and then suggests a rectification that will bring education back into agreement with natural principles. The editor has deleted the sections on examples and imitation so that the reader can move from the principle to its application to education. As a transitional figure between the post-Reformation and the Enlightenment periods, Comenius developed a method for teaching languages and other conventional subjects in the curriculum according to the principles of nature.

FOCUSING QUESTIONS

As you read the selection, you might wish to consider the following questions:

1. How does Comenius relate education to stages of human growth and development? Is his concept of readiness relevant to contemporary education? Explain your answer.
2. What advice does Comenius give to teachers about preparing the classroom environment for instruction? Is his concept of preparing the educational environment relevant to contemporary education? Explain your answer.
3. Comenius argues that schools attempt to teach too many subjects too early in a person's education. Is this criticism relevant to the contemporary curriculum? Explain your answer.
4. Comenius argues that learning is most effective when students really understand what and why something is being taught. Is this principle relevant to contemporary education? Can you provide examples of subjects and skills being taught without students understanding the rationale for learning them?
5. Describe the method Comenius recommends for teaching a subject, and then devise a lesson that follows it.

FROM *THE GREAT DIDACTIC OF JOHN AMOS COMENIUS*

FIRST PRINCIPLE

Nature observes a suitable time. . . .

Deviation.—In direct opposition to this principle, a twofold error is committed in schools.

(i.) The right time for mental exercise is not chosen.

(ii.) The exercises are not properly divided, so that all advance may be made through the several stages needful, without any omission. As long as the boy is still a child he cannot be taught, because the roots of his understanding are still too deep below the surface. As soon as he becomes old, it is too late to teach him, because the intellect and the memory are then failing. In middle age it is difficult, because the forces of the intellect are dissipated over a variety of objects and are not easily concentrated. The season of youth, therefore, must be chosen. Then life and mind are fresh and gathering strength; then everything is vigorous and strikes root deeply.

Rectification.—We conclude, therefore, that

From *The Great Didactic of John Amos Comenius,* translated by M. W. Keatinge. London: Adams and Charles Black, 1907, 112–126.

(i.) The education of men should be commenced in the springtime of life, that is to say, in boyhood (for boyhood is the equivalent of spring, youth of summer, manhood of autumn, and old age of winter).

(ii.) The morning hours are the most suitable for study (for here again the morning is the equivalent of spring, midday of summer, the evening of autumn, and the night of winter).

(iii.) All the subjects that are to be learned should be arranged so as to suit the age of the students, that nothing which is beyond their comprehension be given them to learn.

SECOND PRINCIPLE

Nature prepares the material, before she begins to give it form. . . .

Deviation.—Against this principle schools are offenders: firstly, because they take no care to prepare beforehand the mechanical aids such as books, maps, pictures, diagrams, etc., and to have them in readiness for general use, but at the moment that they need this or that, they make experiments, draw, dictate, copy, etc., and when this is done by an unskilled or careless teacher (and their number increases daily), the result is deplorable. It is just as if a physician, whenever he wishes to administer a medicine, had to wander through gardens and forests, and collect and distil herbs and roots, though medicaments to suit every case should be ready to his hand.

Secondly, because even in school-books the natural order, that the matter come first and the form follow, is not observed. Everywhere the exact opposite is to be found. The classification of objects is unnaturally made to precede a knowledge of the objects themselves, although it is impossible to classify, before the matter to be classified is there. I will demonstrate this by four examples.

(1) Languages are learned in schools before the sciences, since the intellect is detained for some years over the study of languages, and only then allowed to proceed to the sciences, mathematics, physics, etc. And yet things are essential, words only accidental; things are the body, words but the garment; things are the kernel, words the shells and husks. Both should therefore be presented to the intellect at the same time, but particularly the things, since they are as much objects of the understanding as are languages.

(2) Even in the study of languages the proper order is reversed, since the students commence, not with some author or with a skilfully-compiled phrase-book, but with the grammar; though the authors (and in their own way the phrase-books) present the material of speech, namely words, while the grammars, on the other hand, only give the form, that is to say, the laws of the formation, order, and combination of words.

(3) In the encyclopaedic compilations or human knowledge, the arts are always placed first, while the sciences follow after; though the latter teach of the things themselves, the former how to manipulate the things.

(4) Finally: it is the abstract rules that are first taught and then illustrated by dragging in a few examples; though it is plain that a light should precede him whom it lights.

Rectification.—It follows, therefore, that in order to effect a thorough improvement in schools it is necessary:

(i.) That books and the materials necessary for teaching be held in readiness.

(ii.) That the understanding be first instructed in things, and then taught to express them in language.

(iii.) That no language be learned from a grammar, but from suitable authors.

(iv.) That the knowledge of things precede the knowledge of their combinations.

(v.) And that examples come before rules.

THIRD PRINCIPLE

Nature chooses a fit subject to act upon, or first submits one to a suitable treatment in order to make it fit. . . .

Deviation.—Against this principle the schools are offenders: not because they include the weak of intellect (for in our opinion all the young should be admitted into the schools) but far more because:

(1) These tender plants are not transplanted into the garden, that is to say, are not entirely entrusted to the schools, so that none, who are to be trained as men, shall be allowed to leave the workshop before their training is complete.

(2) The attempt is generally made to engraft that noblest graft of knowledge, virtue and piety, too early, before the stock itself has taken root; that is to say, before the desire to learn has been excited in those who have no natural bent in that direction.

(3) The side-shoots or root-suckers are not removed before the grafting takes place; that is to say, the minds are not freed from all idle tendencies by being habituated to discipline and order.

Rectification.—It is therefore desirable:

(i.) That all who enter schools persevere in their studies.

(ii.) That, before any special study is introduced, the minds of the students be prepared and made receptive of it. . . .

(iii.) That all obstacles be removed out of the way of schools.

"For it is of no use to give precepts," says Seneca, "unless the obstacles that stand in the way be removed." But of this we will treat in the following chapter.

FOURTH PRINCIPLE

Nature is not confused in its operations, but in its forward progress advances distinctly from one point to another. . . .

Deviation.—Confusion has arisen in the schools through the endeavour to teach the scholars many things at one time. As, for example, Latin and Greek grammar, perhaps rhetoric and poetic as well, and a multitude of other subjects. For it is notorious that in the classical schools the subject-matter for reading and for composition is changed almost every hour throughout the day. If this be not confusion I should like to know what is. It is just as if a shoemaker wished to make six or seven new shoes at once, and took them up one by one in turn, only to lay them aside in a few minutes; or as if a baker, who wished to place various kinds of bread in his oven, were to take them out again immediately, removing one kind as he put in another. Who would commit such an act of folly? The shoemaker finishes one shoe before he begins another. The baker places no fresh bread in the oven until that already in it is thoroughly baked.

Rectification.—Let us imitate these people and take care not to confuse scholars who are learning grammar by teaching them dialectic, or by introducing rhetoric into their studies. We should also put off the study of Greek until Latin is mastered, since it is impossible to concentrate the mind on any one thing, when it has to busy itself with several things at once.

That great man, Joseph Scaliger, was well aware of this. It is related of him that (perhaps on the advice of his father) he never occupied himself with more than one branch of knowledge at once, and concentrated all his energies on that one. It was owing to this that he was able to master not only fourteen languages, but also all the arts and sciences that lie within the province of man. He devoted himself to these one after the other with such success that in each subject his learning excelled that of men who had given their whole lives to it. And those who have tried to follow in his footsteps and imitate his method, have done so with considerable success.

Schools, therefore, should be organised in such a manner that the scholar shall be occupied with only one object of study at any given time.

FIFTH PRINCIPLE

In all the operations of nature development is from within. . . .

Deviation.—It is on this point that those teachers fall into error who, instead of thoroughly explaining the subjects of study to the boys under their charge, give them endless dictations, and make them learn their lessons off by heart. Even those who wish to explain the subject-matter do not know how to do so, that is to say, do not know how to tend the roots or how to engraft the graft of knowledge. Thus they fatigue their pupils, and resemble a man who uses a club or a mallet, instead of a knife, when he wishes to make an incision in a plant.

Rectification.—It therefore follows

(i.) That the scholar should be taught first to understand things, and then to remember them, and that no stress should be laid on the use of speech or pen, till after a training on the first two points.

(ii.) That the teacher should know all the methods by which the understanding may be sharpened, and should put them into practice skilfully.

SIXTH PRINCIPLE

Nature, in its formative processes, begins with the universal and ends with the particular. . . .

Deviation.—From this it follows that it is a mistake to teach the several branches of science in detail before a general outline of the whole realm of knowledge has been placed before the student, and that no one should be instructed in such a way as to become proficient in any one branch of knowledge without thoroughly understanding its relation to all the rest.

It follows also that arts, sciences, and languages are badly taught unless a general notion of the elements be first given. I remember well that, when we began to learn dialectic, rhetoric, and metaphysics, we were, at the very beginning, overburdened with long-winded rules, with commentaries and notes on commentaries, with comparisons of authors and with knotty questions. Latin grammar was taught us with all the exceptions and irregularities; Greek grammar with all its dialects, and we, poor wretches, were so confused that we scarcely understood what it was all about.

Rectification.—The remedy for this want of system is as follows: at the very commencement of their studies, boys should receive instruction in the first principles of general culture, that is to say, the subjects learned should be arranged in such a manner that the studies that come later introduce nothing new, but only expand the elements of knowledge that the boy has already mastered. Just as a tree, even if it live for a hundred years, puts forth no new branches, but only suffers those that already exist to develope and to spread.

(i.) Each language, science, or art must be first taught in its most simple elements, that the student may obtain a general idea of it. (ii.) His knowledge may next be developed further by placing rules and examples before him. (iii.) Then he may be allowed to learn the subject systematically with the exceptions and irregularities; and (iv.), last of all, may be given a commentary, though only where it is absolutely necessary. For he who has thoroughly mastered a subject from the beginning will have little need of a commentary, but will soon be in the position to write one himself.

SEVENTH PRINCIPLE

Nature makes no leaps, but proceeds step by step. . . .

Deviation.—It is an evident absurdity, therefore, if teachers, for their own sake and that of their pupils, do not graduate the subjects which they teach in such a way that, not only one stage may lead on directly to the next, but also that each shall be completed in a given space of time. For unless goals are set up, means provided for reaching them, and a proper system devised for the use of those means, it is easy for something to be omitted or perverted, and failure is the result.

Rectification.—It follows therefore

(i.) That all studies should be carefully graduated throughout the various classes, in such a way that those that come first may prepare the way for and throw light on those that come after.

(ii.) That the time should be carefully divided, so that each year, each month, each day, and each hour may have its appointed task.

(iii.) That the division of the time and of the subjects of study should be rigidly adhered to, that nothing may be omitted or perverted.

EIGHTH PRINCIPLE

If nature commence anything, it does not leave off until the operation is complete. . . .

Deviation.—It is therefore injurious if boys are sent to school for months or years continuously, but are then withdrawn for considerable periods and employed otherwise; equally so if the teacher commence now one subject, now another, and finish nothing satisfactorily; and lastly, it is equally fatal if he do not fix a certain task for each hour, and complete it, so that in each period his pupil can make an unmistakable advance towards the desired goal. Where such a fire is wanting, everything grows cold. Not without reason does the proverb say "Strike while the iron is hot." For if it be allowed to cool it is useless to hammer it, but it must once more be placed in the fire, and thus much time and iron are wasted. Since every time that it is heated, it loses some of its mass.

Rectification.—It follows therefore

(i.) That he who is sent to school must be kept there until he becomes well informed, virtuous, and pious.

(ii.) That the school must be situated in a quiet spot, far from noise and distractions.

(iii.) That whatever has to be done, in accordance with the scheme of study, must be done without any shirking.

(iv.) That no boys, under any pretext whatever, should be allowed to stay away or to play truant.

NINTH PRINCIPLE

Nature carefully avoids obstacles and things likely to cause hurt. . . .

Deviation.—It is therefore folly to introduce a student to controversial points when he is just beginning a subject, that is to say, to allow a mind that is mastering something new to assume an attitude of doubt. What is this but to tear up a plant that is just beginning to strike root? (Rightly does Hugo say: "He who starts by investigating doubtful points will never enter into the temple of wisdom.") But this is exactly what takes place if the young are not protected from incorrect, intricate, and badly written books as well as from evil companions.

Rectification.—Care should therefore be taken

(i.) That the scholars receive no books but those suitable for their classes.

(ii.) That these books be of such a kind that they can rightly be termed sources of wisdom, virtue, and piety.

(iii.) That neither in the school nor in its vicinity the scholars be allowed to mix with bad companions.

If all these recommendations are observed, it is scarcely possible that schools should fail to attain their object.

SUGGESTIONS FOR FURTHER READING

Busek, Vratislav, ed. *Comenius.* New York: Czechoslovak Society of Arts and Sciences, 1972.

Comenius, John Amos. *The Labyrinth of the World and the Paradise of the Heart.* New York: Arno Press, 1971.

———. *The Orbis Pictus of John Amos Comenius.* Syracuse, N.Y.: C. W. Bardeen Publisher, 1887.

———. *The School of Infancy.* Translated by Ernest M. Eller. Chapel Hill, N.C.: University of North Carolina Press, 1956.

Jakubec, Jan. *Johannes Amos Comenius.* New York: Arno Press, 1971.

Keatinge, M. W. *The Great Didactic of John Amos Comenius.* London: Adam and Charles Black, 1896.

Monroe, Will S. *Comenius and the Beginnings of Educational Reform.* New York: Arno Press, 1971.

Spinka, Matthew. *John Amos Comenius, That Incomparable Moravian.* Chicago: University of Chicago Press, 1943.

Young, Robert F. *Comenius in England.* New York: Arno Press and New York Times, 1971.

NOTES

1. Eve Chyhova Bock, "Seeking a Better Way," *Christian History,* VI (1987), 7.

2. Ibid., 7–8.

3. Josef Smolik, "Comenius: A Man of Hope in a Time of Turmoil," *Christian History,* VI (1987), 16.

4. Paul Heidebrecht, "Learning from Nature: The Educational Legacy of Jan Amos Comenius," *Christian History,* VI (1987), 23.

5. Heidebrecht, 23.

6. Jerome K. Clauser, "The Pansophist: Comenius," in Paul Nash, Andreas M. Kazamias, and Henry J. Perkinson, *The Educated Man: Studies in the History of Educational Thought* (New York: John Wiley and Sons, 1965), 165–88.

7. Lis Le Bar, "What Children Owe to Comenius," *Christian History,* VI (1987), 19.

JEAN-JACQUES ROUSSEAU: PROPHET OF NATURALISM

BIOGRAPHICAL SKETCH

Jean-Jacques Rousseau (1712–1778) is significant in the history and philosophy of education as an iconoclast who challenged traditional ideas, especially that education should be an agency of socialization. Rousseau, who advocated learning according to natural principles—by direct experience and in a permissive environment—anticipated the child-centered tendency in modern education.

The son of Isaac Rousseau, a watchmaker, and Suzanne Bernard Rousseau, Jean-Jacques was born in Geneva, Switzerland. Rousseau's mother died when he was 10 months old, and he was cared for by his father and his aunt. He claimed his highly emotional, impulsive aunt and his irresponsible, fun-loving father provided little guidance or discipline.

Recalling that his father was his first tutor, Rousseau reminisced that he and his father read into the late hours of the night. Their reading, with no definite order, included romantic novels, unsuited for a child, but also such classics as Ovid's *Metamorphoses* and Plutarch's *Lives of Famous Men.* He later commented that his mind was stocked at early age with fantasies. In his own book, *Emile,* he cautioned educators to give children opportunities for direct experience and warned against introducing books too early in a child's life. Though he claims to have had a close relationship with his father, it ended when Rousseau was 10. After a fight with an army officer, Isaac Rousseau hastily departed from Geneva to avoid jail. The young Jean-Jacques was then placed in the guardianship of his uncle, Gabriel Bernard, who sent him to the conventional primary schools.

With this unsettling early childhood as a background, Rousseau then worked as an apprentice in two unsatisfactory training situations. He was first apprenticed to a notary and then an engraver. The notary dismissed Rousseau for neglect of duties. He, in turn, left the engraver, charging unfair treatment. As a youth, Rousseau showed he had difficulty with relationships, especially those in which he was a subordinate.[1]

Rousseau left Geneva in 1728 and eventually found his way to Chambery, in Savoy, where he lived with a wealthy widow, Madame de Waren. She provided the money while he worked at improving his knowledge of the classics and music.

Jean-Jacques Rousseau,
the author of *Emile*.

In 1739, at age 27, Rousseau was hired as tutor to the two sons of M. de Mably. His experience as tutor stimulated him to write his first educational treatise, *The Project of the Education of M. de Sainte-Marie.*[2] Finding his job as tutor unrewarding, Rousseau, in 1741, went to Paris, where he worked at copying music. He began a long relationship with Therese Levasseur, an illiterate servant girl. The couple had five children, all of whom Rousseau placed in an orphanage shortly after their births.[3]

In Paris, the intellectual center of the Enlightenment, Rousseau was drawn to the ideas of such leading thinkers as Diderot and d'Alembert. In 1749, Rousseau's essay "Has the Progress of the Arts and Sciences Contributed More to the Corruption or Purification of Morals?" won first prize.[4] Rousseau's answer, contrary to conventional educational wisdom, is that the arts and sciences corrupt rather than liberate. He also contributed articles for Diderot's *Encyclopedia*. Rousseau's "Discourse on Political Economy" appeared in 1755.

Rousseau's highly important work on politics, *The Social Contract*, was published in 1762. In it, he described the operations of the general will, a kind of grand consensus, as governing the political order. He completed his autobiography, *Confessions*, in 1770. At the invitation of Count Wielhorski, Rousseau wrote a constitution for Poland, *The Government of Poland*, in 1772.

On July 2, 1778, Rousseau died of uremia at Ermenonville and was buried on the Girardin estate. On October 11, 1794, his remains were transferred to the Pantheon in Paris.

OVERVIEW OF IDEAS ON EDUCATION

Rousseau was a philosopher of the "Age of Reason," the eighteenth-century Enlightenment, which emphasized nature as the key to understanding reality. He believed in the power of a naturalistic and secular epistemology to unlock what earlier generations had accepted as mysteries beyond the possibility of human knowing. Rousseau and other Enlightenment philosophers were forward-looking in that they believed it possible to redesign progressively social, political, and economic institutions. Affirming progress, Rousseau hypothesized that the future could be made progressively better than the past.

Although many of his books have educational implications, Rousseau's didactic novel, *Emile*, published in 1762, most directly deals with education. In the spirit of the eighteenth-century Enlightenment, it focuses on nature and the following of naturalist principles in education. The book, which is undergirded by Rousseau's belief in the original goodness of human nature, begins: "Everything is good as it comes from the hands of the Maker of the world but degenerates once it gets into the hands of man." For Rousseau, human beings, at birth, were not initially evil or imperfect, but intrinsically good.

Rousseau wrote *Emile* in the format of a novel about the education of a boy, Emile, by a tutor on an isolated country estate, where the growing boy could experience nature directly. Such a setting illustrated Rousseau's conviction that a child's intrinsic natural goodness is corrupted by society. Thus, Emile is placed in a natural environment, free from corrupting adults, so that his intrinsic natural goodness can develop without being contaminated by a corrupt society. To do this, the child's self-identity is to be developed around the natural instinct of *amour de soi,* or self-esteem, which he contrasts with *amour propre,* the selfishness by which a person manipulates others for his or her own purposes.

The tutor—who is responsible for Emile's moral, mental, and physical education—recognizes that human beings grow by moving through stages of development. For each stage of development, there are appropriate kinds of activities and learning that flow naturally from the readiness of the developmental stage and from the possibilities present in the environment. To make the concept of developmental learning clear and dramatic, Emile's traversing of the developmental stages proceeds naturally without the intrusion or intervention of social agents.

Rousseau identifies infancy as the earliest stage of human development. It begins with birth when the child, an unspoiled primitive, is very close to the original state of nature and extends until age 5. Rousseau advises that the child's nurturing process is intended to build a strong, healthy body. He is to move freely so that his body—especially his senses, muscles, and coordination—is developed. In these first years, the child experiences only pleasure and pain that come from the objects found in the environment. Rousseau tells parents to love their children, to avoid coercing them physically and emotionally, and to give them as much freedom as possible.[5]

Rousseau calls the second stage of Emile's development "boyhood," the period from 5 through 12. Most important at this stage is continued sensory training in which the various senses are used to estimate the size, shape, and dimensions of objects. Physically stronger, Emile, who is able to do more for himself, is becoming increasingly conscious of what causes him to be happy, the experience of pleasure, and what causes unhappiness, pain. Now, two concepts are contesting in Emile's moral development: *amour de soi* and *amour propre*. *Amour de soi*, a natural virtue arising from instinctive self-interests, is to be encouraged. The tendency to *amour propre*, arising from social relationships that make the boy either a manipulator or a manipulated person, is discouraged. At this stage, Rousseau claims that children are incapable of reasoning and judging right from wrong. It is futile to try to make Emile follow moral prescriptions and proscriptions. It is more important that Emile learn that his actions have consequences, in that some will result in pleasure and others in pain.[6]

Rousseau defines the third stage in Emile's education as taking place from ages 12 through 15. Nature studies continue as Emile, observing natural phenomena, asks questions and inductively learns about science. Now, it is important for Emile to learn what objects and activities are useful. He learns about vegetables and flowers by planting a garden. He learns carpentry, a useful skill that combines mental and physical labor. He reads his first book, Daniel Defoe's *Robinson Crusoe*, a tale about the survival of a marooned traveler on a tropical island.

Emile's next stage of development, the years between 15 and 18, might be called adolescence, when Emile's sexual curiosity requires the tutor's special guidance. Emile is now slowly entering society. Taking short trips, where he sees people in unfavorable conditions, he begins to feel compassion for them.

From ages 18 to 20, Emile is in the stage Rousseau calls the "age of humanity," when moral sensitivity grows. Emile is becoming aware of broader issues and concerns. Studying history, he examines conflicts between the human's natural goodness and society's corruptive artificialities. Recommending a natural Deist religion, Rousseau warned against attempting to develop moral principles in the young by trying to teach religious dogma.[7]

At age 20, Emile meets and falls in love with his future wife, Sophie. Reflecting the gender biases of his age, Rousseau says men are active and strong and women passive and weak. A woman's education depends on her relationship to man. She is to win man's affection and provide him with affection, support, and counsel. Rousseau describes Sophie as possessing a "good disposition" and a "pleasing appearance." When the book ends, Emile informs his tutor that he plans to educate his children as he was educated.

Rousseau's *Emile* puts forth an argument for permissiveness—letting children follow their needs and interests as far as possible. Child-centered educators who followed Rousseau have consistently emphasized learning environments that provide the greatest freedom for children's education.

THE PRIMARY SOURCE

The selection consists of excerpts from *Rousseau's Emile or Treatise on Education*, a didactic novel that tells the story of how a young French boy was educated, according to the principles of nature, by an enlightened and permissive tutor. Rousseau asserts that the child is naturally good at birth but, without the kind of natural education that he suggests, will become corrupted as does everything else in human hands. Rousseau argues that the child's natural instincts, coming directly from nature, are good. A negative education that keeps out social artificialities will allow and encourage the full development of these instincts. Rousseau's tutor, letting nature be the principal teacher, is highly permissive. Emile will develop his own skills as he teaches himself to read and acquire his own knowledge directly from the environment, as in the case of geography.

The excerpts in the selection from *Emile* illustrate Rousseau's concepts of key stages of human development. What Rousseau calls infancy, the earliest stage, is from birth to age 5, when the child is helpless and is allowed as much freedom of movement possible to encourage the building of a strong, healthy body. The second stage in Emile's development is from ages 5 through 12, when his increased physical abilities enable him to do more for himself. It is during this stage that Rousseau introduces the concept of "negative education," intended to keep out socially undesirable influences so that the traits to natural goodness can develop. It is important for Emile to learn that his actions have consequences—some of which bring pleasure and others pain. Warning against beginning the teaching of reading too early, Rousseau advises that children should not be pressured into reading. Emile will read when he is ready and needs to read. The third stage in Emile's development and education occurs between ages 12 and 15, when nature studies, such as the one illustrated on geography, are emphasized. Emile's next stage of development, which today is termed "adolescence," occurs between the ages of 15 and 18, when Emile develops sexual interests and requires special guidance. From 18 to 20 is the "age of humanity," when Emile becomes involved in society and makes moral decisions. At age 20, Emile meets and falls in love with his future wife, Sophie.

FOCUSING QUESTIONS
As you read the selection, you might wish to consider the following questions:

1. Why is Rousseau's philosophy called Naturalism? Do you find any evidence of Naturalism in contemporary American education?
2. Rousseau is viewed as an advocate of child permissiveness or permissive education. What is permissiveness? How does Rousseau show his permissiveness in Emile's education? Do you find evidence of permissiveness in contemporary American society and education? What is your opinion regarding permissiveness?
3. Do you find Rousseau's maxims relevant to contemporary education? Explain your answer.
4. What are Rousseau's views on moral education? Do you agree or disagree with them?
5. What is Rousseau's view on the teaching of reading? Is this view relevant to contemporary education?
6. What is Rousseau's view on the teaching of geography? Is this view relevant to contemporary education?

From *Rousseau's Emile or Treatise on Education*

Everything is good as it comes from the hands of the Author of Nature; but everything degenerates in the hands of man. He forces one country to nourish the productions of another; one tree to bear the fruits of another. He mingles and confounds the climates, the elements, the seasons; he mutilates his dog, his horse, and his slave; he overturns everything, disfigures everything; he loves deformity, monsters; he will have nothing as Nature made it, not even man; like a saddle-horse, man must be trained for man's service—he must be made over according to his fancy, like a tree in his garden. . . .

We are born weak; we have need of strength: we are born destitute of everything; we have need of assistance: we are born stupid; we have need of judgment. All that we have not at our birth, but which we need when we are grown, is given us by education.

We derive this education from nature, from men, or from things. The internal development of our faculties and organs is the education of nature; the use which we learn to make of this development is the education of men; while the acquisition of personal experience from the objects that affect us is the education of things. . . .

A child cries as soon as born, and his first years are spent in tears. At one time we trot and caress him to pacify him, and at another we threaten and beat him to keep him quiet. We either do what pleases him, or we exact of him what pleases us; we either subject ourselves to his whims, or subject him to ours. There is no middle ground; he must either give orders or receive them. And so his first ideas are those of domination and servitude. Before knowing how to speak, he commands; and before knowing how to act, he obeys; and sometimes he is punished before he is able to know his faults, or, rather, to commit any. It is thus that, at an early hour, we pour into his young heart the passions that we straightway impute to nature; and that, after having taken the trouble to make him bad, we complain of finding him such.

Would you, then, have him preserve his original form? Guard it from the moment of the child's birth.

As soon as born take possession of him, and do not give him up until he is a man. Save in this way, you will never succeed. As the real nurse is the mother, the real preceptor is the father. Let them agree in the discharge of their functions as well as in the system they follow, and let the child pass from the hands of one into the hands of the other. He will be better educated by a judicious though ignorant father, than by the most skillful teacher in the world; for zeal will much better supply the place of talent than talent the place of zeal. . . .

Do not suffer the child to be restrained by caps, bands, and swaddling-clothes; but let him have gowns flowing and loose, and which leave all his limbs at liberty, not so heavy as to hinder his movements, nor so warm as to prevent him from feeling the impression of the air. By keeping them dressed and within-doors, children in cities are suffocated. Those who have them in charge have yet to learn that cold air, far from doing them harm, invigorates them, and that warm air enfeebles them, makes them feverish, and kills them. Place the child in a wide cradle, well cushioned, where he can move at his ease and without danger. When he begins to grow strong, let him creep about the room and develop his little limbs, by giving them exercise; you will see him gain in strength day by day. Compare him with a child of the same age who has been tightly confined in swaddling-clothes, and you will be astonished at the difference in their progress.

When the child makes the effort and reaches out his hand without saying anything, he expects to reach the object because he does not make a proper estimate of its distance—he has made a mistake; but when he complains and cries while reaching out his hand, he then no longer makes a mistake as to the distance, but is either commanding the object to come to him, or is commanding you to bring him the object. In the first case, carry him to the object slowly, stopping at short intervals; in the second, give no sign whatever of hearing him; the louder he cries the less you should listen to him. It is important to accustom him at an early period neither to command men, for he is not their master, nor things, for they do not hear him. Thus, when a child desires something which he sees or which you wish to give him, it is much better to carry him to the object than to bring this object to him. He draws from this procedure a conclusion suitable to his age, and one which can be suggested to him in no other way. . . .

From *Rousseau's Emile or Treatise on Education,* translated by William B. Payne. New York: A. Appleton and Co., 1907, 1–2, 14–15, 25, 30, 33, 44, 47, 51–52, 59–60, 81–83, 142–143.

MAXIMS

1. Far from having superfluous strength, children do not have enough for all the demands that Nature makes on them. We must therefore grant them the use of all the strength which Nature gives them and of which they can not make a misuse.

2. We must aid them, and supply whatever they lack either in the way of intelligence, or in the way of strength, in whatever concerns their physical need.

3. In the aid which we give them, we must limit ourselves exclusively to the actually useful, without granting anything to caprice or to unreasonable desires; for caprice will not torment them if we have not called it into being, provided it does not have its origin in nature.

4. We must carefully study their language and their signs, to the end that, at an age when they do not know how to dissemble, we may distinguish in their desires what comes immediately from nature and what from opinion.

The spirit of these rules is to grant to children more real liberty and less domination, to leave them more to do on their own account, and to exact less from others. Thus, early accustoming themselves to limit their desires to their powers, they will have but little sense of the privation of what is not within their power. . . .

As children grow in strength, complaining is less necessary for them. As they grow in power to help themselves, they have less frequent need to resort to the assistance of others. Along with their growth in power there is developed the knowledge which puts them in a condition to direct it. It is at this second stage that the life of the individual properly begins. It is then that he takes knowledge of himself. Memory diffuses the feeling of identity over all the moments of his existence. He becomes truly one, the same, and consequently already capable of happiness or misery. It is important, then that we begin to consider him here as a moral being. . . .

In order to strengthen the body and to make it grow, Nature resorts to means which ought never to be thwarted. A child must not be constrained to keep still when he wishes to move, nor to move when he wishes to remain quiet. When the will of children has not been spoiled by our fault, they wish nothing that is to no purpose. They must jump, and run, and scream, whenever they have a mind to do so. All their movements are needs of their constitution which is trying to fortify itself: but we should distrust the desires which they themselves have not the power to satisfy. We must then be careful to distinguish the true or natural need from the fancied need which begins to

appear, or from that which comes merely from that superabundance of life of which I have spoken. . . .

Your child should obtain nothing because he demands it, but only because he has need of it; nor should he do anything from obedience, but from necessity. And so the terms obey and command are proscribed from his vocabulary, and still more the terms duty and obligation; but the terms force, necessity, impotency, and constraint, should have a large place in it. Before the age of reason there can be no idea of moral being, or of social relations. Hence, so far as possible, we must shun the use of the words which express them, for fear that the child may at first attach to these words false ideas which we have not the skill or the power to destroy. The first false idea which enters his head is the germ of error and of vice; and it is to this first step that we must pay particular attention. Proceed in such a way that as long as he is affected only by sensuous things all his ideas shall stop at sensation; so proceed that on every hand he may perceive about him only the world of matter; for, unless you do this, you may be sure that he will not listen to you at all, or that he will form of the moral world of which you speak to him fantastic notions which you will never efface from his life. . . .

The first education, then, ought to be purely negative. It consists not at all in teaching virtue or truth, but in shielding the heart from vice, and the mind from error. If you could do nothing and allow nothing to be done; if you could bring your pupil sound and robust to the age of twelve years without his being able to distinguish his right hand from his left—from your very first lessons the eyes of his understanding would be open to reason. Without prejudice and without habit, he would have nothing in him which could counteract the effect of your endeavors. Ere long he would become in your hands the wisest of men; and, while beginning with doing nothing, you will have produced a prodigy of education.

Take the very reverse of the current practice, and you will almost always do right. As the purpose is not to make of a child a child, but a master of arts, parents and teachers have lost no time in rebuking, correcting, reprimanding, humoring, threatening, promising, instructing, and talking reason. You should do better than this. Be reasonable, and do not reason at all with your pupil, especially to make him approve of what is displeasing to him; for to be always lugging reason into disagreeable things is but to make it wearisome to the child, and at once to bring it into discredit with a mind which is not yet in a condition to listen to it. Exercise his body, his organs, his senses, and his powers, but keep his soul lying fallow as long as you possibly can. Be on your guard against all feelings which precede the judgment that can estimate their value. . . .

In thus relieving children of all their school-tasks, I take away the instruments of their greatest misery, namely, books. Reading is the scourge of infancy, and almost the sole occupation which we know how to give them. At the age of twelve, Émile will hardly know what a book is. But I shall be told that it is very necessary that he know how to read. This I grant. It is necessary that he know how to read when reading is useful to him. Until then, it serves only to annoy him. . . .

Present interest is the grand motive power, the only one which leads with certainty to great results. Émile sometimes receives from his parents, relatives, or friends, notes of invitation for a dinner, a walk, a boat-ride, or to see some public entertainment. These notes are short, clear, concise, and well written. Some one must be found to read them to him, and this person is either not always to be found at the right moment, or he is as little disposed to accommodate the child as the child was to please him the evening before. In this way the moment passes, and the occasion is lost. Finally, the note is read to him, but it is too late. Ah! If one could read for himself! Other notes are received. How short they are! How interesting the matter is! The child would make an attempt to decipher them, and at one time finds some help and at another meets with refusal. Finally, after a great effort, the half of one note is deciphered, and it speaks of going out to eat cream to-morrow; but where or with whom, no one knows. What an effort is now made to read the rest of the note! I do not believe that Émile has need of a cabinet. Shall I speak at present of writing? No; I am ashamed to spend my time with such nonsense in a treatise on education.

I will add this one remark which constitutes an important maxim—viz., we usually obtain very surely and very quickly what we are in no haste to obtain. I am almost certain that Émile will know how to read and write perfectly before the age of ten, precisely because I care but very little whether he learns these things before the age of fifteen. I would much rather he would never know how to read than to buy this knowledge at the price of all that can make it useful. Of what use would reading be to him after he had been disgusted with it forever? . . .

His first two starting-points in geography will be the city where he lives and the country-seat of his father. After these will come the intermediate places, then the neighboring rivers, and lastly the observation of the sun, and the manner of finding one's way. This is the point of reunion. Let him make for himself a map of all this. This map will be very simple, and composed, at first, of only two objects; but to these he will gradually add the others as he ascertains or estimates their distance and position. You already see what advantage we have procured for him in advance by causing him to use his eyes for a compass.

SUGGESTIONS FOR FURTHER READING

Boyd, William, ed. *The Emile of Jean Jacques Rousseau*. New York: Teachers College Press, Columbia University, 1966.

_____. *The Minor Educational Writings of Jean Jacques Rousseau*. New York: Teachers College, Columbia University, 1962.

Compayre, Gabriel. *Jean Jacques Rousseau and Education from Nature*. New York: Burt Franklin, 1971.

Cooper, Laurence D. *Rousseau, Nature, and the Problem of the Good Life*. University Park: Pennsylvania State University Press, 1999.

Cranston, Maurice W. *The Noble Savage: Jean-Jacques Rousseau, 1754–1762*. Chicago: University of Chicago Press, 1991.

_____. *Jean-Jacques: The Early Life and Work of Jean-Jacques Rousseau, 1712–1754*. Chicago: University of Chicago Press, 1991.

Cullen, Daniel. *Freedom in Rousseau's Political Philosophy*. DeKalb: Northern Illinois University Press, 1993.

Davidson, Thomas. *Rousseau and Education According to Nature*. New York: AMS Press, 1971.

Ferrara, Alessandro. *Modernity and Authenticity: A Study in the Social and Ethical Thought of Jean-Jacques Rousseau*. Albany: State University of New York Press, 1992.

Grimsley, Ronald. *Jean-Jacques Rousseau.* Sussex, England: Harvester Press, 1983.

Havens, George R. *Jean-Jacques Rousseau.* Boston: Twayne Publishers, 1978.

Jackson, Susan K. *Rousseau's Occasional Autobiographies.* Columbus: Ohio State University Press, 1992.

Melzer, Arthur M. *The Natural Goodness of Man: On the System of Rousseau's Thoughts.* Chicago: University of Chicago Press, 1990.

Miller, James. *Rousseau: Dreamer of Democracy.* New Haven, Conn.: Yale University Press, 1984.

Misenheimer, Helen E. *Rousseau on the Education of Women.* Washington, D.C.: University Press of America, 1981.

Noble, Richard. *Language, Subjectivity, and Freedom in Rousseau's Moral Philosophy.* New York: Garland Publishers, 1991.

Roosevelt, Grace G. *Reading Rousseau in the Nuclear Age.* Philadelphia: Temple University Press, 1990.

Rousseau, Jean-Jacques. *The Confessions of Jean-Jacques Rousseau.* New York: Modern Library, 1945.

_____. *Discourses on the Origin of Inequality.* Indianapolis: Hackett Publishing Co., 1992.

_____. *Discourses on the Sciences and Arts: (First Discourse and Polemics).* Hanover, N.H.: University Press of New England, 1992.

_____. *Emile; or On Education.* Translated by Allan Bloom. New York: Basic Books, 1979.

_____. *The First and Second Discourses.* Edited by Roger D. Masters. New York: St. Martin's Press, 1964.

_____. *The Government of Poland.* Willmoore Kendall, Indianapolis: Bobbs-Merrill, 1972.

_____. *The Political Writings of J. J. Rousseau.* Edited by C. E. Vaughan. Oxford: Basil Blackwell, 1962.

_____. *The Religious Writings of Rousseau.* Edited by Ronald Grimsley. London: Clarendon Press, 1970.

_____. *The Social Contract.* Translated by Maurice Cranston. Baltimore: Penguin Books, 1969.

Scott, John T., ed. *The Collected Writings of Rousseau, Volume 7: "Essay on the Origin of Languages" and Writings Related to Music.* Hanover, N.H.: University Press of New England, 1999.

Strong, Trace Tracy B. *Jean Jacques Rousseau: The Politics of the Ordinary.* Thousand Oaks, Calif.: Sage Publications, 1994.

Trachtenberg, Zev M. *Making Citizens: Rousseau's Political Theory of Culture.* London and New York: Routledge, 1992.

Weiss, Penny A. *Gendered Community: Rousseau, Sex, and Politics.* New York: New York University Press, 1993.

NOTES

1. William Boyd, ed., *The Minor Educational Writings of Jean Jacques Rousseau* (New York: Teachers College, Columbia University, 1962), 7–23.

2. Ibid., 24–38.

3. William Kessen, "Rousseau's Children," *Daedalus,* 107 (Summer 1978), 155–64.

4. Jean-Jacques Rousseau, *The First and Second Discourses,* edited by Roger D. Masters (New York: St. Martins Press, 1964).

5. Jean-Jacques Rousseau, *Emile; or On Education,* translated by Allan Bloom (New York: Basic Books, 1979), 37–74.

6. Ibid., 77–163.

7. Ibid., 357–480.

JOHANN HEINRICH PESTALOZZI: PROPONENT OF EDUCATING THE HEART AND SENSES

BIOGRAPHICAL SKETCH

Johann Heinrich Pestalozzi (1747–1827), a Swiss educator, is significant for devising a method of education that emphasized sensory learning based on object lessons that took place in emotionally secure educational environments. John Heinrich Pestalozzi was born on January 12, 1747, in Zurich, Switzerland. His father, Johann Baptiste Pestalozzi, a physician, and Susanna Hotz Pestalozzi, his mother, were middle-class Protestants. Pestalozzi's father died in 1751 at age 33, leaving three surviving children, Johann Baptiste, Anna Barbara, and Johann Heinrich, who was then age 5.[1]

In recalling his childhood, Pestalozzi mentioned the important role played by a trusted servant, Barbara Schmidt, who managed the household. His grandfather, Andreas Pestalozzi, a minister in the village of Hongg, also exercised a formative influence. Pestalozzi professed that his grandfather's ministry to the poor inspired him to devote his own life to educating the children of the poor.

Not all of Pestalozzi's childhood memories were happy. Although Babeli, as Barbara Schmidt was called by the family, and his mother were concerned and caring, Pestalozzi believed they were overly protective, keeping him from the peer group activities that were normal for a child of his age. Pestalozzi attributed his social uneasiness and physical awkwardness to the absence of social interaction with other children, especially participation in games and play.

Pestalozzi attended a local primary school, conducted in the vernacular German spoken in Zurich, from 1751 to 1754, where he studied the conventional reading, writing, arithmetic, and religion. In 1754, he commenced his preparatory studies in the classical Latin and Greek languages and literatures at the Schola Abbatissana. He then went to the Schola Carolina, a more advanced classical preparatory school. His university study was at the Collegium Humanitatis where he took courses in Latin, Greek, and Hebrew language and literature, rhetoric, philosophy, and theology. At age 17, Pestalozzi entered the Collegium Carolinum where he concentrated on languages and philosophy.

As a university student, Pestalozzi joined a circle of young Swiss patriots led by Professor Jean Jacques Bodmer (1699–1773), a historian, who preached the need to

Johann Heinrich Pestalozzi teaching students. Note the large charts for teaching number and form.

revitalize Swiss life. Bodmer's young disciples organized the Helvetic Society to carry out his ideas. To disseminate its program, the Helvetic Society published *The Monitor,* a magazine that urged reforms. After some critical articles appeared, Zurich's officials suppressed the magazine. For a short time, Pestalozzi and others who had written articles for the magazine were jailed.

After completing his university studies, Pestalozzi sought to find a suitable career. Though his education in the classics, humanities, and theology provided the academic background to be a minister like his grandfather, he was so unskilled at public speaking that his attempt to preach a sermon proved disastrous. He decided to become a farmer and live the simple natural life that Bodmer had emphasized. He was also inspired by reading Rousseau, who urged a return to nature. What could be more natural than tilling the soil? the life of a farmer?

Pestalozzi, determined to start his own household, married Anna Schulthess, the daughter of an upper-middle-class Zurich family. Described as an attractive, patient, and capable young woman, Anna was 8 years older than her husband. Her family, who regarded Pestalozzi as an eccentric dreamer, reluctantly consented to the marriage. Pestalozzi's only child, Jean Jacques, named after his literary hero Rousseau, was born in 1770. Jean Jacques, a sickly child, suffered from "violent rheumatic attacks," which perhaps were caused by epilepsy. Pestalozzi decided to use Rousseau's *Emile* as a guide for his son's education.[2] However, when Jean Jacques had difficulty in learning to read and write, Pestalozzi decided that Rousseau's ideas needed some revision. Jean Jacques died at the age of 30.

With funds borrowed from friends and his wife's dowry, Pestalozzi purchased a 60-acre farm near the village of Birr in the canton of Bern. Here, he built his home, which he called Neuhof, and began his agricultural and educational experiment.

In 1774, Pestalozzi decided to add a school to his farm. He would turn Neuhof into an experimental agricultural and handicraft school, where the sale of the children's work would support the educational experiment. Pestalozzi accepted orphan children as students and invited poor families in the vicinity to send their children to him for an education. The children, both boys and girls, lived in dormitories. In the summer, they did agricultural chores; in the winter, they did cotton and wool spinning and weaving and made handicraft items. Pestalozzi taught reading, writing, and counting by using a group method that he called "simultaneous instruction."

Despite his own enthusiasm and financial support from friends, Pestalozzi's educational experiment drained his financial resources. Of the 50 children at the school, who ranged in age from 6 to 18, only 14 were capable of working. Pestalozzi's financial losses were aggravated by parents who would withdraw their children after Pestalozzi had provided them with food and clothing. In 1779, Pestalozzi was forced to close his school. However, he was convinced that he had made the correct decision in becoming an educator.

Forced by financial reverses to close his first school, Pestalozzi next turned to writing and publication in order to give his educational ideas a wider audience. His popular novel, *Leonard and Gertrude*, was published in 1781.[3] Following the genre of nineteenth-century didactic novels, the book featured a village mother and heroine who uses natural education to teach her children. *Leonard and Gertrude*, a very popular book, went through numerous reprintings and brought fame to Pestalozzi.

Building on success as a novelist, Pestalozzi wrote other books and articles on sociology and education. His *Christopher and Elizabeth*, a sequel to *Leonard and Gertrude*, was published in 1782 but did not enjoy the earlier novel's success. From 1782 to 1784, Pestalozzi published a journal, *Ein Schweizer Blatt, The Swiss News*, which carried his articles on the need for a new system of education based on natural principles. His sociological treatise, *On Legislation and Infanticide*, in 1783, argued that economic and educational reforms would improve society and eliminate the practice of killing or abandoning unwanted children. He also wrote several children's books: *Illustrations for My ABC Book* in 1787 and *Fables for My ABC Book* in 1795. Pestalozzi attempted to establish a broad philosophical foundation for his educational ideas and practices in his highly abstract *Researches into the Course of Nature in the Development of the Human Race*, published in 1797.

Twenty years after he was forced to close Neuhof, Pestalozzi, in 1799, actively reentered educational practice when the new Swiss government, which included several of his friends, asked him to take charge of the orphanage at Stans. Pestalozzi, at age 59, took charge of the orphanage where he found 80 children, some recently orphaned as a result of war fought on Swiss soil by the opposing French and Austrian armies.[4] It was at Stans that Pestalozzi developed his concept that effective education, teaching and learning, took place in an emotionally healthy environment. He found that many of the orphan children in his charge had suffered emotional trauma from seeing their parents killed and their homes burned. Before he could proceed with his method of natural education based on the senses, he found that the children had to be restored to emotional health. To build emotional security in his young charges, Pestalozzi sought to remake the orphanage into a loving home-life family environment much like that of Gertrude's home. He began to act as a father figure for the children, living with them and providing the security of a caring and loving adult. Unfortunately, Pestalozzi was forced to end his educational mission at Stans when the orphanage was closed on July 8, 1799, as the opposing French and Austrian armies resumed their battles in its vicinity.

Pestalozzi's friends in the Helvetian government again looked out for his welfare. In July 1799, they arranged a job for him in Burgdorf as assistant to Samuel Dysli, the schoolmaster of a working-class primary school. The arrangement between Dysli and Pestalozzi did not work out, and soon the two were clashing over different educational philosophies and teaching methods. Pestalozzi opposed Dysli's emphasis on memorization, the catechism, and use of corporal punishment.

Pestalozzi's allies in the Helvetian government came to his rescue, arranging for him to establish an educational institute in Burgdorf castle. From 1800 to 1804, Pestalozzi was director of the Burgdorf Institute, which included a boarding school for students and a teacher education program for educational interns.

At Burgdorf, he developed his method of learning through the senses. He emphasized what he called *anschauung*, a German word that signified how the human being goes about the process of developing concepts, or clear ideas, from various sensory perceptions of objects. He designed object lessons in which children, guided by teachers, directly examined the form, the shape, the quantity, the number, and the weight of objects, and then learned to name them. To complement classroom teaching, Pestalozzi organized nature study field trips into the surrounding countryside. While at Burgdorf, Pestalozzi completed his most extensive book on educational method, *How Gertrude Teaches Her Children,* published in 1801.[5] In this book, he explained how effective teaching required the implementation of two related phases of method: the general method, which required teachers to create an environment of emotional security and wellness, and the special method, by which children, using their senses, pursued object lessons of form, number, and sound or name.

Pestalozzi's institute at Burgdorf became one of Europe's leading educational centers. Here, he prepared a number of interns in his method of teaching. In turn, they would go out and disseminate the Pestalozzian method throughout Europe and the Americas. Among them was Joseph Neef, who would come to the United States and introduce the Pestalozzian method in the early nineteenth century. Still another intern was Friedrich Froebel, who would devise his own kindergarten method of early childhood education. The American common school leaders Horace Mann and Henry Barnard and the scientist-geologist-philanthropist William Maclure visited Pestalozzi at Burgdorf and observed his teaching methods. Barnard, who became the first U.S. commissioner of education, was especially influential in promoting Pestalozzian education in the United States.

In 1804, when the liberal Helvetian government was replaced by a more conservative federalist regime, Pestalozzi lost his lease at Burgdorf castle. He moved his institute to Yverdon, where the municipal government gave him free use of the local castle. From 1804 until his retirement in 1825, Pestalozzi continued his educational work at Yverdon, where he wrote, prepared teachers, and educated students. In 1827, Pestalozzi died at Neuhof, the site of his very first school.

OVERVIEW OF IDEAS ON EDUCATION

Pestalozzi's philosophy of education was based on his fundamental idea that each person possessed inherent intellectual, moral, and physical powers or potentials. From the mind came intellectual power, from the will moral power, and from the body physical power. Unlike the traditional schools that emphasized intellectual over moral and physical development, Pestalozzi argued that all three powers needed to be developed harmoniously and simultaneously. If the three essential human powers were brought to their full potential, then the society, too, would be improved.

Over the course of his educational practice at Neuhof, Stans, Burgdorf, and Yverdon, Pestalozzi slowly evolved his philosophy of education, which was an eclectic mixture of Enlightenment rationalism, naturalism, and Christian pietism. He arrived at two necessary and related phases of teaching method: the general and the special. The general phase, designed to foster homelike schools characterized by emotional security and wellness, was to be implemented prior to and concurrent with the special phase, which reflected Pestalozzi's *anschauung* principle, direct sensory learning through object lessons.[6]

Pestalozzi's general method flowed from the simple instinctive needs of early childhood, especially infancy, where the good mother satisfied her child's needs for food, warmth, and affection. In the initial stage of human life, a bond or circle of love was created between the nurturing mother and the responding child. From this bond, arising from natural instincts, would come the basis for later emotional security.

Emotional security and wellness then grew outward through circles of positive development. If the relationship between mother and infant was emotionally healthy, then the child would respond positively to other people with love and affection. The next circle, involving a positive bonding with other family members, was portrayed in Gertrude's family. Then came the next circle, which led outward to the members of the community. From this, the next circle of emotional development saw the person moving to a still larger and more abstract concept of the people of the country and then of the world. These broadening circles of love then took on a religious significance. By loving other people, the individual came to love God. Significantly, Pestalozzi made emotional security and health the foundation for morality. Loving persons would also be moral persons. Pestalozzi's philosophy of moral education corresponded to his view of how people developed emotional security. Love first came from basic human instincts rather than abstract principles. In a loving relationship, neither person would injure the other.

Pestalozzi applied his ethical theory to schools. He agreed with earlier educators such as Comenius and Rousseau, who saw traditional schools as places of child confinement. Here, children were treated as depraved savages who needed to be "civilized" by psychologically and physically coercive teachers who ruled their classrooms by corporal punishment. These schools needed to be reformed and made into places where love and emotional security reigned.

Although Pestalozzi had described the ideal or optimum development of emotional security, he knew that many children grew up in dysfunctional situations. Drawing from his experiences at Neuhof and Stans, where he ministered to orphan children, he knew that the mother-child circle could be broken by the mother's death or the breakup of families. In these situations, many children grew up suspicious and mistrustful, and were socially withdrawn or deviant in their behavior. For these children who were the victims of dysfunctional situations, the loving and se-cure climate of the Pestalozzian school would seek to restore emotional health and moral behavior by re-creating the conditions present in the good home.

As the children came to experience greater feeling of emotional security and wellness, then the special method could proceed, as children learned from direct sen-sory experience. Here, Pestalozzi related his epistemology, how we know, to his method of instruction, how we learn. Since human beings know about the objects in the environment through the senses, Pestalozzi reasoned that instruction also should be based on learning through sensory experience. He devised object lessons in which children, aided by their teachers, observed, examined, and analyzed objects found in their immediate environment. Each object was to be studied through a series of "form, number, and name" lessons, which constituted the natural beginning of schooling.[7] Every object had a form, a design, or a structure that could be studied by observing and touching it. In their drawing exercises, children traced the outline of small objects or sketched the shape or design of larger ones. Pestalozzi believed that the tracing and drawing exercises in the form lessons naturally led to writing.

With the form lessons, there were number lessons in which children learned quantity and number. To develop computation skills, children collected marbles, stones, or peas and grouped them, beginning with one object, then two objects, three objects, and so forth. Thus, they learned that the number sign referred to a corre-sponding number of real objects. By using tangible objects, children developed the basic computation skills of adding, subtracting, multiplying, and dividing.

Along with the form and number lessons, Pestalozzi developed a series of name or sound exercises. Each object had a name, and the children were taught to say that name. Each object also had qualities like color, hardness, and softness, and the chil-dren were taught to say these qualities. The names were said slowly and often bro-ken down into simple parts that were repeated over and over again until mastered. The name lessons, with their emphasis on breaking down large words and sentences into their smaller parts, led to reading and to clear speaking.

Pestalozzi devised nature study excursions that were the prototypes of the modern school field trip. Natural science and geography were taught by excursions through the surrounding countryside. Hiking through woodlands and following the streams, they learned how rivers flow and drain the surrounding countryside. They observed the lo-cal topography and geography—locating streams, hills, roads, and buildings. Back at the school, they created a model of the local geography, using clay, sand, paper, and wood. Then they sketched their model on paper, creating a map. They were introduced to the local economy by observing the activities of the farmer, shoemaker, blacksmith, shopkeeper, weaver, and so forth. It was far more meaningful to see people actually working than to memorize the principal products of various countries as was done in conventional schools. They collected plants, stones, and other natural objects that they brought back to the school and classified and arranged as a museum of natural history.

Though his philosophy of education was eclectic and often highly abstract, Pestalozzi developed some very precise and clear principles to guide teaching and learning. Instruction should:

1. Begin with concrete objects in the immediate environment before moving to what was more abstract and remote in the child's experience.
2. Not be hurried or forced but proceed slowly and gradually.

3. Not introduce something new until students have mastered previous lessons.
4. Begin with that which is easy before moving to that which is difficult.
5. Begin with that which is simple before moving to that which is complex.
6. Begin with that which is concrete before moving to that which is abstract.

For education today, Pestalozzi's major contribution was developing a philosophy of natural education that stressed the dignity of children and the importance of a child-centered curriculum. His rejection of child depravity, based on his view of a benevolent human nature, meant that he saw childhood as a uniquely important and special period of human growth. Pestalozzi's general phase of method anticipated modern child psychology. The contemporary doctrines of the child-centered school and child permissiveness had their beginnings with Pestalozzi at Neuhof, Stans, Burgdorf, and Yverdon.

The value of Pestalozzi's special method rested on its relationships to children's experience. Pestalozzi anticipated Dewey in insisting on the importance of maintaining a child's continuity of experience. His stress on the need to maintain a continuum of experience caused him to examine and to use the learning possibilities found in children's immediate environment. When used in such an experiential context, Pestalozzi's instructional strategies of "from the simple to the complex" and "from the near to the far" were valuable contributions to educational methodology.

THE PRIMARY SOURCES

In the selection from *Pestalozzi's Leonard and Gertrude,* set in the small fictional Swiss village of Bonnal, Pestalozzi developed a cast of characters who personified his ideas on social change and education. The heroine, Gertrude, a loving mother, is determined that her children, despite the family's poverty, will be nurtured in an emotionally secure home and become morally, physically, and intellectually well-developed persons. Her husband Leonard, a well-meaning but weak man, is an unemployed stone mason. Like most of village's men, Leonard idles time away in the local tavern, owned by the corrupt bailiff Hummel. Much of the land and other property around the village is owned by Squire Arner, a benign but absent landlord, who is unaware of the village's economic depression and social dysfunction. Through a series of simple episodes, Pestalozzi relates how Gertrude, the good mother-teacher, becomes an agent of social, economic, and educational reform. Pestalozzi uses Gertrude to exemplify the educationai method that he had used at Neuhof. While her children spin and weave, she teaches them reading, writing, and arithmetic. Gertrude's household and her children become an educational model for the village.

Pestalozzi then moves the story to larger social issues, portraying Gertrude as an agent of reform. Gertrude recognizes that her family and household are not isolated but are part of the larger village community. Gertrude, breaking with the tradition that the poor should suffer poverty in silence, goes to Squire Arner to inform him about the deplorable situation in Bonnal. True to the early nineteenth-century story genre, the good squire thanks Gertrude. He did not know that his appointee, Bailiff Hummel, was violating his trust and responsibility. Outraged, Squire Arner goes with Gertrude to the village where he dismisses Hummel. Together with Gertrude, Squire Arner embarks on a program of reform that includes establishing a village school, where the teacher will follow Gertrude's method of natural education. The selections describe Gertrude's method of teaching and the use of the natural method of education in the school.

In the selection titled "The Method, A Report by Pestalozzi" from *How Gertrude Teaches Her Children,* Pestalozzi discusses his method of natural education. Pestalozzi prepared the report to inform the members of an organization that was supporting his educational efforts. The report emphasizes Pestalozzi's guiding principle that all knowledge comes to human beings through their senses. In the cognitive process, two elements are of utmost importance—the human senses and the objects found in the world. Through the senses—seeing, hearing, tasting, feeling—information, or sensory data, is conveyed to the mind, which converts it into concepts or ideas that belong to a class of objects. Pestalozzi called the process of knowing *anschauung,* the forming of clear concepts from sense impressions.

Because human beings came to know the objects present in their environment through the senses, Pestalozzi reasoned that instruction should also be based on the senses. He devised a series of object lessons in which children, with the assistance of the teacher, observed, examined, and analyzed objects found in their immediate environment. Each object could be studied through a series of "form, number, and name" lessons, which constituted the proper beginning of education.

FOCUSING QUESTIONS
As you read the selections, you might wish to consider the following questions:

1. Describe Gertrude's method of simultaneous instruction according to natural principles. Is it relevant for contemporary methods of teaching in the primary grades? Explain your answer.
2. How does Gertrude use the immediate environment as a source of learning?
3. Describe the style of classroom management used by the village schoolteacher. What view of human nature underlies this style of management? Would it be effective in contemporary schools?
4. Describe Pestalozzi's concepts of how we know and how we learn. In your own teaching, what connections do you make between cognition (knowing) and instruction (teaching and learning)?
5. Identify and consider Pestalozzi's principles of instruction. Are they relevant for teaching and learning in contemporary schools?

CHAPTER XXV

GERTRUDE'S METHOD OF INSTRUCTION

It was quite early in the morning when Arner, Glülphi and the pastor went to the mason's cottage. The room was not in order when they entered, for the family had just finished breakfast, and the dirty plates and spoons still lay upon the table. Gertrude was at first somewhat disconcerted, but the visitors reässured her, saying kindly: "This is as it should be; it is impossible to clear the table before breakfast is eaten!"

The children all helped wash the dishes, and then seated themselves in their customary places before their work. The gentlemen begged Gertrude to let everything go on as usual, and after the first half hour, during which she was a little embarrassed, all proceeded as if no stranger were present. First the children sang their morning hymns, and then Gertrude read a chapter of the Bible aloud, which they repeated after her while they were spinning, rehearsing the most instructive passages until they knew them by heart. In the mean time, the oldest girl had been making the children's beds in the adjoining room, and the visitors noticed through the open door that she silently repeated what the others were reciting. When this task was completed, she went into the garden and returned with vegetables for dinner, which she cleaned while repeating Bible-verses with the rest.

It was something new for the children to see three gentlemen in the room, and they often looked up from their spinning toward the corner where the strangers sat. Gertrude noticed this, and said to them: "Seems to me you look more at these gentlemen than at your yarn." But Harry answered: "No, indeed! We are working hard, and you'll have finer yarn to-day than usual."

Whenever Gertrude saw that anything was amiss with the wheels or cotton, she rose from her work, and put it in order. The smallest children, who were not old enough to spin, picked over the cotton for carding, with a skill which excited the admiration of the visitors.

Although Gertrude thus exerted herself to develop very early the manual dexterity of her children, she was in no haste for them to learn to read and

From Pestalozzi's *Leonard and Gertrude,* translated by Eva Channing. Boston: D.C. Heath & Co., 1885), 129–131, 156–159.

write. But she took pains to teach them early how to speak; for, as she said, "of what use is it for a person to be able to read and write, if he cannot speak?—since reading and writing are only an artificial sort of speech." To this end she used to make the children pronounce syllables after her in regular succession, taking them from an old A-B-C book she had. This exercise in correct and distinct articulation was, however, only a subordinate object in her whole scheme of education, which embraced a true comprehension of life itself. Yet she never adopted the tone of instructor toward her children; she did not say to them: "Child, this is your head, your nose, your hand, your finger;" or: "Where is your eye, your ear?"—but instead, she would say: "Come here, child, I will wash your little hands," "I will comb your hair," or: "I will cut your finger-nails." Her verbal instruction seemed to vanish in the spirit of her real activity, in which it always had its source. The result of her system was that each child was skillful, intelligent and active to the full extent that its age and development allowed.

The instruction she gave them in the rudiments of arithmetic was intimately connected with the realities of life. She taught them to count the number of steps from one end of the room to the other, and two of the rows of five panes each, in one of the windows, gave her an opportunity to unfold the decimal relations of numbers. She also made them count their threads while spinning, and the number of turns on the reel, when they wound the yarn into skeins. Above all, in every occupation of life she taught them an accurate and intelligent observation of common objects and the forces of nature.

All that Gertrude's children knew, they knew so thoroughly that they were able to teach it to the younger ones; and this they often begged permission to do. On this day, while the visitors were present, Jonas sat with each arm around the neck of a smaller child, and made the little ones pronounce the syllables of the A-B-C book after him; while Lizzie placed herself with her wheel between two of the others, and while all three spun, taught them the words of a hymn with the utmost patience.

When the guests took their departure, they told Gertrude they would come again on the morrow. "Why?" she returned; "You will only see the same thing over again." But Glülphi said: "That is the best praise you could possibly give yourself." Gertrude blushed at this compliment, and stood confused when the gentlemen kindly pressed her hand in taking leave.

The three could not sufficiently admire what they had seen at the mason's house, and Glülphi was so overcome by the powerful impression made upon him, that he longed to be alone and seek counsel of his own thoughts. He hastened to his room, and as he crossed the threshold, the words broke from his lips: "*I* must be schoolmaster in Bonnal!" All night visions of Gertrude's schoolroom floated through his mind, and he only fell asleep toward morning. Before his eyes were fairly open, he murmured: "I will be schoolmaster!"—and hastened to Arner to acquaint him with his resolution.

CHAPTER XXXII

A GOOD PASTOR AND SCHOOLMASTER; THE OPENING OF A NEW ERA

In his instruction, Glülphi constantly sought to lay the foundation of that equanimity and repose which man can possess in all circumstances of life, provided the hardships of his lot have early become a second nature to him. The success of this attempt soon convinced the pastor that all verbal instruction, in so far as it aims at true human wisdom, and at the highest goal of this wisdom, true religion, ought to be subordinated to a constant training in practical domestic labor. The good man, at the same time, became aware that a single word of the lieutenant's could accomplish more than hours of his preaching. With true humility, he profited by the superior wisdom of the schoolmaster, and remodelled his method of religious instruction. He united his efforts to those of Glülphi and Margaret, striving to lead the children, without many words, to a quiet, industrious life, and thus to lay the foundations of a silent worship of God and love of humanity. To this end, he connected every word of his brief religious teachings with their actual, every-day experience, so that when he spoke of God and eternity, it seemed to them as if he were speaking of father and mother, house and home, in short, of the things with which they were most familiar. He pointed out to them in their books the few wise and pious passages which he still desired them to learn by heart, and completely ignored all questions involving doctrinal differences. He no longer allowed the children to learn any long prayers by rote, saying that this was contrary to the spirit of Christianity, and the express injunctions of their Saviour.

The lieutenant often declared that the pastor was quite unable to make a lasting impression on men, because he spoiled them by his kindness. Glülphi's own principles in regard to education were very strict, and were founded on an accurate knowledge of the world. He maintained that love was only useful in the education of men when in conjunction with fear; for they must learn to root out thorns and thistles, which they never do of their own accord, but only under compulsion, and in consequence of training.

He knew his children better in eight days than their parents did in eight years, and employed this knowledge to render deception difficult, and to keep their hearts open before his eyes. He cared for their heads as he did for their hearts, demanding that whatever entered them should be plain and clear as the silent moon in the sky. To insure this, he taught them to see and hear with accuracy, and cultivated their powers of attention. Above all, he sought to give them a thorough training in arithmetic; for he was convinced that arithmetic is the natural safeguard against error in the pursuit of truth.

Despite the children's rapid progress in their school, the lieutenant did not please everybody in the village, and a rumor soon spread abroad that he was too proud for a schoolmaster. It was in vain that the children contradicted this report; their parents only answered: "Even if he is good to you, he may be proud all the same."It was not until three weeks after the beginning of the school, that an event occurred which accomplished for him what the children's defense had been unable to do.

For the last twenty years the old rotten foot-bridge opposite the schoolhouse had been out of repair, so that in a rainy season the children must get wet above their ankles in crossing the lane to school. The first time the road was in this condition, Glülphi planted himself in the middle of the street in all the rain, and as the children came, lifted them, one after the other, across the brook. Now it happened that some of the very persons who had complained most of the lieutenant's pride, lived just across the way. It amused them greatly to see him get wet through and through in his red coat, and they fancied it would not be many minutes before he would call to them for help. When, however, he kept on patiently lifting the children over, until his hair and clothes were dripping wet, they began to say behind the window-panes: "He must be a good-natured fool, and we were certainly mistaken; if he were proud, he would have given it up long ago." Finally, they came out, and offered to relieve him from his task, while he went home and dried himself. But this was not all; when school was out that day, the children found a foot-bridge built, over which they could go home dry-shod. And from that day forth, not a word more was heard of the schoolmaster's pride.

The school was still not without enemies, the bitterest among them being the old schoolmaster, whose envy and rage at its success would have known no bounds, had he not feared to lose the pension which had been granted him by Arner, on condition that he should not set himself against the new order of things. But the schoolmaster was not the only man in the village who looked back with regret to bygone days. Half of the villagers had been accustomed to spend their evenings at the tavern, and the bitterest complaints were heard on all sides, because, after the affair with Hummel, Arner had caused this house to be closed. As soon as he learned the state of things, and found that many of the former loafers were making their homes miserable by their idle discontent, Arner opened the peat swamps in the vicinity of Bonnal, and at once supplied more than fifty men with good employment.

The condition of the poor people of the village was much improved in various ways. The prospect of tithe-free land brought order and thrift into the houses of many of the spinners, and the poor in general were no longer so servile in their obedience to the whims and exactions of the rich. Renold's wife, who had always been noted for her charity, began to see that more good could be done by leading the people to help themselves, than by all her alms-giving; and now, whenever her aid was asked, her first answer was: "I must go home with you, and see what you really need, and how I can best help you."

Every evening the lieutenant had a half dozen young people at his house, to whom he talked for hours of what Arner and the pastor intended, and showed how their designs had been misunderstood. Among his hearers was one young man, Lindenberger by name, who seemed to comprehend it all at a single word, and whose clear and forcible language served to set things in their true light before many of the villagers.

It was only the old generation, who were hardened in vice, for whom the new era that was opening contained no prospect of anything better. The quack doctor Treufang, who had promised the parson to abstain from his evil practices, could not resolve to leave his old life and lead a good and useful one; the former Baliff Hummel, when freed from the pressure which had been brought to bear upon him in the time of his great humiliation, and deprived of his daily intercourse with the pastor, fell back into his old ways, so far as his changed circumstances would allow; and Hartknopf, after a brief season of repentance, became the same canting hypocrite as ever.

FROM JOHANN H. PESTALOZZI'S *HOW GERTRUDE TEACHES HER CHILDREN*

THE METHOD, A REPORT BY PESTALOZZI

I am trying to psychologize the instruction of mankind; I am trying to bring it into harmony with the nature of my mind, with that of my circumstances and my relations to others. I start from no positive form of teaching, as such, but simply ask myself:—

From Johann H. Pestalozzi's *How Gertrude Teaches Her Children,* translated by Lucy E. Holland and Francis C. Turner. London: Swan Sonnenschein and Co., 1907, 199–211.

"What would you do, if you wished to give a single child all the knowledge and practical skill he needs, so that by wise care of his best opportunities, he might reach inner content?"

I think, to gain this end, the human race needs exactly the same thing as the single child.

I think, further, the poor man's child needs a greater refinement in the methods of instruction than the rich man's child.

Nature, indeed, does much for the human race, but we have strayed away from her path. The poor man is thrust away from her bosom, and the rich destroy themselves both by rioting and by lounging on her overflowing breast.

The picture is severe. But ever since I have been able to see I have seen it so; and it is from this view that the impulse arises within me, not merely to plaster over the evils in schools, which are enervating the people of Europe, but to cure them at their root.

But this can never be done without subordinating all forms of instruction to those eternal laws, by which the human mind is raised from physical impressions of the senses to clear ideas.

I have tried to simplify the elements of all human knowledge according to these laws, and to put them into a series of typical examples that shall result in spreading a wide knowledge of Nature, general clearness of the most important ideas in the mind, and vigorous exercises of the chief bodily powers, even among the lowest classes.

I know what I am undertaking; but neither the difficulties in the way, nor my own limitations in skill and insight, shall hinder me from giving my mite for a purpose which Europe needs so much. And, gentlemen, in laying before you the results of those labours on which my life has been spent, I beg of you but one thing. It is this:—Separate those of my assertions that may be doubtful from those that are indisputable. I wish to found my conclusions entirely upon complete convictions, or at least upon perfectly recognized premises.

The most essential point from which I start is this:—

Sense impression of Nature is the only true foundation of human instruction, because it is the only true foundation of human knowledge.

All that follows is the result of this sense impression, and the process of abstraction from it. Hence in every case where this is imperfect, the result also will be neither certain, safe nor positive; and in any case, where the sense impression is inaccurate, deception and error follow.

I start from this point and ask:—"What does Nature herself do in order to present the world truly to me, so far as it affects me? That is,—By what means does she bring the sense impressions of the most important things around me, to a perfection that contents me?" And I find,—She does this through my surroundings, my wants, and my relations to others.

Thus all the Art (of teaching) men is essentially a result of physico-mechanical laws, the most important of which are the following:—

1. Bring all things essentially related to each other to that connection in your mind which they really have in Nature.

2. Subordinate all unessential things to essential, and especially subordinate the impression given by the Art to that given by Nature and reality.

3. Give to nothing a greater weight in your idea than it has in relation to your race in Nature.

4. Arrange all objects in the world according to their likeness.

5. Strengthen the impressions of important objects by allowing them to affect you through different senses.

6. In every subject try to arrange graduated steps of knowledge, in which every new idea shall be only a small, almost imperceptible addition to that earlier knowledge which has been deeply impressed and made unforgettable.

7. Learn to make the simple perfect before going on to the complex.

8. Recognize that as every physical ripening must be the result of the whole perfect fruit in all its parts, so every just judgment must be the result of a sense impression, perfect in all its parts, of the object to be judged. Distrust the appearance of precocious ripeness as the apparent ripeness of a worm-eaten apple.

9. All physical effects are absolutely necessary; and this necessity is the result of the art of Nature, with which she unites the apparently heterogeneous elements of her material into one whole for the achievement of her end. The Art, which imitates her, must try in the same way to raise the results at which it aims to a physical necessity, while it unites its elements into one whole for the achievement of its end.

10. The richness of its charm and the variety of its free play cause the results of physical necessity to bear the impress of freedom and independence. Here, too, the Art must imitate the course of Nature, and by the richness of its charm and the variety of its free play, try to make its results bear the impress of freedom and independence.

11. Above all, learn the first law of the physical mechanism, the powerful, universal connection between its results and the proportion of nearness or distance between the object and our senses. Never forget this physical nearness or distance of all objects around

you has an immense effect in determining your positive sense impressions, practical ability and even virtue. But even this law of your nature converges as a whole towards another. It converges towards the centre of our whole being, and we ourselves are this centre. Man! never forget it! All that you are, all you wish, all you might be, comes out of yourself. All must have a centre in your physical sense impression, and this again is yourself. In all it does, the Art really only adds this to the simple course of Nature.—That which Nature puts before us, scattered and over a wide area, the Art puts together in narrower bounds and brings nearer to our five senses, by associations, which facilitate the power of memory, and strengthen the susceptibility of our senses, and make it easier for them, by daily practice, to present to us the objects around us in greater numbers, for a longer time and in a more precise way.

The mechanism of Nature as a whole is great and simple. Man! imitate it. Imitate this action of great Nature, who out of the seed of the largest tree produces a scarcely perceptible shoot, then, just as imperceptibly, daily and hourly by gradual stages, unfolds first the beginnings of the stem, then the bough, then the branch, then the extreme twig on which hangs the perishable leaf.

Consider carefully this action of great Nature, how she tends and perfects every single part as it is formed, and joins on every new part to the permanent life of the old.

Consider carefully how the bright blossom is unfolded from the deeply hidden bud. Consider how the bloom of its first day's splendour is soon lost, while the fruit, at first weak but perfectly formed, adds something important every day to all that it is already. So, quietly growing for long months, it hangs on the twig that nourishes it; until, fully ripe and perfect in all its parts, it falls from the tree.

Consider how Mother Nature, with the uprising shoot, also develops the germ of the root, and buries the noblest part of the tree deep in the bosom of the earth; then how she forms the immovable stem from the very heart of the root, and the boughs from the very heart of the stem, and the branches from the very heart of the boughs. How to all, even the weakest, outermost twig she gives enough, but to none useless, disproportionate strength.

The mechanism of physical human nature is essentially subject to the same laws by which physical Nature generally unfolds her powers. According to these laws all instruction should graft the most essential parts of its subject firmly into the very being of the human mind; then join on the less essential gradually, but uninterruptedly, to the most essential, and maintain all the parts of the subject, even to the outermost, in one living proportionate whole.

SUGGESTIONS FOR FURTHER READING

Anderson, Lewis F., ed. *Pestalozzi*. New York: McGraw Hill Book Co., 1931.

Barlow, Thomas A. *Pestalozzi and American Education*. Boulder: Este Es Press, University of Colorado Libraries, 1977.

Barnard, Henry, ed. *Pestalozzi and Pestalozzianism*. New York: F. C.Brownell Publishers, 1862.

Dearborn, Ned H. *The Oswego Movement in American Education*. New York: Teachers College, Columbia University, 1925.

De Guimps, Roger. *Pestalozzi: His Aim and Work*. New York: D. Appleton and Co., 1895.

Downs, Robert B. *Johann Heinrich Pestalozzi: Father of Modern Pedagogy*. Boston: Twayne Publishers, 1975.

Gutek, Gerald L. *Joseph Neef: The Americanization of Pestalozzianism*. University: University of Alabama Press, 1978.

———. *Pestalozzi and Education*. Prospect Heights, Ill.: Waveland Press, 1999.

Heafford, Michael R. *Pestalozzi: His Thought and Relevance Today*. London: Methuen, 1967.

Jedan, Dieter. *Johann Heinrich Pestalozzi and the Pestalozzian Method of Language Teaching*. Bern: Peter Lang, 1981.

Monroe, Will S. *History of the Pestalozzian Movement in the United States.* Syracuse, N.Y.:
C. W. Bardeen Publishers, 1907.

Pestalozzi, Johann H. *The Education of Man—Aphorisms.* New York: Philosophical Library,
1951.

———. *How Gertrude Teaches Her Children.* London: Swan Sonnenschein and Co., 1907.

———. *Leonard and Gertrude.* Translated by Eva Channing. Boston: D. C. Heath and Co.,
1891.

Silber, Kate. *Pestalozzi: The Man and His Work.* London: Routledge and Kegan Paul, 1960.

Walch, Sr. Mary Romana. *Pestalozzi and the Pestalozzian Theory of Education: A Critical
Study.* Washington, D.C.: Catholic University Press, 1952.

NOTES

1. Gerald L. Gutek, *Pestalozzi and Education* (Prospect Heights, Ill.: Waveland Press,
   1999), 21–51.

2. Roger de Guimps, *Pestalozzi: His Aim and Work* (Syracuse, N.Y.: Bardeen, 1889), 6–7.

3. Johann H. Pestalozzi, "Leonard and Gertrude," in Henry Barnard, ed., *Pestalozzi and
   Pestalozzianism* (New York: F. C. Brownell Publishers, 1862).

4. Johann H. Pestalozzi, "Pestalozzi's Account of His Own Educational Experience," in H.
   Barnard, ed., *Pestalozzi and Pestalozzianism,* 674.

5. Johann H. Pestalozzi, *How Gertrude Teaches Her Children* (Syracuse, N.Y.: Bardeen
   Publishers, 1900).

6. Gerald L. Gutek, *Pestalozzi and Education* (Prospect Heights, Ill.: Waveland Press,
   1999), 101–56.

7. Ibid., 93–98.

10

THOMAS JEFFERSON: ADVOCATE OF REPUBLICAN EDUCATION

BIOGRAPHICAL SKETCH

Thomas Jefferson (1743–1826), American statesman and the third president of the United States, is significant in the history and philosophy of education for ideas on the kind of education needed to sustain republican institutions and processes. His political philosophy, his plans for creating public schools in Virginia, and his role in founding the University of Virginia were all elements in his efforts to develop education for the new American republic.

Thomas Jefferson was born on April 13, 1743, at Shadwell, Virginia, the son of Peter Jefferson (1708–1757), a plantation owner, and Jane Randolph (1720–1776), a daughter of one of Virginia's most prominent families. Thomas Jefferson began life with the economic and social advantage of being born into one of Virginia's leading families.

Peter Jefferson took a role in local politics, at various times serving as county sheriff, surveyor, and justice of the peace.[1] He also was elected to the House of Burgesses, Virginia's colonial assembly. An influence on his son, Peter Jefferson's record of public service made him a model that his son Thomas would later emulate.

When Thomas was 5, his father hired a tutor, as was the practice among wealthy southern families, who taught him reading, writing, and arithmetic. He next was enrolled in a Latin grammar school, a preparatory school, conducted by the Reverend William Douglas, an Anglican clergymen. Because the school was some distance from Shadwell, Thomas boarded at the school, where under Douglas' instruction, he studied Latin, Greek, and French.[2] Jefferson learned the classical languages and literatures needed for entry to college.

When Jefferson was 14, his father's death required him to return to his home at Shadwell. He continued his education at a school conducted by the Reverend James Maury, an Anglican minister at Fredericksburg, which was closer to Shadwell. Along with the classics, Jefferson learned religious doctrines and practices of the Church of England. Although interested in religion, Jefferson as an adult doubted that the doctrines of Christianity were divinely inspired. Under Maury's guidance, Jefferson read the books on English literature and history found in his teacher's large library.[3]

Jefferson, in 1760 at age 17, began his studies at the College of William and Mary in the Virginia capital of Williamsburg, where the colonial governor, the General Court, and the House of Burgesses were located. At this time, William and Mary, the South's leading college, enrolled 100 students in its three branches—the grammar, the Indian, and the philosophy schools. The faculty was small, consisting of seven professors, six of whom were Anglican ministers. The seventh professor, Dr. William Small, a mathematician and natural scientist, was Jefferson's adviser.[4]

Jefferson was enrolled in the philosophy school, where he studied mathematics, physics, metaphysics, logic, ethics, rhetoric, and literature.[5] Completing his studies, Jefferson, who decided to become a lawyer, read law with George Wythe, an influential attorney and a member of the House of Burgesses. Jefferson's study with Wythe gave him access to his mentor's experience, library, and wide circle of influential Virginians. Jefferson studied with Wythe for 5 years, and in 1767, he was admitted to the practice of law.

At age 21, Jefferson inherited his father's land, owning 5,000 acres in Ablemarle and adjacent counties. He, like other plantation owners, used enslaved Africans as the plantation's workforce. Jefferson's record on the issue of slavery was ambiguous and tortured. While he disliked slavery as harmful to both blacks and whites, Jefferson, as a political leader, made few efforts to abolish it.[6]

Jefferson, a person of many interests, was fascinated by architecture. He designed and supervised the building of Monticello, his mountain-top mansion retreat. Throughout his life, he continually redesigned and added to Monticello. Interested in horticulture, he created landscape gardens to grace his country estate.

On January 1, 1772, Jefferson married Martha Wayles Skelton (1748–1782), a young widow, who, like Jefferson, was from a socially prominent Virginia family. Jefferson and his wife were the parents of six children. He was devoted to his wife. She died after 10 years of marriage in 1782. Jefferson, experiencing a deep depression, grieved for many months over his loss.

Jefferson was influenced by the eighteenth-century Enlightenment, which was a trans-Atlantic intellectual movement. An intellectual who had many interests—law, politics, religion, architecture, natural science, agriculture, and archaeology—Jefferson read widely. He devoted time and money to creating a large library.[7] His emerging political philosophy was shaped by his reading of John Locke, Anthony Elly, Adam Ferguson, and Charles Montesquieu.

Jefferson's election to the House of Burgesses launched his political career in 1769 during the protests against the taxes imposed by the Townshend Acts. As the American colonists moved closer to rebellion against Great Britain, Jefferson was immersed in the revolutionary cause. In 1773, he was a member of the Committee of Correspondence appointed to plan the colonists' strategy against British domination. In 1775, actual fighting began between British troops and colonial rebels in the Massachusetts towns of Lexington and Concord. As one of Virginia's representatives to the Continental Congress in Philadelphia, Jefferson served on the committee to draft a statement declaring America's independence.[8] As the Declaration's principal author, Jefferson wrote a stirring statement of rights and grievances that was based on John Locke's right of an oppressed people to revolution. Asserting that the colonists' natural rights of "life, liberty, and pursuit of happiness" had been violated by an unjust king, he proclaimed their right to revolt. Affirming that governments derive their "just powers from the consent of the governed," he called on the people to institute a new government.[9]

In October 1776, Jefferson was back in Virginia, serving in the state's General Assembly. An advocate of separation of church and state, he was strongly opposed to state-supported and established churches, such as the Church of England, in his state of Virginia. He introduced a "Bill for Establishing Religious Freedom" in the Virginia Assembly in 1779. Although his first effort did not succeed, a law guaranteeing religious freedom was passed in 1786.

In 1779, Jefferson introduced his bill "for the more general diffusion of knowledge" to create a state school system. Though the bill did not pass, it was significant for charting the future course of education in the United States, especially its affirmation that the state should be responsible for establishing and maintaining public schools.

From 1779 to 1781, Jefferson, serving as Virginia's wartime governor, was pressing the effort against the British. His next national position was as ambassador to France, where he worked to win French recognition and support for the United States. For 5 years the struggle went on between Great Britain and her former colonies. On October 19, 1781, the British General Cornwallis' surrender at Yorktown ended hostilities and the United States was free.

In 1780, Jefferson wrote *Notes on the State of Virginia,* a manuscript that originated as answers to inquiries made by Francois Marbois, the secretary of the French minister, about the state's geography, climate, population, economy, and plants and animals.[10] Jefferson's manuscript is among the most significant scientific and political books on the United States published in the nineteenth century. In particular, Jefferson challenged the theory of the French naturalist Buffon, who claimed that North American people, plants, and animals were steadily degenerating.[11] Jefferson's *Notes* included comments on his educational views and the condition of Virginia's schools and colleges. It gave an early suggestion of his belief on educating an "aristocracy of virtue and talent" that was not based on class.[12] He also expressed his fears that slavery would have deleterious consequences for Virginia. Jefferson's scientific contributions were recognized by the American Philosophical Society, which elected him its president in 1797.

As the United States entered the nineteenth century as a new and independent nation, the early American political party system took shape. Proponents of a strong national government, with limited state power, organized the Federalist party, which included such men as Alexander Hamilton and John Adams. Jefferson, who believed that the federal government should have limited powers, organized the Democratic-Republicans in opposition.

From 1801 to 1809, Jefferson was President of the United States. His administration successfully negotiated the Louisiana Purchase from France for $15 million in 1803. The addition of this vast territory more than doubled the size of the United States and carried the nation's boundaries far across the Mississippi River. In 1804, Jefferson commissioned the transcontinental explorations of Meriwether Lewis and William Clark, which took the two explorers from St. Louis, Missouri, to the Pacific Coast. The exploration was designed to assess the economic potential of and provide scientific information about the new territory.[13]

Leaving the White House in 1809, Jefferson retired to Monticello to pursue his many avocations. Jefferson had once attempted but failed to bring about a reorganization of the College of William and Mary in 1779. After leaving the presidency, Jefferson directed his energy and influence into creating a new state university, the University of Virginia. He wanted to create a modern institution that was open to change, innovative, secular, and scientific. The university Jefferson envisioned was to be state-established and publicly supported and controlled.

In 1818, Jefferson's plan for the University of Virginia moved forward when Governor James P. Preston appointed a commission to recommend the location of the institution. On August 1, 1818, at Rockfish Gap in the Blue Ridge Mountains, the commission, after electing Jefferson its chairman, voted to locate the new university at Charlottesville. The Rockfish Gap Report embodied Jefferson's plan. Even before the Virginia legislature authorized a state university, Jefferson was planning the facilities of an "academical village" of attractive classrooms, libraries, and residences for professors and students in the ancient Greek classical architectural style. The report contained his specifications on curriculum and appointment of faculty.[14] By 1819, construction of the buildings was under way, and Jefferson had been elected the first rector of the University of Virginia. Professors were appointed for natural history or science, mathematics, ancient languages, modern languages, anatomy and medicine, natural philosophy, and moral philosophy. As rector, Jefferson prepared the bylaws that would govern the university, the requirements for examinations and degrees, and even the schedule of classes.[15] On March 7, 1825, the first class of 30 students entered the University of Virginia. Jefferson, dedicating the university to the pursuit of truth, stated the institution would encourage the "illimitable freedom of the human mind. For here we are not afraid to follow truth wherever it may lead, nor to tolerate any error so long as reason is left free to combat it."[16]

Jefferson died on July 4, 1826, 50 years after the proclamation of the Declaration of Independence.

OVERVIEW OF IDEAS ON EDUCATION

Jefferson's quest for knowledge led him to many areas of scholarship—political theory, philosophy, anthropology, history, literature, horticulture, geography, religion, and architecture. He was a generalist with a comprehensive general education, the breadth of which enabled him to have a large vision of what the new nation could be.

Jefferson understood that Americans needed to develop their cultural as well as political identity as an independent people. Although appreciating and enjoying the intellectual, scientific, and cultural achievements of other nations, he believed that the American experience in the New World environment was creating a new people with their own culture. In creating this new cultural identity, education had a key role.

Jefferson's conception of a republican civic education incorporated many ideas from the English philosopher John Locke, especially from his *Second Treatise on Government*.[17] Among the principles that Jefferson accepted from Locke and accommodated to the American experience were:

1. Government arises from the consent of the governed, who—to protect their natural rights of life, liberty, and property—join in a mutual association.
2. Government is representative and is divided into a system of checks and balances between the legislative, judicial, and executive branches.
3. In a republic, officials, elected for a limited term, returned to the people from which they came.
4. Taxes were to be levied only with the consent of the governed.

Jefferson's rendition of Lockean principles had a highly significant meaning for America's republican government and for civic education. Citizens were to be educated to cast their votes intelligently. A workable republic required citizens to have knowledge of its institutions and a commitment to use democratic processes.

Jefferson believed that education, free from arbitrary restraints of church and state, was a necessary prerequisite for a free people who would govern themselves through representative institutions. Jefferson believed that state-supported schools were needed to provide the people with a general education and identify and prepare the most talented persons for leadership roles by providing access to higher education.

In 1779, Jefferson introduced a bill in the Virginia General Assembly concerning "the more general diffusion of knowledge." The bill's intent was the establishment of a state system of elementary and secondary schools.[18] (The bill's provisions are found in the Primary Source section of the chapter.) Although the bill failed to pass, it demonstrates Jefferson's early commitment to public schooling as a component of republican citizenship and as a state responsibility. In the bill, Jefferson grappled with the paradox over equity and excellence, two issues long present in American education. Excellence relates to the goal that schools should identify and cultivate intellectually gifted students. Equity relates to the goal that all children should have the same equal opportunities for education. Although Jefferson's plan would make elementary education available to all free children, secondary schools were highly selective despite some aid for economically disadvantaged students. However, the principle of selectivity did not rest on being a member of a socially or economically advantaged class.

Jefferson's philosophy of civic education was based on the assumption that all citizens needed a general education to provide the skills to participate as citizens of a nation with representative institutions. Although his philosophy had the egalitarian component of providing popular enlightenment, Jefferson also saw it as exercising a highly selective role in identifying and educating those who were to be the nation's leaders.

Foremost, Jefferson, a representative of the Enlightenment in North America, sought to remove the barriers that interfered with freedom of inquiry. He opposed arbitrary government and state-supported churches as institutions that often curtailed freedom of teaching and learning.

THE PRIMARY SOURCE

The selections from *The Papers of Thomas Jefferson* deal with his "Bill for the More General Diffusion of Knowledge" and his "Bill for Establishing Religious Freedom in Virginia." According to Jefferson's plan for the "More General Diffusion of

Knowledge," each of Virginia's counties was to be subdivided into "hundreds," or local districts. In each hundred, an elementary school would be built and maintained at a convenient location at public expense. All free boys and girls would attend these schools at public expense for 3 years. Their curriculum included reading, writing, arithmetic, and the histories of Greece, Rome, Great Britain, and North America. After the first 3 years of elementary schooling, pupils could continue at their parents' expense.

Jefferson's proposal provided that 20 grammar, or secondary, schools be established. The grammar school curriculum was to consist of Latin, Greek, English, geography, and advanced mathematics. From clusters of 10 elementary schools, the most intellectually promising students, whose parents could not afford to pay tuition, would receive a merit scholarship to attend a grammar school. Students whose parents could afford to pay tuition would constitute the majority of the secondary school classes. After 1 year, one-third of the least promising of the state-supported merit students would be dropped. At the completion of the second year, another selection was made with only the most promising merit scholars remaining. In each grammar school for each class, the most intellectually able students would continue to study for an additional 4 years, thus completing the 6 years of grammar school. In any given year, 20 state-supported merit scholars would complete grammar school. Of these 20, the top 10 would continue their education at the College of William and Mary. The lower 10 would become grammar school teachers or enter public service.

Jefferson, an advocate of separation of church and state, was strongly opposed to state-supported and established churches, such as the Church of England, in the state of Virginia. He introduced a "Bill for Establishing Religious Freedom" in the Virginia Assembly in 1779. Although his first effort did not succeed, a law guaranteeing religious freedom was passed in 1786.

FOCUSING QUESTIONS

As you read these selections, you might wish to consider the following questions:

1. How did Jefferson's "Bill for the More General Diffusion of Knowledge" include strategies for achieving both equity and excellence? Do you believe the issue over equity and excellence is still found in contemporary American education?
2. Why was Jefferson concerned with civic education? Do you think his "Bill for the More General Diffusion of Knowledge" satisfactorily addressed the issue of civic education? Explain your answer.
3. From your reading of the selections, identify and analyze Jefferson's major political and educational principles. Are these principles still relevant to contemporary American society?
4. Consider Jefferson's arguments for separation of church and state in the context of contemporary issues such as prayer in public schools, vouchers to attend private schools, and the debate of creationism versus evolution.

A BILL FOR THE MORE GENERAL DIFFUSION OF KNOWLEDGE

Whereas it appeareth that however certain forms of government are better calculated than others to protect individuals in the free exercise of their natural rights, and are at the same time themselves better guarded against degeneracy, yet experience hath shewn, that even under the best forms, those entrusted with power have, in time, and by slow operations, perverted it into tyranny; and it is believed that the most effectual means of preventing this would be, to illuminate, as far as practicable, the minds of the people at large, and more especially to give them knowledge of those facts, which history exhibiteth, that, possessed thereby of the experience of other ages and countries, they may be enabled to know ambition under all its shapes, and prompt to exert their natural powers to defeat its purposes; And whereas it is generally true that that people will be happiest whose laws are best, and are best administered, and that laws will be wisely formed, and honestly administered, in proportion as those who form and administer them are wise and honest; whence it becomes expedient for promoting the public happiness that those persons, whom nature hath endowed with genius and virtue, should be rendered by liberal education worthy to receive, and able to guard the sacred deposit of the rights and liberties of their fellow citizens, and that they should be called to that charge without regard to wealth, birth or other accidental condition or circumstance; but the indigence of the greater number disabling them from so educating, at their own expence, those of their children whom nature hath fitly formed and disposed to become useful instruments for the public, it is better that such should be sought for and educated at the common expence of all, than that the happiness of all should be confided to the weak or wicked: . . .

At every of these schools shall be taught reading, writing, and common arithmetick, and the books which shall be used therein for instructing the children to read shall be such as will at the same time

From *The Papers of Thomas Jefferson*, II (1777–to June 1779), edited by Julius P. Boyd. Princeton, N.J.: Princeton University Press, 1950, 526–529, 531–533, 545–547. Copyright, 1950, by Princeton University Press.

make them acquainted with Graecian, Roman, English, and American history. At these schools all the free children, male and female, resident within the respective hundred, shall be intitled to receive tuition gratis, for the term of three years, and as much longer, at their private expence , as their parents, guardians or friends, shall think proper.

Over every ten of these schools (or such other number nearest thereto, as the number of hundreds in the county will admit, without fractional divisions) an overseer shall be appointed annually by the Aldermen at their first meeting, eminent for his learning, integrity, and fidelity to the commonwealth, whose business and duty it shall be, from time to time, to appoint a teacher to each school, who shall give assurance of fidelity to the commonwealth, and to remove him as he shall see cause; to visit every school once in every half year at the least; to examine the schollars; see that any general plan of reading and instruction recommended by the visiters of William and Mary College shall be observed; and to superintend the conduct of the teacher in every thing relative to his school.

Every teacher shall receive a salary of by the year, which, with the expences of building and repairing the schoolhouses, shall be provided in such manner as other county expences are by law directed to be provided and shall also have his diet, lodging, and washing found him, to be levied in like manner, save only that such levy shall be on the inhabitants of each hundred for the board of their own teacher only. . . .

The said overseers shall forthwith proceed to have a house of brick or stone, for the said grammar school, with necessary offices, built on the said lands, which grammar school-house shall contain a room for the school, a hall to dine in, four rooms for a master and usher, and ten or twelve lodging rooms for the scholars. . . .

In these grammar schools shall be taught the Latin and Greek languages, English grammar, geography, and the higher part of numerical arithmetick, to wit, vulgar and decimal fractions, and the extraction of the square and cube roots. . . .

Every overseer of the hundred schools shall, in the month of September annually, after the most diligent and impartial examination and enquiry, appoint from among the boys who shall have been two years at the least at some one of the schools under his superintendance, and whose parents are too poor to give them farther education, some one of the best and most promising genius and disposition, to proceed to the grammar school of his district; which appointment shall be made in the court-house of the county, on the court day for that month if fair, and if not, then on the next fair day, excluding Sunday, in the presence of the Aldermen, or two of them at the least, assembled on the bench for that purpose, the said overseer being previously sworn by them to make such appointment, without favor or affection, according to the best of his skill and judgment, and being interrogated by the said Aldermen, either on their own motion, or on suggestions from the parents, guardians, friends, or teachers of the children, competitors for such appointment; which teachers shall attend for the information of the Aldermen. On which interregatories the said Aldermen, if they be not satisfied with the appointment proposed, shall have right to negative it; whereupon the said visiter may proceed to make a new appointment, and the said Aldermen again to interrogate and negative, and so toties quoties until an appointment be approved.

Every boy so appointed shall be authorised to proceed to the grammar school of his district, there to be educated and boarded during such time as is hereafter limited; and his quota of the expences of the house together with a compensation to the master or usher for his tuition, at the rate of twenty dollars by the year, shall be paid by the Treasurer quarterly on warrant from the Auditors.

A visitation shall be held, for the purpose of probation, annually at the said grammar school on the last Monday in September, if fair, and if not, then on the next fair day, excluding Sunday, at which one third of the boys sent thither by appointment of the said overseers, and who shall have been there one year only, shall be discontinued as public foundationers, being those who, on the most diligent examination and enquiry, shall be thought to be of the least promising genius and disposition; and of those who shall have been there two years, all shall be discontinued, save one only the best in genius and disposition, who shall be at liberty to continue there four years longer on the public foundation, and shall thence forward be deemed a senior.

The visiters for the districts which, or any part of which, be southward and westward of James river, as known by that name, or by the names of Fluvanna and Jackson's river, in every other year, to wit, at the probation meetings held in the years, distinguished in the Christian computation by odd numbers, and the visiters for all the other districts at their said meetings to be held in those years, distinguished by even numbers, after diligent examination and enquiry as before directed, shall chuse one among the said seniors, of the best learning and most hopeful genius and disposition, who shall be authorised by them to proceed to William and Mary College, there to be educated, boarded, and clothed, three years; the expence of which annually shall be paid by the Treasurer on warrant from the Auditors.

A BILL FOR ESTABLISHING RELIGIOUS FREEDOM

Well aware that the opinions and belief of men depend not on their own will, but follow involuntarily the evidence proposed to their minds; that Almighty God hath created the mind free, *and manifested his supreme will that free it shall remain by making it altogether insusceptible of restraint;* that all attempts to influence it by temporal punishments, or burthens, or by civil incapacitations, tend only to beget habits of hypocrisy and meanness, and are a departure from the plan of the holy author of our religion, who being lord both of body and mind, yet chose not to propagate it by coercions on either, as was in his Almighty power to do, *but to extend it by its influence on reason alone;* that the impious presumption of legislators and rulers, civil as well as ecclesiastical, who, being themselves but fallible and uninspired men, have assumed dominion over the faith of others, setting up their own opinions and modes of thinking as the only true and infallible, and as such endeavoring to impose them on others, hath established and maintained false religions over the greatest part of the world and through all time: That to compel a man to furnish contributions of money for the propagation of opinions which he disbelieves *and abhors,* is sinful and tyrannical; that even the forcing him to support this or that teacher of his own religious persuasion, is depriving him of the comfortable liberty of giving his contributions to the particular pastor whose morals he would make his pattern, and whose powers he feels most persuasive to righteousness; and is withdrawing from the ministry those temporary rewards, which proceeding from an approbation of their personal conduct, are an additional incitement to earnest and unremitting labours for the instruction of mankind; that our civil rights have no dependance on our religious opinions, any more than our opinions in physics or geometry; that therefore the proscribing any citizen as unworthy the public confidence by laying upon him an incapacity of being called to offices of trust and emolument, unless he profess or renounce this or that religious opinion, is depriving him injuriously of those privileges and advantages to which, in common with his fellow citizens, he has a natural right; that it tends also to corrupt the principles of that *very* religion it is meant to encourage, by bribing, with a monopoly of worldly honours and emoluments, those who will externally profess and conform to it; that though indeed these are criminal who do not withstand such temptation, yet neither are those innocent who lay the bait in their way; *that the opinions of men are not the object of civil government, nor under its jurisdiction;* that to suffer the civil magistrate to intrude his powers into the field of opinion and to restrain the profession or propagation of principles on supposition of their ill tendency is a dangerous falacy, which at once destroys all religious liberty, because he being of course judge of that tendency will make his opinions the rule of judgment, and approve or condemn the sentiments of others only as they shall square with or differ from his own; that it is time enough for the rightful purposes of civil government for its officers to interfere when principles break out into overt acts against peace and good order; and finally, that truth is great and will prevail if left to herself; that she is the proper and sufficient antagonist to error, and has nothing to fear from the conflict unless by human interposition disarmed of her natural weapons, free argument and debate; errors ceasing to be dangerous when it is permitted freely to contradict them.

We the General Assembly of Virginia do enact that no man shall be compelled to frequent or support any religious worship, place, or ministry whatsoever, nor shall be enforced, restrained, molested, or burthened in his body or goods, nor shall otherwise suffer, on account of his religious opinions or belief; but that all men shall be free to profess, and by argument to maintain, their opinions in matters of religion, and that the same shall in no wise diminish, enlarge, or affect their civil capacities.

And though we well know that this Assembly, elected by the people for the ordinary purposes of legislation only, have no power to restrain the acts of succeeding Assemblies, constituted with powers equal to our own, and that therefore to declare this act irrevocable would be of no effect in law; yet we are free to declare, and do declare, that the rights hereby asserted are of the natural rights of mankind, and that if any act shall be hereafter passed to repeal the present or to narrow its operation, such act will be an infringement of natural right.

SUGGESTIONS FOR FURTHER READING

Ambrose, Stephen E. *Meriwether Lewis, Thomas Jefferson, and the Opening of the American West.* New York: Simon and Schuster, 1996.

Bestor, Arthur E., Jr., David C. Mearns, and Jonathan Daniels. *Three Presidents and Their Books.* Urbana: University of Illinois Press, 1955.

Boorstin, Daniel J. *The Lost World of Thomas Jefferson.* Boston: Beacon Press, 1960.

Burstein, Meyer L. *Understanding Thomas Jefferson: Studies in Economics, Law and Philosophy.* New York: St. Martin's Press, 1993.

Cunningham, Noble F., Jr. *In Pursuit of Reason: The Life of Thomas Jefferson.* New York: Ballantine Books, 1987.

Fliegelman, Jay. *Declaring Independence: Jefferson, Natural Language & the Culture of Performance.* Stanford, Calif.: Stanford University Press, 1993.

Hellenbrand, Harold. *The Unfinished Revolution: Education and Politics in the Thought of Thomas Jefferson.* Newark: University of Delaware Press, 1990.

Heslep, Robert D. *Thomas Jefferson and Education.* New York: Random House, 1969.

Honeywell, Roy J. *The Educational Work of Thomas Jefferson.* Cambridge, Mass.: Harvard University Press, 1931.

Jefferson, Thomas. *Notes on the State of Virginia.* Edited by William Peden. Chapel Hill, N.C.: University of North Carolina Press, 1954.

Lee, Gordon C. *Crusade Against Ignorance: Thomas Jefferson on Education.* New York: Bureau of Publications, Teachers College, Columbia University, 1961.

Mapp, Alf J., Jr. *Thomas Jefferson: A Strange Case of Mistaken Identity.* Lanham, Md.: Rowman & Little Publishers, 1987.

————.*Thomas Jefferson: Passionate Pilgrim—the Presidency, the Founding of the University, and the Private Battle.* Lanham, Md.: Rowman & Little Publishers, 1991.

Mayer, David N. *The Constitutional Thought of Thomas Jefferson.* Charlottesville, Va.: University Press of Virginia, 1994.

Meltzer, Milton. *Thomas Jefferson, the Revolutionary Aristocrat.* New York: F. Watts, 1991.

Randall, William S. *Thomas Jefferson: A Life.* New York: H. Holt, 1993.

Sheldon, Garrett W. *The Political Philosophy of Thomas Jefferson.* Baltimore: Johns Hopkins University Press, 1991.

Tucker, Robert W. *Empire of Liberty: The Statecraft of Thomas Jefferson.* New York: Oxford University Press, 1990.

NOTES

1. Robert D. Heslep, *Thomas Jefferson and Education* (New York: Random House, 1969), 31–32.
2. Noble E. Cunningham, Jr., *In Pursuit of Reason: The Life of Thomas Jefferson* (New York: Ballantine Books, 1987), 4.
3. Harold Hellenbrand, *The Unfinished Revolution: Education and Politics in the Thought of Thomas Jefferson* (Newark: University of Delaware Press, 1990), 120.
4. Ludwell H. Johnson III, "Sharper Than a Serpent's Tooth: Thomas Jefferson and His Alma Mater," *The Virginia Magazine of History and Biography,* 99, No. 2 (April 1991), 145.
5. Noble E. Cunningham, Jr., *In Pursuit of Reason: The Life of Thomas Jefferson* (New York: Ballantine Books, 1987), 4.
6. Peter S. Onuf, "The Scholar's Jefferson," *The William and Mary Quarterly,* 50 (October 1993), 675.
7. Arthur E. Bestor, Jr., David C. Mearns, and Jonathan Daniels, *Three Presidents and Their Books* (Urbana: University of Illinois Press, 1955).
8. Onuf, 681.
9. "Jefferson's Original Rough Draught of the Declaration of Independence," in Julian P. Boyd et al., eds. *The Papers of Thomas Jefferson,* I (Princeton, N.J.: Princeton University Press, 1950), as quoted in Heslep, *Thomas Jefferson and Education* (New York: Random House), 46.
10. Cunningham, *In Pursuit of Reason,* 76. Also, see Thomas Jefferson, *Notes on the State of Virginia,* William Peden, ed. (Chapel Hill, N.C.: University of North Carolina Press, 1954).
11. Gisela Tauber, "*Notes on the State of Virginia:* Thomas Jefferson's Unintentional Self-Portrait," *Eighteenth Century Studies* 26 (Summer 1993), 637.
12. Ibid., 645.
13. Kathleen Tobin-Schlesinger, "Jefferson to Lewis: The Study of Nature in the West," *Journal of the West,* 29 (January 1990), 54–61.
14. "Report of the Commissioners appointed to Fix the Site of the University of Virginia," in Lee, *Crusade Against Ignorance: Thomas Jefferson on Education* (New York: Bureau of Publications, Teachers College Press, Columbia University, 1961), 114–133.
15. Cunningham, 337–345.
16. Ibid., 344.
17. Garrett W. Sheldon, *The Political Philosophy of Thomas Jefferson* (Baltimore, Md.: Johns Hopkins Press, 1991), 2–3, 45.
18. Thomas Jefferson, "A Bill for the More General Diffusion of Knowledge," in Boyd et al., eds. *The Papers of Thomas Jefferson* II (Princeton, N.J.: Princeton University Press, 1950), 526–533.

11

MARY WOLLSTONECRAFT: PROPONENT OF WOMEN'S RIGHTS AND EDUCATION

Mary Wollstonecraft (1759–1797) is significant as an early proponent of women's rights and education. In the eighteenth century, she challenged existing conventions about women's status and education in European society. Today, she has been rediscovered and enjoys a prominent position in the literature on women's education and education in general.

Mary Wollstonecraft was born on April 27, 1759, in London, the second of seven children of Edward and Elizabeth Dickson Wollstonecraft. Money from her grandfather, a successful weaver, enabled his son, Edward, Mary's father, to buy a country estate in what turned out to be a failed attempt to enter the gentry as a gentleman farmer. The rest of Mary's childhood was the story of growing up in a dysfunctional family, tyrannized by an alcoholic and abusive father. The Wollstonecrafts moved frequently across England and Wales, as Edward tried various schemes at improving his fortune. As a child and adolescent, Mary was often in the middle of family arguments, trying to defend her passive mother from her raging father.[1] As is true of growing up in dysfunctional early childhood situations, Mary's early life shaped her later behavior and insights.

Mary came to resent the subordination of women to men when the Wollstonecraft inheritance, though limited, came to Edward, her eldest brother. She was growing increasingly conscious of the gender discrimination legalized in the law of primogeniture, which gave a family's inheritance to its male heir.

When Mary was 16 in 1774, the Wollstonecrafts were living at Hoxton, near London, where Mary made a close and lasting friendship with Fanny Blood. Fanny would become the model of an idealized heroine in her later writing.

When she was 19, Mary took a job as a companion to a wealthy widow living in Bath. Employment as a governess or companion was one of the few positions open to young middle-class women, like Mary. Uncomfortable in situations of subordination that gave others control over her, Mary was uneasy and anxious.

In 1781, she returned to her family to care for her terminally ill mother. Her situation as a caregiver generated mixed emotions—being a dutiful daughter but also caring for a mother whom she resented for neglecting her. Her mother's death was

91

followed by still another family crisis that involved her younger sister, Eliza, who had recently given birth and was suffering from what was most likely postpartum depression. Mary, seemingly prone to impulsivity, which she called her "incendiary" behavior, decided that she would rescue her sister from the unhappy situation by helping her flee from both her husband, whom Eliza disliked, and the child. The two sisters secretly left and decided they would make their own way, a very rare act for late eighteenth-century women.

To earn their income, Mary, aided by her sisters Eliza and Everina and her friend Fanny Blood, conducted a school, from 1784 to 1786, at Newington Green, near London. Mary's stay in Newington Green was marked by significant intellectual growth. She was a member of a circle of liberal thinkers who were associated with Dr. Richard Price, a social reformer. Gaining a larger perspective on life, Mary began to make connections between her own ideas and feelings on the subjugation of women and the broader issues of social and political freedom.[2] During this time, Fanny Blood, Mary's closest friend, who had married, was living in Portugal, hoping the warmer climate would improve her health. Unfortunately, Fanny's consumption reoccurred and she died in 1785, with Mary at her side.

Forced to close the school, Wollstonecraft turned to writing to earn money and to express her ideas. Her *Thoughts on the Education of Daughters,* in 1787, though providing glimpses into a surfacing feminism, still accepted being a wife and mother as a woman's primary roles.

Wollstonecraft, who needed an income, took a position as governess to the three eldest daughters of Lord and Lady Kingsborough in Ireland. She resented her job, which again placed her in a subordinate position to wealthy employers. In particular, she disliked Lady Kingsborough's idle, aristocratic lifestyle, which to her was unintellectual and trivial. As she would do throughout her life, Wollstonecraft expressed her feelings by writing a novel, *Mary, A Fiction,* an idealized autobiographical version of her childhood and youth. By 1787, she left the Kingsborough household, determined to earn her living as an author.[3]

Wollstonecraft moved to London in 1787 and became assistant editor of the *Analytical Review,* a journal published by Joseph Johnson, who serving as her literary adviser, introduced her to London's most liberal intellectual circles. Wollstonecraft's *Original Stories from Real Life; with Conversations, Calculated to Regulate the Affections, and Form the Mind to Truth and Goodness,* a didactic work designed for the moral education of young women, appeared in 1788. In the book, Mary, drawing on her experience as a governess, examines the relationships between governesses and their charges.

From 1789 to 1790, Wollstonecraft was caught up in the events surrounding the French Revolution. Confirming her beliefs in liberty and equality, she supported the early stages of the Revolution, when moderates such as Lafayette and Condorcet were directing the course of events. Her good friend, Dr. Richard Price, who had acclaimed the revolution in France, had been challenged by the conservative philosopher Edmund Burke, the author of *Reflections on the Revolution in France.*[4] Burke attacked the revolutionaries for destroying the institutions and traditions that provided cultural security. Responding to Burke, Wollstonecraft's *Vindication of the Rights of Men* expressed her long-seething attitudes against the power of rank, aristocracy, privilege, and wealth in limiting human freedom.[5] Burke's condemnation of the French Revolution and his arguments for preservation of the class-based status quo were anathema to Wollstonecraft. She believed that women's rights and equality were part of a movement of general revolutionary change that would liberate human beings from the tyranny of the past. She would reiterate this theme in her most important book, *A Vindication of the Rights of Women*, in 1792.

In December 1792, Wollstonecraft journeyed to France for a firsthand view of the Revolution. At that time, the French political situation was becoming increasingly violent as the Jacobins gained power. Political prisoners had been massacred and the French King, Louis XVI, convicted of treason, had been sentenced to death. Distressed by the rising tide of violent occurrences, Wollstonecraft had doubts about reason's power to direct human history. Regaining her optimism, she expressed her belief in humanity's inevitable progress in *An Historical and Moral View of the Origin and Progress of the French Revolution*.

While in France, Wollstonecraft met and fell passionately in love with Gilbert Imlay, an American financier. An affair followed and Mary became pregnant. In May 1794, her daughter, Fanny Imlay, was born, and in 1795, she returned to England, where the unfaithful Imlay was residing. After Mary failed in a suicide attempt, Imlay, hoping to divert her attentions, sent her, as his business agent, on a trip to the Scandinavian countries. Taking Fanny and a nursemaid with her, Wollstonecraft journeyed through Sweden, Norway, and Denmark.[6] On the basis of her experiences, she wrote *Letters Written During a Short Residence in Sweden, Norway, and Denmark*, published in 1796. When she returned to England in 1795, Wollstonecraft found out that Imlay again had been unfaithful to her. She was rescued from drowning by a passersby when she, in a second suicide attempt, had plunged into the Thames. It was not until the spring of 1797 that she overcame her obsessive love and parted from Imlay.[7]

At an earlier time, Wollstonecraft had met William Godwin, a liberal intellectual leader and author of *Political Justice*. Godwin and Mary became close friends and then fell in love. He wrote of their relationship that "no two persons ever found in each other's society, a satisfaction more pure and refined."[8] When Mary found herself pregnant, she and Godwin were privately married.

Wollstonecraft continued to work on her novel *Maria, or The Wrongs of Women*, a realistic portrayal of the submission of women in a male-dominated society. This semiautobiographical work was a fictional recasting of her own dysfunctional family depicting an abusive tyrannical father, a submissive mother, and four siblings.[9] Further, the heroine, Maria, is the victim of an unfaithful lover.

On August 30, 1797, Mary Wollstonecraft gave birth to a daughter, Mary. The delivery had complications, which led to an infection that claimed her life. She died on September 10, 1797.

Godwin edited and published Wollstonecraft's *Posthumous Works* in 1798 and wrote *Memoirs of the Author of a Vindication of the Rights of Woman*, which expressed his affection and esteem for his wife. Mary Wollstonecraft's literary legacy was carried on by her daughter, Mary Wollstonecraft Shelly, a prolific author in her own right, whose most famous work, *Frankenstein*, was published in 1818.

CHAPTER 11

OVERVIEW OF IDEAS ON EDUCATION

Mary Wollstonecraft's writing asks the persistent question, How can persons, both women and men, create a personal state of being and a society based on love, respect for nature, and education rather than one of power, control, and domination? An early feminist, she wanted to gain and protect women's rights in a society that was male-dominated.

Wollstonecraft's *Thoughts on the Education of Daughters,* her earliest book, dealt with women's upbringing and education. She advised her readers that a woman's education begins with a situation and events over which she has no control—her parents' marriage and family life. Knowing from her own experience the deleterious consequences that unhappy marriages and dysfunctional families have on a child's development, she warns against the lifelong emotional injury this does to children.

Again reflecting on her own unhappy childhood and feelings of rejection by her mother, Wollstonecraft called attention to the crucial importance of early childhood experiences in forming a daughter's character. She wants mothers and daughters to enjoy a close, loving relationship during infancy and early childhood that will create the emotional and intellectual predispositions for later development and life.

Turning to a woman's intellectual education, Wollstonecraft asserted that all persons, both female and male, are born with an innate longing for truth and the potentiality to reason. The rational power can be either stimulated and exercised or dulled and atrophied. Advocating learning based on interaction with the environment, she asserted that an education based on sensory experience can stimulate love of nature, the forming of ideas, and critical thinking.[10]

Contrary to the eighteenth-century traditional way of rearing children, Wollstonecraft advised parents and other adults to include children in their conversations, inviting them to talk about their ideas and feelings. When children ask questions, adults should take their queries seriously and answer them reasonably.

A reader and a writer herself, Wollstonecraft recommended that children, both boys and girls, be encouraged to read. She argued that a "relish for reading, or any of the fine arts, should be cultivated very early in life."[11] However, she did not approve of the so-called women's literature of the period, novels that gave a trivialized and highly romantic and sentimental portrayal of love and marriage.

Wollstonecraft, who waged a lifelong struggle against submitting to the will of others, wanted young women to fulfill their own expectations, rather than those of other people. She resisted and encouraged other women to resist the demands of conventional eighteenth-century society that required young women to be what others—fathers and then husbands—wanted them to be.

Perhaps reflecting her own feelings, in her comments on love and marriage she said that persons "of sense and reflection" are often subject to "violent and constant passions" that may attract them to relationships that their reason would reject. Passion, without mutual respect, she warns, will be temporary or base. However, love of a worthy person, rationally considered, will be the best guide to a woman's own intellectual and moral happiness.[12] Advising against early marriages, Wollstonecraft stated that education and experience are good guides for deferred but happy marriages.

Convinced that knowledge was power, Wollstonecraft concluded that conventional parenting and schooling had not provided women with the education that would develop their intellectual potentiality. Indeed, conventional education had dulled their intellects by deliberately miseducating them. It indoctrinated young women to accept stereotypes that the "ideal" woman was a childlike creature who sought to amuse and please others rather than realize her own potentialities as an intelligent and independent person. A conventional upper- and middle-class young woman's education was often devoted to nonintellectual pursuits such as needlework; reading novels, romances, and poetry; and music—which amused rather than instructed and exercised her reason.

Wollstonecraft did not deny that women, if they so chose, were to be wives and mothers, but she adamantly rejected the conventional wisdom that denied them other alternatives. She argued that women should pursue the whole of knowledge and that a wide range of occupations and professions should be open to them.

Wollstonecraft was a person of wide interests that included government and politics as well as education. She believed that women's issues were embedded in the general social, political, and economic context and that improvement of women's situations required general reform. She made a strong argument for coeducational schooling and insisted that young women should have the same educational opportunities as men.

THE PRIMARY SOURCES

The first selections are from Mary Wollstonecraft's *Thoughts on the Education of Daughters,* her earliest publication. She had just finished duties as a governess when she wrote the book. In it she advises parents on the moral education of daughters and warns against too early marriages.

The second selection from Mary Wollstonecraft's *Original Stories* consists of didactic morality tales. The book, in the genre of eighteenth-century educational "rescue" literature, is intended to provide guidance in rescuing or freeing a person from moral weakness. The principal character is a governess, Mrs. Mason, the narrator and a virtuous exemplar. She instructs two sisters, Mary and Caroline, who are in her care, about the values of benevolence and patience. The sisters, having been brought up largely by servants, have acquired some undesirable behaviors. Mary, age 14, has a "turn for ridicule," and Caroline, age 12, is "vain of her person."

A typical moral lesson in *Original Stories* is provided by the tale of "Jane Fretful," a selfish and continually angry young woman. When Jane was a child, her mother was unwilling to set limits on the little girl's demanding behavior. Trying to satiate Jane's temper, she let Jane have her own way and tried to satisfy her every whim. Although Jane had some "tenderness of heart," this virtue was stunted by the constant appeasement of the child. Jane grew to believe that the "world was made only for her." If her friends had a toy that she wanted, she would cry and demand it. Instead of "being a comfort to her tender, though mistaken mother," Jane caused her tremendous anxiety. When given a dog that she wanted, Jane, in a fit of rage, gave it such a severe blow that she killed it. As a young woman, Jane continued to rage, demand, cajole, and threaten, driving her mother to an early death. When Jane herself died, "no one shed a tear," and she was "soon forgotten."

In her major work, *A Vindication of the Rights of Woman,* Wollstonecraft, sparked by the catalytic French Revolution, wrote her most significant feminist statement. The French National Assembly had taken up Talleyrand's proposal for state-supported schools for boys but not for girls. Hoping to persuade the assembly to include the education of girls in the projected system, Wollstonecraft, addressing the general topic of women's education, called for a revolution in women's educational and social roles. She proposed the establishment of government-sponsored coeducational schools that were to be free and open to all children regardless of class. In the spirit of equality, the pupils were to wear the same type of clothing and receive the same kind of instruction. The curriculum was to include reading, writing, arithmetic, natural science, and some simple experiments in physical science. Religion, history, and politics were to be taught by way of teacher-student conversations.

In *A Vindication of the Rights of Woman,* she argues that many standard books on women's education had been written by men who either misunderstood or deliberately distorted women's rights and needs. Especially offensive is Rousseau, who, in *Emile,* prescribed that women should be pleasing and attractive to men. An early feminist, Wollstonecraft proposed an education for women that would develop their reason and critical judgment as well as heighten their aesthetic tastes and sensibilities.

FOCUSING QUESTIONS

As you read the selections, you might wish to consider the following questions:

1. Identify and analyze Wollstonecraft's admonitions on the early education of daughters. Are these admonitions conventional or revolutionary today?
2. Analyze the story of Jane Fretful for its implications on moral education. Is the story format a useful device in contemporary moral education?
3. Consider Wollstonecraft's comments on Rousseau's advice on women's education. Are there still remnants of Rousseau's arguments in contemporary society? If so, identify them and indicate how Wollstonecraft might react to them.
4. On the basis of the selections, what does Wollstonecraft recommend for women's education and empowerment?

FROM MARY WOLLSTONECRAFT'S *THOUGHTS ON THE EDUCATION OF DAUGHTERS: WITH REFLECTIONS ON FEMALE CONDUCT, IN THE MORE IMPORTANT DUTIES OF LIFE*

MORAL DISCIPLINE

It has been asserted, "That no being, merely human, could properly educate a child." I entirely coincide with this author; but though perfection cannot be attained, and unforeseen events will ever govern human conduct, yet still it is our duty to lay down some rule to regulate our actions by, and to adhere to it, as consistently as our infirmities will permit. To be able to follow Mr. Locke's system (and this may be said of almost all treatises on education) the parents must have subdued their own passions, which is not often the case in any considerable degree.

The marriage state is too often a state of discord; it does not always happen that both parents are rational, and the weakest have it in their power to do most mischief.

How then are the tender minds of children to be cultivated?—Mamma is only anxious that they should love her best, and perhaps takes pains to sow those seeds, which have produced such luxuriant weeds in her own mind. Or, what still more frequently occurs, the children are at first made play-things of, and when their tempers have been spoiled by indiscreet indulgence, they become troublesome, and are mostly left with servants; the first notions they imbibe, therefore, are mean and vulgar. They are taught cunning, the wisdom of that class of people, and a love of truth, the foundation of virtue, is soon obliterated from their minds. It is, in my opinion, a well-proved fact, that principles of truth are innate. Without reasoning we assent to many truths; we feel their force, and artful sophistry can only blunt those feelings which nature has implanted in us as instinctive guards to virtue. Dissimulation and cunning will soon drive all other good qualities before them, and deprive the mind of that beautiful simplicity, which can never be too much cherished.

Indeed it is of the utmost consequence to make a child artless, or to speak with more propriety, not to teach them to be otherwise; and in order to do so we must keep them out of the way of bad examples. Art is almost always practiced by servants, and the same methods which children observe them to use, to shield themselves from blame, they will adopt—and cunning is so nearly allied to falsehood, that it will infallibly lead to it—or some foolish prevaricating subterfuge will occur, to silence any reproaches of the mind which may arise, if an attention to truth has been inculcated.

MATRIMONY

Early marriages are, in my opinion, a stop to improvement. If we were born only "to draw nutrition, propagate and rot," the sooner the end of creation was answered the better; but as women are here allowed to have souls, the soul ought to be attended to. In youth a woman endeavours to please the other sex, in order, generally speaking, to get married, and this endeavour calls forth all her powers. If she has had a tolerable education, the foundation only is laid, for the mind does not soon arrive at maturity, and should not be engrossed by domestic cares before any habits are fixed. The passions also have too much influence over the judgment to suffer it to direct her in this most important affair; and many women, I am persuaded, marry a man before they are twenty, whom they would have rejected some years after. Very frequently, when the education has been neglected, the mind improves itself, if it has leisure for reflection, and experience to reflect on; but how can this happen when they are forced to act before they have had time to think, or find that they are unhappily married? Nay, should they be so fortunate as to get a good husband, they will not set a proper value on him; he will be found much inferior to the lovers described in novels, and their want of knowledge makes them frequently disgusted with the man, when the fault is in human nature.

From Mary Wollstonecraft's *Thoughts on the Education of Daughers: With Reflections on Female Conduct, in the More Important Duties of Life*. London: J. Johnson, 1787, 11–15, 93–95.

FROM MARY WOLLSTONECRAFT'S *ORIGINAL STORIES*

CHAP. IV.

ANGER.—HISTORY OF JANE FRETFUL.

A few days after these walks and conversations, Mrs. Mason heard a great noise in the play-room. She ran hastily to enquire the cause, and found the children crying, and near them, one of the young birds lying on the floor dead. With great eagerness each of them tried, the moment she entered, to exculpate herself, and prove that the other had killed the bird. . . .

The cause of the dispute was easily gathered from what they both let fall. They had contested which had the best right to feed the birds. Mary insisted that she had a right, because she was the eldest; and Caroline, because she took the nest. Snatching it from one side of the room to the other, the bird fell, and was trodden on before they were aware.

When they were a little composed, Mrs. Mason calmly thus addressed them:—I perceive that you are ashamed of your behaviour, and sorry for the consequence; I will not therefore severely reprove you, nor add bitterness to the self-reproach you must both feel,—because I pity you. You are now inferiour to the animals that graze on the common; reason only serves to render your folly more conspicuous and inexcusable. Anger, is a little despicable vice: its selfish emotions banish compassion, and undermine every virtue. It is easy to conquer another; but noble to subdue oneself. Had you, Mary, given way to your sister's humour, you would have proved that you were not only older, but wiser than her. And you, Caroline, would have saved your charge, if you had, for the time, waved your right. . . .

I will tell you a story, that will take stronger hold on your memory than mere remarks.

Jane Fretful was an only child. Her fond weak mother would not allow her to be contradicted on any occasion. The child had some tenderness of heart; but so accustomed was she to see everything give way to her humour, that she imagined the world was only made for her. If any of her playfellows had toys, that struck her capricious sickly fancy, she would cry for

From Mary Wollstonecraft's *Original Stories,* Introduction by E. V. Lucas. London: H. Frowde, 1906, 1–88 (Chapter IV).

them; and substitutes were in vain offered to quiet her, she must have the identical ones, or fly into the most violent passion. When she was an infant, if she fell down, her nurse made her beat the floor. She continued the practice afterwards, and when she was angry would kick the chairs and tables, or any senseless piece of furniture, if they came in her way. I have seen her throw her cap into the fire, because some of her acquaintance had a prettier.

Continual passions weakened her constitution; beside, she would not eat the common wholesome food that children, who are subject to the smallpox and worms, ought to eat, and which is necessary when they grow so fast, to make them strong and handsome. Instead of being a comfort to her tender, though mistaken, mother, she was her greatest torment. The servants all disliked her; she loved no one but herself; and the consequence was, she never inspired love; even the pity good-natured people felt, was nearly allied to contempt.

A lady, who visited her mother, brought with her one day a pretty little dog. Jane was delighted with it; and the lady, with great reluctance, parted with it to oblige her friend. For some time she fondled, and really felt something like an affection for it: but, one day, it happened to snatch a cake she was going to eat, and though there were twenty within reach, she flew into a violent passion, and threw a stool at the poor creature, who was big with pup. It fell down; I can scarcely tell the rest; it received so severe a blow, that all the young were killed, and the poor wretch languished two days, suffering the most excruciating torture.

Jane Fretful, who was now angry with herself, sat all the time holding it, and every look the miserable animal gave her, stung her to the heart. After its death she was very unhappy; but did not try to conquer her temper. All the blessings of life were thrown away on her; and, without any real misfortune, she was continually miserable. . . .

She was, when a child, very beautiful; but anger soon distorted her regular features, and gave a forbidding fierceness to her eyes. But if for a moment she looked pleased, she still resembled a heap of combustible matter, to which an accidental spark might set fire; of course quiet people were afraid to converse with her. And if she ever did a good, or a humane action, her ridiculous anger soon rendered it an intolerable burden, if it did not entirely cancel it.

At last she broke her mother's heart, or hastened her death, by her want of duty, and her many other faults: all proceeding from violent, unrestrained anger.

The death of her mother, which affected her very much, left her without a friend. She would sometimes say, Ah! my poor mother, if you were now alive, I would not tease you—I would give the world to let you know that I am sorry for what I have done: you died, thinking me ungrateful; and lamenting that I did not die when you gave me suck. I shall never—oh! never see you more.

This thought, and her peevish temper, preyed on her impaired constitution. She had not, by doing good, prepared her soul for another state, or cherished any hopes that could disarm death of its terrors, or render that last sleep sweet—its approach was dreadful!—and she hastened her end, scolding the physician for not curing her. Her lifeless countenance displayed the marks of convulsive anger; and she left an ample fortune behind her to those who did not regret her loss. They followed her to the grave, on which no one shed a tear. She was soon forgotten; and I only remember her, to warn you to shun her errors.

FROM MARY WOLLSTONECRAFT'S *A VINDICATION OF THE RIGHTS OF WOMAN*

FROM THE INTRODUCTION

After considering the historic page, and viewing the living world with anxious solicitude, the most melancholy emotions of sorrowful indignation have depressed my spirits, and I have sighed when obliged to confess, that either nature has made a great difference between man and woman, or that the civilization which has hitherto taken place in the world has been very partial. I have turned over various books written on the subject of education, and patiently observed the conduct of parents and the management of schools; but what has been the result?—a profound conviction that the neglected education of my fellow-creatures is the grand source of the misery I deplore; that women, in particular, are rendered weak and wretched by a variety of concurring causes, originating from one hasty conclusion. The conduct and manners of women, in fact, evidently prove that their minds are not in a healthy state; for, like the flowers which are planted in too rich a soil, strength and usefulness are sacrificed to beauty; and the flaunting leaves, after having pleased a fastidious eye, fade, disregarded on the stalk, long before the season when they ought to have arrived at maturity.—One cause of

From Mary Wollstonecraft's *A Vindication of the Rights of Woman,* Introduction by Elizabeth Robbins Pennel. London: Walter Scott, 1891, 1–282.

this barren blooming I attribute to a false system of education, gathered from the books written on this subject by men who, considering females rather as women than human creatures, have been more anxious to make them alluring mistresses than affectionate wives and rational mothers; and the understanding of the sex has been so bubbled by this specious homage, that the civilized women of the present century, with a few exceptions, are only anxious to inspire love, when they ought to cherish a nobler ambition, and by their abilities and virtues exact respect. . . .

. . . the most perfect education, in my opinion, is such an exercise of the understanding as is best calculated to strengthen the body and form the heart. Or, in other words, to enable the individual to attain such habits of virtue as will render it independent. In fact, it is a farce to call any being virtuous whose virtues do not result from the exercise of its own reason. This was Rousseau's opinion respecting men: I extend it to women, and confidently assert that they have been drawn out of their sphere by false refinement, and not by an endeavour to acquire masculine qualities. . . .

Many are the causes that, in the present corrupt state of society, contribute to enslave women by cramping their understandings and sharpening their senses. . . .

This contempt of the understanding in early life has more baneful consequences than is commonly supposed; for the little knowledge which women of strong minds attain, is, from various circumstances, of a more desultory kind than the knowledge of men, and it is acquired more by sheer observations on real life, than from comparing what has been individually observed with the results of experience generalized by speculation. Led by their dependent situation and domestic employments more into society, what they learn is rather by snatches; and as learning is with them, in general, only a secondary thing, they do not pursue any one branch with that persevering ardour necessary to give vigour to the faculties, and clearness to the judgment. In the present state of society, a little learning is required to support the character of a gentleman; and boys are obliged to submit to a few years of discipline. But in the education of women, the cultivation of the understanding is always subordinate to the acquirement of some corporeal accomplishment; even while enervated by confinement and false notions of modesty, the body is prevented from attaining that grace and beauty which relaxed half-formed limbs never exhibit. Besides, in youth their faculties are not brought forward by emulation; and having no serious scientific study, if they have natural sagacity it is turned too soon on life and manners. They dwell on effects, and modifications, without tracing them back to causes; and complicated rules to adjust behaviour are a weak substitute for simple principles. . . .

I, therefore, will venture to assert, that till women are more rationally educated, the progress of human virtue and improvement in knowledge must receive continual checks. And if it be granted that woman was not created merely to gratify the appetite of man, or to be the upper servant, who provides his meals and takes care of his linen, it must follow, that the first care of those mothers or fathers, who really attend to the education of females, should be, if not to strengthen the body, at least, not to destroy the constitution by mistaken notions of beauty and female excellence; . . .

—As for Rousseau's remarks, which have since been echoed by several writers, that they have naturally, that is from their birth, independent of education, a fondness for dolls, dressing, and talking—they are so puerile as not to merit a serious refutation. That a girl, condemned to sit for hours together listening to the idle chat of weak nurses, or to attend at her mother's toilet, will endeavour to join the conversation, is, indeed, very natural; and that she will imitate her mother or aunts, and amuse herself by adorning her lifeless doll, as they do in dressing her, poor innocent babe! is undoubtedly a most natural conse-

quence. For men of the greatest abilities have seldom had sufficient strength to rise above the surrounding atmosphere; and, if the page of genius have always been blurred by the prejudices of the age, some allowance should be made for a sex, who, like kings, always see things through a false medium.

Pursuing these reflections, the fondness for dress, conspicuous in women, may be easily accounted for, without supposing it the result of a desire to please the sex on which they are dependent. The absurdity, in short, of supposing that a girl is naturally a coquette, and that a desire connected with the impulse of nature to propagate the species, should appear even before an improper education has, by heating the imagination, called it forth prematurely, is so unphilosophical, that such a sagacious observer as Rousseau would not have adopted it, if he had not been accustomed to make reason give way to his desire of singularity, and truth to a favourite paradox. . . .

Let an enlightened nation then try what effect reason would have to bring them back to nature, and their duty; and allowing them to share the advantages of education and government with man, see whether they will become better, as they grow wiser and become free. They cannot be injured by the experiment; for it is not in the power of man to render them more insignificant than they are at present.

To render this practicable, day schools, for particular ages, should be established by government, in which boys and girls might be educated together. The school for the younger children, from five to nine years of age, ought to be absolutely free and open to all classes. A sufficient number of masters should also be chosen by a select committee, in each parish. . . .

The school-room ought to be surrounded by a large piece of ground, in which the children might be usefully exercised, for at this age they should not be confined to any sedentary employment for more than an hour at a time. But these relaxations might all be rendered a part of elementary education, for many things improve and amuse the senses, when introduced as a kind of show, to the principles of which, dryly laid down, children would turn a deaf ear. For instance, botany, mechanics, and astronomy. Reading, writing, arithmetic, natural history, and some simple experiments in natural philosophy, might fill up the day; but these pursuits should never encroach on gymnastic plays in the open air. The elements of religion, history, the history of man, and politics, might also be taught by conversations, in the socratic form.

After the age of nine, girls and boys, intended for domestic employments, or mechanical trades, ought to be removed to other schools, and receive instruction, in some measure appropriated to the destination of each individual, the two sexes being still together in the morning; but in the afternoon, the girls should attend a school, where plain-work, mantua-making, millinery, &c. would be their employment.

The young people of superior abilities, or fortune, might now be taught, in another school, the dead and living languages, the elements of science, and continue the study of history and politics, on a more extensive scale, which would not exclude polite literature.

Girls and boys still together? I hear some readers ask: yes. And I should not fear any other consequence than that some early attachment might take place; which, whilst it had the best effect on the moral character of the young people, might not perfectly agree with the views of the parents, for it will be a long time, I fear, before the world will be so far enlightened that parents, only anxious to render their children virtuous, shall allow them to choose companions for life themselves. . . .

I have already inveighed against the custom of confining girls to their needle, and shutting them out from all political and civil employments; for by thus narrowing their minds they are rendered unfit to fulfil the peculiar duties which nature has assigned them. . . .

But these *littlenesses* would not degrade their character, if women were led to respect themselves, if political and moral subjects were opened to them; and, I will venture to affirm, that this is the only way to make them properly attentive to their domestic duties.—An active mind embraces the whole circle of its duties, and finds time enough for all. It is not, I assert, a bold attempt to emulate masculine virtues; it is not the enchantment of literary pursuits, or the steady investigation of scientific subjects, that leads women astray from duty. No, it is indolence and vanity—the love of pleasure and the love of sway, that will reign paramount in an empty mind. I say empty emphatically, because the education which women now receive scarcely deserves the name. For the little knowledge that they are led to acquire, during the important years of youth, is merely relative to accomplishments; and accomplishments without a bottom, for unless the understanding be cultivated, superficial and monotonous is every grace.

SUGGESTIONS FOR FURTHER READING

Alexander, Meena. *Women in Romanticism: Mary Wollstonecraft, Dorothy Wordsworth, and Mary Shelley.* Savage, Md.: Barnes and Noble Books, 1989.

Detre, Jean. *A Most Extraordinary Pair: Mary Wollstonecraft and William Godwin.* New York: Doubleday & Co., 1975.

Ferguson, Moira. *Mary Wollstonecraft.* Boston: Twayne Publishers, 1984.

Flexner, Eleanor. *Mary Wollstonecraft: A Biography.* New York: Coward, McCann and Geoghegan, 1972.

George, Margaret. *One Woman's "Situation": A Study of Mary Wollstonecraft.* Urbana: University of Illinois Press, 1970.

Kelly, Gary. *Revolutionary Feminism: The Mind and Career of Mary Wollstonecraft.* New York: St. Martin's Press, 1992.

Lorch, Jennifer. *Mary Wollstonecraft: The Making of a Radical Feminist.* New York: Berg, 1990.

Nixon, Edna. *Mary Wollstonecraft: Her Life and Times.* London: J. M. Dent and Sons, 1971.

Sapiro, Virginia. *A Vindication of Political Virtue: The Political Theory of Mary Wollstonecraft.* Chicago: University of Chicago Press, 1992.

Sunstein, Emily. *A Different Face: The Life of Mary Wollstonecraft.* New York: Harper & Row, 1975.

Wardle, Ralph. *Mary Wollstonecraft: A Critical Biography.* Lincoln: University of Nebraska Press, 1967.

Wollstonecraft, Mary. *Collected Letters of Mary Wollstonecraft.* Ithaca, N.Y.: Cornell University Press, 1979.

———. *Mary, A Fiction.* London: Joseph Johnson, 1788. Reprinted by New York: Oxford University Press, 1976.

———. *Original Stories from Real Life.* Oxford, U.K., and New York: Woodstock Books, 1990.

———. *Political Writings.* London: W. Pickering, 1993.

———. *Thoughts on the Education of Daughters with Reflections on Female Conduct, in the More Important Duties of Life.* London: Joseph Johnson, 1787. Facsimile by New York: Garland Publishing, Inc., 1974.

———. *A Vindication of the Rights of Men.* Gainesville, Fla.: Scholars' Facsimiles and Reprints, 1960.

———. *A Vindication of the Rights of Woman.* New York: Norton Co., 1975.

———. *The Works of Mary Wollstonecraft.* New York: New York University Press, 1989.

NOTES

1. Moira Ferguson, "Introduction" to Mary Wollstonecraft, *Maria or the Wrongs of Women* (New York: W. W. Norton & Co., 1975), 7–10.

2. Janet M. Todd, ed. *A Wollstonecraft Anthology* (Bloomington: Indiana University Press), 2–4.

3. Ibid., 5–6.

4. Edmund Burke, *Reflections on the Revolution in France* (New York: Liberal Arts Press, 1955).

5. Mary Wollstonecraft, *A Vindication of the Rights of Men* (1790), republished (Gainesville, Fla.: Scholars' Facsimiles and Reprints, 1960).

6. Todd, ed., *A Wollstonecraft Anthology*, 12–13.

7. Ibid., 14–15.

8. William Godwin, *Memoirs of the Author of A Vindication of the Rights of Woman* (London: Joseph Johnson, 1798), 165, as cited in Todd, ed., *A Wollstonecraft Anthology*, 15.

9. Moira Ferguson, "Introduction" to Mary Wollstonecraft, *Maria or the Wrongs of Women* (New York: W. W. Norton & Co., 1975), 13.

10. Mary Wollstonecraft, *Thoughts on the Education of Daughters* (London: J. Johnson, 1787), 17.

11. Ibid., 48.

12. Ibid., 35.

12

HORACE MANN: LEADER OF THE COMMON SCHOOL MOVEMENT

BIOGRAPHICAL SKETCH

In the history of American education, Horace Mann (1796–1859) is often acknowledged as the common school movement's preeminent statesman. A lawyer, politician, and educator, Mann laid the philosophical and organizational foundations of American public schooling.

Horace Mann was born on May 4, 1796, at Franklin, Massachusetts, one of five children of Thomas and Rebecca Mann, who were farmers. The town of Franklin was named for Benjamin Franklin, the self-made inventor and statesman of the revolutionary generation. Franklin gave the town a collection of books that formed a community library. These books would be read by the studious young Horace.[1]

Recalling his childhood, Mann remembered helping to augment the family income by performing numerous farm chores and regularly attending church. In Franklin, the religious doctrines of Calvinism were maintained by the town's minister, the severe and imposing Reverend Nathanael Emmons (1773–1827). The minister's sermons—emphasizing human depravity, sin, and guilt—made a strong and unshakable impression on young Horace.

At the funeral of Mann's brother, Stephen, Reverend Emmons preached about the damnation of those who died unconverted, strongly suggesting that Stephen was among the damned. This event had a lasting impact on Horace, who was 14. As he grew to adulthood, orthodox Calvinism's stern proscriptions would lessen their grip on Mann, who would become a convert to the more liberal Unitarianism.

Mann's formative years as a farm child had a strong influence in reinforcing the values of work, diligence, frugality, and seriousness. Congruent with the Protestant work ethic, Mann saw industriousness, productivity, and punctuality as positive morals that he would emphasize in his educational philosophy. The common school ethos that Mann helped to shape was epitomized in the McGuffey Readers' portrayal of good boys and girls who were always truthful, diligent, and obedient.

Mann attended Franklin's local district school, housed in a one-room schoolhouse and taught by a single male teacher. Mann remembered a drafty building, a leaking roof, and uncomfortable benches. The school year was a brief 10-week term.

The Calvinism of the community was reinforced by the use of the *New England Primer,* which was the text for teaching the alphabet, reading, and moral instruction. Additionally, students memorized the *Westminster Assembly Shorter Catechism,* in which Calvinist doctrine was arranged in question and answer format. Mann recalled that his teachers were "very good people" but poor instructors who neglected children's interests and ignored art and music. Using the recitation method, the teachers stressed memorization.[2]

Reacting to the limited curriculum of his own school days, Mann would later use his position as a common school leader to persistently advocate an enriched curriculum that included history, geography, health, and music as well as the basics of reading, writing, spelling, and arithmetic. He would campaign for increased public taxes to provide better designed, more comfortable school buildings than the one he had attended in Franklin.

In addition to the district school, Horace Mann's early education was shaped by two powerful informal educational forces: his family and the town library. His parents, who valued education, created a home environment that stimulated his interest in learning and motivated him to seek knowledge. Young Horace frequented the town library, eagerly reading books on history and biography.[3]

After his father's death in 1809, prospects that Horace would continue his formal education were dimmed by the family's reduced income. Mann persisted in his goal of further education. Encouraged by his mother, he prepared for entry to Brown University in Providence, Rhode Island. At that time, applicants had to pass examinations in Latin, Greek, and mathematics. Mann engaged private tutors to prepare in these subjects. Passing his entrance examinations, he was admitted as a student to Brown. Mann joined a student body drawn primarily from the middle and lower-middle socioeconomic classes, who came to the college because of its low costs for tuition, room, and board, which came to the modest amount of $100 per year.

Mann's academic program at Brown consisted of the classical Latin and Greek languages and literatures, geometry, geography, English, logic, and public speaking, typical for the period. Mann's elegant prose reflected his study of English. An eloquent speaker, in an age of great orators, Mann proved adept at debate and public speaking. His favorite topics dealt with patriotism and social reform. His annual reports, written as secretary of the Massachusetts Board of Education, which reflected his studied use of language, became eloquent expressions of the public school philosophy.

Mann, a highly motivated student, graduated first in Brown's class of 1819. His valedictory speech, "The Gradual Advancement of the Human Species in Dignity and Happiness," extolled the role that science and education would play in human progress, a persistent theme in Mann's educational philosophy.[4]

After graduating from Brown, Mann decided to become a lawyer. He read law in the office of J. J. Fiske, an attorney in Wrentham, Massachusetts. He took a 2-year hiatus from his legal study to accept a teaching position at his alma mater in 1820, where for $375 a year he taught Latin and Greek and served as librarian. In 1822, he resumed his legal study, this time at Litchfield, Connecticut, where he studied under Judge James Gould, a distinguished jurist. Completing his studies in 1823, Mann located in Dedham, Massachusetts, where he was admitted to the bar.

From 1823 to 1837, Mann, a successful lawyer, earned a reputation as an outstanding orator. Moving in influential circles, he prepared for a political career. He was to marry twice. His first wife, Charlotte Messer, died of consumption after 2 years of marriage. His second marriage was to Mary Peabody, the sister of Elizabeth Peabody, a proponent of kindergarten education in the United States.

Mann was elected to the Massachusetts House of Representatives in 1827, serving until 1833, when he was elected to the state Senate for a 4-year term. During the period 1836–1837, he served as the president of the Senate. As a legislator, Mann developed a concept of responsible republican public service that would later form the foundations of his ideas on civic education. Citizens, he believed, acting on principles of patriotism and altruism, rising "above sectarian and political biases," should make their decisions in an enlightened and disinterested fashion.[5] A determined social reformer, Mann was in the forefront of investigations of conditions in prisons and insane asylums. Armed with statistics, Mann sponsored legislation to improve the care of the insane by establishing the Worcester Asylum in 1833, a model institution. Mann actively supported "An Act Relating to Common Schools," in 1837, which established the Massachusetts Board of Education. As its first secretary, he would become a nationally recognized proponent for public education.[6]

As secretary of the Massachusetts Board of Education, Mann was to compile statistics about schools, diffuse educational information, and offer recommendations for the improvement of public education. He was also charged with preparing reports on education for the state legislature. For example, Mann was to survey the condition of schools throughout the state in order to recommend policies for their improvement.[7]

To gather information, Mann visited and inspected schools throughout Massachusetts. His findings, set out in his first annual report of 1838, revealed that many school buildings were dilapidated and that many local district school committees, which were responsible for education in their localities, were doing little to improve conditions. Mann also found that many districts employed poorly prepared teachers and had low educational standards.[8] His first report asserted his firm conviction that the state was responsible for educating all of its children. He argued that publicly supported schools of high educational quality should be available to all.

As secretary of the Massachusetts Board of Education, Mann wrote 12 annual reports that addressed the condition and improvement of public education. The essential philosophy found in the reports can be summed up in Mann's statement, "Education, then, beyond all other devices of human origin, is the great equalizer of the conditions of men—the balance-wheel of the social machinery."[9] Among the issues addressed in his reports were the kinds of policies needed to improve common schools; the schools' role in preparing a trained, productive, and literate workforce; and the need to educate a responsible citizenry. In addition to these general themes, Mann addressed the specific needs of improving curriculum, reading, penmanship, and other immediate problems. For example, Mann, in his second annual report, advised teachers:

> The best way of inspiring a young child with a desire of learning to read is, to read to him, with proper intervals, some interesting story, perfectly intelligible, yet as full of suggestion as of communication; for the pleasure of discovering is always greater than that of perceiving.[10]

To improve the schools in Massachusetts, Mann developed a strategy to revitalize the existing defective district schools and transform them into an effective system of common or publicly supported and controlled schools. To do this, he defined the nature, purpose, and function of common schools and created a coalition of political support for tax-funded public education.

From 1848 to 1852, Mann served in the U.S. House of Representatives, elected as a Whig candidate. As the nation was coming closer to civil war between the southern slave and the northern free states, Mann took a firm stand against slavery, opposing the extension of slavery into the western territories that were ceded to the United States as a result of the Mexican War. He also opposed the Fugitive Slave Law of 1850 that required federal marshals to recapture and return escaped slaves who had fled to northern states.

In 1853, Mann left his political career to become the first president of Antioch College in Yellow Springs, Ohio. He brought to higher education the same zeal and reform that he had displayed as secretary of the Board of Education in Massachusetts. Worn out from his labors, he died on August 2, 1859.

Overview of Mann's Educational Ideas

Horace Mann's career as a lawyer and politician shaped his belief that the common school was directly related to civic competency and to public service. Subscribing to the Whig ideology and seeing public education as a kind of internal improvement, he believed it could be an agency for national economic development and the maintenance of social and political order.

Mann's common school ideal was based on his belief that the best society was a republic in which people governed themselves through elected officials and representative institutions. Society's well-being depended, he believed, on literate, diligent, productive, and responsible citizens.[11] A proper civic education, Mann argued, should teach basic principles of government, provide insights into representative institutions, and generally form good citizens. The common school would also act as a cultural agency that transmitted the American heritage to young people through literature and history.

Although he saw the common schools as an agency of political socialization, Mann did not want them to be politicized. Using his consensus style of leadership, Mann wanted common schools to cultivate a general political consciousness without being tied to any political party. Public schools were to prepare literate persons who would be intelligent voters and capable of participating in the republic's political institutions and processes.

In the governance and control of common schools, Mann emphasized the New England tradition of local control but gave a larger role to the state. Important for American public education's future, he urged that the governing and supporting of public schools should be a partnership between local districts and states. This policy remains a prominent feature of contemporary public education.

Mann's common school idea sharply differed from the role primary schools played in Europe, where they were used to educate lower socioeconomic class children in reading, writing, and religion. In Europe, upper-class males attended preparatory schools that readied them to enter selective secondary schools and colleges. Rather than segregating children according to socioeconomic class, Mann wanted American common schools to integrate children from diverse social, economic, religious, and ethnic backgrounds into one educational institution. Mann's common school was designed as a completely public institution, supported by public taxes, governed by elected officials, and responsible to the community that it served.

Mann believed the common school curriculum should provide its students with the basic skills and knowledge they needed to function effectively as ethically responsible members of the community, as economically productive managers and workers, and as interested citizens. The common school curriculum, designed to prepare people for practical life and citizenship, included reading, writing, spelling, arithmetic, history, geography, health, music, and art.

Mann's paramount moral values were the Calvinistic ones of hard work, effort, honesty, diligence, thrift, literacy, and a respect for property. But unlike Calvinist predestination, he believed all people were capable of self-reform and enlightenment. His economic values that respected private property and encouraged individual initiative were congenial to the emergent free market capitalism.

Though he wanted the common schools to cultivate moral and ethical values, Mann opposed imposing the doctrines of any particular church or denomination. In his consensus style of leadership, he proposed a compromise on moral education in the common schools, arguing that common schools could cultivate the values of a common Christianity. While his compromise satisfied many but not all of the Protestant clergy, Roman Catholics, who were immigrating in larger numbers to the United States, contended that common Christianity was a stratagem to indoctrinate their children in Protestantism. Of his various compromises, Mann's common Christianity was least successful. To avoid what they regarded as the common schools' "Protestant orientation," Roman Catholics, led by their bishops, established their own separate parochial schools. Later, those who believed public schools should be completely separate from religious influences fashioned the public schools into a secular system.

A skilled and persuasive public speaker, Mann created a public consensus that was favorable to common schools. To do this, he fashioned a broad definition of common schooling that appealed to various social, economic, religious, and ethnic groups and lobbied to persuade the state legislature to levy taxes for public schools. In Massachusetts, where the Protestant clergy was highly influential, he had to convince the ministers that common schools would not be antireligious. He had to walk a delicate balance. While Mann did not want common schools to teach the doctrines of the church, he assured the Protestant ministers that common schools could cultivate the general morality that came from Christianity.

Still, another highly influential group that Mann needed to recruit to support public education was the members of the business community. He argued that they were stewards of economic wealth and productivity and that it was in their interests to pay taxes for common schools. He called public education an investment that would pay dividends in preparing skilled managers and a productive and law-abiding workforce. To win the large class of farmers and tradesmen, Mann called public education the "great equalizer" that would ensure their children's upward social and economic mobility.

Mann knew that the common schools' effectiveness required well-prepared professional teachers, who had expertise in the skills and subjects they taught, were competent in teaching and in managing classes, and were ethical role models. To professionalize teaching, he promoted state establishment of normal schools, teacher education institutions. Mann convinced the state legislature that teacher education would result in higher standards in the common schools, and the Massachusetts legislature created normal schools at Lexington, Barre, and Bridgewater. The normal school curriculum consisted of English composition and grammar, spelling, geography, arithmetic, health, and history (the basic subjects taught in the common schools) as well as the history and philosophy of education, methods of teaching, and clinical experience in a model or demonstration school. An important trend encouraged by the normal schools was that elementary school teaching began to attract more young women. Although they were underpaid and limited in their personal freedom, the entry of women into teaching marked a first step toward entry into other occupations and professions.

THE PRIMARY SOURCE

As secretary of the Massachusetts Board of Education, Mann wrote 12 annual reports on the current condition and needed reforms of public education in the state. His "Twelfth Annual Report," published in the *Life and Works of Horace Mann*, is an important statement of his philosophy of public education. Mann, who believed in education's power to bring about personal and social reform, saw common schools as the agency of creating a healthier, more prosperous, and more moral society. For him, the common schools could educate a people who were committed to the principles of republican government. A society's economic productivity depended, he believed, on literate, diligent, hardworking, and responsible citizens. Mann wanted teachers to be agents in cultivating morally responsible individuals. Faced with religious conflicts, Mann, a conciliator, advised that the common schools, while not indoctrinating the creed of any particular church, could emphasize the general moral values derived from Christianity.

FOCUSING QUESTIONS
As you read the selection, you might consider the following questions:

1. Describe and evaluate Mann's expectations for common schools in the United States. Do you believe that Americans continue to share Mann's expectations for public schools? Explain your answer.
2. Mann considered the diffusion of education to be a means of promoting economic prosperity and reducing class conflict. Examine his concept of education as "the great equalizer" in terms of the general economy and socioeconomic classes in contemporary America.
3. Describe and evaluate Mann's idea of civic education for a republican nation. Is his conception of civic education adequate for contemporary American society? Defend your answer.
4. Describe and evaluate Mann's argument for moral education. Do you agree or disagree with his view that teachers have a responsibility for morally educating their students? Explain your answer.
5. Describe and evaluate Mann's views on the teaching of religion in the common schools. Are Mann's ideas a relevant and adequate solution for such contemporary issues as prayer in public schools, creationism versus evolution, and the use of vouchers to attend private and religious schools?

Without undervaluing any other human agency, it may be safely affirmed that the common school, improved and energized as it can easily be, may become the most effective and benignant of all the forces of civilization. Two reasons sustain this position. In the first place, there is a universality in its operation, which can be affirmed of no other institution whatever. If administered in the spirit of justice and conciliation, all the rising generation may be brought within the circle of its reformatory and elevating influences. And, in the second place, the materials upon which it operates are so pliant and ductile as to be susceptible of assuming a greater variety of forms than any other earthly work of the Creator. The inflexibility and ruggedness of the oak, when compared with the lithe sapling or the tender germ, are but feeble emblems to typify the docility of childhood when contrasted with the obduracy and intractableness of man. It is these inherent advantages of the common school, which, in our own State, have produced results so striking, from a system so imperfect, and an administration so feeble. In teaching the blind and the deaf and dumb, in kindling the latent spark of intelligence that lurks in an idiot's mind, and in the more holy work of reforming abandoned and outcast children, education has proved what it can do by glorious experiments. These wonders it has done in its infancy, and with the lights of a limited experience; but when its faculties shall be fully developed, when it shall be trained to wield its mighty energies for the protection of society against the giant vices which now invade and torment it,—against intemperance, avarice, war, slavery, bigotry, the woes of want, and the wickedness of waste,—then there will not be a height to which these enemies of the race can escape which it will not scale, nor a Titan among them all whom it will not slay.

I proceed, then, in endeavoring to show how the true business of the schoolroom connects itself, and becomes identical, with the great interests of society. The former is the infant, immature state of those interests; the latter their developed, adult state. As "the child is father to the man," so may the training of the schoolroom expand into the institutions and fortunes of the State. . . .

For this thorough diffusion of sanitary intelligence, the common school is the only agency. It is, however, an adequate agency. Let human physiology be introduced as an indispensable branch of study into our public schools; let no teacher be approved who is not master of its leading principles, and of their applications to the varying circumstances of life; let all the older classes in the schools be regularly and rigidly examined upon this study by the school-committees,—and a speedy change would come over our personal habits, over our domestic usages, and over the public arrangements of society. Temperance and moderation would not be such strangers at the table. Fashion, like European sovereigns, if not compelled to abdicate and fly, would be forced to compromise for the continued possession of her throne by the surrender to her subjects of many of their natural rights. A sixth order of architecture would be invented,—the hygienic,—which, without subtracting at all from the beauty of any other order, would add a new element of utility to them all. The "health-regulations" of cities would be issued in a revised code,—a code that would bear the scrutiny of science. And, as the result and reward of all, a race of men and women, loftier in stature, firmer in structure, fairer in form, and better able to perform the duties and bear the burdens of life, would revisit the earth. The minikin specimens of the race, who now go on dwindling and tapering from parent to child, would re-ascend to manhood and womanhood. Just in proportion as the laws of health and life were discovered and obeyed, would pain, disease, insanity, and untimely death, cease from among men. Consumption would remain; but it would be consumption in the active sense. . . .

Poverty is a public as well as a private evil. There is no physical law necessitating its existence. The earth contains abundant resources for ten times—doubtless for twenty times—its present inhabitants. Cold, hunger, and nakedness are not, like death, an inevitable lot. . . .

According to the European theory, men are divided into classes,—some to toil and earn, others to seize and enjoy. According to the Massachusetts theory, all are to have an equal chance for earning, and equal security in the enjoyment of what they earn. . . .

From Horace Mann's "Twelfth Annual Report on Education (1848)," *The Life and Works of Horace Mann*, edited by Mary Mann. Boston: Lee and Shepard Publishers, 1891, 232–313.

The main idea set forth in the creeds of some political reformers, or revolutionizers, is, that some people are poor *because* others are rich. This idea supposes a fixed amount of property in the community, which by fraud or force, or arbitrary law, is unequally divided among men; and the problem presented for solution is, how to transfer a portion of this property from those who are supposed to have too much to those who feel and know that they have too little. At this point, both their theory and their expectation of reform stop. But the beneficent power of education would not be exhausted, even though it should peaceably abolish all the miseries that spring from the co-existence, side by side, of enormous wealth and squalid want. It has a higher function. Beyond the power of diffusing old wealth, it has the prerogative of creating new. It is a thousand times more lucrative than fraud, and adds a thousand-fold more to a nation's resources than the most successful conquests. Knaves and robbers can obtain only what was before possessed by others. But education creates or develops new treasures,—treasures not before possessed or dreamed of by any one. . . .

Now, surely nothing but universal education can counterwork this tendency to the domination of capital and the servility of labor. If one class possesses all the wealth and the education, while the residue of society is ignorant and poor, it matters not by what name the relation between them may be called: the latter, in fact and in truth, will be the servile dependants and subjects of the former. But, if education be equably diffused, it will draw property after it by the strongest of all attractions; for such a thing never did happen, and never can happen, as that an intelligent and practical body of men should be permanently poor. Property and labor in different classes are essentially antagonistic; but property and labor in the same class are essentially fraternal. The people of Massachusetts have, in some degree, appreciated the truth, that the unexampled prosperity of the State—its comfort, its competence, its general intelligence and virtue—is attributable to the education, more or less perfect, which all its people have received: but are they sensible of a fact equally important; namely, that it is to this same education that two-thirds of the people are indebted for not being to-day the vassals of as severe a tyranny, in the form of capital, as the lower classes of Europe are bound to in the form of brute force?

Education, then, beyond all other devices of human origin, is the great equalizer of the conditions of men,—the balance-wheel of the social machinery. I do not here mean that it so elevates the moral nature as to make men disdain and abhor the oppression of their fellow-men. This idea pertains to another of its attributes. But I mean that it gives each man the independence and the means by which he can resist the selfishness of other men. It does better than to disarm the poor of their hostility towards the rich: it prevents being poor. . . .

That political economy, therefore, which busies itself about capital and labor, supply and demand, interest and rents, favorable and unfavorable balances of trade, but leaves out of account the element of a widespread mental development, is nought but stupendous folly. The greatest of all the arts in political economy is to change a consumer into a producer; and the next greatest is to increase the producer's producing power,—an end to be directly attained by increasing his intelligence. . . .

POLITICAL EDUCATION

The necessity of general intelligence,—that is, of education (for I use the terms as substantially synonymous, because general intelligence can never exist without general education, and general education will be sure to produce general intelligence),—the necessity of general intelligence under a republican form of government, like most other very important truths, has become a very trite one. It is so trite, indeed, as to have lost much of its force by its familiarity. Almost all the champions of education seize upon this argument first of all, because it is so simple as to be understood by the ignorant, and so strong as to convince the sceptical. Nothing would be easier than to follow in the train of so many writers, and to demonstrate by logic, by history, and by the nature of the case, that a republican form of government, without intelligence in the people, must be, on a vast scale, what a mad-house, without superintendent or keepers, would be on a small one,—the despotism of a few succeeded by universal anarchy, and anarchy by despotism, with no change but from bad to worse. . . .

Now, as a republican government represents almost all interests, whether social, civil, or military, the necessity of a degree of intelligence adequate to the due administration of them all is so self-evident, that a bare statement is the best argument.

But, in the possession of this attribute of intelligence, elective legislators will never far surpass their electors. By a natural law, like that which regulates the equilibrium of fluids, elector and elected, appointer and appointee, tend to the same level. It is not more certain that a wise and enlightened constituency will refuse to invest a reckless and profligate man with office, or discard him if accidentally chosen, than it is that a foolish or immoral constituency will discard or eject a wise man. This law of assimilation between the choosers and the chosen results, not only from the fact that the voter originally selects his representative according to the affinities of good or of ill, of wisdom or of folly, which exist between them, but if the legislator enacts or favors a law which is too wise for the constituent to understand, or too just for him to approve, the next election will set him aside as certainly as if he had made open merchandise of the dearest interests of the people by perjury and for a bribe. . . . In a republican government, legislators are a mirror reflecting the moral countenance of their constituents. And hence it is, that the establishment of a republican government, without well-appointed and efficient means for the universal education of the people, is the most rash and foolhardy experiment ever tried by man. Its fatal results may not be immediately developed, they may not follow as the thunder follows the lightning; for time is an element in maturing them, and the calamity is too great to be prepared in a day: but, like the slow-accumulating avalanche, they will grow more terrific by delay, and at length, though it may be at a late hour, will overwhelm with ruin whatever lies athwart their path. It may be an easy thing to make a republic; but it is a very laborious thing to make republicans; and woe to the republic that rests upon no better foundations than ignorance, selfishness, and passion! Such a republic may grow in numbers and in wealth. As an avaricious man adds acres to his lands, so its rapacious government may increase its own darkness by annexing provinces and states to its ignorant domain. Its armies may be invincible, and its fleets may strike terror into nations on the opposite sides of the globe at the same hour. Vast in its extent, and enriched with all the prodigality of Nature, it may possess every capacity and opportunity of being great and of doing good. But, if such a republic be devoid of intelligence, it will only the more closely resemble an obscene giant who has waxed strong in his youth, and grown wanton in his strength; whose brain has been developed only in the region of the appetites and passions, and not in the organs of reason and conscience; and who, therefore, is boastful of his bulk alone, and glories in the weight of his heel, and in the destruction of his arm. Such a republic, with all its noble capacities for beneficence, will rush with the speed of a whirlwind to an ignominious end. . . .

However elevated the moral character of a constituency may be, however well informed in matters of general science or history, yet they must, if citizens of a republic, understand something of the true nature and functions of the government under which they live. That any one, who is to participate in the government of a country when he becomes a man, should receive no instruction respecting the nature and functions of the government he is afterwards to administer, is a political solecism. In all nations, hardly excepting the most rude and barbarous, the future sovereign receives some training which is supposed to fit him for the exercise of the powers and duties of his anticipated station. . . .

Hence the Constitution of the United States, and of our own State, should be made a study in our public schools. The partition of the powers of government into the three co-ordinate branches,—legislative, judicial, and executive,—with the duties appropriately devolving upon each; the mode of electing or of appointing all officers, with the reasons on which it was founded; and, especially, the duty of every citizen, in a government of laws, to appeal to the courts for redress in all cases of alleged wrong, instead of undertaking to vindicate his own rights by his own arm; and, in a government where the people are the acknowledged sources of power, the duty of changing laws and rulers by an appeal to the ballot, and not by rebellion,—should be taught to all the children until they are fully understood. . . .

Surely, between these extremes, there must be a medium not difficult to be found. And is not this the middle course, which all sensible and judicious men, all patriots, and all genuine republicans, must approve?—namely, that those articles in the creed of republicanism which are accepted by all, believed in by all, and which form the common basis of our political faith, shall be taught to all. But when the teacher, in the course of his lessons or lectures on the fundamental law, arrives at a controverted text, he is either to read it without comment or remark; or, at most, he is only to say that the passage is the subject of disputation, and that the schoolroom is neither the tribunal to adjudicate, nor the forum to discuss it.

Such being the rule established by common consent, and such the practice observed with fidelity under it, it will come to be universally understood that political proselytism is no function of the school, but that indoctrination into matters of controversy between hostile political parties is to be elsewhere sought for, and elsewhere imparted. Thus may all the children of the Commonwealth receive instruction in all the great essentials of political knowledge,—in those elementary ideas without which they will never be able to investigate more recondite and debatable questions; thus will the only practicable method be adopted for discovering new truths, and for discarding, instead of perpetuating, old errors; and thus, too, will that pernicious race of intolerant zealots, whose whole faith may be summed up in two articles,—that they themselves are always infallibly right, and that all dissenters are certainly wrong,—be extinguished,—extinguished, not by violence, not by proscription, but by the more copious inflowing of the light of truth. . . .

But to all doubters, disbelievers, or despairers in human progress, it may still be said, there is one experiment which has never yet been tried. It is an experiment, which, even before its inception, offers the highest authority for its ultimate success. Its formula is intelligible to all; and it is as legible as though written in starry letters on an azure sky. It is expressed in these few and simple words: *"Train up a child in the way he should go; and, when he is old, he will not depart from it."* This declaration is positive. If the conditions are complied with, it makes no provision for a failure. Though pertaining to morals, yet, if the terms of the direction are observed, there is no more reason to doubt the result than there would be in an optical or a chemical experiment.

But this experiment has never yet been tried. Education has never yet been brought to bear with one-hundredth part of its potential force upon the natures of children, and, through them, upon the character of men and of the race. In all the attempts to reform mankind which have hitherto been made, whether by changing the frame of government, by aggravating or softening the severity of the penal code, or by substituting a government-created for a God-created religion,—in all these attempts, the infantile and youthful mind, its amenability to influences, and the enduring and self-operating character of the influences it receives, have been almost wholly unrecognized. Here, then, is a new agency, whose powers are but just beginning to be understood, and whose mighty energies hitherto have been but feebly invoked; and yet, from our experience, limited and imperfect as it is, we do know, that, far beyond any other earthly instrumentality, it is comprehensive and decisive.

Reformatory efforts hitherto made have been mainly expended upon the oaken-fibred hardihood and incorrigibleness of adult offenders, and not upon the flexibleness and ductility of youthful tendencies. . . . Would any child, on whose heart the horrors and atrocities of the slave-trade had made their natural impression before his arrival at the age of fourteen years, ever connect himself with slavery afterwards?. . . .

Indeed, so decisive is the effect of early training upon adult habits and character, that numbers of the most able and experience teachers—those who have had the best opportunities to become acquainted with the errors and the excellences of children, their waywardness, and their docility—have unanimously declared it to be their belief, that if all the children in the community, from the age of four years to that of sixteen, could be brought within the reformatory and elevating influences of good schools, the dark host of private vices and public crimes which now imbitter domestic peace, and stain the civilization of the age, might, in ninety-nine cases in every hundred, be banished from the world. . . .

All the schemes ever devised by governments to secure the prevalence and permanence of religion among the people, however variant in form they may have been, are substantially resolvable into two systems. One of these systems holds the regulation and control of the religious belief of the people to be one of the functions of government, like the command of the army or the navy, or the establishment of courts, or the collection of revenues. According to the other system, religious belief is a matter of individual and parental concern; and, while the government furnishes all practicable facilities for the independent formation of that belief, it exercises no authority to prescribe, or coercion to enforce it. The former is the system, which, with very few exceptions, has prevailed throughout Christendom for fifteen hundred years. Our own government is almost a solitary example among the nations of the earth, where freedom of opinion, and the inviolability of conscience, have been even theoretically recognized by the law. . . .

Among the infinite errors and enormities resulting from systems of religion devised by man, and enforced by the terrors of human government, have been those dreadful re-actions which have abjured all religion, spurned its obligations, and voted the Deity into nonexistence. This extreme is, if possible, more fatal than that by which it was produced. Between these extremes, philanthropic and godly men have sought to find a medium, which should avoid both the evils of ecclesiastical tyranny and the greater evils of atheism. And this medium has at length been supposed to be found. It is promulgated in the great principle, that government should do all that it can to facilitate the acquisition of religious truth, but shall leave the decision of the question, what religious truth is, to the arbitrament, without human appeal, of each man's reason and conscience: in other words, that government shall never, by the infliction of pains and penalties, or by the privation of rights or immunities, call such decision either into pre-judgment or into review. The formula in which the constitution of Massachusetts expresses it is in these words: "All religious sects and denominations demeaning themselves peaceably and as good citizens shall be equally under the protection of law; and no subordination of one sect or denomination to another shall ever be established by law.". . .

I believed then, as now, that religious instruction in our schools, to the extent which the constitution and laws of the State allowed and prescribed, was indispensable to their highest welfare, and essential to the vitality of moral education. Then as now, also, I believed that sectarian books and sectarian instruction, if their encroachments were not resisted, would prove the overthrow of the schools. . . .

No person, then, in the whole community, could have been more surprised or grieved than myself at finding my views in regard to the extent and the limitation of religious instruction in our public schools attributed to a hostility to religion itself, or a hostility to the Scriptures. . . .

That our public schools are not theological seminaries, is admitted. That they are debarred by law from inculcating the peculiar and distinctive doctrines of any one religious denomination amongst us, is claimed; and that they are also prohibited from ever teaching that what they do teach is the whole of religion, or all that is essential to religion or to salvation, is equally certain. But our system earnestly inculcates all Christian morals; it founds its morals on the basis of religion; it welcomes the religion of the Bible; and, in receiving the Bible, it allows it to do what it is allowed to do in no other system,—*to speak for itself.* But here it stops, not because it claims to have compassed all truth, but because it disclaims to act as an umpire between hostile religious opinions.

SUGGESTIONS FOR FURTHER READING

Binder, Frederick M. *The Age of the Common School, 1830–1865.* New York: John Wiley and Sons, 1974.

Cremin, Lawrence A. *The American Common School: An Historic Conception.* New York: Bureau of Publications, Teachers College Press, Columbia University, 1951.

———. ed. *The Republic and the School: Horace Mann and the Education of Free Men.* New York: Bureau of Publications, Teachers College Press, Columbia University, 1957.

Downs, Robert B. *Horace Mann: Champion of Public Schools.* New York: Twayne Publishers, 1974.

Mann, Horace. *Lectures on Education.* New York: Arno Press, 1969.

Messerli, Johnathan. *Horace Mann: A Biography.* New York: Alfred A. Knopf, 1972.

NOTES

1. Robert B. Downs, *Horace Mann: Champion of Public Schools* (New York: Twayne Publishers, 1974), 11.
2. Mary Mann, *Life of Horace Mann* (Boston: Walker Fuller, 1865), 11–12.
3. Downs, 14.
4. Downs, 17.
5. Johnathan Messerli, *Horace Mann: A Biography* (New York: Alfred A. Knopf, 1972), 119.
6. Downs, 27–30.
7. Downs, 29–30.
8. Lawrence A. Cremin, ed., *The Republic and the School: Horace Mann and the Education of Free Men* (New York: Bureau of Publications, Teachers College Press, Columbia University, 1957), 29–33.
9. Cremin, 87.
10. Cremin, 39.
11. Merle Curti, *The Social Ideas of American Educators* (Paterson, N.J.: Littlefield, Adams, 1959), 101–138.

ROBERT OWEN: UTOPIAN SOCIALIST AND COMMUNITARIAN EDUCATOR

BIOGRAPHICAL SKETCH

Robert Owen (1771–1858) is significant as a utopian theorist, a communitarian, and an educational innovator. Born in Newtown, Wales, in the United Kingdom, Owen was named Robert, after his father, an ironmonger and saddler. Owen's autobiography provides little information about his parents, but he attributed his industriousness to their influence. His reflections on his childhood reveal the self-confident optimism that he possessed throughout his life.[1] In school, he claimed he was the fastest runner, best dancer, and most popular and gifted of his peers.

Leaving home at age 10, Owen set about making his fortune and fame. As an apprentice to a draper in Manchester, Owen became aware of Britain's rapid industrialization and of the economic rewards that an enterprising young man could earn.[2] At 18, Owen had enough money to become a partner in a company manufacturing cotton-spinning machinery. In 1792, he was managing a mechanized cotton mill owned by Peter Drinkwater. Continuing his upward economic ascent, he joined with other young capitalists to organize the Chorlton Twist Company, which in 1799 purchased David Dale's cotton mills in New Lanark, Scotland. While negotiating for the properties, Owen met, was attracted to, and married Dale's daughter Caroline. The self-made Owen had now gained entry into one of nineteenth-century England's leading industrial families.

New Lanark, the locale of Owen's famous social and educational experiment from 1799 to 1824, was an industrial mill town. It consisted of the mill buildings where cotton cloth was manufactured by water-driven machinery, large apartment row houses for the workers, a company store, and the owner's mansion.

At New Lanark, Robert Owen was the manager of 1,000 workers, including men, women, and children. Finding the town rife with delinquency, vice, drunkenness, theft, and vermin, Owen launched a campaign of social and educational reform. Known as the "benevolent Mr. Owen," he proclaimed his reforms were based on his great philosophical discovery that "man's character is made for and not by him."[3] Rejecting the conventional wisdom that saw poverty and vice caused by innate human depravity, Owen asserted that behavior and character were shaped by the environment in which people lived. If you want to reform people, then reform their environment, especially its economic and social aspects. Not yet a communitarian socialist bent on ending private ownership, Owen, still committed to capitalism, believed that an astute entrepreneur could amass profits without exploiting his workers.

Owen launched a well-publicized and concerted program of social reform and community renewal at the Scottish mill town on the banks of the Clyde River. He improved working conditions by improving efficiency and thus reducing the hours of labor. Children under 10 years were not allowed to work in the mills. The streets were swept regularly and debris was removed. Teams, sent by Owen, inspected workers' apartments for cleanliness. Giving high priority to education as an agency for reform, Owen established several schools at New Lanark: an infant school for the early education of children from ages 2 to 6, a general school for older children, and an Institute for the Formation of Character for adults.

Owen's success at reforming the industrial village brought many observers to New Lanark to see his work. Eager to publicize and promote his ideas, he wrote articles and spoke to numerous groups throughout the United Kingdom. Owen, buoyed by the acclaim, decided to disseminate his ideas throughout Europe and the Americas. It was at this stage that he began to articulate his ideology of communitarian socialism and education.

Drawing on his experiences at New Lanark, Owen called for the creation of self-supporting "villages of unity and mutual cooperation," not only for the poor but for all classes and all persons. In these villages, where all property would be owned communally, all accommodations would be arranged in a parallelogram of connected buildings that would include apartments and dormitories, schools, factories, libraries, kitchens, hospitals, dining rooms, and lecture halls.[4]

In 1824, Owen left New Lanark and journeyed to the United States, where at New Harmony in Indiana he sought to establish his new communitarian vision of society and education. One thousand eager, but diverse, enthusiasts joined Owen's experiment in communal living and education on the Indiana frontier. Among them were some of America's leading scholars, scientists, and Pestalozzian educators. They included William Maclure, the pioneer geologist and philanthropist; Thomas Say and Gerard Troost, both eminent natural scientists; and Marie Duclos Fretageot and Joseph Neef, Pestalozzian educators.

Owen planned to create a community of equality at New Harmony where all property would be owned in common. Owen, seeking to make education a focus of community life, planned to develop comprehensive educational institutions, ranging from nursery schools to lectures for adults.[5]

Owen's ambitious plan for a new social order that was to begin at New Harmony did not succeed. The residents of Owen's utopia endlessly debated constitutional revisions, quarreled over a promised division of property that never happened, and argued over social and educational theories and practices. With the community disintegrating, Owen, in 1828, departed from the United States to return to the United Kingdom. Ever optimistic, he believed that the coming of his predicted "new moral world" merely had been postponed. Owen continued to write, lecture, and organize societies to promote communitarianism. Tirelessly, he advocated cooperatives, women's rights, improvement of working conditions, and universal education until his death in 1858.

OVERVIEW OF IDEAS ON EDUCATION

Robert Owen lived during the United Kingdom's early industrialization, when workers, including women and children, were often exploited as factory, mill, and mine workers. An industrialist himself, Owen believed that it was possible to have an industrial, indeed a technological, society free of exploitation. His ideology emphasized the possibility of creating a new kind of community that was free of alienation, class antagonism, and exploitation. After he made his reforms at New Lanark, he developed a plan for creating a new world order in which people lived in villages of mutual cooperation where property was held in common. In these cooperative villages, the inhabitants would lead integrated lives in which their time was devoted to agriculture, industry, education, art, and leisure.

Robert Owen based his plan for a new millennium of peace and prosperity on his often-repeated philosophical principle: "Man's character was made for and not by him." Owen argued that human character was conditioned by the interaction of the person's original nature with the environment. Whoever controlled the environment—especially its social, economic, and educational institutions and processes—could create any kind of character they wished, either a good or a bad one. Owen, who considered himself kindly and benevolent, believed that the completely controlled community was the most effective setting for shaping human character. He believed that human beings, especially children, could be molded into sharing, kindly, altruistic individuals if they were reared and educated in a controlled educational environment.

For Owen, individuals were not responsible for their behavior since they could not choose their parents or control their formative early childhood experiences. Human beings, however, were not fated to be hapless victims of accidents of birth and the unintended consequences that came from a disordered environment. Given the correct surroundings, which Owen believed he knew how to create, individuals could be conditioned into good, kindly, sharing persons. It was imperative, however, that character formation begin as early as possible, even in infancy, and then continue throughout the entire life cycle.

Though his thinking was revolutionary, Owen was not a political organizer or a maker of revolutions. The new moral world would be ushered in peacefully by education, not armed force. He envisioned his cooperative communities as total educational environments that would create the new moral order by educating moral citizens.

Concurrent with the controlled community, Owen regarded children's education as a key element in improving human character. At New Lanark, Owen established an infant school and a general school for the education of older children.

Owen was an early proponent of infant or early childhood education. The earlier that children were educated in a prepared environment, away from the corrupting influences of a dysfunctional society, the better. Although there was a strong underlying current of social control, the curriculum and methods in Owen's infant school were child-centered, play-oriented, and aimed to stimulate children to use their senses in exploring the environment. Teachers created learning centers throughout the classroom and stocked them with objects that piqued the students' curiosity. Owen wanted children to learn through direct, exploratory activities and by casual conversation between teacher and child.

In the general school, which was coeducational, both boys and girls wore a similar uniform, a white Roman-style cotton tunic.[6] The uniformity of dress was based on Owen's belief that schooling should eliminate artificial distinctions and generate feelings of equality.

Within the school, Owen sought to create a permissive but controlled environment in which learning would be a pleasurable experience for the children. There were to be no extrinsic rewards and punishments, which Owen believed caused selfish and competitive behavior. Since people did not make their own character, any reward or punishment that did not result as a natural consequence of a person's action was irrational. A desire for learning and good behavior were to be generated by being a member of a cooperative group. Teachers were to treat all children with kindness and use restraint only to protect young children from physical harm.[7]

In selecting teachers for the New Lanark schools, Owen was more concerned with their attitude toward children than their academic credentials. In the case of music and dancing teachers, however, he made sure that they possessed the appropriate skills.

The general school's curriculum, designed for the 6 to 10 year age cohort, consisted of reading, writing, arithmetic, natural science, geography, history, singing, and dancing. In addition, girls were taught sewing and needlework.

In reading instruction, Owen's guiding principle was that "children should never be directed to read what they cannot understand."[8] Natural science, geography, and history were taught as integrated subjects in which the teacher would first provide a broad general outline of a topic and then work with the pupils to provide the needed supporting details. Owen, who enjoyed singing and dancing, included these skills, which were neglected by conventional schools, in his curriculum.

THE PRIMARY SOURCES

The selections are arranged to illustrate the progression of Owen's social and educational philosophy. The first one, from *A Supplementary Appendix to the First Volume of The Life of Robert Owen,* is from a letter dated July 25, 1817, that contains Owen's testimony about his reforms at New Lanark before a commission gathering information about the employment and education of the poor. It is followed by two excerpts from *The Life of Robert Owen,* in which Owen announces his foundational principle on the formation of human character and then describes his method of education.

FOCUSING QUESTIONS

As you read the selections, you might wish to consider the following questions:

1. Describe and analyze Owen's conclusions on how to improve the conditions of the poor. Do you agree or disagree with him? Explain your answer.
2. Describe and analyze Owen's principles on the formation of human character. Consider contemporary ideas about human behavior and responsibility. Are Owen's principles relevant to contemporary society and education?
3. According to Owen, who should be entrusted with the forming of character? Do you agree or disagree with him? Explain your answer.
4. Describe and analyze Owen's ideas on the instruction of children in schools. Consider their relevance for contemporary education.

FROM *A Supplementary Appendix to the First Volume of The Life of Robert Owen*

Question. Are you the principal proprietor of the works and village of New Lanark, and have you the sole direction and superintendence of them?

Answer. Yes.

Q. How long have you had the management of that establishment?

A. Eighteen years in August next.

Q. Of what description is the population of New Lanark?

A. Of manufacturers of cotton thread chiefly; but also of iron and brass founders, iron and tin smiths, millwrights, turners in wood and metals, sawyers, carpenters, masons, tilers, painters, glaziers, tailors, shoemakers, butchers, bakers, shopkeepers, farmers, labourers, surgeons, ministers of religion, instructors of youth, male and female superintendents of various departments, clerks, and policemen; forming a mixed society of trades and workpeople.

Q. Had you any experience among the working classes before you undertook the management of the works at New Lanark?

A. Yes; I superintended large manufacturing establishments in Manchester and its neighbourhod for about eight years preceding, in which great numbers of men, women, and children were employed.

Q. What has been the chief object of your attention during the number of years that you have had so many persons under your care and superintendence?

A. To discover the means by which the condition of the poor and working classes could be ameliorated, and with benefit to their employers.

Q. To what conclusions have you now come upon this subject?

A. That the situation of these classes may be easily greatly improved; and that their natural powers may be far more beneficially directed, for themselves, and for society at large, without creating injury of any kind, to any class, or to any individual.

Q. Have you generally succeeded in improving the condition and moral habits of those who have been under your care?

A. Yes, and with even fewer exceptions than I anticipated, considering the obstacles I had to encounter, with the nature of the influence that I possessed to enable me to overcome them.

Q. What are those obstacles?

A. The ignorance and ill-training of the people, which had given them the habits of drunkenness, theft, falsehood, and want of cleanliness; with opposition to each other's interests; sectarian feelings; strong national prejudices, both political and religious, against all attempts on the part of a stranger to improve their condition; to which may be added the unhealthy nature of their employment.

Q. On what leading principles did you act, so as to remove those obstacles?

A.—On the principle of prevention solely. Instead of wasting time and talent in considering an endless variety of individual effects, I patiently studied the causes producing those effects, exerting myself to remove them; and by thus acting, it appeared that the same time and talent, when employed under the system of prevention, could produce results very much greater than under the system of coercion and punishment. For instance, in the case of habitual drunkenness, it appeared to me useless to apply to the individuals who had been taught to acquire the practices of intoxication, to desist from it, while they remained surrounded by the circumstances that perpetually tempted them to continue the habit. The first step adopted in that case was to convince the parties when sober, of the advantages they would derive from having the temptation removed; which, when attempted in a mild and proper spirit, was never difficult to accomplish. The next step was to remove the temptation; and then the evil itself, with all its endless injurious consequences, ceased altogether. The whole process, when completely understood, is simplicity itself, and may be easily carried into practice to the fullest extent by those who possess the usual ordinary talents; and society would rapidly improve without any retrogression. But while the notions which have influenced the conduct of mankind up to the present period shall prevail and be acted upon, society cannot substantially and permanently improve. Those notions confine the attention to effects, and, from want of useful inquiry, lead to the conclusion that the causes

From *A Supplementary Appendix to the First Volume of The Life of Robert Owen.* Vol I.A. London: Effingham Wilson, 1858, 66–68, 72–73.

from which they really proceed, however injurious, cannot be altered or controlled by man. Under such notions the world is now governed. Facts, however, prove that the reverse of these notions is true: let men, therefore, attend to facts, and to facts only, and it will be obvious that they can, with ease, remove the real causes which create bad habits, errors, and crimes; and, without difficulty, replace them with other causes, the certain effects of which would be to establish generally throughout society, good habits, correct sentiments, and a kind, charitable, and virtuous conduct, free from the prejudices that would create unkind feelings and thence render them unjust to those who had been taught to differ from them in opinion. It must, therefore, absolutely follow, that to attempt to improve mankind on any other principle whatever, than by a close, accurate, and undeviating attention to facts, is as absurd and as unavailing as to expect that the most barren soil and sterile climate shall spontaneously produce abundance; as to expect that a full and steady light shall issue from the darkest abyss; or that man, immersed in ignorance, surrounded by every vicious temptation, shall be better, wiser, and happier, than when trained to be intelligent and active, amidst circumstances only which would perpetually unite his interests, his duty, and his feelings. While, then, we permit the causes to remain that must leave mankind in ignorance, that must create in them intemperance, idleness, uncharitableness, vice, crime, and every evil passion, and, at the same time, expect or wish them to become the reverse,—there is precisely as much wisdom in such expectation, as to imagine, contrary to all the experience of the world, that effects shall no longer continue to follow their natural causes. To inflict, therefore, upon men, pains and penalties for having vicious qualities (more unfortunate for themselves than others) which are produced in them by the existing circumstances, is to act upon notions devoid of every pretension to sound judgment and rationality.

Q. Has all your practice been founded upon these principles?

A. Yes; and the results have not once disappointed my expectations; on the contrary, in every instance they have exceeded my most sanguine hopes. It is not, as it appears to me, to any natural superiority of mind, or early-acquired advantages, (for I possess none,) that my success in these endeavours can be attributed; but solely to the accidental circumstances of being enabled, early in life, to see, in part, the important benefits that would result to society from the adoption of the system of prevention; and acting uniformly upon the well-known fact "that human "character is always formed *for,* and not *by,* the individual.". . .

Q. But can these establishments be well managed, unless by men of great talents and benevolence, such men not being very numerous?

A. Here also I may be permitted to say, that a mistake exists, in consequence of the principles upon which this plan is founded and ought to be conducted not being as yet sufficiently understood. In the management of workhouses, &c., there is no unity of action; each part is so placed as to feel an interest at variance with the others; they are, in fact, a compound of the same errors that pervade common society, where all are so circumstanced as to counteract each other's intentions, and thus render even extraordinary energies and talents of no avail, which, under another combination, would produce the most extensive and beneficial effects. From my own experience, however, I can aver that such means and regulations may be adopted for the management of these villages, as would enable any one possessing fair talents, so to manage them as to give entire satisfaction to all the parties under his direction and care, with the greatest pleasure to himself, and with unspeakable advantage to the country. Numbers may be found who would soon be competent to such management and who would be satisfied with the living and comforts these villages would offer, without desiring compensation of any kind; and the annual expense of such living would not amount to £20 in value.

Q. Is it not to be feared that such arrangements as you contemplate would produce a dull uniformity of character, repress genius, and leave the world without hope of future improvements?

A. It appears to me that quite the reverse of all this will follow; that the means provided in these establishments will give every stimulus to bring forth and to perfect the best parts only of every character, by furnishing the inhabitants with such valuable instruction as they could not acquire by any other means, and by affording sufficient leisure and freedom from anxiety to promote the natural direction of their powers. When thus prepared by early-imbibed temperate habits, by an accurate knowledge of facts, and by a full conviction that their efforts are directed for the benefit of mankind, it is not easy to imagine, with our present ideas, what may be accomplished by human beings so trained and so circumstanced. As for the probability of a dull uniformity of character being produced, let us for a moment imagine individuals placed as the inhabitants of these villages will be, and contemplate the characters that must be formed solely by the circumstances that will surround them. From the hour they are born, treated with uniform kindness, directed by reason, and not mere caprice, weakness, and imbecility; not one habit acquired to be again unlearned; the physical powers trained and cultivated to attain their natural strength and health; the mental faculties furnished with accurate data, by all the useful facts that the ingenuity and experience of the world have acquired and demonstrated, aided by the power of minds trained to draw only just and consistent conclusions, and each left to declare freely those conclusions, to compare them with others, and thus in the most easy and rapid manner to correct any errors that might otherwise arise;—children so trained, men so circumstanced, would soon become, not a dull uni-

form race, but beings full of health, activity, and energy; endowed by means of instruction with the most kind and amiable dispositions, and who, being trained free from the motives, could not form one *exclusive* wish for themselves. It is only when the obscurities by which society is now enveloped are in some degree removed, that the benefit of these new villages can be even in part appreciated. So far from genius being depressed, it will receive every aid to enable it to exert itself with unrestrained delight, and with the highest benefit to mankind. In short, experience will prove that no objection against the "New View of Society" will be found more futile than that which supposes it not competent, nor calculated, to train men to attain the utmost improvement, in arts, sciences, and every kind of knowledge....

From *The Life of Robert Owen*

The precept or principle of action taught to them from their first day's entrance into the school, ("that they should always endeavor to make each other happy,") the youngest infant easily ceived, and was as easily induced, by the example of those previously so instructed, to apply the precept to undeviating practice. And this principle and practice might with incalculable benefit to all of our race be so deeply impressed at this early period on all infants, that it would become a habit never to be forgotten or unused in the every day transactions of life.

This experiment with the children of all the population of New Lanark cannot be estimated too highly by the advanced minds of the age in all countries; for it at once opens the path by which all from their birth may have the divine parts of their nature so cultivated by their immediate predecessors, that all shall acquire good habits only, and a character as good as the divine parts of each and the existing knowledge of humanity will admit; and these now united in the training, educating, employing, placing, and governing of each, (for all these enter into the formation of the character of every one,) will produce such a change in the condition of society and of humanity, as can be expressed only by a change from a pandemonium to a paradise.

Let the authorities of this age now turn their attention to this subject, and they will discover that they have attained the knowledge of a moral lever by which they can with ease remove ignorance, poverty, disunion, vice, crime, evil passions, and misery, from mankind. Place the human race from birth within superior spiritual and material surroundings, and the evils and sufferings of humanity will be no longer experienced, and will be retained on record only to enhance the pleasures of this new existence for man.

The arrangements to well-form the character of each will of necessity include the entire arrangements to well-form and conduct society; for there can be no part of society which does not enter into the formation of the character of every one.

That which I introduced as new in forming the character of the children of the working class may be thus stated—

1st.—No scolding or punishment of the children.

2nd.—Unceasing kindness in tone, look, word, and action, to all the children without exception, by every teacher employed, so as to create a real affection and full confidence between the teachers and the taught.

3rd.—Instruction by the inspection of realities and their qualities, and these explained by familiar conversations between the teachers and the taught, and the latter always allowed to ask their own questions for explanations or additional information.

From *The Life of Robert Owen*. Vol. 1. London: Effingham Wilson, 1857, 231–233, 266–268.

4th.—These questions to be always answered in a kind and rational manner; and when beyond the teacher's knowledge, which often happened, the want of knowledge on that subject was at once to be fully admitted, so as never to lead the young mind into error.

5th.—No regular in-door hours for school; but the teachers to discover when the minds of the taught, or their own minds, commenced to be fatigued by the in-door lesson, and then to change it for out-of-door physical exercise in good weather; or in bad weather for physical exercise under cover, or exercises in music.

6th.—In addition to music, the children of these workpeople were taught and exercised in military discipline, to teach them habits of order, obedience, and exactness, to improve their health and carriage, and to prepare them at the best time, in the best manner, when required, to defend their country at the least expense and trouble to themselves.

They were taught to dance, and to dance well, so as to improve their appearance, manner, and health. I found by experience that for both sexes the military discipline, dancing, and music, properly taught and conducted, were powerful means to form a good, rational, and happy character; and they should form part of the instruction and exercise in every rationally formed and conducted seminary for the formation of character. They form an essential part of the surroundings to give good and superior influences to the infants, children, and youth, as they grow towards maturity.

7th.—But these exercises to be continued no longer then they were useful and could be beneficially enjoyed by the taught. On the first indications of lassitude, to return to their in-door mental lessons, for which their physical exercises had prepared them, and to which, if properly conducted, they will always return with renewed pleasure. And to receive physical or mental exercise and instruction may always be made to be highly gratifying to the children, when they are rationally treated.

8th.—To take the children out to become familiar with the productions of gardens, orchards, fields, and woods, and with the domestic animals and natural history generally, is an essential part of the instruction to be given to the children of the working classes; and this was the practice in my time with the children at New Lanark.

9th.—It was quite new to train the children of the working class to think and act rationally, and to acquire substantial knowledge which might be useful to them through after life.

10th.—It was quite new to place the child of the working man within surroundings superior to those of the children of any class, as was done in a remarkable manner at New Lanark, by placing them during the day in the first and best institution for the formation of the character of the children of workpeople ever thought of or executed.

But it must be yet some time before these new practical proceedings for the children of the producers of wealth can be duly appreciated; or their importance for the advancement and permanent benefit of society can be comprehended. . . .

If these circumstances did not exist to an extent almost incredible, it would be unnecessary now to contend for a principle regarding Man, which scarcely requires more than to be fairly stated to make it self-evident.

This principle is, that *"Any general character, from the best to the worst, from the most ignorant to the most enlightened, may be given to any community, even to the world at large, by the application of proper means; which means are to a great extent at the command and under the control of those who have influence in the affairs of men."*

The principle as now stated is a broad one, and, if it should be found to be true, cannot fail to give a new character to legislative proceedings, and such a character as will be most favourable to the well-being of society.

That this principle is true to the utmost limit of the terms, is evident from the experience of all past ages, and from every existing fact.

Shall misery, then, most complicated and extensive, be experienced, from the prince to the peasant, throughout all the nations of the world, and shall its cause and the means of its prevention be known, and yet these means withheld? The undertaking is replete with difficulties which can only be overcome by those who have influence in society: who, by foreseeing its important practical benefits, may be induced to contend against those difficulties; and who, when its advantages are clearly seen and strongly felt, will not suffer individual considerations to be put in competition with their attainment. It is true their ease and comfort may be for a time sacrificed to those prejudices; but, if they persevere, the principles on which this knowledge is founded must ultimately universally prevail.

In preparing the way for the introduction of these principles, it cannot now be necessary to enter into the detail of facts to prove that children can be trained to acquire *"any language, sentiments, belief, or any bodily habits and manners, not contrary to human nature"*

For that this has been done, the history of every nation of which we have records, abundantly confirms; and that this is, and may be again done, the facts which exist around us and throughout all the countries in the world, prove to demonstration.

Possessing, then, the knowledge of a power so important, which when understood, is capable of being wielded with the certainty of a law of nature, and which would gradually remove the evils which now chiefly afflict mankind, shall we permit it to remain dormant and useless, and suffer the plagues of society perpetually to exist and increase?

No: the time is now arrived when the public mind of this country, and the general state of the world, call imperatively for the introduction of this all-pervading principle, not only in theory, but into practice.

Nor can any human power now impede its rapid progress. Silence will not retard its course, and opposition will give increased celerity to its movements. The commencement of the work will, in fact, ensure its accomplishment; henceforth all the irritating angry passions, arising from ignorance of the true cause of bodily and mental character, will gradually subside, and be replaced by the most frank and conciliating confidence and good-will.

Nor will it be possible hereafter for comparatively a few individuals, unintentionally to occasion the rest of mankind to be surrounded by circumstances which inevitably form such characters as they afterwards deem it a duty and a right to punish even to death; and that, too, while they themselves have been the instruments of forming those characters. Such proceedings not only create innumerable evils to the directing few, but essentially retard them and the great mass of society from attaining the enjoyment of a high degree of positive happiness. Instead of punishing crimes after they have permitted the human character to be formed so as to commit them, they will adopt the only means which can be adopted to prevent the existence of those crimes; means by which they may be most easily prevented.

Happily for poor traduced and degraded human nature, the principle for which we now contend will speedily divest it of all the ridiculous and absurd mystery with which it has been hitherto enveloped by the ignorance of preceding times: and all the complicated and counteracting motives for good conduct, which have been multiplied almost to infinity, will be reduced to one single principle of action, which, by its evident operation and sufficiency, shall render this intricate system unnecessary, and ultimately supersede it in all parts of the earth. That principle is *the happiness of self, clearly understood and uniformly practised; which can only be attained by conduct that must promote the happiness of the community.*

SUGGESTIONS FOR FURTHER READING

Butt, John, ed. *Robert Owen: Aspects of His Life and Work.* New York: Humanities Press, 1971.

Harrison, John F. C. *Quest for the New Moral World: Robert Owen and the Owenites in Britain and America.* New York: Charles Scribner's Sons, 1969.

_____. *Utopianism and Education: Robert Owen and the Owenites.* New York: Teachers College Press, Columbia University, 1968.

Harvey, Rowland H. *Robert Owen: Social Idealist.* Berkeley: University of California Press, 1949.

Kolmerten, Carol A. *Women in Utopias: The Ideology of Gender in the American Owenite Communities.* Bloomington: Indiana University Press, 1990.

Lockwood, George B. *The New Harmony Movement.* New York: D. Appleton and Co., 1905.

Owen, Robert. *The Life of Robert Owen, Written by Himself with Selections from His Writings and Correspondence.* London: Effingham Wilson, 1857. Reprinted by Augustus M. Kelley, Publishers, New York, 1967.

_____. *Selected Works of Robert Owen.* London: W. Pickering, 1993.

Owen, Robert Dale. *An Outline of the System of Education at New Lanark.* Cincinnati: Deming and Wood, 1825.

_____. *Threading My Way: Twenty-Seven Years of Autobiography*. New York: G. W. Carleton and Co., 1874. Reprinted by Augustus M. Kelley, Publishers, New York, 1967.

Pitzer, Donald E. *Robert Owen's American Legacy*. Indianapolis: Indiana State Historical Society, 1972.

Podmore, Frank. *Robert Owen: A Biography*. London: Hutchinson and Co., 1906. Reprinted by George Allen & Unwin, Ltd. London, 1923. Reprinted by Augustus M. Kelley, Publishers, New York, 1968.

Pollard, Sidney, and John Salt, eds. *Robert Owen: Prophet of the Poor*. Lewisburg, Pa.: Bucknell University Press, 1971.

Silver, Harold, ed. *Robert Owen on Education*. Cambridge: Cambridge University Press, 1969.

NOTES

1. Robert Owen, *The Life of Robert Owen Written by Himself with Selections from His Writings and Correspondence* I (New York: Augustus Kelley, 1967), 1–2.

2. Margaret Cole, "Robert Owen Until New Lanark," in *Robert Owen: Industrialist, Reformer, Visionary, 1771–1858* (London: Robert Owen Bicentenary Association, 1971), 4–14.

3. Harold Silver, "Owen's Reputation as an Educationist," in Sidney Pollard and John Salt, eds., *Robert Owen: Prophet of the Poor* (Lewisburg, Pa.: Bucknell University Press, 1971), 65.

4. Robert Owen, "Report to the Committee of the Association for the Relief of the Manufacturing and Labouring Poor, 1817," and "Report to the County of Lanark, 1820," *A Supplementary Appendix to the First Volume of the Life of Robert Owen* (London: Effingham Wilson, 1858), reprinted by Augustus M. Kelley, Publishers, 1967, 53–54, 263–320.

5. Arthur E. Bestor, Jr., *Backwoods Utopias: The Sectarian and Owenite Phases of Communitarian Socialism in America, 1663–1829* (Philadelphia: University of Pennsylvania Press, 1950), 134–135.

6. Robert Dale Owen, *An Outline of the System of Education at New Lanark* (Cincinnati: Deming and Wood, 1825), 11–14.

7. Frank Podmore, *Robert Owen* (London: Hutchinson and Co., 1906), 136–137.

8. Robert Dale Owen, *An Outline*, 14–17.

FRIEDRICH FROEBEL: FOUNDER OF THE KINDERGARTEN

BIOGRAPHICAL SKETCH

Friedrich Froebel (1782–1852), who was formally christened Friedrich Wilhelm August, was born on April 21, 1782.[1] He was the youngest of five sons of Johann Jacob Froebel, pastor of the Lutheran Church at Oberwiessbach.[2] The village of Oberwiessbach was located in the Thuringian forests of the small principality of Schwarzburg-Rudolstadt, one of the many independent German states.

Froebel's mother died when he was 9 months old. When he was 4, his father remarried. Froebel disliked his stepmother, who he felt neglected him in favor of her own child. Froebel also felt rejected by his father, who he recalled considered him to be "stupid, mischievous, and untrustworthy."[3] As a child, Friedrich was lonely, shy, and isolated. Froebel's unhappy childhood shaped his theory of kindergarten education. The kindergarten teacher would be a loving, kindly, and gentle motherlike figure.

As a young child, living near the Thuringian forests, Froebel was fascinated by the trees, plants, and animals in the natural environment. He enjoyed gardening. When he developed his educational philosophy, the images of growing and blooming plants were used in the language that conveyed his ideas.

Young Friedrich's first schooling was at Oberwiessbach's primary school for girls. His father, who had unsuccessfully attempted to teach Friedrich to read, apparently regarded him as a slow child who needed the more protected atmosphere of the girls' school rather than the more strenuous boys' school. The girls' school followed the conventional curriculum of Bible reading, catechism, reading, writing, and arithmetic. Friedrich had difficulty with the language arts but enjoyed arithmetic. In addition to school, his attendance at his father's church also had an impact on him. He enjoyed the hymns used in the Lutheran religious services and would later make use of their imagery in his own writing of children's songs.

When Friedrich was 10, an uncle, Herr Hoffman, decided to intervene in his nephew's unhappy life. Hoffman, a Lutheran clergyman, invited Friedrich to live with him at Stadt-Ulm. Needing little persuasion, Froebel's father agreed. Friedrich spent the next 5 years at his uncle's home. Finding the affection that was missing from his own household, Froebel described his uncle as a "gentle," "kind-hearted," "loving father."[4] Friedrich attended Stadt-Ulm's town school, where he studied read-

Froebel's fourth kindergarten gift.

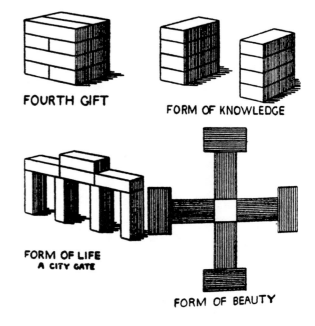

FOURTH GIFT

FORM OF KNOWLEDGE

FORM OF LIFE
A CITY GATE

FORM OF BEAUTY

ing, writing, arithmetic, religion, Latin, and geography. He enjoyed school and began to make friends with his classmates.

When he was 15, Friedrich was apprenticed to a forester and surveyor in the town of Neuhaus. Apprenticeship was popular in Germany, where boys learned a trade by working with master craftsmen. Froebel's apprenticeship lasted 2 years. Although he learned a great deal about trees, Froebel felt that the forester with whom he worked, while having experience in the field, did not know how to teach his skills to others.[5] While serving his apprenticeship, Froebel read widely, especially books on forestry and botany. As he worked outdoors among the trees, he developed a heightened sense of nature and his outlook became increasingly mystical. Common objects, especially plants, came to have a double meaning for him—one of appearance and one of symbol.

After completing his apprenticeship, Froebel, at age 17, began 2 years of study at the University of Jena. His academic interests ranged widely, and he attended lectures in mathematics, mineralogy, physics, chemistry, forestry, architecture, surveying, and botany. Believing it possible to discover a principle that unified all areas of knowledge, he began his search for the underlying foundation of reality.[6]

Once again Froebel, now 19, experienced problems with his father. Because of a loan he made to his brother, Friedrich, unable to pay his own tuition bills, was confined to the university's debtor's prison. His father, reluctantly agreeing to pay Friedrich's bills, arranged for his release. However, the elder Froebel insisted that Friedrich officially renounce his inheritance from the family estate. Froebel agreed. After his father's death in 1802, he never again set foot in his family home.

Without family support, Froebel tried to find a suitable career. For a time, he worked in the Office of Woods and Forests, then as secretary to an estate owner. In 1805, an inheritance from his Uncle Hoffman enabled him to go to Frankfurt to

Kindergarten at The Heines Normal and Industrial Institute, Augusta, Georgia. 1900.

study architecture. His architectural studies helped him to develop a sense of perspective and proportion that he later transferred to his design of the kindergarten's program. In his educational work, Froebel saw children working, like little architects, using building blocks to design and construct their own structures.

While in Frankfurt, Froebel met Anton Gruener, the headmaster of the Frankfurt Model School, which followed Pestalozzian educational principles. Gruener, who believed that Froebel was well suited for teaching, hired him for his school. Gruener also arranged for the 24-year-old Froebel to spend 2 weeks at Johann Heinrich Pestalozzi's educational institute at Yverdon. Pestalozzi enjoyed a reputation as being an innovative educator who had devised a new method of instruction that featured object lessons. Inspired by Rousseau, Pestalozzi, rejecting corporal punishment, argued that learning was most effective in educational situations where children felt emotionally secure.

Froebel was impressed by Pestalozzi's emphasis on children's dignity and the need to create emotionally secure learning environments. Although he saw the value of using objects in instruction, Froebel believed Pestalozzi's object lesson needed to be grounded in a more philosophical base. He would later redesign the directly empirical Pestalozzian object lesson into a highly symbolic version.

After his study with Pestalozzi, Froebel returned to Frankfurt and began instructing at the Model School. Finding teaching a fulfilling endeavor, he determined to devote his life to education. He taught at the Model School for 3 years. In 1808, he resigned his position to return to Yverdon for 2 years of study with Pestalozzi. He learned much from the master Swiss educator but also identified areas he wanted to improve. Two of these areas were play and language acquisition. Convinced that play was highly significant in children's growth and development, Froebel began a search to discover its true meaning. Language acquisition was also a crucial component in early childhood. When he left Yverdon, Froebel was determined to do more advanced study to unlock the doors to understanding play and language development.

In 1810, Froebel was back in Germany, enrolled at the University of Gottingen, where he spent 2 years studying Persian, Hebrew, Arabic, and Greek. His linguistic study convinced him that the various human languages were linked and structurally interconnected. If he could discover the structural linkages in these various languages, he believed he could apply his findings to language teaching. Along with his language studies, Froebel attended lectures in physics, chemistry, mineralogy, geology, history, and economics. He became keenly interested in geology and mineralogy, which in the early nineteenth century were attracting the serious attention of both academic and amateur scientists.

In 1812, caught up in the nationalist fervor, he enlisted in the Lutzow Jagers, an infantry division that fought with the German forces against Napoleon's invading French army. While in the army, Froebel met several other young men who shared an interest in education. Among them were Wilhelm Middendorf and Heinrich Langethal, who would later work with him in the kindergarten.[7]

From 1812 to 1816 Froebel was at the University of Berlin, where he served as an assistant to Professor Christian Samuel Weiss (1780–1856). Weiss, who held the chair of mineralogy at the university, was highly recognized for his pioneering work in crystallography.[8] As he assisted Weiss, Froebel was fascinated by the process of crystallization. He was convinced that crystal formation, following the universal law that governed all creation, went from the simple to the complex through a progression of increasingly intricate geometrical structures.[9] Although Pestalozzi, too, had stressed the movement from simple to complex in his teaching method, Froebel believed that the process of ever increasing complexity was a divinely ordered cosmic law. Human growth and development, too, conformed to this important philosophical principle.

In 1816, Froebel established a school called the Universal German Educational Institute at Griesheim, a small town near Darmstadt. The next year he moved the school to Keilhau, where it had varying success in attracting students. It enrolled 60 pupils at its peak and 5 at its ebb in 1829, when it closed. Froebel's former military comrades, Middendorf and Langethal, also taught at the school. During the 13 years that the institute functioned, Froebel tested some of his educational ideas and developed new insights into child nature and the learning process. Among the principles Froebel developed at the institute were that (1) each child should be recognized as an individual and educated according to his or her own needs and interests, (2) general universal laws existed that governed children's growth and development, and (3) it was possible to develop a method of instruction that recognized the universal laws of child development and also enabled each child to express himself or herself creatively.

Though Froebel's first effort to operate his own school had some important educational successes, his institute had serious administrative problems. Froebel and his teachers faced some hostility in the community, especially from orthodox Lutherans who believed he deviated from traditional religious doctrines. Froebel, like Pestalozzi, lacked the organizational and administrative skills needed to manage a school, especially in funding it. Throughout its 13-year history, the institute was frequently near bankruptcy.

In 1818, Froebel married Henrietta Wilhelmine Hoffmeister (1780–1839), a well-educated woman who had studied with Johann Fichte, a German philosopher. Despite her family's opposition, she married Froebel, sharing a mutual love of children, nature, and education.[10]

In 1831, Froebel accepted an invitation from the Swiss composer Xavier Schnyder to establish an educational institute at his castle at Wartensee on Lake Sempach in the Lucerne Canton. With approval of the Swiss Ministry of Education, Froebel opened his school in Schnyder's castle, enrolling some 30 students who followed a curriculum of arithmetic, languages, history, and gymnastics. The castle, however, proved unsuited for a school, and Froebel relocated at Willisau. Here, the school prospered, and Froebel gained a reputation as a capable educator.

While in Switzerland, Froebel accepted an invitation to establish an orphanage at Burgdorf, a town in which Pestalozzi had once operated an educational institute. At Burgdorf, Froebel was engaged in several lines of educational work. He conducted a school for the town children and a boarding school for those who lived at a distance. He also engaged in teacher-training activities. Anticipating his kindergarten, Froebel grew increasingly interested in early childhood education. He established a nursery school for 3- and 4-year-old children and prepared materials for them. He wrote rhymes and songs and devised physical exercises, activities, and games that could be used in the nursery school. He began experimenting with the objects and materials that would constitute his kindergarten program.[11]

In 1836, Froebel's wife became seriously ill and he decided to return to Blankenburg, a spa town in Germany, where he hoped she would regain her health. Henrietta's health continued to deteriorate, and she died in 1838.

That same year Froebel opened his new educational institution, the kindergarten, the child's garden, at Blankenburg. Using play, songs, stories, and activities, the kindergarten was designed as an educational environment in which children could develop, through their own self-activity, in the right direction, following the divinely established laws of human growth. Froebel's kindergarten was both a natural and cultural environment. Through play, a natural activity, children acted on their interests and satisfied their needs. Froebel designed a series of "gifts," objects that could be used to awaken children's conceptual and symbolic powers. "Occupations,"—such as slats, straws, clay, and paper—would be used in creative and construction activity. Songs, stories, and games, which provided an introduction to the culture, were also used to socialize children through group activities. Froebel's fame as a founder of kindergartens spread throughout the German states, and a number of kindergartens were established.

In 1851, a controversy surrounding the kindergarten developed in Prussia. Karl von Raumer, the Prussian minister of education, who had confused Friedrich Froebel with his nephew Karl, accused him of undermining traditional Prussian values by spreading atheism and socialism. Karl Froebel had written an antigovernment pamphlet. Although Friedrich Froebel denied the charges, von Raumer, unwilling to admit his mistake, banned the kindergarten in Prussia. In the midst of the controversy, Froebel died in 1852. Although kindergartens existed in the other German states, they were not allowed in Prussia until 1860. By the end of the nineteenth century, kindergartens had been established throughout Europe and North America.

OVERVIEW OF FROEBEL'S EDUCATIONAL IDEAS

Froebel's written works were difficult to understand. He expressed his kindergarten philosophy most fully in *The Education of Man* in 1826.[12] In this book, Froebel attempted to weave the strands of philosophical idealism, Christian mysticism, romanticism, and science into a coherent philosophy of education.

Froebel begins by asserting that all existence, including that of humans, originates in and with God. His conception of God combined the traditional Lutheran theology of a personal creator with the Hegelian idealist view of an all-encompassing absolute and universal idea. All creatures, both great and small, have the same spiritual source. Human beings are endowed by their creator with an interior divine or spiritual essence and, at the same time, have a body that makes them part of the natural physical order. It is the spiritual essence, however, that by vitalizing and motivating them leads to human development. Froebel asserts that each child at birth has within him or her a spiritual essence, a life force, that seeks to be externalized. Through the child's own self-activity, the inner spiritual essence is externalized. The kindergarten's gifts, occupations, and activities, especially play, are designed to ensure that this development follows the correct course, which reveals God's plan of development. The human destiny, said Froebel, is to become conscious of the presence of this spiritual essence and to reveal it by externalizing it. In this process of leading the spiritual essence outward, the human being is really growing nearer to God.

Following the idealism that dominated the German intellectual climate in the early nineteenth century, Froebel construed ultimate reality as spiritual rather than physical. All that existed was based on ideational prototypes or concepts in the divine absolute mind. According to idealist metaphysics, all ideas were related to and interconnected with each other and were encompassed in the great all-inclusive idea that was God. All creatures were related to each other in a great chain of being, a universal unity. In educating children, he asserted, the principle of interconnectedness was to be followed. Nothing should be allowed to remain in isolation. In the kindergarten, children were to learn they were members of a great, universal, spiritual community. Froebel saw no conflict between the individual and group, or between individual needs and differences and a universal theory of human development. Each individual is active and autonomous but also associated spiritually with every other person and creature.

For Froebel, child growth and development was essentially based on the doctrine of preformation, the unfolding of that which was already latently present. All the child would become as a man or woman was already present at birth. Using an analogy from the plant world, Froebel reasoned that as a seed contains the roots, stalk, leaves, and blossoms of the mature plant, so the human embryo possesses all that the adult person will become. Just as the seed requires a garden with proper soil, moisture, light, and nutrients to grow in the right direction, so the child needs a special educative environment for growth—the kindergarten. Just as the plant needs the cultivation of a skilled gardener, children need the care of a loving and kindly teacher.

Froebel's kindergarten was a specially prepared educational environment in which children could grow and develop. Similar to Pestalozzi, Froebel used the image of an idealized loving mother for his model of the kindergarten teacher.

Teaching was like a religious vocation in which the kindergarten teacher cooperated with God and nature in facilitating the child's growth and development. Kindergarten teachers were to be quiet observers of children's lives, games, play, and activities. Froebel advised teachers to watch children at play and then base learning on their observations.

In his educational philosophy, Froebel focused primarily on play. Reflecting the symbolism of his mystical idealism, Froebel saw play as the activity by which children expressed their innermost thoughts, needs, and desires in external actions. Froebel's exultation of play contrasted with the view of many traditional nineteenth-century educators who regarded play as a childish diversion from the important matters of life. Froebel, however, saw play as an important part of the design for living. Its nonserious mode permitted children to act on their thoughts without the consequences that work entailed.[13]

Froebel regarded play as a means of cultural recapitulation, imitation of adult activities, and socialization. Froebel believed that the human race, in its collective history, had experienced major epochs of cultural development. In Froebel's theory of cultural recapitulation, each individual human being repeated the general cultural epoch in his or her own personal growth and development. Although the human race had taken centuries to go through these cultural epochs, the individual did so in a much more limited time span of a few years. Children's play provided the means of living through and experiencing the cultural recapitulation process. For example, children enjoy drawing and often sketch pictures on walls. Their drawings are simple and primitive and resemble those of the ancient cave dwellers.

In play, children imitate adult social and economic activities. Froebel believed that children should be encouraged to act out in play such activities as cleaning rooms, serving food, and gardening, which were their means of expressing and acting on their perceptions of adult work.

Play also facilitated children's socialization. Through the kindergarten's activities, each individual child was led into the larger social milieu of group life. Froebel's kindergarten was designed to encourage children to play and interact with other children under the guidance of a loving teacher. Socialization, as a part of play, held a broad symbolic meaning for Froebel. In his idealist conception of reality, the world and its beings were constituents in a great and all-encompassing spiritual community.

A unique feature of Froebel's kindergarten curriculum was the series of gifts and occupations that he developed as teaching and learning materials. The gifts were objects that represented what Froebel defined as fundamental forms. In their concrete appearance, the gifts stimulated the child's senses. Importantly, they also conveyed a symbolic meaning that Froebel believed awakened the child's power of conceptualization. For example, the colored balls, which constituted Froebel's first gift, would be touched and played with. However, the balls conveyed the concept of the sphere, the geometrical form of the circle, an unbroken unity.[14] Froebel attached great symbolic meaning to the sphere. For example, the earth, the sun, the moon, and other planets were spheres. In the kindergarten, a large number of activities and games were played with the balls. Many kindergartens featured a large circle that was painted on the floor. Children would join hands around the circle and move in one direction, then the next. The symbolism of this activity was that it represented the unity of all human beings. The balls, like the other gifts, followed a carefully arranged sequence, which began with the simple undifferentiated sphere or circle and moved to more complex forms.

Each gift led the child to the next in the series. In the order of the sequence in which they were to be introduced to children, the gifts were as follows: (1) 6 soft colored balls; (2) a wooden sphere, cube, and cylinder; (3) a large wooden cube subdivided into 8 smaller cubes; (4) a large wooden cube subdivided into 8 oblong blocks; (5) a large wooden cube subdivided into 21 whole, 6 half, and 12 quarter cubes; (6) a large wooden cube subdivided into 18 whole oblongs; (7) quadrangular and triangular tablets used to arrange figures; (8) sticks for outlining figures; and (9) whole and half wire rings for outlining figures.

The rest of the gifts were materials to be used for drawing, perforating, embroidering, paper cutting, weaving or braiding, paper folding, modeling, and interlacing.[15] Following the idealist predilection for synthesis of opposites, the cylinders represented the integration or fusion of the sphere and the cube. The various cubes and their subdivisions were building blocks that illustrated the relationships between the whole and the part. Children could use them to create geometrical designs or construct buildings. They could use the sticks and rings to trace designs on paper. This activity exercised the small muscles of the hand, developed coordination between hand and eye, and was a first step toward the skill of writing.

In addition to the gifts, the occupations were materials that could be used in making and constructing activities. Among the occupations were paper, pencils, wood, sand, clay, straw, sticks, and other items that children could use to create a picture, an object, or some product.

The kindergarten's activities included games, songs, and stories that involved children in social activities, exercised their bodies, and trained their powers of observation. Froebel prepared a collection of kindergarten songs, the *Mutter-und-Kose-Lieder, Mother's Songs, Games, and Stories,* published in 1843.[16]

Of the various educational innovations of the nineteenth and twentieth centuries, the kindergarten, which has been diffused throughout the world, has been among the most successful. Today, the kindergarten is a part of almost all public school systems in the United States. It can also be found in many other countries.

Froebel's enduring contribution to education was a version of childhood that exalted the dignity of children. For him, childhood had a spiritual quality that needed to be recognized and nurtured. He emphasized play at a time when children were often exploited as laborers and play was disdainfully rejected as a form of idleness.

Today, kindergarten teachers continue to emphasize Froebel's ideas of developing the social side of a child's nature and a sense of readiness for learning.

THE PRIMARY SOURCES

In the first selection from his *Autobiography,* Froebel, recalling his unhappy childhood, writes of his sensitive nature, his fear of punishment, and his attempt to hide his true feelings. In the second selection, he discusses the educational importance of following nature but endows a natural education with a symbolic and dual meaning. There is the external appearance of nature, but underlying the external is the important spiritual dimension. Through activity, children deal with the external, but their very activity is a consequence to give expression to their internal spirituality.

The second selection from Chapter 1 of Froebel's *The Education of Man* is entitled the "Groundwork of the Whole." It reveals the strong mystical idealism that provided the philosophical foundation of his kindergarten. His prose, which is highly abstract and often repetitive, nevertheless conveys his pervasive spirituality. In the selection, Froebel advises his readers that all things, all creation, comes from God and is endowed with a spiritual force. In the case of the human being, education is to draw out and externalize the inner spiritual core.

The third selection, "The Mother in Unity with Her Child," is from *Mother-Play and Nursery Song*. It expresses, in verse, Froebel's powerful belief in the importance of a mother's love for her child as the foundation of emotional security. It should be noted that the book was edited by Elizabeth P. Peabody, who popularized the kindergarten in the United States.

FOCUSING QUESTIONS

As you read the selections, you might wish to consider the following questions:

1. Are reminiscences like that of Froebel in his *Autobiography* useful in creating a personal philosophy of education? What remembrances of childhood have shaped your philosophy of education?

2. In the selection in Chapter 8, Rousseau emphasized nature and the importance of a natural education. Compare and contrast Rousseau's and Froebel's ideas on the importance of nature in education.

3. Identify examples of philosophical idealism in Froebel's "Groundwork of the Whole." Is Froebel's emphasis on the spiritual nature of childhood relevant to contemporary early childhood education? Explain your answer.

4. Consider Froebel's emphasis on the unity of the mother with her child. Is his emphasis relevant to contemporary early childhood education? Explain your answer.

FROM *AUTOBIOGRAPHY OF FRIEDRICH FROEBEL*

This thought, which, as often as it comes into my mind, carries me back even now to the scenes and surroundings of my boyhood, may have been not improbably amongst the last mental impressions of this period, and it may fitly close, therefore, the narrative of my mental development at this age. It became, later, the point whereon my whole life hinged.

From what I have said of my boyish inner life, it might be assumed that my outer life was a happy and

From *Autobiography of Friedrich Froebel*. Translated by Emilie Michaelis and H. Keatley Moore. Syracuse, N.Y.: C. W. Bardeen, Publishers, 1889, 14–15, 76–77.

peaceful one. Such an assumption would, however, not be correct. It seems as if it had always been my fate to represent and combine the hardest and sharpest contrasts. My outer life was really in complete contrast with my inner. I had grown up without a mother; my physical education had been neglected, and in consequence I had acquired many a bad habit. I always liked to be doing something or another, but in my clumsy way I made mistakes as to choice of materials, of time, and of place, and thus often incurred the severe displeasure of my parents. I felt this, being of a sensitive disposition, more keenly and more persistently than my parents; the more so as I felt myself generally to blame in form rather than in substance, and in my inmost heart I could see there was a point of view from whence my conduct would seem, in substance at all events, not altogether wrong, still less blameworthy. The motives assigned to my actions were not those which actuated me, so far as I could tell; and the consciousness of being misjudged made me really what I had been believed to be before, a thoroughly naughty boy. Out of fear of punishment I hid even the most harmless actions, and when I was questioned I made untruthful answers.

In short, I was set down as wicked, and my father, who had not always time to investigate the justice of the accusations against me, remembered only the facts as they were represented to him. My neglected childhood called forth the ridicule of others; when playing with my step-brother, I was always, according to my mother, the cause of anything that went wrong. As the mind of my parents turned more and more away from me, so on my side my life became more and more separated from theirs; and I was abandoned to the society of people who, if my disposition had not been so thoroughly healthy, might have injured me even more than they did. I longed to escape from this unhappy state of things; and I considered my elder brothers fortunate in being all of them away from home. Just at this melancholy time came home my eldest brother. He appeared to me as an angel of deliverance, for he recognised amidst my many faults my better nature, and protected me against ill-treatment. He went away again after a short stay; but I felt that my soul was linked to his, thenceforth, down to its inmost depths; and indeed, after his death, this love of mine for him turned the whole course of my life. . . .

Man is compelled not only to recognise Nature in her manifold forms and appearances, but also to understand her in the unity of her inner working, of her effective force. Therefore he himself follows Nature's methods in the course of his own development and culture, and in his games he imitates Nature at her work of creation. The earliest natural formations, the fixed forms of crystals, seem as if driven together by some secret power external to themselves; and the boy in his first games gladly imitates these first activities of nature, so that by the one he may learn to comprehend the other. Does not the boy take pleasure in building, and what else are the earliest fixed forms of Nature but built-up forms? However, this indication that a higher meaning underlies the occupation and games which children choose out for themselves must for the present suffice. And since these spontaneous activities of children have not yet been thoroughly thought out from a high point of view, and have not yet been regarded from what I might almost call their cosmical and anthropological side, we may from day to day expect some philosopher to write a comprehensive and important book about them. From the love, the attention, the continued interest and the cheerfulness with which these occupations are plied by children other important considerations also arise, of quite a different character.

A boy's game necessarily brings him into some wider or fuller relationship, into relationship with some more elevated group of ideas. Is he building a house?—he builds it so that he may dwell in it like grown-up people do, and have just such another cupboard, and so forth, as they have, and be able to give people things out of it just as they do. And one must always take care of this: that the child who receives a present shall not have his nature cramped and stunted thereby; according to the measure of how much he receives, so much must he be able to give way. In fact, this is a necessity for a simple-hearted child. Happy is that little one who understands how to satisfy this need of his nature, to give by producing various gifts of his own creation! As a perfect child of humanity, a boy ought to desire to enjoy and to bestow to the very utmost, for he dimly feels already that he belongs to the whole, to the universal, to the comprehensive in Nature, and it is as part of this that he lives; therefore, as such would he accordingly be considered and so treated. When he has felt this, the most important means of development available for a human being at this stage has been discovered. With a well-disposed child at such a time nothing has any value except as it may serve for a common possession, for a bond of union between him and his beloved ones. This aspect of the child's character must be carefully noticed by parents and by teachers, and used by them as a means of awakening and developing the active and presentative side of his nature; wherefore none, not even the simplest gifts from a child, should ever be suffered to be neglected.

To sketch my first attempt as an educator in one phrase, I sought with all my powers to give my pupils the best possible instruction, and the best possible training and culture, but I was unable to fulfill my intentions, to attain my end, in the position I then occupied, and with the degree of culture to which I had myself attained.

FROM FRIEDRICH FROEBEL'S *THE EDUCATION OF MAN*

CHAPTER ONE

"GROUNDWORK OF THE WHOLE"

1. In all things there lives and reigns an eternal law. To him whose mind, through disposition and faith, is filled, penetrated, and quickened with the necessity that this can not possibly be otherwise, as well as to him whose clear, calm mental vision beholds the inner in the outer and through the outer, and sees the outer proceeding with logical necessity from the essence of the inner, this law has been and is enounced with equal clearness and distinctness in nature (the external), in the spirit (the internal), and in life which unites the two. This all-controlling law is necessarily based on an all-prevading, energetic, living, self-conscious, and hence eternal Unity. This fact, as well as the Unity itself, is again vividly recognized, either through faith or through insight, with equal clearness and comprehensiveness; therefore, a quietly observant human mind, a thoughtful, clear human intellect, has never failed, and will never fail, to recognize this Unity.

   This Unity is God. All things have come from the Divine Unity, from God, and have their origin in the Divine Unity, in God alone. God is the sole source of all things. In all things there lives and reigns the Divine Unity, God. All things live and have their being in and through the Divine Unity, in and through God. All things are only through the divine effluence that lives in them. The divine effluence that lives in each thing is the essence of each thing.

2. It is the destiny and life-work of all things to unfold their essence, hence their divine being, and, therefore, the Divine Unity itself—to reveal God in their external and transient being. It is the special destiny and life-work of man, as an intelligent and rational being, to become fully, vividly, and clearly conscious of his essence, of the divine effluence in him, and, therefore, of God; to become fully, vividly, and clearly conscious of his destiny and life-work; and to accomplish this, to render it (his essence) active, to reveal it in his own life with self-determination and freedom.

   Education consists in leading man, as a thinking, intelligent being, growing into self-consciousness, to a pure and unsullied, conscious and free representation of the inner law of Divine Unity, and in teaching him ways and means thereto.

3. The knowledge of that eternal law, the insight into its origin, into its essence, into the totality, the connection, and intensity of its effects, the knowledge of life in its totality, constitute *science, the science of life;* and, referred by the self-conscious, thinking, intelligent being to representation and practice through and in himself, this becomes *science of education.*

   The system of directions, derived from the knowledge and study of that law, to guide thinking, intelligent beings in the apprehension of their life-work and in the accomplishment of their destiny, is *the theory of education.*

   The self-active application of this knowledge in the direct development and cultivation of rational beings toward the attainment of their destiny, is *the practice of education.*

   The object of education is the realization of a faithful, pure, inviolate, and hence holy life.

   Knowledge and application, consciousness and realization in life, united in the service of a faithful, pure, holy life, constitute the *wisdom of life,* pure wisdom.

4. *To be wise is the highest aim of man,* is the most exalted achievement of human self-determination.

   To educate one's self and others, with consciousness, freedom, and self-determi-

From Friedrich Froebel's *The Education of Man.* Translated by W. N. Hailmann. New York: Appleton and Co., 1887, 1–10.

nation, is a twofold achievement of wisdom: it *began* with the first appearance of man upon the earth; it *was manifest* with the first appearance of full self-consciousness in man; it *begins now* to proclaim itself as a necessary, universal requirement of humanity, and to be heard and heeded as such. With this achievement man enters upon the path which alone leads to life; which surely tends to the fulfillment of the inner, and thereby also to the fulfillment of the outer, requirement of humanity; which, through a faithful, pure, holy life, attains beatitude.

5. By education, then, the divine essence of man should be unfolded, brought out, lifted into consciousness, and man himself raised into free, conscious obedience to the divine principle that lives in him, and to a free representation of this principle in his life.

Education, in instruction, should lead man to see and know the divine, spirtual, and eternal principle which animates surrounding nature, constitutes the essence of nature, and is permanently manifested in nature; and, in living reciprocity and united with training, it should express and demonstrate the fact that the same law rules both (the divine principle and nature), as it does nature and man.

Education as a whole, by means of instruction and training, should bring to man's consciousness, and render efficient in his life, the fact that man and nature proceed from God and are conditioned by him—that both have their being in God.

Education should lead and guide man to clearness concerning himself and in himself, to peace with nature, and to unity with God; hence it should lift him to a knowledge of himself and of mankind, to a knowledge of God and of nature, and to the pure and holy life to which such knowledge leads.

6. In all these requirements, however, education is based on considerations of the innermost.

The inner essence of things is recognized by the innermost spirit (of man) in the outer and through outward manifestations. The inner being, the spirit, the divine essence of things and of man, is known by its outward manifestations. In accordance with this, all education, all instruction and training, all life as a free growth, start from the outer manifestations of man and things, and proceeding from the outer, act upon the inner, and form its judgments concerning the inner. Nevertheless, education should not draw its inferences concerning the inner from the outer directly, for it lies in the nature of things that always in some relation inferences should be drawn inversely. Thus, the diversity and multiplicity in nature do not warrant the inference of multiplicity in the ultimate cause—a multiplicity of gods—nor does the unity of God warrant the inference of finality in nature; but, in both cases, the inference lies conversely from the diversity in nature to the oneness of its ultimate cause, and from the unity of God to an eternally progressing diversity in natural developments.

The failure to apply this truth, or rather the continual sinning against it, the drawing of direct inferences concerning the inner life of childhood and youth from certain external manifestations of life, is the chief cause of antagonism and contention, of the frequent mistakes in life and education. This furnishes constant occasion for unnumerable false judgments concerning the motives of the young, for numberless failures in the education of children, for endless misunderstanding between parent and child, for so much needless complaint and unseemly arraignment of children, for so many unreasonable demands made upon them. Therefore, this truth, in its application to parents, educators, and teachers, is of such great importance that they should strive to render themselves familiar with its application in its smallest details. This would bring into the relations between parents and children, pupils and educators, teacher and taught, a clearness, a constancy, a serenity which are now sought in vain: for the child that seems good outwardly often is not good inwardly, i.e., does not desire the good spontaneously, or from love, respect, and appreciation; similarly, the outwardly rough, stubborn, self-willed child that seems outwardly not good, frequently is filled with the liveliest, most eager, strongest desire for spontaneous goodness in his actions; and the apparently inattentive boy frequently follows a certain fixed line of thought that withholds his attention from all external things.

7. Therefore, education in instruction and training, originally and in its first principles should necessarily be *passive,* following (only guarding and protecting), not *prescriptive, categorical, interfering. . . .*

21. This feeling of community, first uniting the child with mother, father, brothers, and sisters, and resting on a higher spiritual unity, to which, later on, is added the unmistakable discovery that father, mother, brothers, sisters, human beings in general, feel and know themselves to be in community and unity with a higher principle—with humanity, with God— this feeling of community is the very first germ, the very first beginning of all true religious spirit, of all genuine yearning for unhindered unification with the Eternal, with God. Genuine and true, living religion, reliable in danger and struggles, in times of oppression and need, in joy and pleasure, must come to man in his infancy; for the Divine Spirit that lives and is manifest in the finite, in man, has an early though dim feeling of its divine origin; and this vague sentiment, this exceedingly misty feeling, should be fostered, strengthened, nurtured, and, later on, raised into full consciousness, into clear apprehension.

It is, therefore, not only a touching sight for the quiet and unseen observer, but productive of eternal blessings for the child, when the mother lays the sleeping infant upon his couch with an intensely loving, soulful look to their heavenly Father, praying him for fatherly protection and loving care.

It is not only touching and greatly pleasing, but highly important and full of blessings for the whole present and later life of the child, when the mother, with a look full of joy and gratitude toward the heavenly Father, and thanking him for rest and new vigor, lifts from his couch the awakened child, radiant with joyous smiles; nay, for the whole time of the related life between child and mother this exerts the happiest influence. Therefore, the true mother is loath to let another put the sleeping child to bed, or to take from it the awakened child.

The child thus cared for by his mother is well-conditioned in a human, earthly, and heavenly point of view. Prayer gives peace; through God man rests in God, the beginning and end of all created things.

If father and mother would give to their children, as the choicest portion for life, this never-failing hold, this ever-steady point of support, parent and child must ever be in intimate inner and outer unity, when in prayer—in the silent chamber or in open nature—they feel and acknowledge themselves to be in union with their God and Father. Let no one say, "The children will not understand it," for thereby he deprives them of their greatest good. If only they are not already degenerate, if only they are not already too much estranged from themselves and their parents, they understand it, and will understand it: they understand it not through and in the thought, but through and in the heart. Religious spirit, a fervid life in God and with God, in all conditions and circumstances of life and of the human mind, will hardly, in later years, rise to full vigorous life, if it has not grown up with man from his infancy. On the other hand, a religious spirit thus fostered and nursed (from early infancy) will rise supreme in all storms and dangers of life. This is the fruit of earlier and earliest religious example on the part of the parents, even when the child does not seem to notice it or to understand it. Indeed, this is the case with all living parental example.

FROM FRIEDRICH FROEBEL'S *MOTHER-PLAY AND NURSERY SONGS*

INTRODUCTORY SONG.

THE MOTHER IN UNITY WITH HER CHILD.

Oh child of my heart, so fair and so dear!
All softly the light of knowledge shines here.
What glows now so warm, thy infant form flushing,
And kindles my spirit, like spring's early blushing?
  Pure FAITH it is, enthroned on thy brow,
  That thou a mother's shelter shall know.
  Pure LOVE it is, in thy laughing eyes,
  That light to the mother's soul supplies:
  Bright HOPE it is that throbs in thy breast,
  And makes for the mother life's fountain blessed.
Oh, come then, my darling! each other viewing,
We'll live in springs of life renewing.
Whatever the heart of the child requireth,
The mother's heart alike desireth;
And surely thy faith, thy hope, thy love,
Shall cherished be by spirits above!
Through hoping, believing, and loving 'tis given
To feel the blessings and joys of heaven.

The corresponding sheet music is shown on the next page.

From Friedrich Froebel's *Mother-Play and Nursery Songs*. Edited by Elizabeth P. Peabody and translated by Fannie E. Dwight and Josephine Jarvis. Boston: Lothrop, Lee, and Shepard Co., 1878, 9.

Oh! child of my heart. so fair and so

dear! All soft - ly the light of knowl - edge shines here,

What glows now so warm, thy in - fant form flush - ing? And

SUGGESTIONS FOR FURTHER READING

Blow, Susan. *The Songs and Music of Froebel's Mother Play*. New York: D. Appleton, 1895.

Brosterman, Norman. *Inventing Kindergarten*. New York: Harry N. Abrams, 1997.

Downs, Robert B. *Friedrich Froebel*. Boston: Twayne Publishers, 1978.

Froebel, Friedrich. *Autobiography*. Translated by Emilie Michaelis and H. Keatley Moore. Syracuse, N.Y.: C. W. Bardeen Publishers, 1889.

———.*The Education of Man*. Translated by W. H. Hailman. New York: D. Appleton Sons, 1896.

———.*Mother's Songs, Games, and Stories*. Translated by Francis and Emily Lord. London: W. Rice, 1910.

Hayward, Frank H. *The Educational Ideas of Pestalozzi and Froebel*. Westport, Conn.: Greenwood Press, 1979.

Headley, Neith. *Education in the Kindergarten*. New York: American Book Co., 1966.

Lawrence, Evelyn, ed. *Froebel and English Education*. New York: Schocken Books, 1969.

Lilley, Irene M. *Friedrich Froebel: A Selection from His Writings*. Cambridge: Cambridge University Press, 1967.

Ross, Elizabeth D. *The Kindergarten Crusade: The Establishment of Preschool Education in the United States*. Athens: Ohio University Press, 1976.

Vandewalker, Nina C. *The Kindergarten in American Education*. New York: Arno Press and New York Times, 1971.

Weber, Evelyn. *The Kindergarten: Its Encounter with Educational Thought in America*. New York: Teachers College Press, Columbia University, 1969.

NOTES

1. For his autobiography, see Friedrich Froebel, *Autobiography,* translated by Emilie Michaelis and H. Keatley Moore (Syracuse, N.Y.: C. W. Bardeen Publishers, 1889); a useful biography is Robert B. Downs, *Friedrich Froebel* (Boston: Twayne Publishers, 1978).

2. Froebel, 3–4.

3. Downs, 11–12.

4. Froebel, 17–21.

5. Froebel, 24.

6. Downs, 16–17.

7. Downs, 24–26.

8. John C. Greene and John G. Burke, *The Science of Minerals in the Age of Jefferson, Transactions of the American Philosophical Society,* 68 (Philadelphia: American Philosophical Society, 1978), 16–19.

9. Norman Brosterman, *Inventing Kindergarten* (New York: Harry N. Abrams, 1997), 22–25.

10. Froebel, *Autobiography,* 123.

11. Downs, 34–39.

12. Friedrich Froebel, *The Education of Man,* translated by W. H. Hailman (New York: D. Appleton Sons, 1896).

13. Gerald L. Gutek, *A History of the Western Educational Experience* (Prospects Heights, Ill.: Waveland Press, 1995), 255–69.

14. Froebel's gifts are discussed and beautifully illustrated in Norman Brosterman, *Inventing Kindergarten* (New York: Harry N. Abrams, 1997), 40–89.

15. Downs, 47–50.

16. Friedrich Froebel, *Mother's Songs, Games, and Stores,* translated by Francis and Emily Lord (London: W. Rice, 1910).

JOHN STUART MILL: PROPONENT OF LIBERALISM

BIOGRAPHICAL SKETCH

John Stuart Mill (1806–1873) is significant in the history and philosophy of education as a decided proponent of liberalism and intellectual and academic freedom.[1] He was born on May 20, 1806, in Pentonville, Yorkshire, England, the eldest son of James Mill (1773–1836), a friend and associate of Jeremy Bentham, the founder of Utilitarianism. Bentham and James Mill believed that individual and social reform should be based on the principle of utility—calculating what would bring about the greatest happiness for the greatest number of people. James Mill, a committed Benthamite, decided that he, guided by Bentham, would tutor his son, John Stuart, and educate him to become a future voice for Utilitarianism.

James Mill was a commanding figure in his family. His wife, Harriet Burrow, apparently a quiet and unassertive woman, did not seem to have much of a role in educating her son, John Stuart, the eldest of nine children. John Stuart later remarked that had his mother exercised a greater presence, she might have introduced a more emotional character to his early education to balance his father's rather cold rationalism.[2]

When John Stuart was 3, James Mill moved his family next door to Bentham's home in Westminster so that the Utilitarian philosopher could directly supervise John Stuart's education. James Mill prepared his son for what would be a demanding education by reading classical texts to him when the boy was very young.

James Mill developed a rigorous timetable that scheduled John Stuart's lessons and activities. Mill and Bentham determined John Stuart would study Greek and Latin languages and literature, mathematics, the physical and natural sciences with an emphasis on chemistry, history, and selected literature. Since the senior Mill and Bentham saw little usefulness, or utility, in art, music, and poetry, these areas were neglected. After he had completed his general studies, John Stuart would practice logic and analyze philosophy.

Each day followed a set routine. John Stuart Mill arose at six every morning and studied 3 hours before a short break for breakfast. This was followed by 5 hours of directed study in which he was expected to make applications from his lessons to problems posed by his father. After dinner came 3 more hours of study. John Stuart's physical exercise consisted of a daily walk with his father during which they discussed an intellectual subject.

In his *Autobiography,* John Stuart Mill was emotionally ambivalent about his education and his father. He considered his father a great philosophical mentor who developed his interest and skill in logic. However, he also felt that much of their relationship was so intellectual that there was little love or emotion present. There was little opportunity for or awareness of the play and recreational aspects of life. He most likely was a lonely child, lacking opportunities for association and play with other children, or for enjoying nature, art, or poetry. James Mill was an unbending tutor, a critic, whose method of rewarding his son's academic achievement was to assign another and more demanding lesson.

When he was 14, John Stuart Mill's education involved a study tour of France accompanied by Bentham's brother, Samuel. He now encountered the social, political, and educational philosophies that were popular on the European continent. This sojourn in France gave him a larger and broader perspective on life.

In 1823, James Mill, who was senior director of correspondence with the East India Company, a stock company that controlled large sectors of India, arranged a position for his son. John Stuart Mill, who was employed by the East India Company for the next 35 years, eventually was promoted to the prestigious position of examiner of correspondence with the native states. As had been true with the father, the East India Company provided him with an income but still allowed him enough time to pursue his true interest in philosophical study and writing.

As a young man, John Stuart Mill appeared to be the person his father and Bentham had so carefully trained. Actively involved in the Utilitarian cause, he began working in 1824 with Bentham and his father in editing *The Westminster Review,* the official Utilitarian journal. Inwardly, however, despite his efforts to repress them, John Stuart Mill was experiencing feelings of anxiety and depression. In 1826, at age 20, Mill experienced psychological depression manifested by symptoms of physical exhaustion and loss of interest in philosophy and reform. Though able to work at the East India Company, he could not bring himself to write and edit. Plagued by severe self-doubts, he saw no purpose in his life.

Mill's severe psychological crisis was actually a turning point in his life. In struggling to find his way out of his depression, Mill began to let his feelings come to the surface. He realized that he had emotions as well as intellect. Though still valuing logic, he also enjoyed music and art, the aesthetic experiences that he had not had as a child.

While Utilitarianism remained his philosophical foundation, John Stuart Mill began to humanize his philosophy. He gave the pursuit of happiness a broader meaning than Bentham's philosophical accounting system of adding and subtracting the amounts of pain and pleasure. Mill saw human happiness as an integrated whole—a blending of the intellectual, emotional, cognitive, and affective dimensions of life.

While trying to overcome his psychological depression, Mill met Harriet Taylor, who would become his confidante, companion, and later his wife. When Mill first met her, Harriet was in her early twenties, the wife of John Taylor and the mother of two children. He was strongly attracted to Harriet, who was committed to women's rights, and she, in turn, admired the young intellectual. John Taylor, Harriet's husband, did not oppose their association, which appeared to be a platonic relationship. In 1851, 2 years after John Taylor's death, John Stuart Mill and

Harriet Taylor were married. Their marriage of 7 years was intensely emotional as well as intellectual. With Harriet, John Stuart Mill was able to find the emotional side of his personality that had long been repressed. Intellectually and politically, Harriet impressed on Mill the cause of women's rights and equality. During his service in the British House of Commons, he introduced a bill for women's suffrage, which was defeated. In 1858, Harriet died and was buried near Avignon in southern France. Mill built a small cottage near the cemetery where she was buried; there he would contemplate and write.[5]

The rest of Mill's life was spent in philosophical writing. His *System of Logic* was published in 1843, followed by *Some Questions of Political Economy,* in 1844, and *Principles of Political Economy,* in 1848. His highly influential *On Liberty,* in 1859, expressed Mill's devotion to individual liberty and freedom of expression. His *Utilitarianism,* in 1863, revised Benthamism into a more expansive and generous philosophical position. Challenging the idea that human happiness is strictly measurable and quantitative, Mill saw it in much more complex and qualitative terms.

Mill served one term in the House of Commons, from 1865 to 1868, as the member from Westminster. He supported broadening suffrage by removing property restrictions and giving women the right to vote. However, his efforts did not succeed.

In 1867, Mill's intellectual acclaim led to his appointment as rector of St. Andrews University in Scotland. In his Inaugural Address at St. Andrews, Mill presented his ideas on higher education. He published *The Subjection of Women,* in 1869. Mill died on May 7, 1873, at Avignon and was buried next to the grave of his beloved Harriet.

OVERVIEW OF IDEAS ON EDUCATION

John Stuart Mill was recognized at the end of his life as the foremost philosopher of liberalism. Though committed to Bentham's premise that social policy should aim at the "greatest happiness for the greatest number," he revised Utilitarianism and placed the goal of human happiness in a larger qualitative dimension. Like Bentham and his father, Mill continued to uphold the Utilitarian principle that government had a limited role in bringing about social reform. Mill revised Bentham's premise that reform could be based on rational calculations that estimated the consequences of action in the amount of pleasure and pain generated.

Mill's liberalism emphasized personal freedom and the free expression of ideas as individual rights and as a necessity for human progress. In *On Liberty,* Mill unequivocally states that "the only purpose for which power can be rightfully exercised over any member of a civilized community, against his will, is to prevent harm to others. His own good, either physical or moral, is not a sufficient warrant."[4] Mill asserted the following guiding principles:

1. The individual is interested in promoting his or her own welfare.
2. An individual's welfare lies in promoting the public good.
3. Innovative and creative ideas promoting individual and social progress are often generated by individuals or by members of minorities.
4. In an open society, alternative ideas can be expressed, can compete with each other, and can result in greater freedom and progress.

Mill based his dedication to individual liberty on his belief that society needed critically minded alternative thinkers who challenged the conformism of the status quo. In a truly free society, new and often unpopular ideas could be expressed and tested in a climate of open inquiry.

True to his liberal origins, Mill often gave freedom a negative connotation in that it meant freedom from a coercive government or church or a stifling mass opinion. There should be no restrictions from these authorities on freedom of speech, press, and assembly. In education, teachers should be free to teach and students free to learn. Schooling should not be used to instill conformism in the young but rather be used to cultivate and exercise critical thinking.

Mill's liberal political philosophy was committed to upholding elected representative government in which legislators were responsible to those who had elected them. Civil liberties were best secured and protected by institutions of representative self-government. The proper functioning of representative institutions required that the people have a civic education that encouraged them to make their own decisions on the issues of the day.

Wary of any limitation on freedom of thought and inquiry, Mill was concerned about the danger posed by the "tyranny of the majority," the tendency for a mass public opinion to create a standardized or average judgment on the minority. He would have especially feared the power of the modern opinion poll to set standards that generate a conformity, which, appearing to be popularly based, limits ideas, opinions, and tastes that deviate from the average.

Another fear that Mill had about the future was that representative institutions such as the British House of Commons or the United States Congress might become places where special interest groups influenced legislation rather than the individuals who composed society. Mill looked to education, especially the education of a disinterested group of citizens, to defuse the power of special interests. A "disinterested person" was not uninterested in public affairs but was free of the desire for personal profit and unprejudiced. "Disinterestedness" meant that the person had an educated perspective that made it possible to evaluate an issue objectively.

THE PRIMARY SOURCES

The selections from John Stuart Mill's *Autobiography* provide his reflections on the education he received from his father, James Mill. The rigorous tutelage, based on Jeremy Bentham's Utilitarianism, was highly philosophical. James Mill worked to sharpen his son's powers of logic. John Stuart was challenged to analyze philosophical works, identify their major premises, and examine the consistency of the arguments made. Even though John Stuart Mill would experience a severe psychological depression as a young man, he commented that the rigorous analytical training, demanded by his father, served him well in his later career as a philosopher and spokesman for reform. In particular, he believed that he learned to detect fallacious reasoning and to formulate his ideas logically and clearly.

The selections from Mill's "Inaugural Address" at the University of Saint Andrews on February 1, 1867, set forth his ideas on higher education, especially his emphasis on the need for both the humanities and the sciences in a general education. Mill also carried his ideas on liberty, especially the freedom of thought and expression, into his philosophy of education.

FOCUSING QUESTIONS

As you read the selections, you might wish to consider the following questions:

1. Describe and analyze the educational importance Mill gives to logic. Is logic an important component of education today? Should it be given importance? Explain your answer.

2. Analyze and appraise the educational and emotional relationship that existed between James Mill and his son, John Stuart. If you encountered a student like John Stuart Mill in your class, how would you react as a teacher?

3. What was Mill's opinion of the controversy between the humanities and the sciences and their place in the curriculum? Are there such debates today? What is your opinion?

4. Mill appears to endorse the principle of "the greatest good for the greatest number" and encourages students to reach their own opinion on political issues. Are these principles applicable to contemporary education?

FROM JOHN STUART MILL'S *AUTOBIOGRAPHY*

My own consciousness and experience ultimately led me to appreciate quite as highly as he did, the value of an early practical familiarity with the school logic. I know of nothing, in my education, to which I think myself more indebted for whatever capacity of thinking I have attained. The first intellectual operation in which I arrived at any proficiency, was dissecting a bad argument, and finding in what part the fallacy lay: and though whatever capacity of this sort I attained, was due to the fact that it was an intellectual exercise in which I was most perseveringly drilled by my father, yet it is also true that the school logic, and the mental habits acquired in studying it, were among the principal instruments of this drilling. I am persuaded that nothing, in modern education, tends so much, when properly used, to form exact thinkers, who attach a precise meaning to words and propositions, and are not imposed on by vague, loose, or ambiguous terms. The boasted influence of mathematical studies is nothing to it; for in mathematical processes, none of the real difficulties of correct ratiocination occur. It is also a study peculiarly adapted to an early stage in the education of philosophical students, since it does not presuppose the slow process of acquiring, by experi-

From John Stuart Mill's *Autobiography*. London: Longmans, Green, and Co., 1908, 11–12, 18–21, 27–30, 37–39, 76–77.

ence and reflection, valuable thoughts of their own. They may become capable of disentangling the intricacies of confused and self-contradictory thought, before their own thinking faculties are much advanced; a power which, for want of some such discipline, many otherwise able men altogether lack; and when they have to answer opponents, only endeavour, by such arguments as they can command, to support the opposite conclusion, scarcely even attempting to confute the reasonings of their antagonists; and, therefore, at the utmost, leaving the question, as far as it depends on argument, a balanced one. . . .

There was one cardinal point in this training, of which I have already given some indication, and which, more than anything else, was the cause of whatever good it effected. Most boys or youths who have had much knowledge drilled into them, have their mental capacities not strengthened, but overlaid by it. They are crammed with mere facts, and with the opinions or phrases of other people, and these are accepted as a substitute for the power to form opinions of their own; and thus the sons of eminent fathers, who have spared no pains in their education, so often grow up mere parroters of what they have learnt, incapable of using their minds except in the furrows traced for them. Mine, however, was not an education of cram. My father never permitted anything which I learnt to degenerate into a mere exercise of memory.

He strove to make the understanding not only go along with every step of the teaching, but, if possible, precede it. Anything which could be found out by thinking I never was told, until I had exhausted my efforts to find it out for myself. As far as I can trust my remembrance, I acquitted myself very lamely in this department; my recollection of such matters is almost wholly of failures, hardly ever of success. It is true the failures were often in things in which success, in so early a stage of my progress, was almost impossible. I remember at some time in my thirteenth year, on my happening to use the word idea, he asked me what an idea was; and expressed some displeasure at my ineffectual efforts to define the word: I recollect also his indignation at my using the common expression that something was true in theory but required correction in practice; and how, after making me vainly strive to define the word theory, he explained its meaning, and showed the fallacy of the vulgar form of speech which I had used; leaving me fully persuaded that in being unable to give a correct definition of Theory, and in speaking of it as something which might be at variance with practice, I had shown unparalleled ignorance. In this he seems, and perhaps was, very unreasonable; but I think, only in being angry at my failure. A pupil from whom nothing is ever demanded which he cannot do, never does all he can.

One of the evils most liable to attend on any sort of early proficiency, and which often fatally blights its promise, my father most anxiously guarded against. This was self-conceit. He kept me, with extreme vigilance, out of the way of hearing myself praised, or of being led to make self-flattering comparisons between myself and others. From his own intercourse with me I could derive none but a very humble opinion of myself; and the standard of comparison he always held up to me, was not what other people did, but what a man could and ought to do. He completely succeeded in preserving me from the sort of influences he so much dreaded. I was not at all aware that my attainments were anything unusual at my age. If I accidentally had my attention drawn to the fact that some other boy knew less than myself—which happened less often than might be imagined—I concluded, not that I knew much, but that he, for some reason or other, knew little, or that his knowledge was of a different kind from mine. My state of mind was not humility, but neither was it arrogance. I never thought of saying to myself, I am, or I can do, so and so. I neither estimated myself highly nor lowly: I did not estimate myself at all. If I thought anything about myself, it was that I was rather backward in my studies, since I always found myself so, in comparison with what my father expected from me. I assert this with confidence, though it was not the impression of various persons who saw me in my childhood. They, as I have since found, thought me greatly and disagreeably self-conceited; probably because I was disputatious, and did not scruple to give direct contradictions to things which I heard said. I suppose I acquired this bad habit from having been encouraged in an unusual degree to talk on matters beyond my age, and with grown persons, while I never had inculcated on me the usual respect for them. My father did not correct this ill-breeding and impertinence, probably from not being aware of it, for I was always too much in awe of him to be otherwise than extremely subdued and quiet in his presence. Yet with all this I had no notion of any superiority in myself; and well was it for me that I had not. I remember the very place in Hyde Park where, in my fourteenth year, on the eve of leaving my father's house for a long absence, he told me that I should find, as I got acquainted with new people, that I had been taught many things which youths of my age did not commonly know; and that many persons would be disposed to talk to me of this, and to compliment me upon it. What other things he said on this topic I remember very imperfectly; but he wound up by saying, that whatever I knew more than others, could not be ascribed to any merit in me, but to the very unusual advantage which had fallen to my lot, of having a father who was able to teach me, and willing to give the necessary trouble and time; that it was no matter of praise to me, if I knew more than those who had not had a similar advantage, but the deepest disgrace to me if I did not. I have a distinct remembrance, that the suggestion thus for the first time made to me, that I knew more than other youths who were considered well educated, was to me a piece of information, to which, as to all other things which my father told me, I gave implicit credence, but which did not at all impress me as a personal matter. I felt no disposition to glorify myself upon the circumstance that there were other persons who did not know what I knew; nor had I ever flattered myself that my acquirements, whatever they might be, were any merit of mine: but, now when my attention was called to the subject, I felt that what my father had said respecting my peculiar advantages was exactly the truth and common sense of the matter, and it fixed my opinion and feeling from that time forward.

It is evident that this, among many other of the purposes of my father's scheme of education, could not have been accomplished if he had not carefully kept me from having any great amount of intercourse with other boys. He was earnestly bent upon my escaping not only the corrupting influence which boys exercise over boys, but the contagion of vulgar modes of thought and feeling; and for this he was willing that I should pay the price of inferiority in the accomplishments which schoolboys in all countries chiefly cultivate. The deficiencies in my education were principally in the things which boys learn from being turned out to shift for themselves, and from being brought together in large numbers. From temperance and much walking, I grew up healthy and hardy, though not muscular; but I could do no feats of skill or physical strength, and knew none of the ordinary bodily exercises. It was not that play, or time for it, was refused me. Though no holidays were allowed, lest the habit of work should be broken, and a taste for idleness acquired, I had ample leisure in every day to amuse myself; but as I had no boy companions, and the animal need of physical activity was satisfied by walking, my amusements, which were mostly solitary, were, in general, of a quiet, if not a bookish turn, and gave little stimulus to any other kind even of mental activity than that which was already called forth by my studies: I consequently remained long, and in a less degree have always remained, inexpert in anything requiring manual dexterity; my mind, as well as my hands, did its work very lamely when it was applied, or ought to have been applied, to the practical details which, as they are the chief interest in life to the majority of men, are also the things in which whatever mental capacity they have, chiefly shows itself: I was constantly meriting reproof by inattention, in observance, and general slackness of mind in matters of daily life. My father was the extreme opposite in these particulars: his senses and mental faculties were always on the alert; he carried decision and energy of character in his whole manner and into every action of life: and this, as much as his talents, contributed to the strong impression which he always made upon those with whom he came into personal contact. But the children of energetic parents, frequently grow up unenergetic, because they lean on their parents, and the parents are energetic for them. The education which my father gave me was in itself much more fitted for training me to *know* than to *do*. Not that he was unaware of my deficiencies; both as a boy and as a youth I was incessantly smarting under his severe admonitions on the subject. There was anything but insensibility or tolerance on his part towards such

shortcomings: but, while he saved me from the demoralizing effects of school life, he made no effort to provide me with any sufficient substitute for its practicalizing influences. Whatever qualities he himself, probably, had acquired without difficulty or special training, he seems to have supposed that I ought to acquire as easily. He had not, I think, bestowed the same amount of thought and attention on this, as on most other branches of education; and here, as well in some other points of my tuition, he seems to have expected effects without causes. . . .

My father's moral convictions, wholly disseverated from religion, were very much of the character of those of the Greek philosophers; and were delivered with the force and decision which characterized all that came from him. . . .

My father's moral inculcations were at all times mainly those of the "Socratici viri"; justice, temperance (to which he gave a very extended application), veracity, perseverance, readiness to encounter pain and especially labour; regard for the public good; estimation of persons according to their merits, and of things according to their intrinsic usefulness; a life of exertion in contradiction to one of self-indulgent ease and sloth. These and other moralities he conveyed in brief sentences, uttered as occasion arose, of grave exhortation, or stern reprobation and contempt.

But though direct moral teaching does much, indirect does more; and the effect my father produced on my character, did not depend solely on what he said or did with that direct object, but also, and still more, on what manner of man he was. . . .

His standard of morals was Epicurean, inasmuch as it was utilitarian, taking as the exclusive test of right and wrong, the tendency of actions to produce pleasure or pain. But he had (and this was the Cynic element) scarcely any belief in pleasure; at least in his later years, of which alone, on this point, I can speak confidently. He was not insensible to pleasures; but he deemed very few of them worth the price which, at least in the present state of society, must be paid for them. The greater number of miscarriages in life he considered to be attributable to the overvaluing of pleasures. Accordingly, temperance, in the large sense intended by the Greek philosophers—stopping short at the point of moderation in all indulgences—was with him, as with them, almost the central point of educational precept. His inculcations of this virtue fill a large place in my childish remembrances. He thought human life a poor thing at best, after the freshness of youth and of unsatisfied curiosity had gone by. This was a topic on which he did not often speak, especially, it may be supposed, in the presence of young persons: but when he did, it was with an air of settled and profound conviction. He would sometimes say that if life were made what it might be, by good government and good education, it would be worth having: but he never spoke with anything like enthusiasm even of that possibility. He never varied in rating intellectual enjoyments above all others, even in value as pleasures, independently of their ulterior benefits. . . . For passionate emotions of all sorts, and for everything which has been said or written in exaltation of them, he professed the greatest contempt. He regarded them as a form of madness. "The intense" was with him a bye-word of scornful disapprobation. He regarded as an aberration of the moral standard of modern times, compared with that of the ancients, the great stress laid upon feeling. Feelings, as such, he considered to be no proper subjects of praise or blame. Right and wrong, good and bad, he regarded as qualities solely of conduct—of acts and omissions; there being no feeling which may not lead, and does not frequently lead, either to good or to bad actions: conscience itself, the very desire to act right, often leading people to act wrong. . . .

No one prized conscientiousness and rectitude of intention more highly, or was more incapable of valuing any person in whom he did not feel assurance of it. But he disliked people quite as much for any other deficiency, provided he thought it equally likely to make them act ill. He disliked, for instance, a fanatic in any bad cause, as much as or more than one who adopted the same cause from self-interest, because he thought him even more likely to be practically mischievous. . . .

It will be admitted, that a man of the opinions, and the character, above described, was likely to leave a strong moral impression on any mind principally formed by him, and that his moral teaching was not likely to err on the side of laxity or indulgence. The element which was chiefly deficient in his moral relation to his children was that of tenderness. I do not believe that this deficiency lay in his own nature. I believe him to have had much more feeling than he habitually showed, and much greater capacities of feeling than were ever developed. He resembled most Englishmen in being ashamed of the signs of feeling, and, by the absence of demonstration, starving the feelings themselves. If we consider further that he was in the trying position of sole teacher, and add to this that his temper was constitutionally irritable, it is impossible not to feel true pity for a father who did, and strove to do, so much for his children, who would have so valued their affection, yet who must have been constantly feeling that fear of him was drying it up at its source. This was no longer the case later in life, and with his younger children. They loved him tenderly: and if I cannot say so much of myself, I was always loyally devoted to him. As regards my own education, I hesitate to pronounce whether I was more a loser or gainer by his severity. It was not such as to prevent me from having a happy childhood. And I do not believe that boys can be induced to apply themselves with vigour, and—what is so much more difficult—perseverance, to dry and irksome studies, by the sole force of persuasion and soft words. Much must be done, and much must be learnt, by children, for which rigid discipline, and known liability to punishment, are indispensable as means. It is, no doubt, a very laudable effort, in modern teaching, to render as much as possible of what the young are required to learn, easy and interesting to them. But when this principle is pushed to the length of not requiring them to learn anything *but* what has been made easy and interesting, one of the chief objects of education is sacrificed. I rejoice in the decline of the old brutal and tyrannical system of teaching, which, however, did succeed in enforcing habits of application; but the new, as it seems to me, is training up a race of men who will be incapable of doing anything which is disagreeable to them. I do not, then, believe that fear, as an element in education, can be dispensed with; but I am sure that it ought not to be the main element; and when it predominates so much as to preclude love and confidence on the part of the child to those who should be the unreservedly trusted advisers of after years, and perhaps to seal up the fountains of frank and spontaneous communicativeness in the child's nature, it is an evil for which a large abatement must be made from the benefits, moral and intellectual, which may flow from any other part of the education. . . .

My previous education had been, in a certain sense, already a course of Benthamism. The Benthamic standard of "the greatest happiness" was that which I had always been taught to apply; . . . Yet in the first pages of Bentham it burst upon me with all the force of novelty. What thus impressed me was the chapter in which Bentham passed judgment on the common modes of reasoning in morals and legislation, deduced from phrases like "law of nature," "right reason," "the moral sense," "natural rectitude," and the like, and characterized them as dogmatism in disguise, imposing its sentiments upon others under cover of sounding expressions which convey no reason for the sentiment, but set up the sentiment as its own reason. It had not struck me before, that Bentham's principle put an end to all this. The feeling rushed upon me, that all previous moralists were superseded, and that here indeed was the commencement of a new era in thought. This impression was strengthened by the manner in which Bentham put into scientific form the application of the happiness principle to the morality of actions, by analysing the various classes and orders of their consequences. . . . Logic and the dialectics of Plato, which had formed so large a part of my previous training, had given me a strong relish for accurate classification. This taste had been strengthened and enlightened by the study of botany, on the principles of what is called the Natural Method, which I had taken up with great zeal, though only as an amusement, during my stay in France; and when I found scientific classification applied to the great and complex subject of Punishable Acts, under the guidance of the ethical principle of Pleasurable and Painful Consequences, followed out in the method of detail introduced into these subjects by Bentham, I felt taken up to an eminence from which I could survey a vast mental domain, and see stretching out into the distance intellectual results beyond all computation. As I proceeded further, there seemed to be added to this intellectual clearness, the most inspiring prospects of practical improvement in human affairs. To Bentham's general view of the construction of a body of law I was not altogether a stranger, having read with attention that admirable compendium, my father's article on Jurisprudence: but I had read it with little profit, and scarcely any interest, no doubt from its extremely general and abstract character, and also because it concerned the form more than the substance of the *corpus juris*, the logic rather than the ethics of law. But Bentham's subject was Legislation, of which Jurisprudence is only the formal part: and at every page he seemed to open a clearer and broader conception of what human opinions and institutions ought to be, how they might be made what they ought to be, and how far removed from it they now are. . . .

It gave unity to my conceptions of things. I now had opinions; a creed, a doctrine, a philosophy; in one among the best senses of the word, a religion; the inculcation and diffusion of which could be made the principal outward purpose of a life. And I had a grand conception laid before me of changes to be effected in the condition of mankind through that doctrine. . . .

From the winter of 1821, when I first read Bentham, and especially from the commencement of the *Westminster Review,* I had what might truly be called an object in life; to be a reformer of the world. My conception of my own happiness was entirely identified with this object. The personal sympathies I wished for were those of fellow labourers in this enterprise. I endeavoured to pick up as many flowers as I could by the way; but as a serious and permanent personal satisfaction to rest upon, my whole reliance was placed on this; and I was accustomed to felicitate myself on the certainty of a happy life which I enjoyed, through placing my happiness in something durable and distant, in which some progress might be always making, while it could never be exhausted by complete attainment. This did very well for several years, during which the general improvement going on in the world and the idea of myself as engaged with others in struggling to promote it, seemed enough to fill up an interesting and animated existence. But the time came when I awakened from this as from a dream. It was in the autumn of 1826. I was in a dull state of nerves, such as everybody is occasionally liable to; unsusceptible to enjoyment or pleasurable excitement; one of those moods when what is pleasure at other times, becomes insipid or indifferent; the state, I should think, in which converts to Methodism usually are, when smitten by their first "conviction of sin." In this frame of mind it occurred to me to put the question directly to myself: "Suppose that all your objects in life were realized; that all the changes in institutions and opinions which you are looking forward to, could be completely effected at this very instant: would this be a great joy and happiness to you?" And an irrepressible self-consciousness distinctly answered, "No!" At this my heart sank within me: the whole foundation on which my life was constructed fell down. All my happiness was to have been found in the continual pursuit of this end. The end had ceased to charm, and how could there ever again be any interest in the means? I seemed to have nothing left to live for.

FROM JOHN STUART MILL'S "INAUGURAL ADDRESS, UNIVERSITY OF SAINT ANDREWS, FEBRUARY 1, 1867"

Let me first say a few words on the great controversy of the present day with regard to the higher education, the difference which most broadly divides educational reformers and conservatives; the vexed question between the ancient languages, and the modern sciences and arts; whether general education should be classical—let me use a wider expression, and say literary—or scientific. A dispute as endlessly, and often as fruitlessly agitated as that old controversy which it resembles, made memorable by the names of Swift and Sir William Temple in England, and Fontenelle in France—the contest for superiority between the ancients and the moderns. This question, whether we should be taught the classics or the sciences, seems to me, I confess, very like a dispute whether painters should cultivate drawing or coloring, or, to use a more homely illustration, whether a tailor should make coats or trousers. I can only reply by the question, Why not both? Can anything deserve the name of a good education which does not include literature and science too? If there were no more to be said than that scientific education teaches us to think, and literary education to express our thoughts, do we not require both? and is not any one a poor, maimed, lopsided fragment of humanity who is deficient in either? We are not obliged to ask ourselves whether it is more important to know the languages or the sciences. Short as life is, and shorter still as we make it by the time we waste on things which are neither business, nor meditation, nor pleasure, we are not so badly off that our scholars need be ignorant of the laws and properties of the world they live in, or our scientific men destitute of poetic feeling and artistic cultivation. I am amazed at the limited conception which many educational reformers have formed to themselves of a human being's power of acquisition. The study of science, they truly say, is indispensable: our present education neglects it: there is truth in this too, though it is not all truth: and they think it impossible to find room for the studies which they desire to encourage, but by turning out, at least from general education, those which are now chiefly cultivated. How absurd, they say, that the whole of boyhood should be taken up in acquir-

ing an imperfect knowledge of two dead languages. Absurd indeed: but is the human mind's capacity to learn, measured by that of Eton and Westminster to teach? I should prefer to see these reformers pointing their attacks against the shameful inefficiency of the schools, public and private, which pretend to teach these two languages and do not. I should like to hear them denounce the wretched methods of teaching, and the criminal idleness and supineness, which waste the entire boyhood of the pupils without really giving to most of them more than a smattering, if even that, of the only kind of knowledge which is even pretended to be cared for. Let us try what conscientious and intelligent teaching can do, before we presume to decide what cannot be done. . . .

In this brief outline of a complete scientific education, I have said nothing about direct instruction in that which it is the chief of all the ends of intellectual education to qualify us for—the exercise of thought on the great interests of mankind as moral and social beings—ethics and politics, in the largest sense. These things are not, in the existing state of human knowledge, the subject of a science, generally admitted and accepted. Politics cannot be learned once for all, from a text-book, or the instructions of a master. What we require to be taught on that subject, is to be our own teachers. It is a subject on which we have no masters to follow; each must explore for himself, and exercise an independent judgment. Scientific politics do not consist in having a set of conclusions ready made, to be applied everywhere indiscriminately, but in setting the mind to work in a scientific spirit to discover in each instance the truths applicable to the given case. And this, at present, scarcely any two persons do in the same way. Education is not entitled, on this subject, to recommend any set of opinions as resting on the authority of established science. But it can supply the student with materials for his own mind, and helps to use them. It can make him acquainted with the best speculations on the subject, taken from different points of view; none of which will be found complete, while each embodies some considerations really relevant, really requiring to be taken into the account. Education may also introduce us to the principal facts which have a direct bearing on the subject, namely, the different modes or stages of civilization that have been found among mankind, and the characteristic properties of each.

From John Stuart Mill's "Inaugural Address, University of Saint Andrews, February 1, 1867," in *Dissertations and Discussions: Political, Philosophical and Historical*. IV. New York: Henry Holt and Co., 1874, 339–40, 381–82.

SUGGESTIONS FOR FURTHER READING

Bain, Alexander. *James Mill: A Biography*. London: Longmans, Green, and Co., 1882.

Burston, W. H. *James Mill on Education*. London: Cambridge University Press, 1969.

Carlisle, Janice. *John Stuart Mill and the Writing of Character*. Athens: University of Georgia Press, 1991.

Cavenagh, F. A., ed. *James and John Stuart Mill on Education*. London: Cambridge University Press, 1931.

Cohen, Marshall, ed. *The Philosophy of John Stuart Mill*. New York: The Modern Library, 1961.

Donner, Wendy. *The Liberal Self: John Stuart Mill's Moral and Political Philosophy*. Ithaca, N.Y.: Cornell University Press, 1991.

Ellery, John B. *John Stuart Mill*. New York: Twayne Publishers Inc., 1964.

Garforth, Francis W. *Educative Democracy: John Stuart Mill on Education in Society*. Oxford: Oxford University Press, 1980.

———. ed. *John Stuart Mill on Education*. New York: Teachers College Press, Columbia University, 1971.

Glassman, Peter J. *J. S. Mill: The Evolution of a Genius*. Gainesville: University of Florida Press, 1985.

Hamburger, Joseph. *John Stuart Mill on Liberty and Control*. Princeton, N.J.: Princeton University Press, 1999.

Jackson, Julius. *A Guided Tour of John Stuart Mill's Utilitarianism*. Mountain View, Calif.: Mayfield Publishing Co., 1993.

Kurer, Oskar. *John Stuart Mill: The Politics of Progress*. New York: Garland Publishing Co., 1991.

Mazlish, Bruce. *James and John Stuart Mill*. New York: Basic Books, 1975.

Mill, John Stuart. *Autobiography*. Edited by John J. Coss. New York: Columbia University Press, 1944.

———. *Essays on Equality, Law, and Education*. Edited by John M. Robson. Toronto: University of Toronto Press, 1984.

———. *On Liberty*. Edited by Alburey Castell. Wheeling, Ill.: Harlan Davidson, 1947.

———. *Utilitarianism, Liberty, and Representative-Government*. Edited by A. D. Londsay. New York: E. P. Dutton and Co., 1951.

Mill, John Stuart, and Harriet Taylor Mill. *Essays on Sex Equality*. Edited by Alice S. Rossi. Chicago: University of Chicago Press, 1970.

Ryan, Alan. *John Stuart Mill*. New York: Pantheon Books, 1970.

Strasser, Mark P. *The Moral Philosophy of John Stuart Mill: Toward Modifications of Contemporary Utilitarianism*. Wakefield, N.H.: Longwood Academic Publishers, 1991.

Thomas, William. *Mill*. Oxford: Oxford University Press, 1985.

NOTES

1. There are many editions of John Stuart Mill's *Autobiography*. For example, see John Stuart Mill, *The Autobiography of John Stuart Mill* (New York: Columbia University Press, 1944). Among biographies are Alan Ryan, *John Stuart Mill* (New York: Pantheon Books, 1970); Peter J. Glassman, *J. S. Mill: The Evolution of a Genius* (Gainesville: University of Florida Press, 1985); Richard J. Halliday, *John Stuart Mill* (London: Allen and Unwin, 1976).

2. John Stuart Mill, *Autobiography of John Stuart Mill*, edited by John J. Cross (New York: Columbia University Press, 1944), 2.

3. John Stuart Mill and Harriet Taylor Mill, *Essays on Sex Equality,* edited by Alice S. Rossi (Chicago: University of Chicago Press, 1971), 6.

4. John Stuart Mill, *On Liberty,* edited by Alburey Castell (Wheeling, Ill.: Harlan Davidson, 1947), 9–10.

16

HERBERT SPENCER: ADVOCATE OF INDIVIDUALISM, SCIENCE, AND SOCIAL DARWINISM

BIOGRAPHICAL SKETCH

Herbert Spencer (1820–1903), an eminent British sociologist, is significant as a proponent of individual competition, science in the curriculum, and social Darwinism in society. Spencer was born on April 17, 1820, in Derby, in the United Kingdom.[1] His father, William George Spencer, an educator and writer, was the author of *Inventional Geometry,* a textbook on the basic principles of geometry. Spencer's father, the dominant member of the family and a strong formative influence on Herbert, was an outspoken critic of English society and education. Advocating critical thinking, William Spencer encouraged his son to think for himself and defend his ideas by logical argument. Herbert would demonstrate these characteristics throughout his life. Spencer's mother appears to have been a rather passive person who devoted herself to caring for her family. The Spencers, who dissented from the Church of England, valued individualism of every sort.

Although destined to be a writer on education, Herbert Spencer had but a brief period of formal schooling. He was educated primarily at home by his father, a strong critic of the existing schools. In particular, William Spencer opposed their overemphasis on Greek and Latin and their neglect of science.[2] William taught his son reading, writing, and arithmetic and devoted much time to mathematics and science. Reflecting on the tutoring he received from his father, Herbert said that he knew virtually nothing of Latin, Greek, ancient history, and literature.[3] The elder Spencer passed on his educational beliefs to his son, who, in his later writing on education, would proclaim science to be the most worthwhile study.

Along with the lessons that he taught his son, William Spencer also encouraged Herbert to be a critical thinker who was willing to question the then-accepted authorities, especially the educational assumptions based on the ancient classics and philosophy. William rejected the Victorian adage that "children should be seen but not heard." He expected and encouraged Herbert to participate in adult conversations, especially those dealing with controversial issues. Thus, the boy acquired the predispositions to skepticism, criticism, and science that would become his life work.

In 1832, when Herbert was 13, William Spencer engaged his brother, the Reverend Spencer, to tutor his son. While his uncle taught him some Latin and Greek, he, too, like his brother, was more inclined to mathematics and science. Herbert especially enjoyed his studies in Euclid's geometry and trigonometry. History, literature, and languages, which the Spencers disdained as ornamental and largely a waste of time, were purposefully minimized.

Largely educated by his father and uncle, Herbert Spencer at age 17 began working as a civil engineer, a career he pursued until he was 27. Engineering suited his tendency to apply mathematics and science to practical affairs, a predilection that shaped his later thinking on education. He increasingly began to think about the larger possibilities afforded by applying mathematics and science to broader social, economic, and educational issues.

In 1842, Spencer began his career as a writer for *The Economist,* a leading British journal. A prolific author, he wrote a large number of essays, articles, and books. With his scientific background and temperament, he decided that he would create a new social science, a comprehensive sociology of knowledge. To this end, he began his monumental work, *The Synthetic Philosophy,* in 1860, a project that would occupy the next 36 years of his life.

Spencer's writings first appeared as lectures, articles, and essays, which he would then organize and edit into books. His *First Principles of a New System of Philosophy,* seeking to apply the Darwinian theory of evolution to society, analyzed the structure and function of social institutions. His *Social Statics* gave a strong endorsement to classical liberal ideas of the freedom of individuals in the laissez-faire, free enterprise market economy. His *Essays: Scientific, Political, and Speculative* proclaimed that scientific inquiry should be free from government interference. He expressed his philosophy of education in *Education: Intellectual, Moral, and Physical,* which sought to answer his famous query, What knowledge is of most worth?

Herbert Spencer, educated by both his father and himself, was not part of the educational milieu of the generally educated, cultivated English gentleman. He disdained what he regarded to be a dying breed, an archaic and obsolete residue of the past.

OVERVIEW OF IDEAS ON EDUCATION

Spencer's philosophy of education was shaped by his lifelong interest in mathematics and science and their application to society and the economy. For him, mathematics and science were the most valuable kind of knowledge. However interesting they might be as fields of human inquiry, Spencer believed that mathematics and science had immense power for industrial and technological development. However, an archaic curriculum—Latin, Greek, theology, and metaphysically oriented philosophy—in England's public schools, which were really prestigious private preparatory institutions, and the historically great universities of Oxford and Cambridge were blocking the entry of mathematics and science into education. Spencer used his logic and the power of his pen to attack the old educational order and to argue for a new, scientifically oriented curriculum.

The period when Spencer was most active as a writer was also the time when Charles Darwin proposed his theory of biological evolution in the *Origin of the*

Species by Means of Natural Selection in 1859.[4] In some ways, Spencer, asserting the doctrine of "the survival of the fittest," had anticipated the theory of evolution. Darwin's evolutionary thesis exerted a powerful influence on Spencer's social thinking. Spencer applied Darwin's hypothesis—that plants and animals had slowly evolved as a result of a process of natural selection—to society. Spencer was especially taken by Darwin's conjecture that species which were successful in surviving transmitted favorable adaptive characteristics to their offspring.

Spencer applied Darwin's evolutionary theory to society. His social Darwinism earned him a highly respected position in the United States, which was experiencing profound industrial and technological change in the second half of the nineteenth century. Spencer's social Darwinism was a handy ideological rationale for the business activities of dominant industrialists such as Andrew Carnegie and John D. Rockefeller. It was a sociological justification, a "scientific" rationale, for an expansive American capitalism.

Spencer, a proponent of unregulated individualism and competition, applied the theory of evolution to society. For him, the brightest and the best of the human race would come forward and take their positions as leaders by winning the race of life. Individual competition, unregulated by altruistic do-gooders or paternalistic government, would bring about an inevitable human progress. The kind of education that encouraged individual initiative and competition was exactly what was needed in an industrializing and modernizing society.

In Spencer's educational philosophy, a key term was "adjustment," the ability of the individual to adjust effectively and efficiently to changes in the environment. The key to efficiency was to apply mathematics and science, in an engineering mode of operations, to society, politics, the economy, and education. The curriculum that Spencer endorsed would incorporate and emphasize the scientific method for efficient adjustment.

In society and in school, it was crucial that the fittest individuals, the gifted and able, be encouraged to compete and to excel. They should not be held back by those who were slower to learn. For Spencer, ethics meant that the fittest were allowed to win. Government welfare programs in society and in school were doomed to fail in that they violated the natural order of evolution. They not only maintained the unfit but held back the progress of the gifted, the fittest, who by their inventiveness and creativity would bring about a more prosperous society and economy.

Spencer's educational rationale for a scientific curriculum appeared in "What Knowledge Is of Most Worth?" published in 1855.[5] In his interpretation of the history of education, Spencer argued that much of the curriculum was still dominated by a tradition that emphasized the Latin and Greek classics, which, once useful, had lost their relevance in a modern industrial society. Not only were the classical languages archaic residues of a now irrelevant past, but they inefficiently took the resources—time, money, and energy—that should be used for mathematics and science.

To devise a curriculum for the modern age, Spencer advised educators to determine which subjects were most useful and then devote their resources to teaching them. Spencer asked curriculum makers to find answers to the following questions:

1. What do we need to know and do to keep healthy?
2. What do we need to know and do to develop our minds?

3. What do we need to know and do to manage our economic, social, political, and educational affairs efficiently?
4. What do we need to know and do to rear and educate our children correctly and effectively?
5. What do we need to know and do to act as responsible citizens?
6. What do we need to know and do to use our natural resources efficiently and scientifically?

Spencer then identified the human activities needed to answer these questions and made them the basis for constructing a curriculum. The key human activities were those related to:

1. Self-preservation—the human body's physical health.
2. Indirect self-preservation of human life by providing the necessities of life and earning a living.
3. Rearing and educating children.
4. Maintaining proper social and political relationships.
5. Leisure time that provides enjoyment through art, literature, drama, poetry, and music.

Underlying all of these activities, Spencer affirmed the importance of science. Scientific knowledge could be applied to all the activities that sustained human life. For example, knowledge of anatomy and physiology enhanced physical health. Industrial productivity was spurred by the application of knowledge from mathematics, chemistry, botany, and zoology. While Spencer's argument for the entry of mathematics and science into the curriculum may seem unremarkable today, it was a bold proposal in the nineteenth century.

Though committed to what seemed to be the ruthlessness of social Darwinism, Spencer shared the naturalist orientation of Rousseau and Pestalozzi regarding human growth and development. Rather than relying on tradition, Spencer advised educators to base their instruction on educational psychology. According to Spencer, instruction is more effective when based on a child's direct experience in the real world rather than on the verbalism of books. He advised teachers to organize instruction according to the following principles:

1. Begin with children's direct experience.
2. Use concrete situations before moving to more abstract problems.
3. Let children learn from the natural consequences of their actions rather than from artificial rewards and punishments.
4. Avoid rote memorization.
5. Impress on children the practical application of what they are learning.

Civic education, Spencer advised, should be based on sociology rather than on history. Sociology provided information about the evolution of human societies and the role and functions of social and economic institutions. True to his social Darwinist ideology, Spencer believed that social change resulted as the fittest individuals efficiently adapted to a changing environment. A genuinely scientific civic education would convince individuals to reject the utopian delusions of do-gooders, socialists, and other misguided reformers.

Spencer gave scant attention to the humanities, art, literature, and music, which he described as fitted for leisure time activities. Science, industry, and technology were his major preoccupations.

THE PRIMARY SOURCE

In this selection from *Education, Intellectual, Moral, and Physical*, Herbert Spencer raised a question that is highly significant in constructing the curriculum—What knowledge is of most worth? He sought to answer his own question in terms of the essential human activities that people perform in their daily life. These essential activities included maintaining health; developing the mind; managing practical economic, social, political, and educational affairs; rearing and educating children; acting as civically responsible citizens; and using natural resources effectively. Spencer then organized the curriculum around the following human activities:

1. Preserving health.
2. Providing the necessities of life such as earning a living.
3. Rearing and educating children.
4. Maintaining responsible social and political relationships.
5. Miscellaneous activities such as art, literature, and drama.

FOCUSING QUESTIONS
As you read the selection, you might consider the following questions:

1. Spencer believed that too much time was spent in schools on teaching useless subjects. How did he distinguish between a useful and a useless subject? Do you agree or disagree with him? Are contemporary schools committing the same error?
2. How did Spencer go about constructing a curriculum? Do you agree or disagree with his approach? How would you construct a curriculum?
3. How would you answer the question, What knowledge is of most worth? Why did you answer the question as you did?
4. Examine Spencer's concept of what constitutes a "miscellaneous activity." Do you agree with him? Why, or why not?

FROM HERBERT SPENCER'S *EDUCATION: INTELLECTUAL, MORAL, AND PHYSICAL*

In education, then, this is the question of questions, which it is high time we discussed in some methodic way. The first in importance, though the last to be con-

Importance of the subject.

sidered, is the problem—how to decide among the conflicting claims of various subjects on our attention. Before there can be a rational *curriculum*, we must settle which things it most concerns us to know; or, to use a word of Bacon's, now unfortunately obsolete—we must determine the relative values of knowledges.

From Herbert Spencer's *Education: Intellectual, Moral, and Physical*. Syracuse, N.Y.: C. W. Bardeen Publisher, 1894, 20–26, 45–47.

To this end, a measure of value is the first requisite.
The measure of value. And happily, respecting the true measure of value, as expressed in general terms, there can be no dispute. Every one in contending for the worth of any particular order of information, does so by showing its bearing upon some part of life. In reply to the question, "Of what use is it?" the mathematician, linguist, naturalist, or philosopher, explains the way in which his learning beneficially influences action—saves from evil or secures good—conduces to happiness.

When the teacher of writing has pointed out how great an aid writing is to success in business—that is, to the obtainment of sustenance—that is, to satisfactory living—he is held to have proved his case. And when the collector of dead facts (say a numismatist) fails to make clear any appreciable effects which these facts can produce on human welfare, he is obliged to admit that they are comparatively valueless. All then, either directly or by implication, appeal to this as the ultimate test.

How to live?—that is the essential question for us. Not how to live in the mere material **The problem of right living.** sense only, but in the widest sense. The general problem which comprehends every special problem is—the right ruling of conduct in all directions under all circumstances. In what way to treat the body; in what way to treat the mind; in what way to manage our affairs; in what way to bring up a family; in what way to behave as a citizen; in what way to utilize all those sources of happiness which nature supplies—how to use all our faculties to the greatest advantage of ourselves and others—how to live completely? And this being the great thing needful for us to learn, is, by consequence, the great thing which education has to teach. *To prepare us for complete living* is the function which education has to discharge; and the only rational mode of judging of an educational course is to judge in what degree it discharges such function.

This test, never used in its entirety, but rarely even partially used, and used then in a **Importance of right selection of studies.** vague, half conscious way, has to be applied consciously, methodically, and throughout all cases. It behooves us to set before ourselves, and ever to keep clearly in view, complete living as the end to be achieved, so that in bringing up our children we may choose subjects and methods of instruction with deliberate reference to this end. Not only ought we to cease from the mere unthinking adoption of the current fashion in education, which has no better warrant than any other fashion, but we must also rise above that rude, empirical style of judging displayed by those more intelligent people who do bestow some care in overseeing the cultivation of their children's minds. It must not suffice simply to *think* that such or such information will be useful in after life, or that this kind of knowledge is of more practical value than that, but we must seek out some process of estimating their respective values, so that as far as possible we may positively *know* which are most deserving of attention.

Doubtless the task is difficult—perhaps never to be more than approximately achieved. But, considering the vastness of the interests at stake, its difficulty is no reason for pusillanimously passing it by, but rather for devoting every energy to its mastery. And if we only proceed systematically we may very soon get at results of no small moment.

Our first step must obviously be to classify, in the **Kinds of activity.** order of their importance, the leading kinds of activity which constitute human life. They may be naturally arranged into:—

1. Those activities which directly minister to self-preservation.
2. Those activities which, by securing the necessaries of life, indirectly minister to self-preservation.
3. Those activities which have for their end the rearing and discipline of offspring.
4. Those activities which are involved in the maintenance of proper social and political relations.
5. Those miscellaneous activities which fill up the leisure part of life, devoted to the gratification of the tastes and feelings.

That these stand in something like their true order of subordination it needs no long consideration to show. The actions and precautions by which, from moment to moment, we secure personal safety, must clearly take precedence of all others. Could there be a man, ignorant as an infant of all surrounding objects and movements, or how to guide himself among them, he would pretty certainly lose his life the first time he went into the street: notwithstanding any amount of learning he might have on other matters. And as entire ignorance in all other directions would be less promptly fatal than entire ignorance in this direction, it must be admitted that knowledge immediately conducive of self-preservation is of primary importance.

That next after direct self-preservation comes the indirect self-preservation which consists in acquiring the means of living, none will question. That a man's industrial functions must be considered before his parental ones, is manifest from the fact that, speaking generally, the discharge of the parental functions is made possible only by the previous discharge of the industrial ones. The power of self-maintenance necessarily preceding the power of maintaining offspring, it follows that knowledge needful for self-maintenance has stronger claims than knowledge needful for family welfare—is second in value to none save knowledge needful for immediate self-preservation.

2d, self-maintenance.

As the family comes before the State in order of time—as the bringing up of children is possible before the State exists, or when it has ceased to be, whereas the State is rendered possible only by the bringing up of children—it follows that the duties of the parent demand closer attention than those of the citizen. Or, to use a further argument—since the goodness of a society ultimately depends on the nature of its citizens; and since the nature of its citizens is more modifiable by early training than by anything else—we must conclude that the welfare of the family underlies the welfare of society. And hence knowledge directly conducing to the first, must take precedence of knowledge directly conducing to the last.

3d, parental duties.

Those various forms of pleasurable occupation which fill up the leisure left by graver occupations—the enjoyments of music, poetry, painting, etc.—manifestly imply a pre-existing society. Not only is a considerable development of them impossible without a long-established social union, but their very subject-matter consists in great part of social sentiments and sympathies. Not only does society supply the conditions to their growth, but also the ideas and sentiments they express. And, consequently, that part of human conduct which constitutes good citizenship is of more moment than that which goes out in accomplishments or exercise of the tastes; and, in education, preparation for the one must rank before preparation for the other.

4th, good citizenship.

Such then, we repeat, is something like the rational order of subordination:—That education which prepares for direct self-preservation; that which prepares for indirect self-preservation; that which prepares for parenthood; that which prepares for citizenship; that which prepares for the miscellaneous refinements of

5th, the refinements.

life. We do not mean to say that these divisions are definitely separable. We do not deny that they are intricately entangled with each other in such way that there can be no training for any that is not in some measure a training for all. Nor do we question that of each division there are portions more important than certain portions of the preceding divisions; that, for instance, a man of much skill in business but little other faculty, may fall further below the standard of complete living than one of but moderate ability in money-getting but great judgment as a parent; or that exhaustive information bearing on right social action, joined with entire want of general culture in literature and the fine arts, is less desirable than a more moderate share of the one joined with some of the other. But, after making due qualifications, there still remain these broadly-marked divisions; and it still continues substantially true that these divisions subordinate one another in the foregoing order, because the corresponding divisions of life make one another *possible* in that order. . . .

And if already the loss from want of science is so frequent and so great, still greater and more frequent will it be to those who hereafter lack science. Just as fast as productive processes become more scientific, which competition will inevitably make them do, and just as fast as joint-stock , undertakings spread, which they certainly will, so fast must scientific knowledge grow necessary to every one.

That which our school courses leave almost entirely out, we thus find to be that which most nearly concerns the business of life. All our industries would cease were it not for that information which men begin to acquire as they best may after their education is said to be finished. And were it not for this information, that has been from age to age accumulated and spread by unofficial means, these industries would never have existed. Had there been no teaching but such as is given in our public schools, England would now be what it was in feudal times. That increasing acquaintance with the laws of phenomena which has through successive ages enabled us to subjugate Nature to our needs, and in these days gives the common laborer comforts which a few centuries ago kings could not purchase, is scarcely in any degree owed to the appointed means of instructing our youth. The vital knowledge—that by which we have grown as a nation to what we are, and which now underlies our whole existence—is a knowledge that has got itself taught in nooks and corners; while the ordained agencies for teaching have been mumbling little else but dead formulas.

Schools have taught dead formulas.

Suggestions for Further Reading

Beale, Truxtun, ed. *The Man Versus the State: A Collection of Essays by Herbert Spencer.* New York: Mitchell Kennerley, 1916.

Elliot, Hugh. *Herbert Spencer.* New York: Henry Holt and Co., 1917.

Kazamias, Andreas M., ed. *Herbert Spencer on Education.* New York: Teachers College Press, Teachers College, Columbia University, 1966.

Kennedy, James G. *Herbert Spencer.* Boston: G. K. Hall and Co., 1978.

Peel, John D. Y. *Herbert Spencer: The Evolution of a Sociologist.* New York: Basic Books, 1971.

Rumney, Jay. *Herbert Spencer's Sociology: A Study in the History of Social Theory.* New York: Atherton Press, 1966.

Spencer, Herbert. *An Autobiography,* 2 vols. New York: D. Appleton and Co., 1904.

———. *Education: Intellectual, Moral and Physical.* New York: Appleton-Century-Crofts, 1889.

———. *Essays on Education and Kindred Subjects.* New York: AMS Press, 1977.

———. *Political Writings.* Cambridge, U.K.: Cambridge University Press, 1993.

———. *Essays: Scientific, Political, and Speculative.* New York: D. Appleton Co., 1910.

———. *Facts and Comments.* New York: D. Appleton and Co., 1902.

———. *First Principles.* New York: D. Appleton and Co., 1880.

———. *Social Statics.* New York: D. Appleton and Co., 1886.

Taylor, Michael W. *Men Versus the State: Herbert Spencer and Late Victorian Individualism.* New York: Oxford University Press, 1992.

Notes

1. For the life of Herbert Spencer, see Herbert Spencer, *An Autobiography,* 2 vols. (New York: D. Appleton and Co., 1904); David Duncan, *Life and Letters of Herbert Spencer,* 2 vols. (D. Appleton and Co., 1908); Josiah Royce, *Herbert Spencer: An Estimate and Review* (New York: Fox, Dufield and Co., 1904); and John D. Y. Peel, *Herbert Spencer: The Evolution of a Sociologist* (New York: Basic Books, 1971).

2. William H. Hudson, *Herbert Spencer* (London: Archibald and Constable, 1908), 3–12.

3. Spencer, *An Autobiography,* vol. 1, 100.

4. Jonathan Howard, *Darwin* (New York: Oxford University Press, 1982); and Michael Ruse, *The Darwinian Revolution* (Chicago: University of Chicago Press, 1979).

5. Andreas M. Kazamias, ed., *Herbert Spencer on Education* (New York: Teachers College Press, Columbia University, 1966), 121–159.

JANE ADDAMS: ADVOCATE OF SOCIALIZED EDUCATION

BIOGRAPHICAL SKETCH

Jane Addams (1860–1935), founder of Hull House and a pioneering figure in social work and the movement for women's rights, is significant in the history and philosophy of education for her work with urban immigrants and for her progressive philosophy of "socialized education."

Jane Addams was born on September 6, 1860, in Cedarville, Illinois. She was the daughter of John Huy Addams, a prominent local businessman and Republican Party leader, and Sarah Weber Addams. Her mother died when Jane was 2 years old, and the fear of separation caused her to be socially reserved throughout her life. Her attitudes toward social and civic commitment were learned from her father, who was dedicated to public service.

When Jane was 8, John Addams married Anna Haldeman, a well-educated and cultivated widow. Unlike Jane, who would challenge women's traditionally ascribed roles as wife and mother, Anna delighted in being a homemaker.[1]

In 1877, Jane Addams, at age 17, enrolled at Rockford Seminary, a Presbyterian and Congregational women's college. An academically talented student, she took a wide range of courses such as Greek, Latin, German, geology, astronomy, botany, medieval history, civil government, music, literature, Bible studies, and moral philosophy. She was awarded the bachelor of arts degree in 1882.[2]

In 1881, when Jane was 21, her father died, and she began to experience the bouts of psychological depression and physical illness that she suffered for much of her life. Feeling closed in by the limiting roles assigned to middle-class young women, she began a struggle to free herself and to define her own purpose in life. As a part of this search, Addams took two extended tours of Europe. In the United Kingdom, she visited, in 1888, a social settlement, Toynbee Hall, established by Canon Samuel A. Barnett, a Church of England clergyman, and staffed by students from Oxford University. Toynbee Hall would later become the model for her own settlement house, Hull House, in Chicago.[3]

Making the decision that would define her life, Jane Addams and Ellen Gates Starr, her longtime friend, established Hull House on Chicago's near west side in 1889. The neighborhood Hull House served contained a wide variety of recent im-

Jane Addams with children at
Hull House in Chicago.

migrants—Italians, Bohemians, Poles, Greeks, and Russian Jews. What developed
at Hull House was a reciprocal educational affair. Hull House was a two-way street
as Addams and her cadre of young middle-class women educated the immigrants
and, in turn, were educated by them. At Hull House progressive social and educational theory was made practical as Addams and her coworkers helped the immigrant community find jobs, pay rent, find health care, and educate their children.
While art, music, and cultural activities were included in the Hull House program,
there was also a focus on the applied economic, social, and political skills that made
it possible to survive in the new world. Hull House became a multifunctional institution with a nursery school, kindergarten, savings bank, labor museum, craft center, and medical dispensary. Addams was advised by such leading progressive aca-
demicians as Richard T. Ely, professor of economics at the University of Wisconsin,
and John Dewey, professor of philosophy, psychology, and pedagogy at the University of Chicago.[4]

While Addams' Hull House was the centerpiece of her work that put her philosophy of socialized education into practice, she had many other achievements. She
was active in progressive politics and supported Theodore Roosevelt's "Bull Moose"
campaign for President in 1912. She opposed American entry into World War I and
worked throughout her life for world peace. She pressed for women's rights, especially the right to vote. A pioneering feminist, she took a leading role in the international struggle for women's rights.

A child laborer, a "bobbin' girl," in the early twentieth century. Jane Addams opposed this kind of child labor.

Jane Addams' career took her from being the socially reserved graduate of a small women's college to a progressive social reformer and settlement house pioneer. When she died in 1935, she was recognized throughout the world as champion of peace, education, and social reform.

ADDAMS' IDEAS ON EDUCATION

Jane Addams developed a philosophy called "socialized education." Her broad, progressive, and pragmatic philosophy encompassed a wide range of educational agencies. It included the informal and nonformal education of the immigrants at Hull House as well as formal schooling.

Addams' philosophy of "socialized education" evolved from her work at Hull House in urban and immigrant education. Socialized education sought to restore a sense of community to an America that was experiencing a difficult transformation as it evolved from a rural agrarian, small-town society to an urban, industrialized nation. The country also faced the tremendous challenge of assimilating the thousands of new immigrants from southern and eastern Europe.

On the basis of her idea that society was a vast network of interrelated groups and activities, Addams believed that education was multiagency and multifunctional. The school, as a community agency, was connected to the settlement house; the social worker was connected to the teacher. To really do their multifunctional work, Addams believed that schools needed progressive reform to reduce their isolation from social realities. The school curriculum should be redesigned to provide a broadened experience that explored children's immediate environment in a way that highlighted connections with an industrial society. For example, the curriculum might include the manual arts and industrial history. Addams believed the settlement house, like the progressive school, was an experimental setting for solving the social, economic, psychological, and political problems of modern urban life. As a complement to public schooling, the settlement house's educational program, intended for both adults and children, was to reach out into the community.

Addams was not nostalgic for the small-town past. She readily accepted the challenges of industrialization and modernity, which she believed had dramatically enlarged the definition and purpose of education. To Addams, the occupations of a modern industrial economy needed to be infused with a meaning that portrayed how life and work were interconnected and had a large social purpose. Modern industrial workers needed the kind of education that explored social relationships and connections and built the network of interconnections needed to re-create a sense of community.[5]

Although she believed children should be introduced to the various occupations as part of their general education, Addams strongly opposed child labor. Fighting against it, she organized the National Child Labor Committee and lobbied for compulsory school attendance laws. Addams' opposition to child labor rested on her belief that children needed to enjoy the experiences of childhood. When forced into adult work, they were denied the opportunities for play and schooling and lost the needed experiences that contributed to growth and development. Further, child labor unfairly divided children on a socioeconomic class basis. While upper- and middle-class children enjoyed the benefits of childhood, working-class children were denied them.

An early proponent of multiculturalism, Addams, in her work at Hull House, sought to make connections between the immigrant and the larger American experience. Such connections, she believed, could be established by linking the immigrants' customs, arts, and crafts to American life and society. Although her philosophy rested on the belief that immigrants needed to be assimilated into American culture, she was not an American monoculturalist. Rather, she believed, like a true progressive, that a plurality of cultures could coexist within the larger national cultural fabric. What was important for her was that all Americans share a common commitment to democratic processes. Anticipating contemporary multicultural education, Addams wanted the public schools to include the history, customs, songs, crafts, and stories of various ethnic and racial groups in the curriculum.[6] A concrete application of her theory came with the establishment of the Hull House Labor Museum, where there were exhibits of the artifacts and demonstrations of the handicraft skills that characterized the immigrants' life in Europe.

Addams was a proponent of women's rights. As a young woman, she rebelled against the restrictions society placed on women. She rejected the traditional curriculum that was designed to make upper- and middle-class women into genteel social ornaments. For her, a true women's education was the kind of education that all people should have. It should make the connections with the issues and problems of a changing and modernizing society. In the spirit of progressivism, it should educate women, who, with a commitment to social service, were engaged in the reforms that would make the world a better place.

Addams was a firm believer in the progressive view that knowledge should be applied to the problems of society. While research was done at Hull House, it was not for the purpose of generating theory. The goal was to use theory to influence the enactment of progressive legislation and to inform practice.

THE PRIMARY SOURCES

In the first selection from *Democracy and Social Ethics,* Addams develops her ideas on educational methods in a democratic society. A progressive social and political thinker as well as activist, Addams based her ideas on educational method on her philosophy of "socialized education," by which each individual was connected to others in a greater community. She argues that modern education in an industrial society needs to make the larger connections between industrial production and social life.

In the second selection from *The Spirit of Youth and the City Streets,* Addams develops an early argument for multicultural education. From her activities with immigrants at Hull House, she believed that the customs and arts of each ethnic group were a valuable contribution to an enlarged American experience.

FOCUSING QUESTIONS
As you read the selections, you might wish to consider the following question:

1. Identify and analyze Addams' concepts of social connections and progress. Are these concepts relevant in contemporary American society and schools?
2. Examine and reflect on Addams' argument that modern education needs to be more than the basics and that it needs to make connections between industry and society. Are her ideas relevant to the contemporary information age technological society?
3. Examine and reflect on Addams' discussion that schools should incorporate ethnic customs and arts in their program. Are her ideas relevant for contemporary schools, particularly as a part of multicultural education?
4. How did Addams' philosophy of socialized education seek to enlarge the concept of what constitutes American society?

FROM JANE ADDAMS' *DEMOCRACY AND SOCIAL ETHICS*

CHAPTER VI

EDUCATIONAL METHODS

As democracy modifies our conception of life, it constantly raises the value and function of each member of the community, however humble he may

From Jane Addams, *Democracy and Social Ethics.* New York: Macmillian Co., 1905, 178–181, 212–214.

be. We have come to believe that the most "brutish man" has a value in our common life, a function to perform which can be fulfilled by no one else. We are gradually requiring of the educator that he shall free the powers of each man and connect him with the rest of life. We ask this not merely because it is the man's right to be thus connected, but because we have become convinced that the social order cannot afford to get along without his special contribution.

Just as we have come to resent all hindrances which keep us from untrammelled comradeship with our fellows, and as we throw down unnatural divisions, not in the spirit of the eighteenth-century reformers, but in the spirit of those to whom social equality has become a necessity for further social development, so we are impatient to use the dynamic power residing in the mass of men, and demand that the educator free that power. We believe that man's moral idealism is the constructive force of progress, as it has always been; but because every human being is a creative agent and a possible generator of fine enthusiasm, we are sceptical of the moral idealism of the few and demand the education of the many, that there may be greater freedom, strength, and subtilty of intercourse and hence an increase of dynamic power. We are not content to include all men in our hopes, but have become conscious that all men are hoping and are part of the same movement of which we are a part.

Many people impelled by these ideas have become impatient with the slow recognition on the part of the educators of their manifest obligation to prepare and nourish the child and the citizen for social relations. The educators should certainly conserve the learning and training necessary for the successful individual and family life, but should add to that a preparation for the enlarged social efforts which our increasing democracy requires. The democratic ideal demands of the school that it shall give the child's own experience a social value; that it shall teach him to direct his own activities and adjust them to those of other people. We are not willing that thousands of industrial workers shall put all of their activity and toil into services from which the community as a whole reaps the benefit, while their mental conceptions and code of morals are narrow and untouched by any uplift which the consciousness of social value might give them.

We are impatient with the schools which lay all stress on reading and writing, suspecting them to rest upon the assumption that the ordinary experience of life is worth little, and that all knowledge and interest must be brought to the children through the medium of books. Such an assumption fails to give the child any clew to the life about him, or any power to usefully or intelligently connect himself with it. . . .

Manufacturers, as a whole, however, when they attempt educational institutions in connection with their factories, are prone to follow conventional lines, and to exhibit the weakness of imitation. We find, indeed, that the middle-class educator constantly makes the mistakes of the middle-class moralist when he attempts to aid working people. The latter has constantly and traditionally urged upon the workingman the specialized virtues of thrift, industry, and sobriety—all virtues pertaining to the individual. When each man had his own shop, it was perhaps wise to lay almost exclusive stress upon the industrial virtues of diligence and thrift; but as industry has become more highly organized, life becomes incredibly complex and interdependent. If a workingman is to have a conception of his value at all, he must see industry in its unity and entirety; he must have a conception that will include not only himself and his immediate family and community, but the industrial organization as a whole. It is doubtless true that dexterity of hand becomes less and less imperative as the invention of machinery and subdivision of labor proceeds; but it becomes all the more necessary, if the workman is to save his life at all, that he should get a sense of his individual relation to the system. Feeding a machine with a material of which he has no knowledge, producing a product, totally unrelated to the rest of his life, without in the least knowing what becomes of it, or its connection with the community, is, of course, unquestionably deadening to his intellectual and moral life. To make the moral connection it would be necessary to give him a social consciousness of the value of his work, and at least a sense of participation and a certain joy in its ultimate use; to make the intellectual connection it would be essential to create in him some historic conception of the development of industry and the relation of his individual work to it.

FROM JANE ADDAMS' THE SPIRIT OF YOUTH AND THE CITY STREETS

We are only beginning to understand what might be done through the festival, the street procession, the band of marching musicians, orchestral music in public squares or parks, with the magic power they all possess to formulate the sense of companionship and solidarity. The experiments which are being made in public schools to celebrate the national holidays, the changing seasons, the birthdays of heroes, the planting of trees, are slowly developing little ceremonials which may in time work out into pageants of genuine beauty and significance. No other nation has so unparalleled an opportunity to do this through its schools as we have, for no other nation has so widespreading a school system, while the enthusiasm of children and their natural ability to express their emotions through symbols, gives the securest possible foundation to this growing effort.

The city schools of New York have effected the organization of high school girls into groups for folk dancing. These old forms of dancing which have been worked out in many lands and through long experiences, safeguard unwary and dangerous expression and yet afford a vehicle through which the gaiety of youth may flow. Their forms are indeed those which lie at the basis of all good breeding, forms which at once express and restrain, urge forward and set limits.

One may also see another center of growth for public recreation and the beginning of a pageantry for the people in the many small parks and athletic fields which almost every American city is hastening to provide for its young. These small parks have innumerable athletic teams, each with its distinctive uniform, with track meets and match games arranged with the teams from other parks and from the public schools, choruses of trade unionists or of patriotic societies fill the park halls with eager listeners. Labor Day processions are yearly becoming more carefully planned and more picturesque in character, as the desire to make an overwhelming impression with mere size gives way to a growing ambition to set forth the significance of the craft and the skill of the workman. At moments they almost rival the dignified showing of the processions of the German Turn Vereins which are also often seen in our city streets.

The many foreign colonies which are found in all American cities afford an enormous reserve of material for public recreation and street festival. They not only celebrate the feasts and holidays of the fatherland, but have each their own public expression for their mutual benefit societies and for the observance of American anniversaries. From the gay celebration of the Scandinavians when war was averted and two neighboring nations were united, to the equally gay celebration of the centenary of Garibaldi's birth; from the Chinese dragon cleverly trailing its way through the streets, to the Greek banners flung out in honor of immortal heroes, there is an infinite variety of suggestions and possibilities for public recreation and for the corporate expression of stirring emotions. After all, what is the function of art but to preserve in permanent and beautiful form those emotions and solaces which cheer life and make it kindlier, more heroic and easier to comprehend; which lift the mind of the worker from the harshness and loneliness of his task, and, by connecting him with what has gone before, free him from a sense of isolation and hardship?

Were American cities really eager for municipal art, they would cherish as genuine beginnings the tarentella danced so interminably at Italian weddings; the primitive Greek pipe played throughout the long summer nights; the Bohemian theaters crowded with eager Slavophiles; the Hungarian musicians strolling from street to street; the fervid oratory of the young Russian preaching social righteousness in the open square.

Many Chicago citizens who attended the first annual meeting of the National Playground Association of America, will never forget the long summer day in the large playing field filled during the morning with hundreds of little children romping through the kindergarten games, in the afternoon with the young men and girls contending in athletic sports; and the evening light made gay by the bright colored garments of Italians, Lithuanians, Norwegians, and a dozen other nationalities, reproducing their old dances and festivals for the pleasure of the more stolid Americans. Was this a forecast of what we may yet see accomplished through a dozen agencies promoting public recreation which are springing up in every city of America, as they already are found in the large towns of Scotland and England?

From Jane Addams, *The Spirit of Youth and the City Streets*. New York: Macmillan Co., 1909, 98–103.

Let us cherish these experiments as the most precious beginnings of an attempt to supply the recreational needs of our industrial cities. To fail to provide for the recreation of youth, is not only to deprive all of them of their natural form of expression, but is certain to subject some of them to the overwhelming temptation of illicit and soul-destroying pleasures. To insist that young people shall forecast their rose-colored future only in a house of dreams, is to deprive the real world of that warmth and reassurance which it so sorely needs and to which it is justly entitled; furthermore, we are left outside with a sense of dreariness, in company with that shadow which already lurks only around the corner for most of us—a skepticism of life's value.

SUGGESTIONS FOR FURTHER READING

Addams, Jane. *Democracy and Social Ethics.* Edited by Anne F. Scott. Cambridge, Mass.: Harvard University Press, 1964.

_____.*The Long Road of Woman's Memory.* New York: Macmillan Publishing Company, 1916.

_____. *Newer Ideals of Peace.* New York: Macmillan Publishing Company, 1907.

_____. *The Second Twenty Years at Hull-House.* New York: Macmillan Publishing Company, 1930.

_____. *The Spirit of Youth and the City Street.* New York: Macmillan Publishing Company, 1909.

_____. *Twenty Years at Hull-House.* New York: Macmillan Publishing Company, 1910.

Davis, Allen F. *American Heroine: The Life and Legend of Jane Addams.* New York: Oxford University Press, 1973.

_____. *Spearheads for Reform: The Social Settlements and the Progressive Movement, 1890–1914.* New York: Oxford University Press, 1967.

Diliberto, Gioia. *A Useful Woman: The Early Life of Jane Addams.* New York: Scribner, A Lisa Drew Book, 1999.

Farrell, John C. *Beloved Lady: A History of Jane Addams' Ideas on Reform and Peace.* Baltimore: Johns Hopkins University Press, 1967.

Lagemann, Ellen Condliffe. *A Generation of Women: Education in the Lives of the Progressive Reformers.* Cambridge, Mass.: Harvard University Press, 1979.

Lagemann, Ellen Condliffe, ed. *Jane Addams on Education.* New York: Teachers College Press, Columbia University, 1985.

NOTES

1. Allen F. Davis, *American Heroine: The Life and Legend of Jane Addams* (New York: Oxford University Press, 1973), 6–7.

2. Winifred E. Wise, *Jane Addams of Hull-House* (New York: Harcourt Brace and Jovanovich, 1935), 61–74, 77–80.

3. Ellen Condliffe Lagemann, ed., *Jane Addams on Education* (New York: Teachers College Press, Columbia University, 1985), 16–17.

4. Ibid., 33–34.

5. Jane Addams, *Democracy and Social Ethics,* edited by Anne F. Scott (Cambridge, Mass.: Harvard University Press, 1964), 178–220.

6. Lagemann, 136–42.

18

JOHN DEWEY: PRAGMATIST PHILOSOPHER AND PROGRESSIVE EDUCATOR

BIOGRAPHICAL SKETCH

John Dewey (1859–1952), one of America's most influential philosophers and educators, is significant in the history and philosophy of education as a forceful proponent of pragmatism, progressivism, and liberalism. His ideas have left an enduring impact on pragmatism as an educational philosophy and on how we view experience in education.

John Dewey was born in Burlington, Vermont, on October 20, 1859, the son of Archibald Sprague Dewey and Lucina Artemisia Rich Dewey.[1] His father had left farming to operate a grocery store in Burlington.[2] The Deweys attended the local Congregational Church in which his mother was especially active. Small-town life had an important formative impact on Dewey, who was inspired in his own quest to devise a revitalized American community by New England's town meeting type of participatory democracy.

Dewey, a studious child, entered the local public elementary school in 1867, where he studied the conventional elementary subjects—reading, writing, spelling, arithmetic, history, and geography. In 1872, he entered Burlington High School, where he studied the college preparatory subjects of Latin, Greek, French, English, mathematics, and literature.[3]

In 1875, Dewey entered the University of Vermont, where the curriculum was still classically oriented. Here, he enrolled in such courses as Greek, Latin, rhetoric, and English literature. As an undergraduate, Dewey developed his interest in political and social philosophy, especially the positivism of Auguste Comte.[4]

After receiving his bachelor of arts degree in 1879, Dewey took a position as a high school teacher in Oil City, Pennsylvania, an important center in the petroleum industry. Dewey taught Latin, algebra, and natural science in the Oil City High School for 2 years. He then returned to Vermont, his home state, as a teacher at the Lake View Seminary in Charlotte. He also enrolled in the graduate program in philosophy at the University of Vermont and received his master's degree in 1881.[5]

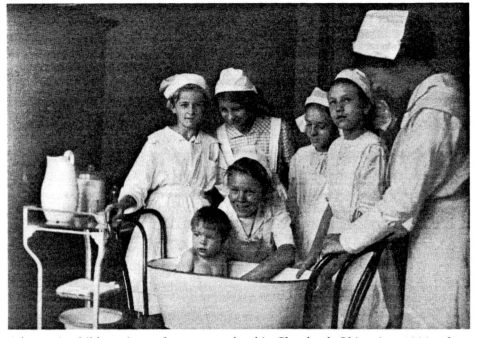

A lesson in childcare in an elementary school in Cleveland, Ohio, circa 1920s, that illustrates the progressive concept of connecting education to life.

In 1882, Dewey was admitted to the Ph.D. program in philosophy at Johns Hopkins University. At this new graduate institution, based on the German research model, highly promising students, directed by distinguished professors, investigated specialized topics. Dewey's adviser was Professor George Sylvester Morris, an academically recognized interpreter of the German idealist philosopher Georg Wilhelm Hegel. Morris, an influential mentor, encouraged Dewey's work in philosophy. Although Dewey later abandoned Hegel's abstract metaphysics, his own pragmatic experimentalism showed a Hegelian inclination to unify contradictions, or dualisms, into general concepts such as experience, democracy, and community. Indeed, Dewey showed a continuing attraction to the Hegelian theme of a unifying "great community," which, with the New England town meeting, became the democratic society. Along with Morris, his mentor in philosophy, Dewey also enrolled in courses taught by G. Stanley Hall, the pioneering American psychologist, and Charles S. Peirce, who developed pragmaticism, a new approach to philosophy that emphasized testing ideas by acting on them.[6]

In 1884, Dewey embarked on his long career as a professor of philosophy, joining that department at the University of Michigan. At Ann Arbor, he met and wed Harriet Alice Chipman in 1886. Alice shared Dewey's interests in intellectual and educational matters. She would later be the principal of Dewey's Laboratory School at the University of Chicago.

In 1888, Dewey went to the University of Minnesota as professor of mental and moral philosophy. However, 1 year later, in 1889, Dewey, a recognized scholar, returned to the University of Michigan, where he chaired the philosophy department.

In 1894, Dewey accepted an appointment as chairman of the Department of Philosophy, Psychology, and Pedagogy at the University of Chicago, a relatively new institution that had been established 4 years earlier with support from John D. Rockefeller. Sr. William Rainey Harper, the founding president of the University of Chicago, recruited a faculty of academic "super stars," including Dewey, to make the institution the preeminent center in scholarly research and publication.[7]

Dewey's department at the University of Chicago was composed of leading professors in philosophy, psychology, and pedagogy—the disciplines foundational for education. At Chicago, Dewey established his famous Laboratory School, which functioned from 1896 to 1904 as an experimental setting to test his ideas on education.[8] Dewey described his school, which enrolled students from 6 through 16, as a "miniature society" and an "embryonic community" in which children learned collaboratively by solving problems. Conflicts between Dewey and Harper about the administration of the Laboratory School and other matters led to his resignation in 1904.

In 1905, Dewey accepted a position in the Department of Philosophy at Columbia University, which he held until his retirement in 1930. At Columbia, Dewey was closely associated with such prominent progressive professors of education as William Heard Kilpatrick, the founder of the project method, George S. Counts, the originator of social reconstructionism, and Harold Rugg, a pioneer in issue-based social studies.

Dewey, a distinguished philosopher and educator, enjoyed an international reputation and was invited to lecture in foreign countries. From 1919 through 1921, Dewey lectured in Japan and China. In 1928, he was in the Soviet Union. Soviet educators had introduced some of Dewey's educational ideas, especially his emphasis on cooperative learning. He, in turn, was intrigued by the Soviet use of planning as part of their modernization process. Dewey, a committed liberal democrat, however, was staunchly anti-Communist, consistently opposing the American Communist Party and speaking out against Stalin's despotic regime in the Soviet Union. As a result, Dewey's books were banned in the USSR.

For 22 years after his retirement from Columbia University until his death in 1952, Dewey was a voice speaking for social and educational reform and renewal. His reputation has remained that of a committed pragmatist and progressive.

OVERVIEW OF IDEAS ON EDUCATION

Dewey is often identified with the American pragmatists—Charles S. Peirce, William James, and George H. Mead—who argued that philosophy should deal with real human problems rather than metaphysical speculation. Dewey, like these pragmatists, rejected universal and eternal truths. He believed that human beings can arrive at tentative warranted assertions. These assertions are developed as we test and verify our ideas by acting upon them to resolve problems.

Dewey's philosophy of education challenged Western philosophy's traditional proclivity to dualism—to seeing reality in two dimensions—one that was perfect, timeless, unchanging, and universal and the other that was temporary, finite, and changing.[9]

Dewey contended that the Western philosophical and theological tradition sought to alleviate the human fear of death and disappearance by professing that the human being's spiritual essence or soul would live forever. Western philosophy had come to emphasize a perfect world, beyond human experience, and had ignored the issues of everyday living. This tendency to dualism separated mind and body, and theory and practice. Dewey's theory of knowledge rested on a continuum of human experience that united, rather than separated, thinking and acting.[10] Rejecting this kind of dualism, Dewey advised people to develop a way of dealing with the problems arising in experience.

Rejecting the possibility of a universal certainty, Dewey argued that we live in a highly uncertain and relative world. In a world of continual change, Dewey advised that we have the possibility to plan and direct our lives by using the scientific method.[11]

Dewey's philosophy was shaped, in part, by Charles Darwin's theory of evolution that hypothesized that various species had evolved slowly over the course of time. Dewey used the concepts of the "organism" in interaction with the "environment" in building his philosophy of education. He reasoned that the human organism had life-sustaining needs and impulses. Possessing a highly developed brain, the power of speech, and the ability to create tools, the human being was able to make plans by projecting and weighing the possible results that would be caused by an action. This planning capability, which involved knowing the relationship between cause and effect, was the basis for human intelligence. Humans live in an environment that both supports and threatens life.

Human life was sustained through successful interactions with the environment, which Dewey called "experience." In the course of these interactive episodes, thinking, reflection on cause, effects, and consequences takes place. When we find ourselves in a situation where an obstacle blocks our activity, we are in what Dewey called a "problematic situation." When we have gone through the process that solves our problem, we have engaged in thinking. Dewey designed a series of five problem-solving steps, called the "complete act of thought," which he felt replicated the scientific method. Dewey's problem-solving steps were as follows:

1. We encounter something different or new in experience that blocks our ongoing activity and involves us in a "problematic situation."
2. To begin to solve the problem, we need to locate it in our experience and define it as specifically and exactly as we can.
3. Once we have defined the problem, we can do the research that we need to gather the information that will help us solve the problem.
4. On the basis of the information that we have, we can formulate some tentative hypotheses, informed guesses, about what we can do to solve the problem and what effects our action is likely to have.
5. After choosing the hypothesis we think will solve our problem and give us the effects we want, we need to test it by acting on it. If we used the process successfully, our problem will be solved; if not, we need to identify our mistakes and try again.

For Dewey, the complete act of thought, or problem solving according to the scientific method, is the way in which we think effectively and also the most effective strategy for teaching and learning. Because of his emphasis on the scientific method, Dewey's philosophy is called experimentalism.

Dewey's experimentalism, which accentuates the person as a member of society, places special emphasis on the group in education. For Dewey, humans developed their intelligence as they interacted with each other to solve mutual problems and create the human community, or society. For Dewey, genuine communities were developed as the human group went through three stages:

1. Common tools and objects are used and shared in common activities.
2. The association generated in pursuing common activities produces a sense of identification or membership, which results in communication, talking about common problems and endeavors.
3. Communication leads to the third stage, a commonly shared society and culture—the basis of community.

For Dewey, the group, with its associative activities, possessed immensely rich educational potentialities. Collaborative group problem solving, planning, and implementation reduce the isolation of the individual from others and through mutual activities produce an enriched social intelligence. Democracy provides the fullest opportunities for full human association since it is free of the impediments that block free interaction between people.

Dewey organized the curriculum around three general kinds of activities: making and doing, history and geography, and science. Making and doing, activities children perform in their first years of schooling, were designed to lead youngsters from their immediate families and homes into the larger society. Dewey emphasized the need to maintain continuity, with home experiences leading easily into school experiences, without isolating either from the other. Then came history and geography to enlarge children's perspective of time and space. The third stage of curriculum, science, referred to inquiry into the various subjects in the mode of interdisciplinary problem solving.

By using the scientific method in a collaborative group setting, Dewey's students would develop practical intelligence, a sense of reflective inquiry, and the values needed for life in a democratic community. They would not fear change but would be eager to direct it, flexible in their attitudes, open to experimentation, critical in their thinking, and socially involved and tolerant of others.

THE PRIMARY SOURCE

The excerpts from Dewey's *Democracy and Education,* published in 1916, convey his view of an experimentalist philosophy of education. For Dewey, the concept of the human being in interaction or transaction with the environment was a basic building block in his philosophy. For the human being this interaction gave rise to experience.

A liberal and progressive, Dewey advocated a democratic society as the environment most conducive for using the scientific method and for creating a truly sharing community. His *Democracy and Education* indicates his emphasis on democratic processes. A democratic environment was free of absolutes that blocked truly experimental inquiry. No subject, custom, or value was so sacrosanct as to escape critical inquiry. Ideally, the social setting, including the school, was to be free of coercive and authoritarian persons who would jeopardize freedom of thought, inquiry, and experimentation.

In the interactive episode between the person and the environment, thinking occurs and, from that, education takes place. Dewey designed a series of problem-solving steps, or reflective experience, that approximate the scientific method. Referred to as the "complete act of thought," Dewey's process-oriented experimental method consisted of the following five steps: (1) encountering the problematic situation; (2) locating and defining the problem; (3) gathering information, doing research, and consulting previous experience to aid in solving the problem; (4) conjecturing tentative hypotheses of possible action that may solve the problem; (5) testing the selected hypothesis by acting on it. For Dewey, problem solving according to the scientific method is the way in which we think most intelligently and is also the most effective strategy for teaching and learning.

FOCUSING QUESTIONS

As you read the selection, you might wish to answer the following questions:

1. What importance does Dewey give to the group in learning? Examine the contemporary emphasis on collaborative learning as an example of the educative power of the group.
2. Identify and examine Dewey's principles that relate to the role of the school as a learning environment. Are these principles relevant to contemporary theories about the role of the school?
3. According to Dewey, what is the purpose of education? Compare and contrast Dewey's statement of the purpose of education with contemporary statements of educational goals.
4. Why does Dewey prefer a democratic society as the social context of education? Is his vision of democracy relevant to contemporary society and education?
5. What is Dewey's complete act of thought? Why is it called a complete act of thought? Is the complete act of thought relevant for contemporary education?

FROM JOHN DEWEY'S *DEMOCRACY AND EDUCATION: AN INTRODUCTION TO THE PHILOSOPHY OF EDUCATION*

The Nature and Meaning of Environment. We have seen that a community or social group sustains itself through continuous self-renewal, and that this renewal takes place by means of the educational growth of the immature members of the group. By various agencies, unintentional and designed, a society trans-

forms uninitiated and seemingly alien beings into robust trustees of its own resources and ideals. Education is thus a fostering, a nurturing, a cultivating, process. All of these words mean that it implies attention to the conditions of growth. We also speak of rearing, raising, bringing up—words which express the difference of level which education aims to cover. Etymologically, the word education means just a process of leading or bringing up. When we have the outcome of the process in mind, we speak of education as shaping, forming, molding activity—that is, a shaping into the standard form of social activity. . . .

The School as a Special Environment. The chief importance of this foregoing statement of the educative process which goes on willynilly is to lead us to note that the only way in which adults consciously control the kind of education which the immature get is by controlling the environment in which they act, and hence think and feel. We never educate directly, but indirectly by means of the environment. Whether we permit chance environments to do the work, or whether we design environments for the purpose makes a great difference. And any environment is a chance environment so far as its educative influence is concerned unless it has been deliberately regulated with reference to its educative effect. An intelligent home differs from an unintelligent one chiefly in that the habits of life and intercourse which prevail are chosen, or at least colored, by the thought of their bearing upon the development of children. But schools remain, of course, the typical instance of environments framed with express reference to influencing the mental and moral disposition of their members.

Roughly speaking, they come into existence when social traditions are so complex that a considerable part of the social store is committed to writing and transmitted through written symbols. Written symbols are even more artificial or conventional than spoken; they cannot be picked up in accidental intercourse with others. In addition, the written form tends to select and record matters which are comparatively foreign to everyday life. The achievements accumulated from generation to generation are deposited in it even though some of them have fallen temporarily out of use. Consequently as soon as a community depends to any considerable extent upon what lies beyond its own territory and its own immediate generation, it must rely upon the set agency of schools to insure adequate transmission of all its resources. To take an obvious illustration: The life of the ancient Greeks and Romans has profoundly influenced our own, and yet the ways in which they affect us do not present themselves on the surface of our ordinary experiences. In similar fashion, peoples still existing, but remote in space, British, Germans, Italians, directly concern our own social affairs, but the nature of the interaction cannot be understood without explicit statement and attention. In precisely similar fashion, our daily associations cannot be trusted to make clear to the young the part played in our activities by remote physical energies, and by invisible structures. Hence a special mode of social intercourse is instituted, the school, to care for such matters.

This mode of association has three functions sufficiently specific, as compared with ordinary associations of life, to be noted. First, a complex civilization is too complex to be assimilated *in toto*. It has to be broken up into portions, as it were, and assimilated piecemeal, in a gradual and graded way. The relationships of our present social life are so numerous and so interwoven that a child placed in the most favorable position could not readily share in many of the most important of them. Not sharing in them, their meaning would not be communicated to him, would not become a part of his own mental disposition. There would be no seeing the trees because of the forest. Business, politics, art, science, religion, would make all at once a clamor for attention; confusion would be the outcome. The first office of the social organ we call the school is to provide a simplified environment. It selects the features which are fairly fundamental and capable of being responded to by the young. Then it establishes a progressive order, using the factors first acquired as means of gaining insight into what is more complicated.

In the second place, it is the business of the school environment to eliminate, so far as possible, the unworthy features of the existing environment from influence upon mental habitudes. It establishes a purified medium of action. Selection aims not only at simplifying but at weeding out what is undesirable. Every society gets encumbered with what is trivial, with dead wood from the past, and with what is positively perverse. The school has the duty of omitting such things from the environment which it supplies, and thereby doing what it can to counteract their influence in the ordinary social environment. By selecting the best for its exclusive use, it strives to reinforce the power of this best. As a society becomes more enlightened, it realizes that it is responsible *not* to transmit and conserve the whole of its existing achievements, but only such as make for a better future society. The school is its chief agency for the accomplishment of this end.

In the third place, it is the office of the school environment to balance the various elements in the social environment, and to see to it that each individual gets an opportunity to escape from the limitations of the social group in which he was born, and to come into living contact with a broader environment. Such words as "society" and "community" are likely to be misleading, for they have a tendency to make us think there is a single thing corresponding to the single word. As a matter of fact, a modern society is many societies more or less loosely connected. Each household with its immediate extension of friends makes a society; the village or street group of playmates is a community; each business group, each club, is another. Passing beyond these more intimate groups, there is in a country like our own a variety of races, religious affiliations, economic divisions. Inside the modern city, in spite of its nominal political unity, there are probably more communities, more differing customs, traditions, aspirations, and forms of government or control, than existed in an entire continent at an earlier epoch. . . .

Since in reality there is nothing to which growth is relative save more growth, there is nothing to which education is subordinate save more education. It is a commonplace to say that education should not cease when one leaves school. The point of this commonplace is that the purpose of school education is to insure the continuance of education by organizing the powers that insure growth. The inclination to learn from life itself and to make the conditions of life such that all will learn in the process of living is the finest product of schooling. . . .

The Democratic Ideal. The two elements in our criterion both point to democracy. The first signifies not only more numerous and more varied points of shared common interest, but greater reliance upon the recognition of mutual interests as a factor in social control. The second means not only freer interaction between social groups (once isolated so far as intention could keep up a separation) but change in social habit—its continuous readjustment through meeting the new situations produced by varied intercourse. And these two traits are precisely what characterize the democratically constituted society.

Upon the educational side, we note first that the realization of a form of social life in which interests are mutually interpenetrating, and where progress, or readjustment, is an important consideration, makes a democratic community more interested than other communities have cause to be in deliberate and systematic education. The devotion of democracy to education is a familiar fact. The superficial explanation is that a government resting upon popular suffrage cannot be successful unless those who elect and who obey their governors are educated. Since a democratic society repudiates the principle of external authority, it must find a substitute in voluntary disposition and interest; these can be created only by education. But there is a deeper explanation. A democracy is more than a form of government; it is primarily a mode of associated living, of conjoint communicated experience. The extension in space of the number of individuals who participate in an interest so that each has to refer his own action to that of others, and to con-

sider the action of others to give point and direction to his own, is equivalent to the breaking down of those barriers of class, race, and national territory which kept men from perceiving the full import of their activity. These more numerous and more varied points of contact denote a greater diversity of stimuli to which an individual has to respond; they consequently put a premium on variation in his action. They secure a liberation of powers which remain suppressed as long as the incitations to action are partial, as they must be in a group which in its exclusiveness shuts out many interests.

The widening of the area of shared concerns, and the liberation of a greater diversity of personal capacities which characterize a democracy, are not of course the product of deliberation and conscious effort. On the contrary, they were caused by the development of modes of manufacture and commerce, travel, migration, and intercommunication which flowed from the command of science of natural energy. But after greater individualization on one hand, and a broader community of interest on the other have come into existence, it is a matter of deliberate effort to sustain and extend them. Obviously a society to which stratification into separate classes would be fatal, must see to it that intellectual opportunities are accessible to all on equable and easy terms. A society marked off into classes need be specially attentive only to the education of its ruling elements. A society which is mobile, which is full of channels for the distribution of a change occurring anywhere, must see to it that its members are educated to personal initiative and adaptability. Otherwise, they will be overwhelmed by the changes in which they are caught and whose significance or connections they do not perceive. The result will be a confusion in which a few will appropriate to themselves the results of the blind and externally directed activities of others. . . .

So much for the general features of a reflective experience. They are (*i*) perplexity, confusion, doubt, due to the fact that one is implicated in an incomplete situation whose full character is not yet determined; (*ii*) a conjectural anticipation—a tentative interpretation of the given elements, attributing to them a tendency to effect certain consequences; (*iii*) a careful survey (examination, inspection, exploration, analysis) of all attainable consideration which will define and clarify the problem in hand; (*iv*) a consequent elaboration of the tentative hypothesis to make it more precise and more consistent, because squaring with a wider range of facts; (*v*) taking one stand upon the projected hypothesis as a plan of action which is applied to the existing state of affairs: doing something overtly to bring about the anticipated result, and thereby testing the hypothesis. It is the extent and accuracy of steps three and four which mark off a distinctive reflective experience from one on the trial and error plane. They make *thinking* itself into an experience. Nevertheless, we never get wholly beyond the trial and error situation. Our most elaborate and rationally consistent thought has to be tried in the world and thereby tried out. And since it can never take into account all the connections, it can never cover with perfect accuracy all the consequences. Yet a thoughtful survey of conditions is so careful, and the guessing at results so controlled, that we have a right to mark off the reflective experience from the grosser trial and error forms of action.

SUGGESTIONS FOR FURTHER READING

Chambliss, Joseph J. *The Influence of Plato and Aristotle on John Dewey's Philosophy.* Lewiston: E. Mellen Press, 1990.

Coughlan, Neil. *Young John Dewey: An Essay in American Intellectual History.* Chicago: University of Chicago Press, 1975.

Dewey, John. *A Common Faith.* New Haven, Conn.: Yale University Press, 1934.

_____. *Democracy and Education: An Introduction to the Philosophy of Education.* New York: Macmillan Publishing Company, 1964.

_____. *Experience and Education.* New York: Collier Books, 1963.

_____. *Individualism Old and New.* New York: Capricorn Books, 1962.

_____. *Lectures on Ethics, 1900–1901.* Carbondale: Southern Illinois University Press, 1991.

_____. *Liberalism and Social Action.* New York: Capricorn Books,1963.

_____. *Philosophy and Education in Their Historic Relations.* Boulder, Colo.: Westview Press, 1993.

_____. *The Political Writings.* Indianapolis: Hackett Publishing Co., 1993.

_____. *The Quest for Certainty: A Study of the Relation of Knowledge and Action.* New York: G. P. Putnam's Sons, 1960.

Dykhuizen, George. *The Life and Mind of John Dewey.* Carbondale: Southern Illinois University Press, 1973.

Feffer, Andrew. *The Chicago Pragmatists and American Progressivism.* Ithaca, N.Y.: Cornell University Press, 1993.

Hendley, Brian P. *Dewey, Russell, Whitehead: Philosophers as Educators.* Carbondale: Southern Illinois University Press,1986.

Hichman, Larry A. *John Dewey's Pragmatic Technology.* Bloomington: Indiana University Press, 1990.

Hook, Sidney. *John Dewey: An Intellectual Portrait.* Westport, Conn.: Greenwood Press, 1971.

Kulp, Christopher B. *The End of Epistemology: Dewey and His Current Allies on the Spectator Theory of Knowledge.* Westport, Conn.: Greenwood Press, 1992.

Paringer, William A. *John Dewey and the Paradox of Liberal Reform.* Albany: State University of New York Press, 1990.

Rice, Daniel F. *Reinhold Niebuhr and John Dewey: An American Odyssey.* Albany: State University of New York Press, 1992.

Rockefeller, Steven C. *John Dewey: Religious Faith and Democratic Humanism.* New York: Columbia University Press, 1991.

Ryan, Alan. *John Dewey and the High Tide of American Liberalism.* New York: W. W. Norton & Co., 1995.

Sleeper, R. W. *The Necessity of Pragmatism: John Dewey's Conception of Philosophy.* New Haven: Yale University Press, 1986.

Stuhr, John J., ed. *Philosophy and the Reconstruction of Culture: Pragmatic Essays After Dewey.* Albany: State University of New York Press, 1993.

Tanner, Laurel N. *Dewey's Laboratory School. Lessons for Today.* New York: Teachers College Press, 1997.

Welchman, Jennifer. *Dewey's Ethical Thought.* Ithaca, N.Y.: Cornell University Press, 1995.

Westbrook, Robert B. *John Dewey and American Democracy.* Ithaca, N.Y.: Cornell University Press, 1991.

Wirth, Arthur G. *John Dewey as Educator: His Design for Work in Education (1894–1904).* New York: John Wiley and Sons, 1966.

Xu, Di. *A Comparison of the Educational Ideas and Practices of John Dewey and Mao Zedong in China: Is School Society or Society School?* San Francisco: Mellen Research University Press, 1992.

NOTES

1. Biographical studies of Dewey are George Dykhuizen, *The Life and Mind of John Dewey* (Carbondale: Southern Illinois University Press, 1973); Neil Coughlan, *Young John Dewey: An Essay in American Intellectual History* (Chicago: University of Chicago Press, 1975); Robert B. Westbrook, *John Dewey and American Democracy* (Ithaca, N.Y.: Cornell University Press, 1991).

2. Dykhuizen, *The Life and Mind of John Dewey,* 4–9.

3. Ibid.

4. Ibid., 11–18.

5. Ibid., 19–23.

6. Ibid., 27–31.

7. Thomas W. Goodspeed, *A History of the University of Chicago: The First Quarter-Century* (Chicago: University of Chicago Press, 1972), 98–104.

8. For Dewey's Laboratory School, see Arthur G. Wirth, *John Dewey as Educator: His Design for Working in Education (1894–1904)* (New York: John Wiley and Sons, 1966); and Herbert M. Kliebard, *The Struggle for the American Curriculum 1893–1958* (Boston and London: Routledge & Kegan Paul, 1986).

9. John Dewey, *The Quest for Certainty: A Study of the Relation of Knowledge and Action* (New York: G. P. Putnam's Sons, 1960).

10. Hilary Putnam and Ruth Anna Putnam, "Education for Democracy," *Educational Theory,* 43, No. 4 (Fall 1993), 364.

11. Robert B. Westbrook, *John Dewey and American Democracy* (Ithaca, N.Y.: Cornell University Press, 1991), 141.

MARIA MONTESSORI: PROPONENT OF EARLY CHILDHOOD EDUCATION

BIOGRAPHICAL SKETCH

Maria Montessori (1870–1952), a pioneering leader in early childhood education, is significant in the history and philosophy of education for developing a distinctive method that can be found around the world. In addition to her educational work, she was a highly motivated woman who successfully overcame many of the barriers that limited women's educational opportunities in the late nineteenth and early twentieth centuries.

Born in Chiaravalle, an Italian hill town in the Ancona province, on August 31, 1870, Maria Montessori was the daughter of middle-class parents: Alessandro Montessori, a civil servant, and Renilde Stoppani, a well-educated young woman. Signor Montessori, who exemplified the style of an "old-fashioned gentleman," was an official in the tobacco industry, a state monopoly.[1]

The Montessori family moved to Rome in 1875, where Maria, the family's only child, attended the state primary school located on the Via di San Nicolo da Tolentino. When she was 12, Maria, displaying her tendency to make her own choices, announced that she wanted to go to a technical secondary school rather than a girls' finishing school. Her announcement about her future was a radical departure from the general Italian educational expectations for young women.

Maria, an independent young woman, persuaded her parents to allow her to enroll in a technical school. In 1883, Maria Montessori, age 13, enrolled in the Regia Scuola Technica Michelangelo Buonarroti, a state technical school. She followed a 7-year curriculum that included Italian literature, French, mathematics, algebra, geometry, natural science, chemistry, physics, history, and geography. Upon completing her secondary studies at the Scuola Technica, Maria Montessori entered the Regio Instituto Technico Leonardo da Vinci to pursue engineering.

In 1890, Montessori, in a serious departure from the traditional pattern of an Italian woman's education, made another important decision. She decided to leave her engineering studies to enter medical school. Overcoming many bureaucratic obstacles, she was the first woman admitted to the University of Rome's School of Med-

A class in Montessori school, using didactic materials.

icine. As a student in a male-dominated profession, she encountered regulations and practices that discriminated against women. She could not enter a classroom until all the male students had been seated. She could do laboratory work in anatomy only in the evenings when the male students were no longer present. Nevertheless, she demonstrated her academic ability, winning scholarships in surgery, pathology, and medicine.[2] While a medical student, she was an intern at the Children's Pediatric Hospital, which stimulated her interest in child development. In 1896, she became the first woman in Italy to receive the degree of doctor of medicine.

Montessori, a 26-year-old physician, accepted a position at the university's San Giovanni Hospital and began a private practice. She also worked at the University of Rome's Clinica Psichiatrica, where she did research on mental illness. Reading widely in the literature on psychological disorders, she encountered the writings of Jean-Marc Gaspard Itard (1774–1838) and Edouard Seguin (1812–1880), two French psychologists who had worked with mentally deficient children. Seguin had based instruction on developmental stages, had used special materials, and had trained children to perform practical skills to achieve some degree of independence.[3] Seguin's writings stimulated Montessori's own thinking on educating children with special needs.

At the Clinica Psichiatrica, Maria Montessori worked with Giuseppe Montesano, a young physician with whom she developed a close personal relationship. Montessori never married, and her protégé, Mario Montessori, was the couple's son.[4]

Between 1904 and 1908, Montessori lectured at the University of Rome's School of Pedagogy. Her lectures were interdisciplinary, drawing information from a variety of disciplines ranging from medicine to anthropology and psychology. She wrote *Pedagogical Anthropology*, an interdisciplinary book that drew conclusions from pediatric medicine, child psychology, and cultural anthropology and applied them to children's development and education.

Montessori opened her first school on January 6, 1907. The Casa dei Bambini, the Children's House, which enrolled pupils from ages 3 to 7, was located in a large tenement in Rome's poverty-ridden San Lorenzo district. (Montessori's account of this school is found in the primary source selections in the chapter.) She enjoyed such success at the Casa dei Bambini that three more schools were established in Rome. She gained support from the Humanitarian Society of Italy, which began to popularize the Montessori method.

By 1910, the Montessori method was attracting attention throughout Europe and the United States. Her book, *The Montessori Method*, an account of her work at the Casa dei Bambini and a discussion of her method, was published in 1912 and translated in 10 languages. She attracted a steady stream of visitors who attended her lectures, interviewed her, and observed her schools. Some of these visitors became dedicated disciples who introduced the Montessori method to their own countries. Montessori established a training school to prepare Montessori directresses, as she called her teachers.

The United States, where over a 100 Montessori schools were functioning in 1913, was especially receptive to the Italian educator. Her American supporters organized a national association, called the Montessori Educational System, to promote her ideas. The association arranged a speaking tour, in 1913, so that Montessori could promote her method in the United States. She spoke in the major American cities—Washington, D.C., New York, Philadelphia, Boston, Chicago, and San Francisco. Although she enjoyed large and receptive audiences, several critics attacked her method as unsuited to American children. A leading critic was William Heard Kilpatrick, a prominent professor at Columbia University's Teachers College, who attacked the Montessori method as insufficient in encouraging socialization, creativity, and problem-solving skills.[5] These attacks dampened the reception of Montessori's ideas in the United States.

Montessori made a second tour of the United States in 1917 to promote her new book, *Dr. Montessori's Own Handbook*, and to exhibit her didactic instructional materials. She attracted audiences, but the tour did not generate the support she envisioned. It would not be until the 1950s that the Montessori method would attract a large number of American supporters, which led to the establishment of hundreds of Montessori schools in the United States.

The Montessori method enjoyed greater success in Europe. The Spanish government invited Montessori to lecture and to establish two schools in Barcelona. From 1915 to 1927, Montessori worked in Spain, where she established a training school.

In 1927, Benito Mussolini's Fascist government invited Montessori to establish schools and training centers in Italy. Although basically a nonpolitical person, Montessori accepted the invitation and returned to Italy. Mussolini wanted to showcase prominent Italians as supporters of his Fascist government. Cooperation between the Fascist government and Montessori was uneasy. In 1934, the Association

Montessori Internationale, an international organization, was established to coordinate Montessori schools and activities. The Fascists wanted to use the association for political purposes, but Montessori refused. Mussolini ordered Montessori's schools closed, and Montessori left Italy as an exile.

When World War II began in 1939, Montessori was in India on a lecture tour. Although Italy and the United Kingdom were at war, the British authorities in India permitted Montessori the freedom to carry on her educational activities. As a result, a large number of Montessori schools were established in India. Many of her books were also published in that country.

When the war ended, Montessori, in 1946, went to the Netherlands, where an international headquarters was established to disseminate and coordinate her work. Her lectures took her to a number of countries. She continued her writing, teaching, and lecturing until her death on May 6, 1952.

In the 1950s, the Montessori method was rediscovered and enjoyed a significant revival in the United States. By the decade's end, more than 200 Montessori schools and several large training schools were operating in the United States.

Overview of Ideas on Education

Montessori's educational philosophy and method emerged as she gained insights from her work in medicine, anthropology, and pedagogy. Her multidisciplinary approach to education led her to develop an educational method designed to educate the whole child—physically, mentally, and emotionally.

Montessori's philosophy of education asserted that every child is to be respected as a person with individual needs and interests. Children, by their nature, have an innate sensitivity and intellectual capacity for absorbing information from the environment. They naturally possessed a strong capacity for mental concentration. If truly interested in their activity, children would concentrate their attention and their energy.

Montessori believed that children developed and learned through their own self-activity. While children were stimulated by their own interior potentiality, their self-activity was not to be wasted in purposeless commotion but was a potential to be exercised in conjunction with their motor, intellectual, and social development. She believed that children, disliking chaotic situations, preferred an orderly and structured environment.

Furniture and equipment in the Montessori school were proportioned to the size of the student. Montessori made sure that tables and chairs were child-sized so that classroom furniture did not interfere with children's freedom of movement. The school's rooms were lined with cupboards, positioned so that children had easy access to materials and could return them to their proper location.

Desiring to master new skills, children would practice a task, repeating it until they had learned it. Children understood that proficiency in such practical skills as tying a shoelace, buttoning a jacket, and putting on gloves and overshoes without the help of an adult gave them freedom and independence.

Montessori was convinced that children progressed through a series of developmental stages, each of which required an appropriate and specifically designed kind of learning. The first stage, the period of the absorbent mind, was from birth through age 6, when children were especially sensitive to learning from their environment. The second stage, from ages 7 through 18, saw the child moving through adolescence to adulthood.

Because of her interest in early childhood education, Montessori was primarily concerned with the "absorbent mind," during which children absorbed sensory impressions from the environment. She divided this period into two stages. During the early stage, from ages 1 to 3, a child's mind functions unconsciously and learning occurs from interaction with stimuli in the environment. During the later stage, from 3 to 6, children are more aware of and directive of their intellectual operations. Since absorption was heavily influenced by the learning possibilities found in the environment, the Montessori school, as a specially prepared environment, was rich in the materials and activities that stimulated a child's learning.

During the period of the absorbent mind, Montessori's students are working to put their information into some kind of order so that it makes sense to them. To do this, they learn that they need to know more about the larger world in which they live so that their ideas have a relationship to themselves and to the world. While children have a great capacity for acquiring and ordering their ideas, what they are learning needs to be appropriate to their readiness and development. It was therefore highly important to recognize when a child was sensitive, or ready, to acquire a new skill or body of information. On the basis of her theory of sensitive periods, Montessori designed her curriculum to develop children in three broad areas: motor and sensory development, the skills of practical life, and the formal literary and computational subjects. For each of these areas, she developed didactic materials and learning episodes.

By using the didactic apparatus in repeated exercises, children developed motor skills and physical coordination. The sensory exercises were intended to develop the ability to make comparisons, to discern color and hue, and to heighten sensitivity to smell and sound. Like objects were grouped; colors and shades were distinguished by using color tablets; tone bells were used to cultivate tonal sensitivity and discrimination.

Children learned such "generic" or practical skills as tying, lacing, buckling, zipping, and buttoning that are performed daily and could be applied to related tasks. Thus, they learned to be independent and lace and tie their own shoes, button their coats, and set a table with dishes and silverware—all without the help of adults.

Next came reading, writing, and arithmetic, which Montessori claimed were learned when, at ages 4 and 5, children "burst spontaneously into writing." To create readiness for writing and reading, Montessori devised letters cut from cardboard and covered with sandpaper. As the children touched and traced these letters, the Montessori directress voiced their sounds. Children discovered reading when they understood the sounds of the letters they were tracing and then wrote them to form words. A series of colored rods of varying lengths were used to teach arithmetic.

Children learned about the natural environment by planting and cultivating gardens. Small animals in the school introduced them to the animal kingdom. Gymnastics, group games, songs, and stories were included in the school day for socialization.

The prepared Montessori environment provided the milieu for instruction that emphasizes freedom of choice within an orderly structure. Children are free to pursue their interests and activities at their own rate without competition from their peers. No one is permitted to interfere with the work of others, to disrupt the school's order and routine, or to damage or misuse the equipment. Children are free to observe, but not interfere with, the work of peers, in order to learn from it.

THE PRIMARY SOURCE

In the selection from *The Montessori Method,* Maria Montessori discusses her first school, the Casa dei Bambini, or Children's House, which opened in Rome's poverty-ridden San Lorenzo district on January 6, 1907. Emphasizing that the school's success required parental involvement and community support, Montessori announced clear expectations in the guidelines that governed the school. The educational program of Montessori's Children's House, which enrolled students from ages 3 to 7, was based on her conception that children learned most effectively in a prepared environment that was structured and orderly. In preparing the school's environment, Montessori made certain that its physical arrangements—the tables, chairs, and apparatus—were appropriate to the children's needs. Tables and chairs were sized according to children's heights and weights. Washstands were accessible to the younger children. Classrooms were lined with low cupboards where children could reach instructional materials and return them to their proper location. The Montessori school was designed to cultivate children's sensory skills and manual dexterity, to allow them a degree of choice within a structured environment, and to cultivate independence and self-assurance in performing skills.

FOCUSING QUESTIONS

As you read the selection, you might wish to consider the following questions:

1. Consider the contemporary needs for early childhood education in the United States. Are Montessori's expectations and guidelines relevant to the American situation? Explain your answer.
2. Is Montessori's description of the educational directress relevant for contemporary society and schools? Does the description fit the profile of contemporary public school primary teachers? Explain your answer.
3. Montessori described her method as being based on pedagogical or educational science. Consider your courses in educational psychology, the exceptional child, and methods of teaching. In terms of these contemporary courses, is Montessori's approach scientific? Explain your answer.
4. Consider Montessori's specifications about furnishing her school. Are her ideas relevant for contemporary schools? Explain your answer.

FROM MARIA MONTESSORI'S *THE MONTESSORI METHOD*

But in striving to realise its ideal of a semi-gratuitous maintenance of its buildings, the Association met with a difficulty in regard to those children under school age, who must often be left alone during the entire day

From Maria Montessori's *The Montessori Method.* Translated by Anne E. George. New York: Frederick A. Stokes Co., 1912, 60–83.

while their parents went out to work. These little ones, not being able to understand the educative motives which taught their parents to respect the house, became ignorant little vandals, defacing the walls and stairs. And here we have another reform the expense of which may be considered as indirectly assumed by the tenants as was the care of the building. This reform may be considered as the most brilliant transformation of a tax which progress and civilization have as yet devised. The "Children's House" is earned by the parents through the care of the building. Its expenses are met by the sum that the Association would have otherwise been forced to spend upon repairs. A wonderful climax, this, of moral benefits received! Within the "Children's House," which belongs exclusively to those children under school age, working mothers may safely leave their little ones, and may proceed with a feeling of great relief and freedom to their own work. But this benefit, like that of the care of the house, is not conferred without a tax of care and of good will. The Regulations posted on the walls announce it thus:

"The mothers are obliged to send their children to the 'Children's House' clean, and to co-operate with the Directress in the educational work."

Two obligations: namely, the physical and moral care of their own children. If the child shows through its conversation that the educational work of the school is being undermined by the attitude taken in his home, he will be sent back to his parents, to teach them thus how to take advantage of their good opportunities. Those who give themselves over to low-living, to fighting, and to brutality, shall feel upon them the weight of those little lives, so needing care. They shall feel that they themselves have once more cast into the darkness of neglect those little creatures who are the dearest part of the family. In other words, the parents must learn to *deserve* the benefit of having within the house the great advantage of a school for their little ones.

"Good will," a willingness to meet the demands of the Association is enough, for the directress is ready and willing to teach them how. The regulations say that the mother must go at least once a week, to confer with the directress, giving an account of her child, and accepting any helpful advice which the directress may be able to give. The advice thus given will undoubtedly prove most illuminating in regard to the child's health and education, since to each of the "Children's Houses" is assigned a physician as well as a directress.

The directress is always at the disposition of the mothers, and her life, as a cultured and educated person, is a constant example to the inhabitants of the house, for she is obliged to live in the tenement and to be therefore a co-habitant with the families of all her little pupils. This is a fact of immense importance. Among these almost savage people, into these houses where at night no one dared go about unarmed, there

has come not only to teach, *but to live the very life they live,* a gentlewoman of culture, an educator by profession, who dedicates her time and her life to helping those about her! A true missionary, a moral queen among the people, she may, if she be possessed of sufficient tact and heart, reap an unheard-of harvest of good from her social work.

This house is verily *new;* it would seem a dream impossible of realization, but it has been tried. It is true that there have been before this attempts made by generous persons to go and live among the poor to civilise them. But such work is not practical, unless the house of the poor is hygienic, making it possible for people of better standards to live there. Nor can such work succeed in its purpose unless some common advantage or interest unites all of the tenants in an effort toward better things.

This tenement is new also because of the pedagogical organisation of the "Children's House." This is not simply a place where the children are kept, not just an *asylum,* but a true school for their education, and its methods are inspired by the rational principles of scientific pedagogy.

The physical development of the children is followed, each child being studied from the anthropological standpoint. Linguistic exercises, a systematic sense-training, and exercises which directly fit the child for the duties of practical life, form the basis of the work done. The teaching is decidedly objective, and presents an unusual richness of didactic material.

It is not possible to speak of all this in detail. I must, however, mention that there already exists in connection with the school a bathroom, where the children may be given hot or cold baths and where they may learn to take a partial bath, hands, face, neck, ears. Wherever possible the Association has provided a piece of ground in which the children may learn to cultivate the vegetables in common use.

It is important that I speak here of the pedagogical progress attained by the "Children's House" as an institution. Those who are conversant with the chief problems of the school know that to-day much attention is given to a great principle, one that is ideal and almost beyond realization,—the union of the family and the school in the matter of educational aims. But the family is always something far away from the school, and is almost always regarded as rebelling against its ideals. It is a species of phantom upon which the school can never lay its hands. The home is closed not only to pedagogical progress, but often to social progress. We see here for the first time the possibility of realising the long-talked-of pedagogical ideal. We have put *the school within the house;* and this is not all. We have placed it within the house as the *property of the collectivity,* leaving under the eyes of the parents the whole life of the teacher in the accomplishment of her high mission.

This idea of the collective ownership of the school is new and very beautiful and profoundly educational.

The parents know that the "Children's House" is their property, and is maintained by a portion of the rent they pay. The mothers may go at any hour of the day to watch, to admire, or to meditate upon the life there. It is in every way a continual stimulus to reflection, and a fount of evident blessing and help to their own children. We may say that the mothers *adore* the "Children's House," and the directress. How many delicate and thoughtful attentions these good mothers show the teacher of their little ones! They often leave sweets or flowers upon the sill of the schoolroom window, as a silent token, reverently, almost religiously, given.

And when after three years of such a novitiate, the mothers send their children to the common schools, they will be excellently prepared to co-operate in the work of education, and will have acquired a sentiment, rarely found even among the best classes; namely, the idea that they must *merit* through their own conduct and with their own virtue, the possession of an educated son.

Another advance made by the "Children's House" as an institution is related to scientific pedagogy. This branch of pedagogy, heretofore, being based upon the anthropological study of the pupil whom it is to educate, has touched only a few of the positive questions which tend to transform education. For a man is not only a biological but a social product, and the social environment of individuals in the process of education, is the home. Scientific pedagogy will seek in vain to better the new generation if it does not succeed in influencing also the environment within which this new generation grows! I believe, therefore, that in opening the house to the light of new truths, and to the progress of civilisation we have solved the problem of being able to modify directly, the *environment* of the new generation, and have thus made it possible to apply, in a practical way, the fundamental principles of scientific pedagogy.

The "Children's House" marks still another triumph; it is the first step toward the *socialisation of the house.* The inmates find under their own roof the convenience of being able to leave their little ones in a place, not only safe, but where they have every advantage.

And let it be remembered that *all* the mothers in the tenement may enjoy this privilege, going away to their work with easy minds. Until the present time only one class in society might have this advantage. Rich women were able to go about their various occupations and amusements, leaving their children in the hands of a nurse or a governess. To-day the women of the people who live in these remodeled houses, may say, like the great lady, "I have left my son with the governess and the nurse." More than this, they may add, like the princess of the blood, "And the house physician watches over them and directs their sane and sturdy growth." These women, like the most advanced class of English and American mothers, possess a "Biographical Chart," which, filled for the mother by the directress and the doctor, gives her the most practical knowledge of her child's growth and condition.

We are all familiar with the ordinary advantages of the communistic transformation of the general environment. For example, the collective use of railway carriages, of street lights, of the telephone, all these are great advantages. The enormous production of useful articles, brought about by industrial progress, makes possible to all, clean clothes, carpets, curtains, table-delicacies, better tableware, etc. The making of such benefits generally tends to level social caste. All this we have seen in its reality. But the communising of *persons* is new. That the collectivity shall benefit from the services of the servant, the nurse, the teacher—this is a modern ideal. . . .

ENVIRONMENT: SCHOOLROOM FURNISHINGS

The method of *observation* must undoubtedly include the *methodical observation* of the morphological growth of the pupils. But let me repeat that, while this element necessarily enters, it is not upon this particular kind of observation that the method is established.

The method of observation is established upon one fundamental base—*the liberty of the pupils in their spontaneous manifestations.*

With this in view, I first turned my attention to the question of environment, and this, of course, included the furnishing of the schoolroom. In considering an ample playground with space for a garden as an important part of this school environment, I am not suggesting anything new.

The novelty lies, perhaps, in my idea for the use of this open-air space, which is to be in direct communication with the schoolroom, so that the children may be free to go and come as they like, throughout the entire day. I shall speak of this more fully later on.

The principal modification in the matter of school furnishings is the abolition of desks, and benches or stationary chairs. I have had tables made with wide, solid, octagonal legs, spreading in such a way that the tables are at the same time solidly firm and very light, so light, indeed, that two four-year-old children can easily carry them about. These tables are rectangular and sufficiently large to accommodate two children on the long side, there being room for three if they sit rather close together. There are smaller tables at which one child may work alone.

I also designed and had manufactured little chairs. My first plan for these was to have them cane seated, but experience has shown the wear on these to be so great, that I now have chairs made entirely of wood. These are very light and of an attractive shape. In addition to these, I have in each schoolroom a number of comfortable little armchairs, some of wood and some of wicker.

Another piece of our school furniture consists of a little washstand, so low that it can be used by even a three-year-old child. This is painted with a white waterproof enamel and, besides the broad, upper and lower shelves which hold the little white enameled basins and pitchers, there are small side shelves for the soap-dishes, nail-brushes, towels, etc. There is also a receptacle into which the basins may be emptied. Wherever possible, a small cupboard provides each child with a space where he may keep his own soap, nail-brush, tooth-brush, etc.

In each of our schoolrooms we have provided a series of long low cupboards, especially designed for the reception of the didactic materials. The doors of these cupboards open easily, and the care of the materials is confided to the children. The tops of these cases furnish room for potted plants, small aquariums, or for the various toys with which the children are allowed to play freely. We have ample blackboard space, and these boards are so hung as to be easily used by the smallest child. Each blackboard is provided with a small case in which are kept the chalk, and the white cloths which we use instead of the ordinary erasers.

Above the blackboards are hung attractive pictures, chosen carefully, representing simple scenes in which children would naturally be interested. Among the pictures in our "Children's Houses" in Rome we have hung a copy of Raphael's "Madonna della Seggiola," and this picture we have chosen as the emblem of the "Children's Houses." For indeed, these "Children's Houses" represent not only social progress, but universal human progress, and are closely related to the elevation of the idea of motherhood, to the progress of woman and to the protection of her offspring. In this beautiful conception, Raphael has not only shown us the Madonna as a Divine Mother holding in her arms the babe who is greater than she, but by the side of this symbol of all motherhood, he has placed the figure of St. John, who represents humanity. So in Raphael's picture we see humanity rendering homage to maternity,—maternity, the sublime fact in the definite triumph of humanity. In addition to this beautiful symbolism, the picture has a value as being one of the greatest works of art of Italy's greatest artist. And if the day shall come when the "Children's Houses" shall be established throughout the world, it is our wish that this picture of Raphael's shall have its place in each of the schools, speaking eloquently of the country in which they originated.

The children, of course, cannot comprehend the symbolic significance of the "Madonna of the Chair," but they will see something more beautiful than that which they feel in more ordinary pictures, in which they see mother, father, and children. And the constant companionship with this picture will awaken in their heart a religious impression.

This, then, is the environment which I have selected for the children we wish to educate.

SUGGESTIONS FOR FURTHER READING

Fisher, Dorothy Canfield. *Montessori for Parents.* Cambridge, Mass.: Robert Bentley, 1965.

_____. *The Montessori Manual.* Cambridge, Mass.: Robert Bentley, 1964.

Gitter, Lena L. *Montessori's Legacy to Children.* Johnstown, Pa.: Mafex Associates, 1970.

_____. *The Montessori Way.* Seattle: Special Child Publications, 1970.

Gross, Michael J. *Montessori's Concept of Personality.* Lantham, Md.: University Press of America, 1986.

Hainstock, Elizabeth G. *The Essential Montessori.* New York: New American Library, 1978.

Kilpatrick, William H. *The Montessori System Examined.* New York: Arno Press and New York Times, 1971.

Kramer, Rita. *Maria Montessori: A Biography.* Reading, Mass.: Perseus Books, 1988.

Lillard, Paul P. *Montessori: A Modern Approach.* New York: Schocken Books, 1972.

Montessori, Maria. *The Absorbent Mind.* New York: Henry Holt and Co., 1995.

_____. *Childhood Education.* Translated by A. M. Joosten. Chicago: Henry Regnery Press, 1949.

_____. *The Child in the Family.* Translated by Nancy Rockmore Cirillo. Chicago: Henry Regnery Press, 1970.

_____. *The Discovery of the Child.* Translated by Mary A. Johnstone. Madras, India: Theosophical Press, 1948.

_____. *Dr. Montessori's Own Handbook.* New York: Frederick A. Stokes, 1914. Reprinted by Robert Bentley, 1967.

_____. *Education and Peace.* Translated by Helen R. Lane. Chicago: Henry Regnery Press, 1949.

_____. *From Childhood to Adolescence.* New York: Schocken Books, 1948.

_____. *The Montessori Method.* Translated by Anne E. George. New York: Frederick A. Stokes, 1912. Reprinted by Robert Bentley, 1967.

_____. *Pedagogical Anthropology.* Translated by Frederick T. Cooper. New York: Frederick A. Stokes, 1913.

_____. *The Secret of Childhood.* Translated by Barbara Barclay Carter. New York: Frederick A. Stokes, 1939.

_____. *Spontaneous Activity in Education.* Translated by Florence Simmonds. New York: Frederick A. Stokes, 1917. Reprinted by Robert Bentley, 1967.

Oren, R. C. *Montessori Today.* New York: G. P. Putnam's Sons, 1971.

_____. *Montessori: Her Method and the Movement—What You Need to Know.* New York: G. P. Putnam's Sons, 1974.

Standing, E. M. *Maria Montessori: Her Life and Work.* New York: A Plume Book, Penguin Group, 1998.

Ward, Florence E. *The Montessori Method and the American School.* New York: Arno Press and New York Times, 1971.

NOTES

1. Rita Kramer, *Maria Montessori* (New York: G. P. Putnam's Sons, 1976), 22–24.
2. Lena L. Gitter, *The Montessori Way* (Seattle: Special Child Publications, 1970), 7.
3. Kathrina Myers, "Seguin's Principles of Education as Related to the Montessori Method," *Journal of Education* 77 (May 1913), 538–41.
4. Kramer, 214.
5. William H. Kilpatrick, *The Montessori Method Examined* (Boston: Houghton Mifflin, 1914).

MOHANDAS GANDHI: FATHER OF INDIAN INDEPENDENCE

Mohandas Gandhi (1869–1948), the father of Indian independence, is significant in world history as a leader who developed and used a strategy of nonviolent resistance to bring about social and political change. As a moral leader, Gandhi designed his ideas to foster a climate of mutual respect and cooperation between people. He developed a plan of basic education that anticipated today's theory of sustainable development.

Mohandas K. Gandhi was born on October 2, 1869, at Porbandar, in Kathiawad, India. He was the son of Karmachand and Puthbai Gandhi, higher caste parents. Both his grandfather and father had been ministers in the government of Kathiawad. Gandhi attended the local primary school at Rajkot, where his family had moved. As was the custom, he was betrothed at age 7 to marry Kasturbai, daughter of the merchant Kokuldas Makanji. After he completed secondary school in Rajkot, he married his betrothed in 1883.

For his higher education, Gandhi began undergraduate studies at Sarmaldas College in Bhavnager in 1887, but after a semester he left to study law in the United Kingdom. He remained in England for 3 years, completed his legal studies, and returned to India in 1891 to begin practicing law in Bombay.

Gandhi then went to South Africa as legal counsel for an Indian commercial firm. From 1893 to 1901, except for brief visits to India, he was in South Africa, which had a large Indian population consisting of laborers and small shopkeepers. The white South African government had enacted policies against the Indians that restricted their personal liberties. Gandhi organized and led the Natal Indian Congress, which sought to repeal the laws that discriminated against the Indian population. It was during this period that Gandhi developed his strategies of nonviolent passive resistance. He also established several ashrams, communal settlements, that contained schools.

In 1901, Gandhi and his family returned to India. He resumed his legal practice in Bombay but soon joined the young independence movement. Largely British educated, Gandhi sought to reestablish his roots in his native country, traveling extensively to meet the local people and encourage the leaders of the Indian National Congress party.

Gandhi returned to South Africa in response to a plea from the Indian community, asking him to represent them as they faced more repression from the South African government. From 1902 to 1904, Gandhi represented the Indian minority, organizing them to resist the government's official repression. As he sought to marshal his personal resources against the South Africa government's discrimination, Gandhi read the works of John Ruskin (1819–1900), the English writer and ethicist, and Leo Tolstoy (1828–1910), the Russian author of *War and Peace,* both of whom were proponents of social justice. Facing a system of unjust law, Gandhi came to believe that the only course was a moral struggle based on nonviolent resistance. To educate his followers for the coming campaign of nonviolent resistance, Gandhi established Phoenix Farm, near Durban. Phoenix Farm, Tolstoy Farm, and other centers for social and moral education that Gandhi would later establish were based on the ancient Vedic concept of the ashram, a school where students sought the truth guided by an enlightened teacher. Gandhi based his ashrams on his philosophy that called for the well-rounded intellectual, moral, and physical development of the whole person.

Gandhi believed moral development rested upon a spiritual foundation. While his spirituality was universalist rather than sectarian, each child was to be educated in the principles of his or her religion and to read and study the scriptures appropriate for that creed. Within the general moral and spiritual climate of the school, Gandhi believed children should learn the academic skills and subjects of reading, writing, arithmetic, English, history, geography, and singing. They were to be taught in the language they spoke at home whenever possible. Gandhi included vocational education, which was to emphasize the dignity of work and to teach the skills for earning a living. Vocational education would offset the residues of the ancient Indian scholarly tradition, British education, and the caste system, which relegated those who did manual labor to the bottom rungs of society. The teachers, including Gandhi, worked among the children at gardening, did chores, and learned handicraft production.

Between 1905 and 1910, Gandhi led South Africa's Indian community against an oppressive government. His weapon was *satyagraha,* the consciousness of the "soul force" in each person. This spiritual force took the form of nonviolent civil disobedience, passive resistance, and noncooperation against the state's police and military power. Gandhi's concept of satyagraha had the following important implications for moral education:

1. All persons possessed the interior spiritual power to resist social injustice but needed to bring it to consciousness.
2. "Soul power" had to be disciplined by training to subdue the urge to do violence to revenge repression and injustice.
3. A complete spiritual education would prepare the person to participate in the cause of liberation.

Between 1906 and 1914, Gandhi was imprisoned on several occasions for leading three major satyagraha campaigns against the South African government. In 1914, passage of the Indian Relief Act eliminated some of the restrictions against the Indian population.

In 1915, Gandhi returned to India to mobilize the independence movement to which he devoted the rest of his life. On the basis of his experiences in South Africa, he again established an ashram, Satyagraha Ashram, to prepare his followers for their long struggle against British rule. He organized local satyagraha campaigns and edited *Young India,* an English language weekly, and *Navajivan,* a weekly published in Gujarati, one of the Indian languages.

In 1937, an all-India conference of educators met at Wardha where Gandhi made the following specific educational proposals.

1. Education should be free and compulsory for 7 years throughout India.
2. Instruction at the primary level should be in the child's mother tongue, the vernacular spoken in the home.
3. Instruction should be craft-centered.[1]

The Wardha Conference adopted a resolution in support of Gandhian basic education, which was also endorsed by the Indian National Congress party. After independence, some basic education schools were established, but their impact was small.

For more than three decades, Gandhi was the leading voice calling for an independent India. His campaign sought to persuade the British to voluntarily grant independence. Gandhi would call for an all-India satyagraha, a campaign of massive civil disobedience, often accompanied by a cessation of work and transportation. The British would respond, often arresting Gandhi and the Congress party leaders. Gandhi would be released and the scenario would be repeated. During his lifetime, Gandhi spent a total of 2,338 days in prison. As a result of his patient but persistent strategy, India became independent in 1947 when the British voluntarily left.

Gandhi worked desperately against the casteism and sectarianism that traditionally divided Indians on ethnic, language, and religious lines. His ability to keep the Muslims in his movement was always shaky and broke down when India received independence in 1947. At that time, an independent Muslim state, headed by Mohammed Ali Jinnah, was established as Pakistan. At various times, violent communal riots between the Hindus and Muslims depressed the apostle of nonviolence. When such outbreaks occurred, Gandhi would suspend his activities and begin a fast, which on several occasions became life threatening, until the communal rioting and violence had ceased.

Although independence was won, the process of achieving freedom was perilous. Though Gandhi wanted a united India, two independent nations—India and Pakistan—were created when the British left the subcontinent. When the two nations were created, the Hindu and Sikh religious groups living in Pakistan began a painful exodus to India, and many Muslims in India migrated to Pakistan. In the midst of the relocation of millions of displaced persons, communal rioting broke out between the religious factions, resulting in massacres and pillaging. Gandhi began a fast that lasted until the rioting subsided. On January 30, 1948, Gandhi was assassinated by Vinayak Godse, a fanatical Hindu nationalist. Thus, the man who preached and practiced nonviolence was a victim of the violence he so deplored.

OVERVIEW OF IDEAS ON EDUCATION

Gandhi's social and educational philosophy was a mosaic of spiritual, political, economic, and educational elements. He claimed he was not a systematic philosopher but was trying to live according to the eternal truths that governed the universe.[2]

Some of Gandhi's philosophical beliefs came from Hinduism, especially the metaphysics that held the universe was inherently spiritual. This perspective emphasized the inner self, a spiritual essence, to be at the core of the human being. The universe, a manifestation of God, a supreme spiritual presence, was governed by unalterable laws. In Hindu cosmology, the purpose of human existence was to be reabsorbed into God and to end the trials of earthly life. The Hindu concept of reincarnation—successive births and deaths in either higher or lower orders of life depending upon one's performance in the previous existence—emphasized the sacredness of all life. In his social and educational philosophy, Gandhi referred to the universal principles and truths of all the world's great religions that bind people all over the world.[3]

Grounded in spirituality, Gandhi believed in well-rounded, harmonious human development that was intellectual and physical as well as spiritual. In the *India of My Dreams,* he discussed his concept of holistic education:

> The true education of the intellect can only come through a proper exercise and training of the bodily organs. . . . In other words, an intelligent use of the bodily organs in a child provides the best and quickest way of developing his intellect. But unless the development of the mind and body goes hand in hand with a corresponding awakening of the soul, the former alone would prove to be a poor lop-sided affair. By spiritual training I mean education of the heart. A proper and all-round development of the mind, therefore, can take place only when it proceeds . . . with the education of the physical and spiritual faculties of the child. They constitute an indivisible whole.[4]

This kind of holistic development, Gandhi believed, took place in a peaceful and nonviolent world order. However, neither his native India, which was subject to British colonialism and sectarian contention, nor the world, then torn by war, was a peaceful society. He felt he could not retreat inwardly but rather had to manifest his inner spirituality outwardly to struggle against violence and injustice. His convictions brought him into politics and education as agencies that might correct unjust political, social, and economic conditions.

As part of a worldview, Gandhi's underlying philosophy was a movement against imperialism and colonialism. Advocating human freedom, he did not believe that people achieve self-realization under exploitative systems. For him, all people had the right to political and economic self-determination. The peoples of Asia and Africa and, indeed, all oppressed people needed to be liberated from conditions of dependency and submission. His anti-imperialism had important implications for education. The kind of schooling and training the Europeans had imposed on subject peoples was designed for servitude and dependency rather than self-reliance and independence. A liberating education was to awaken a sense of cultural and national identity that came from studying the history, language, and literature of one own's country in a self-affirming way but not in one that generated nationalism and hatred of others.

Gandhi opposed not only foreign-imposed domination but also the forms of discrimination that a people might create within their own indigenous society. The caste system—which rigidly ascribed a person's status, role, and function—was such a form of subordination. The system fell most heavily on the untouchables, who were a large marginalized group relegated to the most burdensome jobs as sweepers and scavengers and confined to the poorest and most squalid sections of cities and villages. Gandhi strongly opposed untouchability. He renamed the untouchables the harijans, or people of God, and argued for the removal of disabilities because of caste. His teachings and actions consistently opposed discrimination of all kinds.

Gandhi, an early proponent of the theory of sustainable development, wanted to bring about a revitalization of the Indian villages where the great mass of the population lived. Village India was characterized by illiteracy, poverty, and unemployment. Gandhi's proposal for basic education was designed to renew village life and economy. He wanted economic development to begin at the grassroots level, where the local people planned and created their own small-scale industries. He saw small-scale industries that centered on handicraft production as a key to such an economic revitalization.

In terms of schooling, Gandhi developed a program called "basic education."[5] In his plan, primary schooling was to be craft-centered, conducted in the child's own language, and compulsory for all children between the ages of 7 and 14. The craft taught in the particular school was to be one of the major occupations found in the locality, and instruction was to center around the craft. He also believed the sale of the items made in the schools could help support them. Basic education, according to Gandhi, would inculcate a spirit of cooperation, unity, and group responsibility. Gandhi saw basic education as providing a common foundation that would reduce the gap between urban and rural India.

THE PRIMARY SOURCE

India is a multilanguage country, where there are more than 17 languages, many of which are state or regionally based. In multilanguage countries, educational policy regarding language instruction is frequently controversial and politically charged. In the selections from *The Moral and Political Writings of Mahatma Gandhi*, Gandhi comments on the need for instruction to be in the child's own vernacular language.

In Indian society a strong dichotomy existed between intellectual and physical work. In his educational philosophy, Gandhi emphasized the importance and the dignity of physical labor.

Gandhi believed both traditional Indian education and British education were too verbal and passive. He proposed a plan for basic education that was craft-centered. For example, the craft might be cotton spinning and manufacturing, which, he believed, had a number of correlated educational possibilities. It related to botany and to agriculture in that children could observe and participate in planting, cultivating, and harvesting cotton. It related to small-scale industry in that children could observe and participate in ginning cotton—separating the fiber from the seeds and spinning the fiber into thread. Children could also participate in weaving the thread into cloth. Further, the cloth could be made into clothing. Thus, the participation of children in craft education—from planting the seed to manufacturing the clothing, in the case of cotton—would enable them to understand the full process of production. Further, the finished product was something they could see and appreciate as the tangible manifestation of their work.

FOCUSING QUESTIONS

As you read the selections, you might wish to consider the following questions:

1. On the basis of the selection, identify and comment on Gandhi's principles of education, especially as they related to language, untouchability, manual work, and women's education.
2. Why was Gandhi a proponent of craft-centered education?
3. Reflect on Gandhi's theory of nonviolent protest. How has this theory been applied in the American experience?
4. How did Gandhi hope to revitalize village India?

FROM *THE MORAL AND POLITICAL WRITINGS OF MAHATMA GANDHI*

In Europe, every cultured man learns, not only his language, but also other languages, certainly three or four. And even as they do in Europe, in order to solve the problem of language in India, we, in this Ashram, make it a point to learn as many Indian vernaculars as we possibly can. And I assure you that the trouble of learning these languages is nothing compared to the trouble that we have to take in mastering the English language. We never master the English language; with some exceptions, it has not been possible for us to do so; we can never express ourselves as clearly as we can in our own mother tongue. How dare we rub out of our memory all the years of our infancy? But that is precisely what we do when we commence our higher life, as we call it, through the medium of a foreign tongue. This creates a breach in our life for bridging which we shall have to pay dearly and heavily.

And you will see now the connection between these two things—education and untouchableness—this persistence of the spirit of untouchableness even at this time of the day in spite of the spread of knowledge and education. Education has enabled us to see the horrible crime. But we are seized with fear also and, therefore, we cannot take this doctrine to our homes. And we have got a superstitious veneration for our family traditions and for the members of our family. You say, 'My parents will die if I tell them that I, at least, can no longer partake of this crime.' I say that Prahlad never considered that his father would die if

From *The Moral and Political Writings of Mahatma Gandhi* II, edited by Raghavan Iyer. Oxford: Clarendon Press, 1986, 530–531, 541–543, 608–612, 632.

he pronounced the sacred syllables of the name of Vishnu. On the contrary, he made the whole of that household ring, from one corner to another, by repeating that name even in the sacred presence of his father. And so you and I may do this thing in the sacred presence of our parents. If, after receiving this rude shock, some of them expire, I think that would be no calamity. It may be that some rude shocks of the kind might have to be delivered. So long as we persist in these things which have been handed down to us for generations, these incidents may happen. But there is a higher law of Nature, and in due obedience to that higher law, my parents and myself should make that sacrifice, and then we follow hand-weaving.

You may ask: 'Why should *we* use our hands?' and say 'the manual work has got to be done by those who are illiterate. I can only occupy myself with reading literature and political essays.' I think that we have to realize the dignity of labour. If a barber or shoemaker attends a college, he ought not to abandon the profession of barber or shoe-maker. I consider that a barber's profession is just as good as the profession of medicine.

VII. NATIONAL EDUCATION

An attempt is made in the Ashram to impart such education as is conducive to national welfare. In order that spiritual, intellectual and physical development may proceed side by side, an atmosphere of industry has been created, and letters are not given more than their due importance. Character-building is attended to in the smallest detail. 'Untouchable' children are freely admitted. Women are given special attention with a view to improving their status, and they are accorded the same opportunities for self-culture as the men. The Ashram accepts the following principles of the Gujarat Vidyapith:

1. The principal object of the Vidyapith shall be to prepare workers of character, ability, education and conscientiousness, necessary for the conduct of the movements connected with the attainment of *swaraj*.
2. All the institutions conducted by and affiliated to the Vidyapith shall be fully non-co-operating and shall therefore have nothing to do with any help from Government.
3. Whereas the Vidyapith has come into being in connection with the *swaraj* movement, and Non-violent Non-co-operation as a means thereof, its teachers and trustees shall restrict themselves to those means only which are not inconsistent with truth and non-violence and shall consciously strive to carry them out.
4. The teachers and the trustees of the Vidyapith, as also all the institutions affiliated to it, shall regard untouchability as a blot on Hinduism, shall strive to the best of their power for its removal, and shall not exclude a boy or a girl for reason of his or her untouchability nor shall give him or her differential treatment having once accorded admission to him or her.
5. The teachers and the trustees of and all the institutions affiliated to the Vidyapith shall regard hand-spinning as an essential part of the *swaraj* movement and shall therefore spin regularly, except when disabled, and shall habitually wear *khadi*.
6. The language of the province shall have the principal place in the Vidyapith and shall be the medium of instruction.

EXPLANATION. Languages other than Gujarati may be taught by direct method.

7. The teaching of Hindi-Hindustani shall be compulsory in the curricula of the Vidyapith.
8. Manual training shall receive the same importance as intellectual training and only such occupations as are useful for the life of the nation shall be taught.
9. Whereas the growth of the nation depends not on cities but its villages, the bulk of the funds of the Vidyapith and a majority of the teachers of the Vidyapith shall be employed in the propagation of education conducive to the welfare of the villagers.
10. In laying down the curricula, the needs of village dwellers shall have principal consideration.
11. There shall be complete toleration of all established religions in all institutions conducted by and affiliated to the Vidyapith, and for the spiritual development of the pupils, religious instruction shall be imparted in consonance with truth and non-violence.
12. For the physical development of the nation physical exercise and physical training shall be compulsory in all the institutions conducted by and affiliated to the Vidyapith.

NOTE. Hindi-Hindustani means the language commonly spoken by the masses of the North—both Hindu and Mussalman—and written in the Devanagari or the Arabic script.

The Ashram school has so far sent forth 15 boys and 2 girls. . . .

I have my own perhaps peculiar views on education which have not been accepted by my colleagues in full, and here they are:

1. Young boys and girls should have co-education till they are eight years of age.
2. Their education should mainly consist in manual training under the supervision of an educationist.
3. The special aptitudes of each child should be recognized in determining the kind of work he or she should do.
4. The reasons for every process should be explained when the process is being carried on.
5. General knowledge should be imparted to each child as he begins to understand things. Learning to read or write should come later.
6. The child should first be taught to draw simple geometrical figures, and when he has learnt to draw these with ease, he should be taught to write the alphabet. If this is done he will write a good hand from the very first.
7. Reading should come before writing. The letters should be treated as pictures to be recognized and later on to be copied.

8. A child taught on these lines will have acquired considerable knowledge according to his capacity by the time he is eight.

9. Nothing should be taught to a child by force.

10. He should be interested in everything taught to him.

11. Education should appear to the child like play. Play is an essential part of education.

12. All education should be imparted through the mother tongue.

13. The child should be taught Hindi–Urdu as the national language, before he learns letters.

14. Religious education is indispensable and the child should get it by watching the teacher's conduct and by hearing him talk about it.

15. Nine to sixteen constitutes the second stage in the child's education.

16. It is desirable that boys and girls should have co-education during the second stage also as far as possible.

17. Hindu children should now be taught Sanskrit, and Muslim children Arabic.

18. Manual training should be continued during the second stage. Literary education should be allotted more time according to necessity.

19. The boys during this stage should be taught their parents' vocation in such a way that they will by their own choice obtain their livelihood by practising the hereditary craft. This does not apply to the girls.

20. During this stage the child should acquire a general knowledge of world history and geography, botany, astronomy, arithmetic, geometry, and algebra.

21. Each child should now be taught to sew and to cook.

22. Sixteen to twenty-five is the third stage, during which every young person should have an education according to his or her wishes and circumstances.

23. During the second stage (9–16) education should be self-supporting; that is, the child, all the time that he is learning, is working upon some industry, the proceeds of which will meet the expenditure of the school.

24. Production starts from the very beginning, but during the first stage it does not still catch up with the expenditure.

25. Teachers should be paid not very high salaries but only a living wage. They should be inspired by a spirit of service. It is a despicable thing to take any Tom, Dick or Harry as a teacher in the primary stage. All teachers should be men of character.

26. Big and expensive buildings are not necessary for educational institutions.

27. English should be taught only as one of several languages. As Hindi is the national language, English is to be used in dealing with other nations and international commerce.

As for women's education I am not sure whether it should be different from men's and when it should begin. But I am strongly of opinion that women should have the same facilities as men and even special facilities where necessary.

There should be night schools for illiterate adults. But I do not think that they must be taught the three R's; they must be helped to acquire general knowledge through lectures, etc., and if they wish, we should arrange to teach them the three R's also.

Experiments in the Ashram have convinced us of one thing, viz., that industry in general and spinning in particular should have pride of place in education, which must be largely self-supporting as well as related to and tending to the betterment of rural life.

In these experiments we have achieved the largest measure of success with the women, who have imbibed the spirit of freedom and self-confidence as no other class of women have done to my knowledge. This success is due to the Ashram atmosphere. Women in the Ashram are not subject to any restraint which is not imposed on the men as well. They are placed on a footing of absolute equality with the men in all activities. Not a single Ashram task is assigned to the women to the exclusion of the men. Cooking is attended to by both. Women are of course exempted from work which is beyond their strength; otherwise men and women work together everywhere. There is no such thing as *purdah* or *laj* in the Ashram. No matter from where she has come, a woman, as soon as she enters the Ashram, breathes the air of freedom and casts out all fear from her mind. And I believe that the Ashram observance of *brahmacharya* has made a big contribution to this state of things. Adult girls live in the Ashram as virgins. We are aware that this experiment is fraught with risk but we feel that no awakening among women is possible without incurring it.

Women cannot make any progress so long as there are child marriages. All girls are supposed to be in duty bound to marry and that too before menstruation commences, and widow remarriage is not permitted. Women, therefore, when they join the Ashram, are told that these social customs are wrong and irreligious. But they are not shocked as they find the Ashram practising what it preaches.

Not much of what is usually called education will be observed in the Ashram. Still we find that the old as well as the young, women as well as men are eager to acquire knowledge and complain that they have no time for it. This is a good sign. Many who join the Ashram are not educated or even interested in education. Some of them can hardly read or write. They had no desire for progress so long as they had not joined the Ashram. But when they have lived in the Ashram for a little while, they conceive a desire for increasing their knowledge. This is a great thing, as to create a desire for knowledge is very often the first step to be taken. But I do not regret it very much that there are insufficient facilities in the Ashram calculated to satisfy this desire. The observances kept in the Ashram will perhaps prevent a sufficient number of qualified teachers from joining it. We must therefore rest satisfied with such Ashramites as can be trained to teach. The numerous activities of the Ashram may come in the way of their acquiring the requisite qualifications at all or at an early date. But it does not matter much, as the desire for knowledge can be satisfied later as well as sooner, being independent of a time-limit. Real education begins after a child has left school. One who has appreciated the value of studies is a student all his life. His knowledge must increase from day to day while he is discharging his duty in a conscientious manner. And this is well understood in the Ashram.

The superstition that no education is possible without a teacher is an obstacle in the path of educational progress. A man's real teacher is himself. And nowadays there are numerous aids available for self-education. A diligent person can easily acquire knowledge about many things by himself and obtain the assistance of a teacher when it is needed. Experience is the biggest of all schools. Quite a number of crafts cannot be learnt at school but only in the workshop. Knowledge of these acquired at school is often only parrot-like. Other subjects can be learnt with the help of books. Therefore what adults need is not so much a school as a thirst for knowledge, diligence and self-confidence.

The education of children is primarily a duty to be discharged by the parents. Therefore the creation of a vital educational atmosphere is more important than the foundation of numerous schools. When once this atmosphere has been established on a firm footing the schools will come in due course.

This is the Ashram ideal of education which has been realized to some extent, as every department of Ashram activity is a veritable school.

SUGGESTIONS FOR FURTHER READING

Andrews, C. F. *Mahatma Gandhi at Work.* New York: Macmillan Publishing Company, 1931.

Ashe, Geoffrey. *Gandhi.* New York: Stein and Day, 1968.

Duncan, Ronald. *Gandhi: Selected Writings.* New York: Harper and Row, 1972.

Erikson, Erik. *Gandhi's Truth.* New York: Norton, 1972.

Fischer, Louis. *The Essential Gandhi: His Life, Work, and Ideas: An Anthology.* New York: Vintage Books, 1962.

_____. *The Life of Mahatma Gandhi.* New York: Harper and Row, 1952.

Gandhi, M. K. *India of My Dreams.* Ahmedabad: Navajivan Publishing House, 1947.

_____. *An Autobiography or the Story of My Experiments with Truth.* Boston: Beacon Press, 1957.

Iver, Raghavan. *The Moral and Political Writings of Mahatma Gandhi.* Oxford, England: Clarendon Press, 1986.

Patel, M. *The Educational Philosophy of Mahatma Gandhi.* Ahmedabad: Navajivan Publishing House, 1953.

Ramanathan, G. *Education from Dewey to Gandhi.* London: Asia Publishing House, 1965.

Shirer, William. *Gandhi: A Memoir.* New York: Simon and Schuster, 1979.

NOTES

1. G. Ramanathan, *Education from Dewey to Gandhi* (London: Asia Publishing House, 1965), 4–5.
2. Shriman Narayan, ed., *The Selected Works of Mahatma Gandhi,* VI (Ahmedabad: Navajivan Publishing House, 1968), 94.
3. S. P. Chaube, *Recent Educational Philosophies in India* (Agra: Ram Pradad and Sons, 1967), 116.
4. M. K. Gandhi, *India of My Dreams* (Ahmedabad: Navajivan Publishing House, 1947), 185.
5. K. G. Saiyidain, *The Humanist Tradition in Modern Indian Educational Thought* (Madison, Wis.: Dembar Educational Research Services, 1967), 89.

W. E. B. DU BOIS: SCHOLAR AND ACTIVIST FOR AFRICAN AMERICAN RIGHTS

BIOGRAPHICAL SKETCH

William E. B. Du Bois (1868–1963), a sociologist and historian, is significant for his scholarship and activism, which helped to raise African American consciousness. His scholarship laid the foundations for Pan Africanism and the Afrocentric curriculum.

Du Bois was born on February 23, 1868, in Great Barrington, Massachusetts. Alfred Du Bois, his father was born in Haiti. Mary Silvina Burghardt, his mother, was from a family that had lived in Great Barrington since the late colonial period. Du Bois' father, who left Great Barrington when William was a year old, never returned to the family. William was raised by his mother, who supported the household and encouraged her son's education.[1] The Du Bois family were among a small number of African Americans living in Great Barrington, a small New England town with few racial tensions. Raised in a religious atmosphere, William and his mother attended the First Congregational Church.

Du Bois attended his local elementary school, enrolling at age 6, where as a child he earned a reputation of being a serious student. He then enrolled in Great Barrington's high school, where the principal, Frank Hosmer, encouraged Du Bois to enroll in the college preparatory curriculum.[2] He was very active in extracurricular activities. He served as coeditor of the school newspaper, *The Howler,* and organized a literary society, the "Sons of Freedom." As a teenager, Du Bois worked at a number of part-time jobs to supplement his mother's income. A talented writer, young William Du Bois was also a part-time newspaper reporter for the Great Barrington-Springfield *Republican.*[3]

In 1884, W. E. B. Du Bois graduated from high school, receiving his diploma with high honors and delivering a commencement address on Wendell Phillips, the New England abolitionist.[4] Du Bois' mother died in March 1885, and it appeared that he would be forced to abandon his plans for a college education. However, Hosmer and several other community leaders raised funds to support Du Bois' enrollment at Fisk University, an African American institution under Congregational Church control in Nashville, Tennessee.[5]

The 17-year-old Du Bois made his first journey to the South in 1885 to begin classes at Fisk. The university faculty, composed of dedicated Congregationalists, were still inspired by New England abolitionism. Fisk's classical curriculum included Greek, Latin, French, German, theology, natural sciences, music, moral philosophy, and history.[6] Du Bois earned high grades in his courses. Interested in journalism and editing, he worked on the *Fisk Herald,* the university newspaper, becoming editor-in-chief in his senior year.

In 1886, Du Bois enrolled in teacher education courses at the Lebanon Teachers' Institute. Passing the elementary teachers' examination, he was issued a teaching certificate. In the summers of 1886 and 1887, Du Bois taught in a small rural black elementary school near Alexandria in east Tennessee. The school, located in an abandoned storage barn, had 15 students, ranging in age from 6 to 20.[7] His teaching experience gave Du Bois an understanding of the economically depressed conditions of African Americans in the rural South.

In June 1888, Du Bois graduated from Fisk University. In his commencement address, an oration on Otto von Bismarck, the iron chancellor of Germany, Du Bois argued that African Americans needed leaders like Bismarck who could mobilize a disciplined people.[8]

In 1888, Du Bois enrolled at Harvard, admitted with junior standing and a scholarship. He was awarded his bachelor's degree cum laude on June 25, 1890, with a concentration in philosophy.[9] He now began graduate study in history at Harvard, with Professor Albert Bushnell Hart as his major adviser. Du Bois' work with Hart was particularly useful in developing his competency in historical research that he would later combine with sociology. In 1891, Du Bois received his master of arts degree in history and began work on his doctorate in social science. His research dissertation was titled "Suppression of the African Slave Trade to the United States of America, 1638–1870."[10]

It was the custom for aspiring American graduate students who wanted careers as professors to go to Germany to complete higher academic studies. Du Bois, too, went to Germany for advanced study. He enrolled at Berlin's Friedrich Wilhelm University, where until 1894 he studied the emerging social sciences—political science, economics, and sociology—with leading experts. Despite his excellent academic record at the Friedrich Wilhelm University, the majority of the faculty voted that Du Bois was ineligible for doctoral examinations because he had not met residency requirements. He then returned to the United States to complete a Harvard doctorate. Du Bois' European experience broadened his intellectual worldview, and he began to see race relations beyond the problems that blacks faced in the United States. He saw African American culture in the United States as part of a larger global Pan Africanism.

In 1894, his funds depleted, W. E. B. Du Bois returned to the United States. In 1895, Harvard University accepted his doctoral dissertation on the African slave trade, which was later published as a book in the Harvard Historical Studies Series.[11]

From 1894 through 1896, Du Bois was a professor of classics at Wilberforce University, an institution affiliated with the African Methodist Episcopal Church, in Zenia, Ohio. Here, he taught Latin, Greek, and German. He was not happy with his situation at Wilberforce. He disliked the university's religious orientation and preferred a position where he could teach his specialties of history and sociology. At Wilberforce, Du Bois met and married Nina Gomer, an undergraduate student from Cedar Rapids, Iowa.

In 1896, Du Bois took a position at the University of Pennsylvania, where he directed a historical and sociological study of Philadelphia's African American population, which at 40,000 was then the nation's largest northern black community. A pioneering work in sociology, Du Bois' study examined family structure, neighborhoods, social organizations, educational institutions, political involvement, and economic roles. His findings appeared in *The Philadelphia Negro,* in 1899.[12] Du Bois found that racial discrimination was a powerful determinant that limited African American socioeconomic and educational opportunities.

In 1897, Du Bois accepted a position as a professor of economics and history at Atlanta University, an African American institution of higher education in Georgia, where he taught history, sociology, and economics. Du Bois coordinated the annual Atlanta University Conference on Negro Problems, which documented the history, condition, and problems of African Americans. He examined the African American educational situation, documenting growing disparities in the funding and resources allocated to black and white schools.

Du Bois was a prolific author. His book *The Souls of Black Folk,* consisting of essays on African American life and culture, was published in 1903.[13] In 1909, *John Brown,* his biography of the radical abolitionist who led an abortive attempt to free the slaves at Harper's Ferry, appeared.[14]

At the beginning of the twentieth century, tensions developed between the long-established African American leader and educator Booker T. Washington, the founder of the Tuskegee Institute, and Du Bois. For a time, the two had maintained cordial relations, with Washington offering Du Bois a position at Tuskegee, which he declined. Washington, the recognized leader of African Americans, had developed an influential network called the "Tuskegee Machine" that was connected to the white establishment and controlled the appointment of African Americans to political and educational positions. Du Bois strongly disagreed with two of Washington's guiding strategies: (1) avoiding a direct challenge to racial segregation and (2) concentrating on industrial training rather than higher and professional education. For Du Bois, the higher education of able African Americans was necessary for black empowerment. For Washington, industrial education and the ownership of small businesses was the more realistic course. Du Bois was determined that Washington's compromising accommodationist policy had to be challenged and discredited and that African Americans needed to take a more activist course to secure civil rights. Du Bois' relationship with Washington moved from disagreement to open antagonism.

In 1905, Du Bois joined with blacks and whites who wanted to restore civil rights to African Americans at a conference at Fort Erie, Ontario. The group, called the "Niagara Movement," named Du Bois its general secretary. Many of those in the Niagara Movement would create the larger National Association for the Advancement of Colored People (NAACP) in 1911. The NAACP, with Moorfield Storey as its president, united leading blacks and whites to work for the civil, social, and educational progress of African Americans. Rejecting Washington's accommodationism, the NAACP took an activist stand to inform the public about the conditions of discrimination faced by African Americans and to begin a legal battle to end racial segregation in the United States.

Du Bois, in 1910, was made director of publicity and research and editor of *The Crisis,* the NAACP's journal. He also served on the NAACP's board of directors. Under his editorial direction, *The Crisis* addressed the major issues relating to racial discrimination in the United States. Despite the demands of his commitment to the NAACP, Du Bois continued his scholarship and publication. In 1911, his book *The Quest for the Silver Fleece* appeared. It was followed by *The Negro,* in 1915; *Darkwater: Voices from Within the Veil,* in 1920; and *The Gift of Black Folk,* in 1924.[15]

Actively promoting African American culture, Du Bois, in the 1920s and 1930s, encouraged African American writers, artists, poets, and actors, such as Countee Cullen, Jean Toomer, Langston Hughes, and Claude McKay, who were part of the Harlem Renaissance. Helping to arrange conferences, performances, and concerts, he facilitated meetings and appointments with publishers and sponsors.

Recognizing the importance of education, Du Bois wrote articles and books that were acknowledged sources in African American history and culture. With Jessie Redmond Fauset, a teacher in the New York City public schools, Du Bois published *The Brownies' Book,* a children's monthly magazine.[16]

Politically, Du Bois joined the American Socialist party, led by Eugene V. Debs, in 1911. His belief that American blacks were victims of capitalist exploitation was leading him in the direction of Marxism. In later years, Du Bois often supported left-wing political organizations and movements.

Du Bois, a person of strong convictions, was often embroiled in disputes with more conservative members of the NAACP. In 1934, he resigned from the NAACP's board of directors and as editor of *The Crisis* and resumed his professorship at Atlanta University, where he chaired of the sociology department. Ten years later in 1944, reconciled with the NAACP directors, he returned to that organization as director of special research. He wrote *Black Reconstruction: An Essay Toward a History of the Part Which Black Folk Played in the Attempt to Reconstruct Democracy in America, 1860–1880,* in 1935; *Black Folk Then and Now,* in 1939; and *Dusk of Dawn: An Essay Toward an Autobiography of a Race Concept,* in 1940.

In the post-World War II era, Du Bois gave increasing attention to world affairs. He was especially interested in ending colonialism and bringing independence to the European nations' African and Asian colonies. He also worked in developing Pan Africanism as a worldwide movement. His books *Color and Democracy: Colonies and Peace,* in 1945, and *The World and Africa: An Inquiry into the Part Which Africa Has Played in World History,* in 1947, represented his Afrocentric ideas.

While the general political atmosphere in the United States during the Cold War was growing more anti-Communist, Du Bois moved steadily toward the left. He was accused of being a Soviet sympathizer and a member of Communist front organizations. Internal tensions resurfaced in the NAACP, and in 1949, Du Bois was dismissed as director of special research.

Convinced that the Soviet Union was promoting racial equality, Du Bois, in 1950, attended the All-Union Conference of Peace Proponents in Moscow. In the early 1950s, the United States was experiencing the McCarthy era, when investigations were directed against alleged subversives in the U.S. government and in educational institutions. Du Bois, who did not conceal his positive view of the Soviet Union, was among the suspects. In 1951 the U.S. Department of Justice demanded that Du Bois and the Peace Information Center, of which he was a member, register as agents of a foreign government. Refusing to comply with what he regarded as a violation of his civil rights, Du Bois and other center officers were indicted and tried. The case eventually reached the U.S. Supreme Court, where Du Bois and his associates were acquitted on the grounds that the Justice Department had not proved its allegations. In 1952, Du Bois told his version in his book *In Battle for Peace: The Story of My 83rd Birthday*.[17] He also wrote a trilogy—*The Ordeal of Mansart*, in 1957, *Mansart Builds a School*, in 1959, and *The Worlds of Color*, in 1961.[18]

Nina Du Bois, William Du Bois' wife of 54 years, died on July 1, 1950. In February 1951, the 83-year-old Du Bois married Shirley Graham, a close friend and coworker from the Peace Information Center. From 1952 to 1958, the U.S. government refused to issue a passport to Du Bois, who had been invited to visit many of the newly independent African nations. In 1958, passports were finally issued to Du Bois and his wife, Shirley Graham-Du Bois, who embarked on a world tour. In the Soviet Union, Du Bois was awarded the Lenin Peace Prize. In 1961, Du Bois accepted the invitation of President Kwame Nkrumah of Ghana to direct a project to prepare a comprehensive African encyclopedia. In 1963, he became a Ghanese citizen and died on August 27 of that year at the age of 95.

OVERVIEW OF IDEAS ON EDUCATION

Du Bois' educational ideas were part of his overall strategy to achieve equality of opportunity and full civil rights for African Americans. An initial point of departure in his elaboration of educational ideas came from his disagreement with Booker T. Washington, the president of Tuskegee Institute. Washington's educational philosophy was based on his belief that African Americans had to create an economic base prior to their entry into the social and political arena. An accommodationist, Washington cautioned African Americans to move gradually and incrementally and avoid any challenge to the white power structure. Du Bois argued that Washington's political passivity, gradualism, and policy of industrial education would perpetuate a racially based caste system in the United States.

Du Bois made access to higher education an important element in his philosophy. Using the phrase the "talented tenth," Du Bois argued that all races, including blacks, had an intellectually gifted elite. This elite, the talented tenth, should have the advantage of higher and professional education. In the struggle for racial justice, the talented tenth would act as the vanguard of the movement. In colleges, universities, and professional schools, the African American intellectual elite, the talented tenth, would be prepared to lead their race. For Du Bois, social progress was "more often a pull than a push" caused by the efforts of the exceptional man to lift "his duller brethren slowly and painfully to his vantage-ground."[19]

Though he gave a special emphasis to higher education, Du Bois recognized the importance of general education in shaping a person's knowledge base, worldview, and behavior. The early years of schooling, regardless of a child's race or class, should cultivate basic literacy and communication skills and broaden the horizons of space, time, and events.[20]

Though he recognized some value in Washington's industrial education, Du Bois warned against premature vocational education that turned children's early education into specific training for the trades, farming, or domestic service. Vocational training, commenced too early in a child's general education, could limit expectations and future career choice. For Du Bois, all children should learn to read, write, calculate, and broaden their horizons by studying history, geography, and literature rather than being trained for particular jobs.

Du Bois, an early proponent of African American history and cultural studies as well as Pan Africanism, was especially concerned that many textbook treatments of world history and culture exclusively emphasized the Western European and North American experience and ignored African contributions. His book *The Negro*, in 1915, was a seminal work for Afrocentric scholarship.[21] His books *Africa—Its Place in Modern History*, in 1930; *Africa—Its Geography, People, and Products*, in 1930; and *The World and Africa: An Inquiry into the Part Which Africa Has Played in World History*, in 1947, created a usable knowledge base from which to bring the study of Africa into the curriculum.[22]

Du Bois' Pan Africanism contained an international dimension that emphasized multiculturalism in the larger world society. He advised African Americans to use education as a means of relocating themselves in their African origins and roots. While taking pride in their African heritage, African American children were to learn they were citizens of a larger multicultural and multiracial world.

Du Bois' books on black history and culture in both the United States and Africa were important sources that anticipated the Afro-American and black studies programs that developed at many colleges and universities. Du Bois, who was always concerned with historical accuracy and sociological validity in his research and writing, made a valuable contribution to these disciplines.

THE PRIMARY SOURCE

In *The Souls of Black Folk,* Du Bois examines the social, cultural, and educational aspects of black life in America. He appeals to African American intellectuals to take the initiative in working for voting rights, civil rights, and equal access to colleges and universities. He criticizes Booker T. Washington for weakening black political power, for jeopardizing American civil rights, and for discouraging the entry of black youth into institutions of higher education. As a result of Washington's accommodationist strategy, blacks had been politically disenfranchised.

The selections from *The Souls of Black Folk* provide a clear insight into Du Bois' thinking about the condition and problems of African Americans at the beginning of the twentieth century. His critique and challenge of the leadership of Booker T. Washington sparked a dramatic conflict between the two men. He pointed out the inequities in funding white and black schools that resulted from the "separate but equal doctrine" of *Plessy v. Ferguson*. Du Bois' theory of the "talented tenth" was intended to create a leadership elite, but he was also concerned that blacks receive the best elementary and secondary education their talents would allow. In making a strong argument for the access of larger numbers of African Americans to colleges and universities, Du Bois expresses his belief in the "talented tenth."

FOCUSING QUESTIONS

As you read the selections, you might consider the following questions:

1. What were Du Bois' principal objections to Booker T. Washington's educational philosophy and policy? How do you think Washington might respond? What was Du Bois' agenda for change?

2. What did Du Bois consider to be the function of common schools and colleges and universities in general and for African Americans in particular?

3. In Du Bois reasoning, what social, economic, and educational role would be played by the "talented tenth"? Consider his argument for the talented tenth both in the context of the early twentieth century and in the contemporary period. Do you agree with the idea?

FROM W. E. B. DU BOIS' *THE SOULS OF BLACK FOLK: ESSAYS AND SKETCHES*

It startled the nation to hear a Negro advocating such a programme after many decades of bitter complaint; it startled and won the applause of the South, it interested and won the admiration of the North; and after a confused murmur of protest, it silenced if it did not convert the Negroes themselves.

To gain the sympathy and coöperation of the various elements comprising the white South was Mr. Washington's first task; and this, at the time Tuskegee was founded, seemed, for a black man, well-nigh impossible. And yet ten years later it was done in the word spoken at Atlanta: "In all things purely social we can be as separate as the five fingers, and yet one as the hand in all things essential to mutual progress." This "Atlanta Compromise" is by all odds the most notable thing in Mr. Washington's career. The South interpreted it in different ways: the radicals received it as a complete surrender of the demand for civil and political equality; the conservatives, as a generously conceived working basis for mutual understanding. So both approved it, and to-day its author is certainly the most distinguished Southerner since Jefferson Davis, and the one with the largest personal following.

Next to this achievement comes Mr. Washington's work in gaining place and consideration in the North. Others less shrewd and tactful had formerly essayed to sit on these two stools and had fallen between them; but as Mr. Washington knew the heart of the South from birth and training, so by singular insight he intuitively grasped the spirit of the age which was dominating the North. And so thoroughly did he learn the speech and thought of triumphant commercialism, and the ideals of material prosperity, that the picture of a lone black boy poring over a French grammar amid the weeds and dirt of a neglected home soon seemed to

him the acme of absurdities. One wonders what Socrates and St. Francis of Assisi would say to this.

And yet this very singleness of vision and thorough oneness with his age is a mark of the successful man. It is as though Nature must needs make men narrow in order to give them force. So Mr. Washington's cult has gained unquestioning followers, his work has wonderfully prospered, his friends are legion, and his enemies are confounded. To-day he stands as the one recognized spokesman of his ten million fellows, and one of the most notable figures in a nation of seventy millions. One hesitates, therefore, to criticise a life which, beginning with so little, has done so much. And yet the time is come when one may speak in all sincerity and utter courtesy of the mistakes and shortcomings of Mr. Washington's career, as well as of his triumphs, without being thought captious or envious, and without forgetting that it is easier to do ill than well in the world. . . .

Mr. Washington represents in Negro thought the old attitude of adjustment and submission; but adjustment at such a peculiar time as to make his programme unique. This is an age of unusual economic development, and Mr. Washington's programme naturally takes an economic cast, becoming a gospel of Work and Money to such an extent as apparently almost completely to overshadow the higher aims of life. Moreover, this is an age when the more advanced races are coming in closer contact with the less developed races, and the race-feeling is therefore intensified; and Mr. Washington's programme practically accepts the alleged inferiority of the Negro races. Again, in our own land, the reaction from the sentiment of war time has given impetus to race-prejudice against Negroes, and Mr. Washington withdraws many of the high demands of Negroes as men and American citizens. In other periods of intensified prejudice all the Negro's tendency to self-assertion has been called forth; at this period a policy of submission is advocated. In the history of nearly all other races and peoples the doctrine preached at such crises

From: W. E. B. Du Bois' *The Souls of Black Folk: Essays and Sketches.* Chicago: A. C. McClurg and Co., 1903, 37–38, 43–46, 50, 70–71, 84–88, 146–147.

has been that manly self-respect is worth more than lands and houses, and that a people who voluntarily surrender such respect, or cease striving for it, are not worth civilizing.

In answer to this, it has been claimed that the Negro can survive only through submission. Mr. Washington distinctly asks that black people give up, at least for the present, three things,—

First, political power,

Second, insistence on civil rights,

Third, higher education of Negro youth,—

and concentrate all their energies on industrial education, the accumulation of wealth, and the conciliation of the South. This policy has been courageously and insistently advocated for over fifteen years, and has been triumphant for perhaps ten years. As a result of this tender of the palm-branch, what has been the return? In these years there have occurred:

1. The disfranchisement of the Negro.
2. The legal creation of a distinct status of civil inferiority for the Negro.
3. The steady withdrawal of aid from institutions for the higher training of the Negro.

These movements are not, to be sure, direct results of Mr. Washington's teachings; but his propaganda has, without a shadow of doubt, helped their speedier accomplishment. The question then comes: Is it possible, and probable, that nine millions of men can make effective progress in economic lines if they are deprived of political rights, made a servile caste, and allowed only the most meagre chance for developing their exceptional men? If history and reason give any distinct answer to these questions, it is an emphatic *No*. And Mr. Washington thus faces the triple paradox of his career:

1. He is striving nobly to make Negro artisans business men and property-owners; but it is utterly impossible, under modern competitive methods, for workingmen and property-owners to defend their rights and exist without the right of suffrage.
2. He insists on thrift and self-respect, but at the same time counsels a silent submission to civic inferiority such as is bound to sap the manhood of any race in the long run.
3. He advocates common-school and industrial training, and depreciates institutions of higher learning; but neither the Negro common-schools, nor Tuskegee itself, could remain open a day were it not for

teachers trained in Negro colleges, or trained by their graduates.

This triple paradox in Mr. Washington's position is the object of criticism by two classes of colored Americans. One class is spiritually descended from Toussaint the Savior, through Gabriel, Vesey, and Turner, and they represent the attitude of revolt and revenge; they hate the white South blindly and distrust the white race generally, and so far as they agree on definite action, think that the Negro's only hope lies in emigration beyond the borders of the United States. And yet, by the irony of fate, nothing has more effectually made this programme seem hopeless than the recent course of the United States toward weaker and darker peoples in the West Indies, Hawaii, and the Philippines,—for where in the world may we go and be safe from lying and brute force?

The other class of Negroes who cannot agree with Mr. Washington has hitherto said little aloud. They deprecate the sight of scattered counsels, of internal disagreement; and especially they dislike making their just criticism of a useful and earnest man an excuse for a general discharge of venom from small-minded opponents. Nevertheless, the questions involved are so fundamental and serious that it is difficult to see how men like the Grimkes, Kelly Miller, J. W. E. Bowen, and other representatives of this group, can much longer be silent. Such men feel in conscience bound to ask of this nation three things:

1. The right to vote.
2. Civic equality.
3. The education of youth according to ability.

They acknowledge Mr. Washington's invaluable service in counselling patience and courtesy in such demands; they do not ask that ignorant black men vote when ignorant whites are debarred, or that any reasonable restrictions in the suffrage should not be applied; they know that the low social level of the mass of the race is responsible for much discrimination against it, but they also know, and the nation knows, that relentless color-prejudice is more often a cause than a result of the Negro's degradation; they seek the abatement of this relic of barbarism, and not its systematic encouragement and pampering by all agencies of social power from the Associated Press to the Church of Christ. They advocate, with Mr. Washington, a broad system of Negro common schools supplemented by thorough industrial training; but they are surprised that a man of Mr. Washington's insight cannot see that no such educational system ever has rested or can rest on any other basis than that of the well-equipped college and university, and they insist that there is a demand for a few such institutions throughout the South to train the best of the Negro youth as teachers, professional men, and leaders. . . .

The South ought to be led, by candid and honest criticism, to assert her better self and do her full duty to the race she has cruelly wronged and is still wronging. The North—her co-partner in guilt—cannot salve her conscience by plastering it with gold. We cannot settle this problem by diplomacy and suaveness, by "policy" alone. If worse come to worst, can the moral fibre of this country survive the slow throttling and murder of nine millions of men?

The black men of America have a duty to perform, a duty stern and delicate,—a forward movement to oppose a part of the work of their greatest leader. So far as Mr. Washington preaches Thrift, Patience, and Industrial Training for the masses, we must hold up his hands and strive with him, rejoicing in his honors and glorying in the strength of this Joshua called of God and of man to lead the headless host. But so far as Mr. Washington apologizes for injustice, North or South, does not rightly value the privilege and duty of voting, belittles the emasculating effects of caste distinctions, and opposes the higher training and ambition of our brighter minds,—so far as he, the South, or the Nation, does this,—we must unceasingly and firmly oppose them. By every civilized and peaceful method we must strive for the rights which the world accords to men, clinging unwaveringly to those great words which the sons of the Fathers would fain forget: "We hold these truths to be self-evident: That all men are created equal; that they are endowed by their Creator with certain unalienable rights; that among these are life, liberty, and the pursuit of happiness."

The function of the university is not simply to teach bread-winning, or to furnish teachers for the public schools, or to be a centre of polite society; it is, above all, to be the organ of that fine adjustment between real life and the growing knowledge of life, an adjustment which forms the secret of civilization. Such an institution the South of to-day sorely needs. She has religion, earnest, bigoted:—religion that on both sides the Veil often omits the sixth, seventh, and eighth commandments, but substitutes a dozen supplementary ones. She has, as Atlanta shows, growing thrift and love of toil; but she lacks that broad knowledge of what the world knows and knew of human living and doing, which she may apply to the thousand problems of real life to-day confronting her. The need

of the South is knowledge and culture,—not in dainty limited quantity, as before the war, but in broad busy abundance in the world of work; and until she has this, not all the Apples of Hesperides, be they golden and bejewelled, can save her from the curse of the Boeotian lovers. . . .

Fifty years ago the ability of Negro students in any appreciable numbers to master a modern college course would have been difficult to prove. To-day it is proved by the fact that four hundred Negroes, many of whom have been reported as brilliant students, have received the bachelor's degree from Harvard, Yale, Oberlin, and seventy other leading colleges. Here we have, then, nearly twenty-five hundred Negro graduates, of whom the crucial query must be made, How far did their training fit them for life? It is of course extremely difficult to collect satisfactory data on such a point,—difficult to reach the men, to get trustworthy testimony, and to gauge that testimony by any generally acceptable criterion of success. In 1900, the Conference at Atlanta University undertook to study these graduates, and published the results. First they sought to know what these graduates were doing, and succeeded in getting answers from nearly two-thirds of the living. The direct testimony was in almost all cases corroborated by the reports of the colleges where they graduated, so that in the main the reports were worthy of credence. Fifty-three per cent of these graduates were teachers,—presidents of institutions, heads of normal schools, principals of city school-systems, and the like. Seventeen per cent were clergymen; another seventeen per cent were in the professions, chiefly as physicians. Over six per cent were merchants, farmers, and artisans, and four per cent were in the government civil-service. Granting even that a considerable proportion of the third unheard from are unsuccessful, this is a record of usefulness. Personally I know many hundreds of these graduates, and have corresponded with more than a thousand; through others I have followed carefully the life-work of scores; I have taught some of them and some of the pupils whom they have taught, lived in homes which they have builded, and looked at life through their eyes. Comparing them as a class with my fellow students in New England and in Europe, I cannot hesitate in saying that nowhere have I met men and women with a broader spirit of helpfulness, with deeper devotion to their life-work, or with more consecrated determination to succeed in the face of bitter difficulties than among Negro college-bred men. They have, to be sure, their proportion of ne'er-do-weels, their pedants and lettered fools, but they have a surprisingly small proportion of them; they have not that culture of manner which we instinctively associate with university men, forgetting that in reality it is the heritage from cultured homes, and that no people a generation removed from slavery can escape a certain unpleasant rawness and *gaucherie,* despite the best of training.

With all their larger vision and deeper sensibility, these men have usually been conservative, careful leaders. They have seldom been agitators, have withstood the temptation to head the mob, and have worked steadily and faithfully in a thousand communities in the South. As teachers, they have given the South a commendable system of city schools and large numbers of private normal-schools and academies. Colored college-bred men have worked side by side with white college graduates at Hampton; almost from the beginning the backbone of Tuskegee's teaching force has been formed of graduates from Fisk and Atlanta. And to-day the institute is filled with college graduates, from the energetic wife of the principal down to the teacher of agriculture, including nearly half of the executive council and a majority of the heads of departments. In the professions, college men are slowly but surely leavening the Negro church, are healing and preventing the devastations of disease, and beginning to furnish legal protection for the liberty and property of the toiling masses. All this is needful work. Who would do it if Negroes did not? How could Negroes do it if they were not trained carefully for it? If white people need colleges to furnish teachers, ministers, lawyers, and doctors, do black people need nothing of the sort?

If it is true that there are an appreciable number of Negro youth in the land capable by character and talent to receive that higher training, the end of which is culture, and if the two and a half thousand who have had something of this training in the past have in the main proved themselves useful to their race and generation, the question then comes, What place in the future development of the South ought the Negro college and college-bred man to occupy? That the present social separation and acute race-sensitiveness must eventually yield to the influences of culture, as the South grows civilized, is clear. But such transformation calls for singular wisdom and patience. If, while the healing of this vast sore is progressing, the races are to live for many years side by side, united in economic effort, obeying a common government, sensitive to mutual thought and feeling, yet subtly and silently separate in many matters of deeper human in-

timacy,—if this unusual and dangerous development is to progress amid peace and order, mutual respect and growing intelligence, it will call for social surgery at once the delicatest and nicest in modern history. It will demand broad-minded, upright men, both white and black, and in its final accomplishment American civilization will triumph. So far as white men are concerned, this fact is to-day being recognized in the South, and a happy renaissance of university education seems imminent. But the very voices that cry hail to this good work are, strange to relate, largely silent or antagonistic to the higher education of the Negro.

Strange to relate! for this is certain, no secure civilization can be built in the South with the Negro as an ignorant, turbulent proletariat. Suppose we seek to remedy this by making them laborers and nothing more: they are not fools, they have tasted of the Tree of Life, and they will not cease to think, will not cease attempting to read the riddle of the world. By taking away their best equipped teachers and leaders, by slamming the door of opportunity in the faces of their bolder and brighter minds, will you make them satisfied with their lot? or will you not rather transfer their leading from the hands of men taught to think to the hands of untrained demagogues? We ought not to forget that despite the pressure of poverty, and despite the active discouragement and even ridicule of friends, the demand for higher training steadily increases among Negro youth: there were, in the years from 1875 to 1880, 22 Negro graduates from Northern colleges; from 1885 to 1890 there were 43, and from 1895 to 1900, nearly 100 graduates. From Southern Negro colleges there were, in the same three periods, 143, 413, and over 500 graduates. Here, then, is the plain thirst for training; by refusing to give this Talented Tenth the key to knowledge, can any sane man imagine that they will lightly lay aside their yearning and contentedly become hewers of wood and drawers of water?

No. The dangerously clear logic of the Negro's position will more and more loudly assert itself in that day when increasing wealth and more intricate social organization preclude the South from being, as it so largely is, simply an armed camp for intimidating black folk. Such waste of energy cannot be spared if the South is to catch up with civilization. And as the black third of the land grows in thrift and skill, unless skillfully guided in its larger philosophy, it must more and more brood over the red past and the creeping, crooked present, until it grasps a gospel of revolt and revenge and throws its new-found energies athwart the current of advance. Even to-day the masses of the Negroes see all too clearly the anomalies of their position and the moral crookedness of yours. You may marshal strong indictments against them, but their counter-cries, lacking though they be in formal logic, have burning truths within them which you may not wholly ignore, O Southern Gentlemen! If you deplore their presence here, they ask, Who brought us? When you cry, Deliver us from the vision of intermarriage, they answer that legal marriage is infinitely better than systematic concubinage and prostitution. And if in just fury you accuse their vagabonds of violating women, they also in fury quite as just may reply: The wrong which your gentlemen have done against helpless black women in defiance of your own laws is written on the foreheads of two millions of mulattoes, and written in ineffaceable blood. And finally, when you fasten crime upon this race as its peculiar trait, they answer that slavery was the arch-crime, and lynching and lawlessness its twin abortion; that color and race are not crimes, and yet they it is which in this land receives most unceasing condemnation, North, East, South, and West. . . .

It is the public schools, however, which can be made, outside the homes, the greatest means of training decent self-respecting citizens. We have been so hotly engaged recently in discussing trade-schools and the higher education that the pitiable plight of the public-school system in the South has almost dropped from view. Of every five dollars spent for public education in the State of Georgia, the white schools get four dollars and the Negro one dollar; and even then the white public-school system, save in the cities, is bad and cries for reform. If this is true of the whites, what of the blacks? I am becoming more and more convinced, as I look upon the system of common-school training in the South, that the national government must soon step in and aid popular education in some way. To-day it has been only by the most strenuous efforts on the part of the thinking men of the South that the Negro's share of the school fund has not been cut down to a pittance in some half-dozen States; and that movement not only is not dead, but in many communities is gaining strength. What in the name of reason does this nation expect of a people, poorly trained and hard pressed in severe economic competition, without political rights, and with ludicrously inadequate common-school facilities? What can it expect but crime and listlessness, offset here and there by the dogged struggles of the fortunate and more determined who are themselves buoyed by the hope that in due time the country will come to its senses?

SUGGESTIONS FOR FURTHER READING

Andrews, William L., ed. *Critical Essays on W. E. B. Du Bois.* Boston: G. K. Hall & Co., 1985.

Broderick, Francis L. *W. E. B. Du Bois: Negro Leader in a Time of Crisis.* Stanford, Calif.: Stanford University Press, 1959.

Du Bois, W. E. B. *Africa—Its Geography, People, and Products.* Girard, Kans.: Haldeman-Julius, 1930.

_____. *Africa—Its Place in Modern History.* Girard, Kans.: Haldeman-Julius, 1930.

_____. *The Autobiography of W. E. B. Du Bois: A Soliloquy on Viewing My Life from the Last Decade of Its First Century.* Herbert Aptheker, ed. New York: International Publishers, 1968.

_____. *Black Folk Then and Now: An Essay in the History and Sociology of the Negro Race.* New York: Henry Holt and Co., 1939.

_____. *Black Reconstruction: An Essay Toward a History of the Part Which Black Folk Played in the Attempt to Reconstruct Democracy in America, 1860–1880.* New York: Harcourt Brace Jovanovich, 1935.

_____. *Color and Democracy: Colonies and Peace.* New York: Harcourt Brace Jovanovich, 1945.

_____. *Darkwater: Voices from Within the Veil.* New York: Harcourt Brace Jovanovich, 1920.

_____. *Dusk of Dawn: An Essay Toward an Autobiography of a Race Concept*. New York: Harcourt Brace Jovanovich, 1940.

_____. *The Gift of Black Folk: Negroes in the Making of America*. Boston: Stratford Publishing Co., 1924.

_____. *In Battle for Peace: The Story of My 83rd Birthday*. New York: Masses and Mainstream, 1952.

_____. *John Brown*. Philadelphia: George W. Jacobs, 1909.

_____. *The Negro*. New York: Henry Holt and Co., 1915.

_____. *The Philadelphia Negro: A Social Study*. Boston: Ginn and Co., 1899.

_____. *The Souls of Black Folk: Essays and Sketches*. Chicago: A. C. McClurg and Co., 1903.

_____. *The Souls of Black Folk*. Edited by David W. Blight and Robert Gooding-Williams. New York: Bedford Books, 1997.

_____. *The World and Africa: An Inquiry into the Part Which Africa Has Played in World History*. New York: Viking Press, 1947.

Foner, Philip S. *W. E. B. Du Bois Speaks: Speeches and Addresses, 1920–1963*. New York: Pathfinder Press, 1970.

Hamilton, Virginia. *W. E. B. Du Bois: A Biography*. New York: Thomas Y. Crowell Co., 1972.

Harlan, Louis. *Booker T. Washington: The Making of a Black Leader: 1856–1901*. New York: Oxford University Press, 1972.

Horne, Gerald. *Black and Red: W. E. B. Du Bois and the Afro-American Response to the Cold War*. Albany: State University of New York Press, 1986.

Lewis, David Levering. *W. E. B. Du Bois: Biography of a Race, 1868–1919*. New York: Henry Holt and Co., 1993.

Marable, Manning. *W. E. B. Du Bois: Black Radical Democrat*. Boston: Twayne Publishers, 1986.

Paschal, Andrew G., ed. *A W. E. B. Du Bois Reader*. New York: Macmillan Publishing Company, 1971.

Rampersad, Arnold. *The Art and Imagination of W. E. B. Du Bois*. New York: Schocken Books, 1990.

NOTES

1. Manning Marable, *W. E. B. Du Bois: Black Radical Democrat* (Boston: Twayne Publishers, 1986), 2–3.
2. Virginia Hamilton, *W. E. B. Du Bois: A Biography* (New York: Thomas Y. Crowell Co., 1972), 15.
3. Marable, 4–6.
4. David Levering Lewis, *W. E. B. Du Bois: Biography of a Race, 1868–1919* (New York: Henry Holt and Co., 1993), 50.
5. Marable, 7.
6. Lewis, 58–59.
7. Ibid., 68–69.
8. Ibid., 77.
9. Ibid., 84–88.
10. Marable, 15.
11. W. E. B. Du Bois, *The Suppression of the African Slave-Trade to the United States of America, 1638–1870* (New York: Longmans, Green, and Co., 1896).
12. W. E. B. Du Bois, *The Philadelphia Negro: A Social Study* (Boston: Ginn and Co., 1899).

13. W. E. B. Du Bois, *The Souls of Black Folk: Essays and Sketches* (Chicago: A. C. McClurg and Co., 1903).

14. W. E. B. Du Bois, *John Brown* (Philadelphia: George W. Jacobs, 1909).

15. W. E. B. Du Bois, *The Quest of the Silver Fleece: A Novel* (Chicago: A. C. McClurg, 1911); Du Bois, *The Negro* (New York: Henry Holt, 1915); Du Bois, *Darkwater: Voices from Within the Veil* (New York: Harcourt Brace Jovanovich, 1920); Du Bois, *The Gift of Black Folk: Negroes in the Making of America* (Boston: Stratford Publishing Co., 1924).

16. Hamilton, 133.

17. W. E. B. Du Bois, *In Battle for Peace: The Story of My 83rd Birthday* (New York: Masses and Mainstream, 1952).

18. W. E. B. Du Bois, *The Ordeal of Mansart* (New York: Mainstream, 1957); and Du Bois, *Worlds of Color* (New York: Mainstream, 1959).

19. Du Bois, *Souls of Black Folks*, 84.

20. Henry Lee Moon, *The Emerging Thought of W. E. B. Du Bois* (New York: Simon and Schuster, 1972), 127.

21. Lewis, 462.

22. W. E. B. Du Bois, *Africa—Its Place in Modern History* (Girard, Kans.: Haldeman-Julius, 1930); Du Bois, *Africa—Its Geography, People and Products* (Girard, Kans.: Haldeman-Julius, 1930).

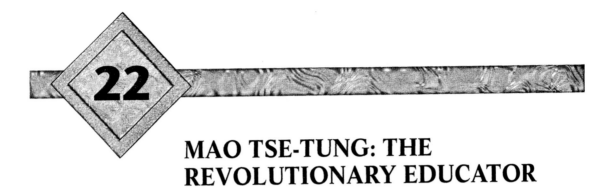

MAO TSE-TUNG: THE REVOLUTIONARY EDUCATOR

BIOGRAPHICAL SKETCH

Mao Tse-tung was born on December 26, 1893, in the village of Shao Shan-ch'ung in China's Hunan province. He was the son of Mao Jen-sheng, an ambitious farmer, who was determined to enlarge the family's land.[1] Mao recalled that his mother, Wen Ch'i mei, though unschooled, was a kindly woman and a devout Buddhist.[2] As a young child, Mao Tse-tung was devoted to his mother but feared and disliked his father.

During Mao's childhood, Confucian philosophy shaped the traditional Chinese outlook on life. Confucius (551–478) had devised an ethical system that emphasized traditional values and customs. Hierarchical relationships, in families and the larger society, were esteemed as appropriately regulating behavior. In such a patriarchal family, the wife was to be subordinate to her husband and sons to their father. Mao, however, rebelled against these inherited family and social patterns.

Mao's childhood was one of tension in a family where his father, in the Confucianist tradition, was the household's undisputed ruler, holding his wife and children in subjection. Even as a child, Mao displayed his revolutionary temperament, challenging his father whom he recalled as "a severe task master, a hot-tempered man who gave us no money whatsoever and the most meager food."[3] While the father expected Mao, his eldest son, to heed the Confucianist protocol and eventually head the household, the son thought otherwise. Mao, who wanted to become a scholar, resented the work his father imposed. An avid reader, Mao was constantly scolded by his father, who regarded reading as idleness. During the Cultural Revolution, Mao told the Red Guards that if his father were still alive, he would have been condemned as an enemy of the people and punished. Though detesting his father's materialism, Mao came to value hard work and to despise the intellectuals who looked down on physical labor.

Using the Marxist dialectic, Mao interpreted events as a clash of opposing forces, a thesis and antithesis, that culminated in a new synthesis. He even interpreted family conflicts dialectically, perceiving family members as opposing factions locked in struggle. His father was the "ruling power," while his mother, siblings, and he formed the opposition "united front." He regarded his mother as his protector who helped him under-

A Red Guard demonstration in China during the Cultural Revolution.

mine an authoritarian father.[4] When his mother died, Mao experienced a long period of grief and loss. A poet, Mao wrote that his mother's "mind was attentive and sophisticated, logical and reasonable; Never a plan miscalculated, nor a thing overlooked."[5]

As a youth, Mao rebelled against the traditional role he was expected to play in an extended family. It was assumed that as the eldest son he would inherit the family farm and be responsible for his younger siblings' welfare. Then, he, too, as an old man, following Confucianist ethics, would pass the estate and family responsibilities to his eldest son. Mao, however, broke with tradition. He became a Marxist revolutionary who left not a patrimony but an ideological cause to his siblings. As adults, his two brothers and sister met violent deaths because of their support for their elder brother's revolutionary cause. Mao's first wife was arrested and executed in 1930 when he was away on Communist Party business.

From ages 8 to 13, Mao attended the village primary school, studying the Chinese language and history and Confucian classics. His teachers emphasized the Confucian values of obedience to one's father, respect for elders, submission to those in authority, and veneration of one's ancestors. The teachers used group recitations in which students recited passages in unison.[6] Contrary to his teachers' expectations, Mao learned to resent the Confucianist tradition's emphasis on patient submission to authority figures.

Mao, at age 14, entered the larger urban Tungshan Primary School to pursue a more comprehensive curriculum that included literature, writing, mathematics, history, and geography. After a year's study, he moved on to the Fourth Normal School, a teacher preparation institution in Changsha.[7]

In 1911, Dr. Sun Yat-sen led a republican revolution to overthrow the decrepit imperial Manchu dynasty. Caught up in the republican cause, Mao joined the revolt. The imperial government quickly fell to be replaced by Yuan Shih-kai, a general, who, becoming president, installed himself as dictator.

In 1912, Mao was back at school, enrolled in the Provincial Middle School, but left after six months, deciding he could educate himself. His self-education took him to the Hunan Provincial Library, where he read books on history, politics, and biography. The next year, the 19-year-old Mao returned to formal education. From 1913 to 1918, he attended the Fourth Teachers Training School. Joining the New Citizen's Society, he volunteered as a literacy instructor to educate peasants and workers. During the Cultural Revolution, Mao would criticize his own formal education, especially the many years needed to learn what he condemned as largely useless subjects.

Finishing his studies, Mao went to China's capital, Beijing, to work at the National University Library. Here, he joined a Marxist group that was developing a program to improve the condition of China's impoverished rural agricultural workers. A Soviet agent, Grigori Voitinsky, who joined the group, maneuvered them into a more active revolutionary posture. In 1921, Mao and his associates organized the Beijing Communist Party. He then went to Changsha to teach at the First Normal School, where he continued his political activities.

During the 1920s, China's political situation grew increasingly destabilized. Yuan Shih-kai, the dictator, had died. General Chiang Kai-shek, the leader of the Kuomintang, or Nationalist Party, launched a military campaign to reestablish central political authority by defeating the war lords who controlled several of the provinces. During this uncertain political period Mao, in 1921, attended and took a leadership role at the first Chinese Communist Congress.[8]

In 1927, following a brief period of cooperation, Chiang's Kuomintang and the Communists confronted each other as resolute enemies. Chiang and Mao began their long battle for control of China. Desperately struggling to survive against the better equipped Kuomintang army, Mao and his troops and followers, in 1934, began their famous "Long March," a 6,000-mile forced march of 368 days that took them to a refuge in northern China's remote Shensi region. During the Long March, which would be immortalized in Communist ideology, Mao's beleaguered forces fought off constant attacks from the Kuomintang army. Of the estimated 200,000 who began the march, less than 20,000 reached their destination on October 29, 1935.[9] In the remote safety of Yenan, an isolated area of 3 million inhabitants, Mao, proclaiming the Chinese Soviet Republic, proceeded to devise and implement the strategy that would eventually create the People's Republic of China.

In 1936, Mao's Communists and Chiang's Nationalists called a truce so that they could concentrate on defeating the Japanese invaders who had occupied much of China. After Japan's defeat in World War II, the Communists and Kuomintang resumed the civil war. This time, the Kuomintang suffered a series of defeats that forced Chiang's flight to Taiwan. On October 1, 1949, Mao, savoring the Communist victory, proclaimed the People's Republic of China in Beijing.

Consolidating power, Mao's Communists commenced to build a Marxist collectivist state. Convinced that literacy was indispensable in forming the new Chinese Communist man and woman, Mao began a massive effort to eradicate illiteracy among the workers and peasants, the core supporters of the new social order. To eliminate suspected enemies, the Communist regime staged purge trials, especially of landlords and businessmen. It confiscated the property of these suspected enemies and placed it under state control. Farmland was collectivized into state-held agricultural communes. Foreign and privately owned industries were seized and run as state enterprises.

Initially, the leaders of the People's Republic, emphasizing heavy industry rather than consumer goods, saw the Soviet Union as a model for building their Communist state. Schools and teachers were to eliminate the traditional Confucianist orientation that valued intellectual effort over manual labor. University students were to engage in productive labor to avoid the traditional error of separating thinking and working.[10]

By 1958, relations between the two Communist giants, the Soviet Union and the People's Republic of China, had soured. Distrusting China's reliance on Soviet assistance, Mao decided to lead China on its own path to Communism. Proclaiming that China with its immense natural and human resources would stand on its own economic and military feet, Mao launched "the Great Leap Forward." China, through its own grassroots efforts, would, he said, transform itself from a backward agricultural economy into an industrial giant. Quickly mobilized, millions of peasants threw up improvised backyard smelters to make iron and steel. To double crop production, farmers were ordered to plant two instead of one rice crop. The results were calamitous. Instead of a Great Leap Forward, Mao's policies, aggravated by natural calamities, caused a massive famine with 20 million deaths.[11]

Educationally, too, Mao's Great Leap Forward had its consequences. Mao called for rapid educational progress to completely eradicate illiteracy and to universalize education. To expand schooling, spare and part-time schools were established on agricultural communes and in factories.

After the disaster of his Great Leap Forward, Mao Tse-tung, though remaining China's revolutionary father, was relegated to a figurehead position. From 1960 to 1965, the government and Party labored to recover from the losses caused by the Great Leap Forward. They emphasized large, well-run, efficient industries, concentrated in industrial zones. To restore academic quality, many of the hastily established schools on communes and in factories were closed.

In 1965, Chairman Mao, marshaling all the resources at his command, resurfaced and called for a new "great proletarian cultural revolution" to completely eradicate old ideas, customs, and habits and replace them with a totally new culture.[12] Telling them that "destruction must come before construction," Mao urged school-aged children and youth to leave their studies and join the Red Guards, new China's young vanguard.[13] The Red Guards' destruction of the old culture degenerated into a rampage as temples were sacked and libraries were emptied of books condemned as anti-Maoist and counterrevolutionary. The turbulence in the schools became so intense that instruction virtually ended between 1966 and 1968.[14]

Between 1966 and 1970, most universities were closed and the Ministry of Higher Education was abolished. In 1970, 90 politically correct universities, run by University Revolutionary Committees, reopened. The Revolutionary Committees abolished the old admission requirements, especially entrance examinations. The new admission requirements were reduced to secondary school graduation; 2 years of work experience in industry, agriculture, or the army; single marital status; and ages ranging from 20 to 25. To purify the faculties, the Revolutionary Committees staged trials of administrators and professors suspected of anti-Maoist tendencies.[15] The new teachers and professors were to come from the ranks of workers and peasants, with the most important qualification being allegiance to Maoist ideology. Teachers, forced to engage in self-criticism sessions, were persuaded to confess lapses of bourgeois sentimentality and traditional scholasticism.

As the Cultural Revolution grew more turbulent, Red Guard factions, turning on themselves, fought pitched battles. With the country's political and economic system in chaos, the Communist Party and the army started to curb the Red Guards and bring the Cultural Revolution to a halt. The aging Mao was again pushed to the margins of power as the government and Communist Party apparatus reasserted control over China.

By the mid-1970s, the Cultural Revolution had ended. As Mao grew increasingly ill, his wife, Chiang Ch'ing, still tried to influence policy. In early September 1976, Mao died. His wife and her associates, condemned as the Gang of Four, were purged and then tried.

In 1977, the Chinese government and the Communist Party—in a concerted effort to overcome the scientific, technological, and educational losses caused by the Cultural Revolution—launched "the Four Modernizations." They sought to modernize four key sectors—agriculture, industry, national defense, and science and technology. The government, to modernize the country, opened it to Western technology. An important part of the program involved restoring the universities' academic quality by improving science, technology, and engineering education.

By the 1980s, the government began to encourage a limited market economy that privatized some industries and businesses. In agriculture, too, state control was decreased.

Though the government and Party believed they controlled the modernization process, new ideas entered into politics, culture, society, and art. University students, organized as the Pro-Democracy Movement, staged a sit-in at Tiananmen Square in Beijing to press their demands for liberalization. The response was the ruthless suppression of the Pro-Democracy Movement by the army with the massacre of students in Tiananmen Square in 1989.

Modern China, in the twenty-first century, appears to be moving toward a modified state-sanctioned capitalism. While the Communist Party remains in control, China is no longer the proletarian state envisioned by Mao Tse-tung.

OVERVIEW OF IDEAS ON EDUCATION

For Mao, a truly revolutionary education had two purposes: (1) to eliminate false consciousness by eradicating traditional beliefs and values; and (2) to create a true consciousness based on Marxist ideology. He arrived at his ideas on education by interpreting Karl Marx's philosophy to fit, what he regarded as, China's historical, political, and economic context. Marx, a nineteenth-century German theorist, had developed a philosophy of dialectical materialism. For Marx, history, the record of class struggle, followed a dialectical process in which a thesis generated an antithesis, which, in turn, produced a synthesis or new thesis. Inevitably, Marx reasoned that the dialectical struggle would lead to a massive conflict of historic proportions that pitted the capitalists, the thesis, against their proletarian opponents, the antithesis. Inevitably, the working class proletariat would triumph, Marx reasoned.

Mao used the Marxist dialectic to interpret both personal and political events. Recalling his childhood, he saw himself in dialectical conflict with his father. During China's civil war, Mao's Communists, the proletariat, were in a life and death struggle against Chiang's Nationalists, representing bourgeois capitalism. During the Cultural Revolution, Mao believed that Confucianist traditional scholarship was in conflict with the proletarian mass culture.

Mao enthusiastically accepted Marx's argument that a violent but resolutely guided revolution would be needed to overthrow the capitalists. Both Marx and Mao discounted that they could attain their objectives through peaceful parliamentary processes. Mao continually mobilized the proletarian peasants to destroy the remnants of the old prerevolutionary order. Believing that the Communist revolution had lost its zeal, he launched the Cultural Revolution to revivify the movement.

Marx hypothesized that a genuinely revolutionary education was needed to expose and eradicate false consciousness from the workers' minds. False consciousness resulted from a fraudulent education that was used to indoctrinate workers and their children to accept the exploitative socioeconomic status quo. For both Marx and Mao, a true revolutionary education would alert workers to the dangers of false consciousness and create a proletarian consciousness based on their real interests.

Mao reinterpreted Marx's ideology to fit the Chinese context. In the first half of the twentieth century, China, with its massive illiteracy and depressed agricultural economy, lacked what Marx had identified as necessary prerevolutionary conditions—an industrial economy exploited by a capitalist class and a restive working class. Though Marx predicted that industrial workers would incite the revolution, Mao decided that in China's context the mission would fall to the rural peasants. For Mao, the Communist Party's mission was to mobilize China's working classes into a revolutionary army.

Mao was concerned with schooling the young to assume their places in the new China. For him, education was ideologically connected to the political and economic goals of his envisioned revolutionary society. Education in the new China was "to develop morally, intellectually and physically" well-educated workers with "socialist consciousness."[16]

Though a poet, ideologist, and visionary, Mao, valuing practice over theory, believed that traditional schooling had deliberately separated thought from action.[17] He condemned the disconnection of academic subjects from politics and the economy. The Cultural Revolution that he engineered dramatically attacked academic theoreticians.

The schools Mao wanted for China were based on political and economic foundations. He was more concerned with "redness," or politically correct Marxist-Maoism, than educating scientists, engineers, and technicians. Despite the revolution's victory, Mao believed that China's educational system, especially its secondary and higher schools, continued to encourage an elitism removed from practical life. He especially disliked university entrance examinations, which be condemned as a sorting device that separated intellectuals from the working masses.[18] Despite his personal prominence and power, Mao had opponents in the government and Party bureaucracy who believed that if China were to become a great world power, it needed trained scientific, technological, and engineering experts. Expertise, for them, was more important than Maoist ideological political correctness.

During the Cultural Revolution, Mao put forth his ideas on what would be truly revolutionary schools. Nursery schools would begin indoctrination of little children in Marxist-Maoist thought and proletarian behavior and values. This would be followed by 5 years of primary school, where students would learn reading, writing, basic arithmetic, and science and, most importantly, continue their political formation according to Mao's book, *Red Little Soldiers*. The secondary schools would offer a curriculum of political formation, mathematics, chemistry, foreign languages, and socially useful labor. Then, most students would work from 1 to 3 years in rural areas with the peasants. After completing their schooling and training, students would work on farms or in factories. Adult education, taking place on agricultural communes, would consist of literacy studies and Marxist-Maoist political indoctrination.

Mao believed that only a very small percentage of students should go to universities. Instead of being attended by family members of government and Party bureaucrats, Mao wanted university spaces filled by young workers and peasants. Believing that university entrance examinations discriminated against workers and peasants, he called for their elimination.[19] Universities were to be thoroughly politicized according to Maoist ideology.

THE PRIMARY SOURCE

The primary source contains selected quotations from *Chairman Mao Talks to the People*, which appeared as a dialogue with other officials during the Cultural Revolution. The comments of the other officials have been deleted so that the selection appears as a running commentary by Mao on education.

The selection is set in the Great Proletarian Cultural Revolution, which Mao unleashed in 1965 when the aging revolutionary sought to inflame China's masses, especially its youth, to rekindle China's lagging revolutionary zeal. Mao mobilized China's children and young people to rebel against the government and Communist Party bureaucracy. Thousands of Chinese youth, organized as Red Guards, streamed out of secondary schools and universities to eradicate anti-Maoist remnants of scholasticism and Confucianism in education and the arts. Their favorite targets were teachers, professors, and administrators, who were tried at student-conducted public trials.

The Red Guards' attacks on the "old culture" degenerated into a destructive rampage. Temples were sacked and destroyed, and libraries were emptied of books condemned as counterrevolutionary. The turmoil in the schools was so intense that instruction virtually ended between 1966 and 1968.[20] During the Cultural Revolution, Chairman Mao was exalted as an infallible leader. His speeches and sayings became the Red Guards' revolutionary catechism. Students, carrying the *Little Red Book of Mao Tse-Tung*, conducted a mass campaign to educate the peasants and workers in Maoist ideology.

Mao believed too much time was wasted in schools studying useless subjects that were far removed from practical life. To the applause of the Red Guards, Mao condemned university entrance examinations, which he said discriminated against the children of workers and peasants, as "tickling enemies" and "surprise attacks" full of obscure questions.[21] *Quotations from Chairman Mao Tse-Tung* contains a picture of students, standing before a large portrait of Mao, pledging: "We are determined to win honor for you and for our great socialist motherland . . . our consciousness of continuing the revolution will not change . . . our loyalty to you will never change."[22]

In the selection, Mao, arguing that students waste too much time studying too many subjects, recommends shortening the curriculum. He further attacks examinations, urging ways to reduce their emphasis and the stress produced on students. He advises that more time should be spent on Marx rather than on the Confucian classics. Opposing scholasticism, the separation of theory and practice in universities, he wants higher education to emphasize politics and practicalities.

FOCUSING QUESTIONS
As you read the selection, you might wish to consider the following questions:

1. On the basis of the selection, describe Mao's philosophy or ideology of education. How were his educational ideas driven by his political ideology?
2. Why did Mao urge a reduction in the time spent in school and the subjects being studied? What would have been the social, political, and economic consequences of his recommendations?
3. Analyze Mao's comments on examinations. Are they relevant to contemporary education, especially at the college and university level? Consider the impact that ACT and SAT scores have in college and university selections and acceptances in the United States.
4. Mao displayed a strong distrust of some intellectuals, especially those who were highly scholastic. Do you find any evidence of this kind of distrust in contemporary society, either in the United States or in other countries?

FROM CHAIRMAN MAO TALKS TO THE PEOPLE: TALKS AND LETTERS: 1956–1971

Chairman Mao: That's not important; those who are not old enough for military service can also experience military life. Not only male students, but also female students can undergo military service. We can form a red women's detachment. Girls of sixteen or seven-

From *Chairman Mao Talks to the People: Talks and Letters: 1956–1971*, edited by Stuart Schram, translated by John Chinnery and Tieyun. New York: Pantheon Books, Random House, 1974, 203–210, 236–237. Copyright © 1974 by Stuart Schram. Reprinted by permission of Pantheon Books, a Division of Random House, Inc.

teen can also experience six months to a year of military life, and at seventeen they can also serve as soldiers. . . .

Chairman Mao: At present, there is too much studying going on, and this is exceedingly harmful. There are too many subjects at present, and the burden is too heavy, it puts middle-school and university students in a constant state of tension. Cases of short sight are constantly multiplying among primary and middle-school students. This can't be allowed to go on unchanged. . . .

Chairman Mao: The syllabus should be chopped in half. The students should have time for recreation, swimming, playing ball, and reading freely outside their course work. Confucius only professed the six arts—rites, music, archery, chariot-driving, poetry and history—but he produced four sages: Yen Hui, Tseng-tzu, Tzu Lu and Mencius. It won't do for students just to read books all day, and not to go in for cultural pursuits, physical education, and swimming, not to be able to run around, or to read things outside their courses, etc. . . .

Chairman Mao: Our present method of conducting examinations is a method for dealing with the enemy, not a method for dealing with the people. It is a method of surprise attack, asking oblique or strange questions. This is still the same method as the old eight-legged essay. I do not approve of this. It should be changed completely. I am in favour of publishing the questions in advance and letting the students study them and answer them with the aid of books. For instance, if one sets twenty questions on the *Dream of the Red Chamber,* and some students answer half of them and answer them well, and some of the answers are very good and contain creative ideas, then one can give them 100 per cent. If some other students answer all twenty questions and answer them correctly, but answer them simply by reciting from their textbooks and lectures, without any creative ideas, they should be given 50 or 60 per cent. At examinations whispering into each other's ears and taking other people's places ought to be allowed. If your answer is good and I copy it, then mine should be counted as good. Whispering in other people's ears and taking examinations in other people's names used to be done secretly. Let it now be done openly. If I can't do something and you write down the answer, which I then copy, this is all right. Let's give it a try. We must do things in a lively fashion, not in a lifeless fashion. There are teachers who ramble on and on when they lecture; they should let their students doze off. If your lecture is no good, why insist on others listening to you? Rather than keeping your eyes open and listening to boring lectures, it is better to get some refreshing sleep. You don't have to listen to nonsense, you can rest your brain instead. . . .

Chairman Mao: We must drive actors, poets, dramatists and writers out of the cities, and pack them all off to the countryside. They should all periodically go down in batches to the villages and to the factories. We must not let writers stay in the government offices; they will never get anything written if they do not go down. Whoever does not go down will get no dinner; only when they go down will they be fed. . . .

Chairman Mao: Primary-school teaching should not go on too long, either. Gorki had only two years of primary school; his learning was all self-taught. Franklin of America was originally a newspaper seller, yet he discovered electricity. Watt was a worker, yet he invented the steam-engine. Both in ancient and modern times, in China and abroad, many scientists trained themselves in the course of practice. . . .

Chairman Mao: Nowadays, first, there are too many classes; second, there are too many books. The pressure is too great. There are some subjects which it is not necessary to examine. For example, it is not necessary to examine the little logic and grammar which is learned in middle school. Real understanding must be acquired gradually through experience at work. It is enough to know what logic and grammar are. . . .

Chairman Mao: This is scholasticism. The annotations to the Four Books and the Five Classics are exceedingly scholastic, and nowadays they have all become completely indigestible. Scholasticism must inevitably die out. For example, in the study of the classics very many commentaries were written, but now they have disappeared. I think that students trained by this method, no matter whether it be in China, in America or in the Soviet Union, will all disappear, will all move towards their opposites. The same applies to the Buddhist classics, of which there are so many. The version of the *Diamond Sutra* edited by Hsüan-tsang of the T'ang dynasty was comparatively simplified, only a thousand-odd words, and it still exists. Another version, edited by Kumarajiva, was too long, and has died out. Won't the Five Classics and the Thirteen Classics also come to the end of the road? They have been very copiously annotated, and as a result nobody reads them. In the fourteenth and fifteenth centuries they indulged in scholastic philosophy; only in the seventeenth, eighteenth and nineteenth centuries did [the world] enter the age of enlightenment and the Renaissance take place. We shouldn't read too many books. We should read Marxist books, but not too many of them either. It will be enough to read a dozen or so. If we read too many, we can move towards our opposites, become bookworms, dogmatists, revisionists. In the writings of Confucius, there is nothing about agriculture. Because of this, the limbs of his students were not accustomed to toil, and they could not distinguish between the five grains. We must do something about this. . . .

You should gradually get into contact with reality, live for a while in the countryside, learn a bit of agricultural science, botany, soil technology, fertilizer technology, bacteriology, forestry, water conservancy, etc. There's no need to read big tomes. It's sufficient to read little books and get a bit of general knowledge.

Now about this university education. From entering primary school to leaving college is altogether sixteen or seventeen years. I fear that for over twenty years people will not see rice, mustard, wheat or millet growing; nor will they see how workers work, nor how peasants till the fields, nor how people do business. Moreover their health will be ruined. It is really terribly harmful. I said to my own child: 'You go down to the countryside and tell the poor and lower-middle peasants, "My dad says that after studying a few years we became more and more stupid. Please, uncles and aunts, brothers and sisters, be my teachers. I want to learn from you."' In point of fact pre-school children have a lot of contact with society up to the age of seven. At two they learn to speak and at three they have noisy quarrels. When they grow a little bigger, they dig with toy hoes to imitate grown-ups working. This is the real world. By then the children have already learned concepts. 'Dog' is a major concept. 'Black dog' and 'yellow dog' are minor concepts. His family's yellow dog is concrete. Man is a concept which has shed a great deal of meaning. Man or woman, great or small, Chinese or foreigner, revolutionary or counter-revolutionary—all these distinctions are absent. What is left are only the characteristics which differentiate man from the other animals. Who has ever seen 'man'? You can only see Mr. Chang and Mr. Li. You cannot see the concept 'house' either, only actual houses, such as the foreign-style buildings of Tientsin or the courtyard houses of Peking.

CHAPTER 22

We should reform university education. So much time should not be spent attending classes. Not to reform arts faculties would be terrible. If they are not reformed, can they produce philosophers? Can they produce writers? Can they produce historians? Today's philosophers can't turn out philosophy, writers can't write novels, and historians can't produce history. All they want to write about is emperors, kings, generals and ministers. Ch'i Pen-yü's article is excellent, I read it three times. Its defect is that it does not name names. Yao Wen-yüan's article is also very good: it has had a great impact on theatrical, historical and philosophical circles. Its defect is that it did not hit the crux of the matter. The crux of *Hai Jui Dismissed from Office* was the question of dismissal from office. The Chia Ch'ing emperor dismissed Hai Jui from office. In 1959 we dismissed P'eng Te-huai from office. And P'eng Te-huai is Hai Jui too.

We must reform the arts faculties in the universities. The students must go down and engage in industry, agriculture and commerce. The engineering and science departments are different. They have factories for practical work and also laboratories. They can work in their factories and do experiments in their laboratories. After they have finished high school they should first do some practical work. Only to go to the countryside is not enough. They should also go to factories, shops, army companies. They can do this kind of work for a few years and then study for two years. This will be enough. If the university has a five-year system, they should go down for three years. Teachers should also go down and work and teach at the same time. Can't they teach philosophy, literature and history there too? Must they have big foreign-style buildings to teach them in?

SUGGESTIONS FOR FURTHER READING

Carter, Peter. *Mao.* New York: Viking Press, 1979.

Ch'en, Theodore H. *The Maoist Educational Revolution.* New York: Praeger, 1974.

Chu, Don-Chean. *Chairman Mao: Education of the Proletariat.* New York: Philosophical Library, 1980.

Clayre, Alasdair. *The Heart of the Dragon.* Boston: Houghton Mifflin Co., 1985.

Fitzgerald, Charles P. *Mao Tse-tung and China.* New York: Holmes and Meier Publications, 1976.

Hawkins, John N. *Mao Tse-tung and Education: His Thoughts and Teachings.* Hamden: Linnet Books, 1974.

Hayhoe, Ruth. *Contemporary Chinese Education*. Armonk, N.Y.: M. E. Sharpe, Inc., 1984.

Hollingworth, Clare. *Mao and the Men Against Him*. London: J. Cape, 1985.

Karnow, Stanley. *Mao and China: From Revolution to Revolution*. New York: Viking Press, 1972.

Pye, Lucian W. *Mao Tse-tung: The Man in the Leader*. New York: Basic Books, 1976.

Schram, Stuart R. *Mao Tse-tung*. New York: Simon and Schuster,1966.

Snow, Edgar. *Red Star Over China*. New York: Grove Press, 1968.

Tse-tung, Mao. *Selected Works*. London: Lawrence and Wishart, 1954.

Wilson, Richard. *Mao Tse-tung in the Scales of History: A Preliminary Assessment*. Cambridge, U.K., and New York: Cambridge University Press, 1977.

NOTES

1. Stuart Schram, *Mao Tse-tung* (New York: Simon and Schuster, 1966), 15.

2. Lucian W. Pye, *Mao Tse-tung: The Man in the Leader* (New York: Basic Books, 1976), 75.

3. Edgar Snow, *Red Star Over China* (New York: Grove Press, 1968), 132.

4. Ibid., 132–134.

5. Pye, 84.

6. George Poloczi-Horvath, *Mao Tse-Tung: Emperor of the Blue Ants,* (London: Secker and Warburg, 1962), 24–25.

7. Siao-Yu, *Mao Tse-Tung and I Were Beggars* (Syracuse: Syracuse University Press, 1959), 38–41.

8. Li Jui, *The Early Revolutionary Activities of Comrade Mao Tse-Tung,* Anthony W. Sariti, trans., James C. Hsiun, ed. (New York: M. E. Sharpe, 1977), 178–179.

9. Mao Tse-Tung, *Selected Works,* I (London: Lawrence and Wishart, 1954), 161.

10. Erica Jen, "An Experience with Peking Youth," in Terrill Ross, ed., *The China Difference* (New York: Harper Colophon Books, 1972), 147.

11. Alasdair Clayre, *The Heart of the Dragon* (Boston: Houghton-Mifflin Co., 1985), 25–27.

12. Richard Wilson, *Mao Tse-Tung in the Scales of History: A Preliminary Assessment* (London: Cambridge University Press, 1977), 291.

13. Clare Hollingworth, *Mao and the Men Against Him* (London: J. Cape 1985), 140.

14. Ruth Hayhoe, *Contemporary Chinese Education* (Armonk, N.Y.: M. E. Sharpe, 1984), 48.

15. Jurgen Henze, "Higher Education: Tension Between Quality and Equality," in Ruth Hayhoe, *Contemporary Chinese Education* (Armonk, N.Y.: M. E. Sharpe, 1984), 105–119.

16. Mao ZeDong, "On the Correct Handling of Contradictions Among People," in *Four Essays on Philosophy* (Peking: Foreign Language Press, 1968), 110.

17. John N. Hawkins, *Mao Tse-Tung and Education: This Thoughts and Teachings* (Hamden: Linnet Books, 1974), 71–75.

18. Theodore Hsi-en Chen, *The Maoist Educational Revolution* (New York: Praeger Publishers, 1974), 4.

19. Ibid., 220–221.

20. Hayhoe, 48.

21. Chen, 220–221.

22. Mao Tse-Tung, *Quotations from Chairman Mao Tse-Tung* (Peking: Foreign Language Press, 1966), 276–277.

Index

Absorbent mind, stage of, 182
African American rights, 198–203
Afrocentric curriculum, 198, 201, 203
"Allegory of the Cave" (Plato), 3
Anschauung principle, 70, 71, 74
Athenian philosophers; *see* Greek philosophers
Autobiography, from John Stuart Mill's, 144–148
Autobiography of Friedrich Froebel, from, 132–133

Bible, The, in education, 43–44, 51; *see also* Religion in education
"Bill for the more general diffusion of knowledge" (Jefferson), 83, 85, 86

Calvinism, 103, 104, 107
  origins of, 41–45
Caste system in India, 190–192
Catechism in education, 43, 45, 70
Chairman Mao Talks to the People: Talks and Letters: 1956–1971, from, 218–220
Child labor, 163
Childhood development; *see* Early childhood development
Civic education, 85, 106, 155
Colloquies of Erasmus, The, from, 37–38
Common school movement, 70, 103, 106–107
Communitarian socialism, 114–117

Compendium of the Summa Theologica of St. Thomas Aquinas, from Berardus Bonjoannes', 28–31
Confucianism, 211, 212, 216–218
Corporal punishment, 70, 71, 126
Cultural Revolution, 211, 213, 215–217

Darwinian theory of evolution, 153–154, 171
Democracy, importance of, in education, 172
Democracy and Social Ethics, from Jane Addams', 164–165
Dialectical materialism, 215–216
Dualism, principle of, 11, 170–171

Early childhood education
  Comenius on, 52
  Du Bois on, 202
  Froebel on, 124–132
  Montessori on, 178–183
  Owen on, 116
  Pestalozzi on, 71–73
  Plato on, 4
  Quintilian on, 20
  Rousseau on, 58, 60
  Tse-Tung on, 217
Education, Intellectual, Moral, and Physical, from Herbert Spencer's, 156–158
Education of Man, The, from Friedrich Froebel's, 134–136
Educational philosophy
  of Aquinas, 25–27

  of Aristotle, 10–11
  of Calvin, 43–45
  of Comenius, 51–52
  of Dewey, 170–172
  of Du Bois, 202–203
  of Erasmus, 36–37
  of Froebel, 129–131
  of Gandhi, 190–192
  of Jefferson, 84–86
  of Mann, 106–108
  of Mill, 142–143
  of Montessori, 181–182
  of Owen, 116–117
  of Pestalozzi, 71–73
  of Plato, 3–5
  of Quintilian, 19–20
  of Rousseau, 60–61
  of Spencer, 153–156
  of Tse-Tung, 215–217
  of Wollstonecraft, 94–95
"Effective schooling," 52
Enlightenment, 60
  influence of, on Jefferson, 82, 85
Evangelical Protestantism, 43, 44
Experimentalism, 171–172

French Revolution, 92–93, 96

Gifts, use of, in kindergarten, 125, 128–131
Great Didactic of John Amos Comenius, The, from, 53–56
Great Leap Forward, 214
Greek philosophers
  Aristotle, 9–12
  Plato, 1–5

Hegelian theme, 169
Helvetic Society, 68

How Gertrude Teaches Her Children, from Johann H. Pestalozzi's, 77–79
Hull House, 160–164
Humanism, 33, 36, 44

Idealism, philosophy of, 3, 129
"Inaugural Address, University of Saint Andrews, February 1, 1867," from John Stuart Mill's, 149
Indian independence, 188–192
Individualism, 152, 154
Industrialization, impact of, on education, 163
International education, 51

John Dewey's Democracy and Education: An Introduction to the Philosophy of Education, from, 173–176

Kindergarten, 70, 105, 124–132

Laboratory School, 169, 170
Language development, importance of, 127
Learning theory, 20
Liberalism, philosophy of
Dewey on, 168
Mill on, 140, 142–143
Life of Robert Owen, The, from, 120–122

Mary Wollstonecraft's Original Stories, from, 98–99
Mathematics in curriculum, 153, 155
Medieval Christian synthesis, 24, 25
Metaphysics, 10, 11, 129, 191
Model School, 126
Montessori Method, The, from Maria Montessori's, 183–186
Montessori schools, 180–182
Moral and Political Writings of Mahatma Gandhi, The, from, 193–196
Moral development, 61, 71, 107, 116, 189

Mother-Play and Nursery Songs, from Friedrich Froebel's, 137–138
Mothers, importance of, in child development
Froebel on, 124, 129, 132
Pestalozzi on, 71, 73–74
Multiculturalism, 163, 203

National Association for the Advancement of Colored People (NAACP), 200–201
Natural education, 61–62, 69–74
Natural progression, theory of, 9
Naturalism, 58, 60–62, 155
New Harmony, community at, 115
New Lanark, community at, 114–117
Niagara Movement, 200
Nicomachean Ethics of Aristotle, The, from, 12–17
Nonviolent resistance, 188, 189, 191

Oratory, 19–20

Pan Africanism, 198, 199, 201, 203
Pansophism, 51–52
Papers of Thomas Jefferson, The, from, 87–89
Pestalozzi's Leonard and Gertrude, from, 75–77
Play, importance of, in childhood, 126–127, 130
Pragmaticism, 168–170
Praise of Folly, from Desiderius Erasmus', 39
Problem-solving steps, 171–173
Pro-Democracy Movement, 215
Progressivism, 168, 170
Protestant Reformation, 41–45
Protestant work ethic, 44–45, 103
Public schools, importance of
Jefferson on, 83, 85, 86
Mann on, 103, 105–108
Punishment, corporal, 70, 71, 126

Quintilian's Institutes of Oratory, from, 21–23

Reading, importance of
Montessori on, 182
Owen on, 117
Rousseau on, 58
Wollstonecraft on, 94
Realism, philosophy of, 9–12, 25, 51
Red Guards, 214, 215, 217, 218
Religion in education
Calvin on, 43–45
Gandhi on, 191
Jefferson on, 83, 86
Mann on, 107, 108
Renaissance, 33, 36
Republic of Plato, The, from, 5–8
Republican education, 81, 84–85
Rhetoric, 19–20
Rockfish Gap Report, 84
Rousseau's Emile or Treatise on Education, from, 63–65

Satyagraha, 189–190
Science in curriculum, 152, 153, 155, 156
Scientific method, 171, 172
Sensory learning, 60, 67, 70–72, 74, 94, 182
"Simultaneous instruction," 69
Social Darwinism, 152–155
Socialized education, 160–164
Socratic method, 2
Sophists, 2, 3
Souls of Black Folk: Essays and Sketches, The, from W. E. B. Du Bois, 204–208
Spirit of Youth and the City Streets, The, from Jane Addam's, 166–167
Supplementary Appendix to the First Volume of The Life of Robert Owen, A, from, 118–120

"Talented tenth," 202, 203
Thomism, philosophy of, 25–27
Thoughts on the Education of Daughters: With Reflections on Female Conduct, In the More Important Duties of Life, from Mary Wollstonecraft's, 97

Tracts and Treatises on the Doctrine and Worship of the Church, from John Calvin's, 46–48
Tuskegee Institute, 200, 202
"Twelfth Annual Report on Education (1848)," from Horace Mann's, 109–113

University of Virginia, 81, 84
Utilitarianism, 140–142
Utopian theory, 114, 115

Vindication of the Rights of Woman, A, from Mary Wollstonecraft's, 99–101
Vocational training, Du Bois on, 200, 202

Women, education of
    Addams on, 163
    Rousseau on, 61
    Wollstonecraft on, 91, 92, 94–96
Women's rights, 141–142
    Addams on, 160–161, 163
    Wollstonecraft on, 91–96